Toward a General Theory of Social Control
Volume 1
FUNDAMENTALS

STUDIES ON LAW AND SOCIAL CONTROL

DONALD BLACK *Series Editor*

Center for Criminal Justice
Harvard Law School
Cambridge, Massachusetts 02138

Toward a General Theory of Social Control

Volume 1

FUNDAMENTALS

Edited by

Donald Black

Center for Criminal Justice
Harvard Law School
Cambridge, Massachusetts

 1984
ACADEMIC PRESS, INC.
(Harcourt Brace Jovanovich, Publishers)
Orlando San Diego San Francisco New York London
Toronto Montreal Sydney Tokyo São Paulo

ACADEMIC PRESS, INC.
Orlando, Florida 32887

United Kingdom Edition published by
ACADEMIC PRESS, INC. (LONDON) LTD.
24/28 Oval Road, London NW1 7DX

Library of Congress Cataloging in Publication Data
Main entry under title:

Toward a general theory of social control.

    (Studies on law and social control)
    Includes bibliographies and indexes.
    Contents: v. 1. Fundamentals – v. 2. Selected prob-
lems.
    1. Sociological jurisprudence–Addresses, essays, lec-
tures. 2. Social control--Addresses, essays, lectures.
3. Deviant behavior--Addresses, essays, lectures.
I. Black, Donald J. II. Series.
K376.T68 1984   340'.115   83-11886
ISBN 0−12−102801−1 (v. 1)

PRINTED IN THE UNITED STATES OF AMERICA

84 85 86 87   9 8 7 6 5 4 3 2 1
                        4/2/85

Contents

3
From Disputing to Complaining   71
LAURA NADER

4
Liability and Social Structure   95
KLAUS-FRIEDRICH KOCH

5
The Social Organization of Vengeance   131
JONATHAN RIEDER

10

Rethinking Gossip and Scandal   271

SALLY ENGLE MERRY

11

Social Control from Below   303

M. P. BAUMGARTNER

Contributors

Numbers in parentheses indicate the pages on which the authors' contributions begin.

M. P. Baumgartner (303), Center for Criminal Justice, Harvard Law School, Cambridge, Massachusetts 02138

Donald Black (1), Center for Criminal Justice, Harvard Law School, Cambridge, Massachusetts 02138

William L. F. Felstiner (251), The Rand Corporation, Santa Monica, California 90406

Peter N. Grabosky (163), Australian Institute of Criminology, Woden, Australian Capital Territory 2606, Australia

John Griffiths (37), Faculty of Law, University of Groningen, Groningen, The Netherlands

Allan V. Horwitz (211), Department of Sociology, Rutgers–The State University of New Jersey, New Brunswick, New Jersey 08903

Klaus-Friedrich Koch* (95), Department of Anthropology, Northwestern University, Evanston, Illinois 62201

Sally Engle Merry (271), Department of Anthropology, Wellesley College, Wellesley, Massachusetts 02181

*Deceased.

Laura Nader (71), Department of Anthropology, University of California, Berkeley, Berkeley, California 94720

Jonathan Rieder (131), Department of Sociology, Yale University, New Haven, Connecticut 06520

Vivian J. Rohrl (191), Department of Anthropology, San Diego State University, San Diego, California 92182

Preface

Social control includes all of the practices by which people define and respond to deviant behavior. Even so, the scientific study of this subject matter has long been preoccupied with the phenomenon of law. Perhaps this is understandable, for in recent centuries the legal form of social control—that which is an appendage of the state—seems to have enjoyed especially favorable conditions for its growth and prominence, while many other forms have tended to fade into the background. We might easily forget that for most of human history (until the past 100 centuries or so) people managed without law and that, all along, other species of social control have continued to inhabit every society in great variety and profusion. Today as in the past, people with grievances might beat, banish, or kill one another; they might demand restitution, seize or destroy one another's property, or take hostages; they might protest, nag, ridicule, or gossip; they might resort to third parties such as mediators, arbitrators, or judges; they might avoid one another, negotiate, run away, fast, or commit suicide; they might weep, frown, or merely stare. All of these practices are worthy of scientific attention.

The following collection of essays—divided into two volumes—is designed to extend the study of social control beyond law. Moreover, it seeks to establish a conception of social control as a dependent variable, that is, as a thing to be predicted and explained. It also seeks to further a theoretical strategy suitable to this end, the fundamental assumption of which is that social control varies with its location and direction in social space. This strategy—which first appeared in my earlier work, *The Behavior of Law* (New York: Academic Press, 1976)—takes natural science as an appropriate model for social science, disregards the psychological aspects of social life, and incorporates a number of sociological traditions and theories into a single framework. While not all of the authors included in the collection explicitly follow this strategy, their writings are largely consistent with it.

Each of the essays is published here for the first time, though earlier versions of two (Chapters 1 and 3 in Volume 2) appeared elsewhere. Most were written in response to my invitation to the authors to venture beyond their usual realm of study to a more general problem. A few were recruited after I happened upon them in preliminary form, such as in a doctoral dissertation or conference presentation, and several more were proposed by the authors themselves after I invited them to join the project. Volume 1 (*Fundamentals*) opens with progammatic statements about the subject matter and then offers a number of inquiries into the conditions under which particular modes of social control occur. Volume 2 (*Selected Problems*) contains a set of investigations of social control in situations that may be especially interesting from a theoretical standpoint, as well as several essays on explanation and methodology. It should be obvious to the reader that these volumes are only a beginning, primitive in many respects, and that they will inevitably become obsolete as our knowledge expands.

Acknowledgments

I am grateful to the authors for their contributions. Because invitations to participate in the project were extended as early as 1978, and the first chapters were received within the year, most of the authors deserve additional credit for tolerating a long wait before publication. During the planning and preparation of the collection, I benefited immensely from the assistance of M. P. Baumgartner. Mark Cooney also made valuable suggestions, and Michael Oshima prepared a comprehensive Subject Index for each volume. I thank the administrative staff of Harvard Law School's Center for Criminal Justice, notably Kathleen Keeffe and Patricia Keating, for their services as well. And for providing a supportive environment for my work in general, I thank the Center's directors during the past several years: James Vorenberg, Lloyd E. Ohlin, and Philip Heymann.

Contents of Volume 2

1

Social Control as
a Dependent Variable*

DONALD BLACK

This essay introduces the general theory of social control.[1] Although little theory of this kind presently exists, several developments in social science lead naturally in its direction, and the time has come to announce its appearance, plan its future, and encourage its growth. The following pages advance a concept of social control, survey its variable nature, offer formulations that predict and explain the degree of variability in social control from one setting to another, and suggest how we might construct models that apply across particular cases of human conflict and across larger social formations such as communities and societies. First, however, it should be noted how recent developments in social science appear to invite the program of theory and research contemplated here.

Beyond Law

After a flurry of attention during the early years of social science (e.g., Durkheim, 1893; Ross, 1901; Weber, 1925; Malinowski, 1926), the phe-

*Support for this work was provided by the National Science Foundation Program in Law and Social Science.

[1]The concept of social control is discussed at some length later in this chapter. Suffice it to say for now that here *social control* refers to any process by which people define and respond to deviant behavior. Accordingly, a general theory of social control is a body of formulations that predict and explain variation in how people define and respond to deviant behavior.

1

nomenon of social control was largely neglected until the second half of the twentieth century, and even then scholarly work concentrated on a single category of this broader class: law. An emphasis on law—or governmental social control (Black, 1972: 1096)—has been particularly characteristic of sociologists, political scientists, and lawyers, most of whom have further narrowed their concern to legal life as it appears in modern societies such as the United States. This work has resulted in a sizable body of information about diverse aspects of social control through law, especially criminal justice but also such processes as the operation of regulatory agencies, the distribution of legal services, civil litigation, and adjudication (see, e.g., the materials collected in Aubert, 1969; Black and Mileski, 1973; Sanders and Daudistel, 1976; Friedman and Macaulay, 1977; see also Vago, 1981). Anthropologists have similarly concentrated on what they regard as law—typically the most formal and dramatic aspects of social control in tribal and other simple societies—although this often includes nongovernmental as well as governmental processes (for overviews and collections see, e.g., Hoebel, 1954; Nader, 1965; Bohannan, 1967; Nader and Todd, 1978; Roberts, 1979). In fact, a major portion of the literature in legal anthropology pertains to stateless societies where law, by definition, cannot exist (e.g., Barton, 1919; Llewellyn and Hoebel, 1941; Gulliver, 1963; Koch, 1974).[2] Finally, it might be added that in recent years historians have turned increasingly to the study of legal life, particularly to criminal justice in early Europe (e.g., Macfarlane, 1970; Samaha, 1974; Hay, Linebaugh, Rule, Thompson, and Winslow, 1975; but see also Baumgartner, 1978; Abel, 1979; Reid, 1980; Kagan, 1981; Snyder, 1981).

Leaving aside the question of why law has so dominated the study of social control (terminologically[3] and otherwise), we can at least appreciate that the growth of knowledge about how people define and respond to deviant behavior has been considerable. Moreover, the many facts that have accumulated provide a substantial foundation for theoretical development. How does law vary across social space? When does it

---

[2]A qualification: Although stateless societies cannot have law on a permanent basis, they may have it temporarily, such as during warfare, communal hunts, and other collective undertakings (see, e.g., Karsten, 1923: 8; MacLeod, 1937; Lowie, 1948; see also Black, 1976: 87–91).

[3]A number of scholars have long insisted on classifying as "law" many instances of social control that have no connection to government in a formal sense, so that law is said to exist even in stateless societies (e.g., Barton, 1919; Howell, 1954; Pospisil, 1958). Nongovernmental social control has often been called "customary law" or "unwritten law," though a number of other labels are sometimes preferred, including "folk law," "people's law," "unofficial law," and "indigenous law" (see, e.g., Fuller, 1971: 171–186; Berman, 1978; Galanter, 1981). Another strategy is to treat the "legalness" of social control as a matter of degree (see Griffiths, Chapter 2 of this volume).

come into play, how, against whom, and with what consequences? What predicts and explains who is arrested by the police? Who brings lawsuits? Who wins? A number of formulations addressing questions of this sort have already appeared, following as well as stimulating research about how law behaves as a natural phenomenon (see Black, 1976). At the same time, it has increasingly come to be recognized that law is but one among many kinds of social control.

The more we study law, indeed, the more we realize how little people actually use it to handle their conflicts (see, e.g., Kawashima, 1963; Macaulay, 1963; Biderman, 1967; Curran, 1977: chap. 4; Baumgartner, 1984). And as we discover the radically uneven pattern by which it appears across the social landscape—every society has settings in which law is virtually never used—we wonder precisely what is the range of mechanisms to which people resort when they have grievances against one another. What, beyond law, constitutes the larger universe of social control? How is it situated in social space? To be more specific: It is now abundantly clear, for example, that people of lower status, such as the poor and the disreputable, rarely use law against their social superiors (see Black, 1976: chaps. 2–6). In fact, some of those at the very bottom of society, such as slaves and children, are generally not permitted to use law at all, whereas some of the highest, such as feudal lords and monarchs, are practically immune to it. How, then, do people of lower status express grievances against those above them? It happens that "social control from below" is not nearly so uncommon as might be supposed and is in its own way quite as orderly as law itself (see Baumgartner, Chapter 11 of this volume). Moreover, people at the bottom use relatively little law among themselves, but this does not mean that they do not express grievances against one another. Far from it. A significant part of their social control, however, especially that which is violent, is regarded as crime by the authorities (see Black, Chapter 1, Volume 2 of this work).

Besides social status, another condition associated with the distribution of law is intimacy: People who are very close, such as blood relatives and married couples, use comparatively little law against one another;[4] at the opposite extreme, the same applies to those who are separated by the greatest distances in social space, such as those from

---

[4]A seeming exception to this principle in some societies is the frequent resort to law by married people seeking a divorce. On closer examination, however, it may be seen that divorce generally is a legal matter only where the state participates in and guarantees the marriage contract. Where this is not the case, people simply end their marriages when one or both partners are so inclined—a practice seen in many tribal societies (e.g., Turnbull, 1965: 140, 274–275; Reid, 1970: 117–118; Lee, 1979: 452–453) as well as in modern societies among couples who live together without certification by the state.

different tribes or nations (Black, 1976: 40–46). But, again, a scarcity of law does not necessarily imply that other kinds of social control are unavailable. In the case of intimates such as members of the same family, people typically have numerous means by which to express grievances against one another, including direct criticism, ridicule, ostracism, deprivation, resort to third parties (e.g., another relative, a friend, or a psychotherapist), desertion, self-destruction,[5] and violence. In the case of total strangers such as people from alien tribes or nations, the variety of social control is not so lush, but its scale and severity may be enormous. An invasion of one society by another, for instance, often expresses a grievance, and so, in general, does war. In any event, as we acquire knowledge of the limited conditions under which legal life appears and flourishes, new questions arise concerning what people do when they are uninclined or possibly unable to have recourse to law. The scientific study of legal life thus leads naturally to the study of other species of social control, to normative life in general, to all that expresses how people ought to behave.[6] What is more, scholarship on the social nature of law has produced a rich endowment of intellectual resources that can readily be applied to other processes involving right and wrong—in and between families, organizations, or nations, and among friends, colleagues, neighbors, or strangers. A program of theory and research embracing all of this at once, including law, is now feasible.

The Concept of Social Control

First advanced at the turn of the century by Edward Alsworth Ross (1901), the concept of social control has long been associated with the normative aspect of social life. In one usage, which dominated the earlier literature, social control refers broadly to virtually all of the human practices and arrangements that contribute to social order and, in particular, that influence people to conform (see, e.g., Ross, 1901; Park and Burgess, 1921: chap. 10; Mannheim, 1940: 274–311; Hollingshead, 1941; LaPiere, 1954; Cohen, 1966: 39; for an overview of this conception, see Gibbs, 1981: chap. 3). These practices may be intentional, as when someone is punished in order to deter others from similar misconduct, or unintentional, as when adults unconsciously implant habits of behavior in their children. In a second and more recent usage, which is followed

[5]For discussions of suicide as social control, see Jeffreys (1952), Koch (1974: 75–76), Counts (1980), and Baumgartner (Chapter 11 of this volume).

[6]Just as the sociology of law is also known as legal sociology, so a larger sociology of social control might appropriately be known as normative sociology.

throughout this essay, social control refers more narrowly to how people define and respond to deviant behavior (Black, 1976: 105; see also Clark and Gibbs, 1965).[7] It thus includes punishment of every kind— such as the destruction or seizure of property, banishment, humiliation, beating, and execution—as well as the demand for compensation by a victim of misconduct, sorcery, gossip, scolding, or a facial expression of disapproval such as a scowl or stare. It also includes various modes of intervention by third parties, such as mediation, arbitration, and adjudication. In this sense, social control is present whenever and wherever people express grievances against their fellows.[8]

When social control is understood as a kind of influence, the central problem in its study is the degree to which it has an impact on human conduct. How much does each means of social control contribute to social order? How effective is each? What are the consequences of each? To what extent, for example, does punishment deter deviant behavior? Scientifically speaking, in this broader view social control is approached primarily as an independent variable. It predicts and explains something

[7]For these purposes, *deviant behavior* refers to any conduct regarded as undesirable from a normative standpoint, that is, any conduct that *ought not* to occur. Although to some readers the concept of deviant behavior may seem to suggest conduct that is subject to penal or possibly therapeutic responses (such as psychiatric care), any connotations or limitations of this sort are unintended here (see Black, 1979a: 97, n. 2). Similarly, although the concept of social control may also seem to have penal or even coercive connotations, these are unintended in this discussion as well. Unfortunately, at present there does not appear to be any word or phrase that adequately captures the wide range of phenomena to which the concept of social control is meant to refer. Alternatives such as *dispute settlement* and *conflict management*—favored by many anthropologists and lawyers—do not seem appropriate in the context of penal and therapeutic modes of normative life and thus appear to be no more inclusive, if not less so, than the concept of social control. Another possibility, *social ordering* (Fuller, 1978: 357), implies an outcome that might better remain problematic—namely, whether social control necessarily results in "order"—and still another, *reglementation* (Moore, 1978: 1–31), would seem not only to suggest an orderly result but also to place what may be an overly restrictive emphasis on explicit expectations about how people should behave, or "rules." It should not be assumed that people always define and respond to deviant behavior according to rules. This may occur under limited social conditions and should be treated as a problem for investigation (see, e.g., Toulmin, 1982).

[8]Even so, social control should not be conceived entirely at the case level, where one individual complains about another. It also appears—and invites study—in larger units that transcend particular cases. Social control includes prescriptions, proscriptions, and other kinds of exhortations and promulgations that define how people should or should not behave, for example, and it includes all manner of mechanisms and arrangements for processing people with complaints and people defined as deviants, such as courts, police forces, mental hospitals, witch finders, and lawyers. The varieties of punishment might be studied as well, and so might strategies of therapy or mediation, modes of fighting or dueling, and so on.

else: how people behave. When conceived more narrowly as a reaction to deviant behavior, however, social control invites analysis as a dependent variable.[9] From this point of view, every manifestation of social control itself requires study. Why, for example, does punishment occur at all? Why is one person punished more severely than another? Under what conditions might the wrongdoer be asked to pay compensation to the aggrieved party, to enter psychotherapy, or just to go away? Why does a third party intervene in one conflict but not another? When are rules invoked? When does law occur? Vengeance? Gossip? Now the question of the extent to which these phenomena influence human behavior is left aside, and the impact of each on conformity and social order is ignored. But this is not because it is claimed that social control has no such influence or impact. Nor is it because the consequences of social control are thought to be uninteresting or unworthy of study. Rather, it is simply because a different question is being asked: What predicts and explains social control itself? This question acknowledges that social control is a thing in its own right, variable in its own way, and worthy of study for its own sake. Furthermore, precisely how it varies in social space is the central problem of a general theory of social control.[10]

[9]This is not to say that any concept such as social control logically implies the approach to be pursued in its study. In principle, one could conceive of social control as a process of influence and investigate why it occurs, or conceive of it as a reaction and investigate its impact on other phenomena. Even so, those who have conceptualized social control as influence have generally been more concerned with its consequences than with the social conditions under which it occurs, whereas the view that social control is a reaction to conduct regarded as deviant seems to lead in the opposite direction, to the question of why reactions of a particular kind come into being.

It should also be noted that a single approach might understand social control as both an independent and a dependent variable. For example, social control might be regarded as a reaction to deviant behavior that counteracts its disequilibrating effects on the social system in which it occurs (see Homans, 1950: 301–312; Parsons, 1951: 297–321).

[10]This usage assumes that the identity of a scientific theory resides in what it seeks to predict and explain, so that, for instance, a theory of earthquakes or cancer tells us when and why these phenomena occur. It treats them as dependent variables. Accordingly, a theory that inquires into the impact of social control on other aspects of social life such as deviant behavior or social order is not a theory of social control but rather a theory of those other phenomena (see Gibbs, 1981: chap. 6). A theory of the conditions under which punishment deters crime, for example, is a theory of crime, not a theory of social control.

To speak of *a* general theory of social control is not to suggest that the formulations comprising this theory should be considered final or complete. Instead, what is meant is a body of theory about social control, an organic network of formulations, more or less interrelated, forever subject to revision and refinement. It might therefore be more appropriate to speak of *the* general theory of social control, rather than *a* general theory of social control, in this context.

Finally, we are concerned here entirely with the development of sociological theory about social control and not in any way whatsoever with the psychology—or subjective aspect—of this phenomenon.

Varieties of Normative Behavior

Across societies and history, and from one conflict to another, the phenomenon of social control appears in many different structures, levels of complexity, and magnitudes. Leaving aside for now how such diversity might be understood, this section briefly outlines several kinds of variation that a general theory of social control might address.

FORM

A form of social control is a mechanism by which a person or group expresses a grievance. It is a mode of conducting normative business, such as a court of law, a face-to-face discussion, a public protest, or an act of violence. It might involve a small number of people, each with a specialized role, as in a judicial process; large numbers with similar roles, as in a war or a lynching; or simply a lone individual showing displeasure toward another. It might possibly occur without the knowledge of the offending party, as in gossip, or it might have other elements of secrecy, as in anonymous complaints. It might entail many stages or episodes, spaced over time, so that the pursuit of a grievance requires weeks, months, years, or even lifetimes of commitment; or it might begin and end literally in a matter of seconds with a scowl, glare, rebuke, or other situational display. The forms of social control thus vary dramatically, and an exhaustive classification of all that have been observed would be a challenge in itself.

For present purposes, suffice it to say that the forms of social control divide into two major categories: those involving only the principals, with or without the help of supporters, and those involving also a third side who relates to the conflict as an agent of settlement.[11] In the first category, social control may be unilateral, flowing in one direction alone, from the aggrieved to the offending party—as when a parent scolds a child or a citizen assassinates a government official—or it may be bilateral, flowing in both directions at once—as in a duel, fight, or feud—where each side pursues a grievance against the other (called "negative reciprocation" by Warner, 1958: 162; compare Sahlins, 1965: 148–149). The second category, trilateral social control, appears only with the intervention of a settlement agent who relates authoritatively to both sides, even if ultimately a preference is expressed for one or the

---

[11]A "side" of a conflict may be an individual, a group, or an aggregate. Hence, nothing is assumed here about the number of people who participate in cases of social control, though surely most involve only two and occur in face-to-face encounters. Regardless of the number involved, however, it seems that most (if not all) such cases exhibit a two- or three-sided structure.

other. Examples of settlement agents are peacemakers, mediators, and judges. Considering these possibilities, we may speak of a theory of self-help that addresses the conditions under which people aggressively pursue their own grievances, such as by unilaterally admonishing or injuring their antagonists or by entering bilaterally into a verbal or phys-ical fight (see Black, Chapter 1, Volume 2 of this work), and a theory of avoidance that addresses the conditions under which people simply withdraw—whether unilaterally or bilaterally—when conflict erupts (see Homans, 1950: 308; Fürer-Haimendorf, 1967: 22; Felstiner, 1974; Baumgartner, Chapter 4, Volume 2 of this work; see also Baumgartner, forthcoming). We may also speak of a theory of support that specifies when and how third parties relate to conflict as partisans and a theory of settlement that specifies when and how they become involved as non-partisans (see generally Black and Baumgartner, 1983). Each form of social control is worthy of study in its own right and worthy of its own theory.

STYLE

Another variable aspect of social control is its style, or the language and logic by which it defines and responds to deviant behavior. Four of these styles have been identified: penal, compensatory, therapeutic, and conciliatory (Black, 1976: 4–6; see also Horwitz, 1982: 122–127). In mod-ern societies, for example, the penal style is seen in criminal law, the compensatory style in tort and contract law, the therapeutic style in juvenile justice and psychiatric care, and the conciliatory style in nego-tiation, mediation, and arbitration of marital, labor–management, and international affairs. Each style has its own standards, questions, and solutions. Thus, each attributes a different identity to the person or group who enters its jurisdiction. Whereas in the penal style the deviant is regarded as an offender who has violated a prohibition and who should therefore suffer pain, deprivation, or humiliation, in the com-pensatory style the party in jeopardy becomes a debtor, liable for damages resulting from a failure to fulfill an obligation. In the therapeu-tic style, the deviant is understood as a victim who needs help, and in the conciliatory style, as a disputant in a conflict that needs to be settled.

Each style also involves a different focus. When the penal style is applied, the point of reference is the conduct itself, typically a particular act. Punishment may be justified as a means of discouraging similar conduct by the offender or others (designated, respectively, as "specific deterrence" and "general deterrence" by Andenaes, 1966), or it may be levied for its own sake, as vengeance. In the compensatory style, the focus is not so much the conduct as its consequences, and because identical acts may have different consequences, they may require different amounts of compensation. The same act might result in a death in one case but a lesser injury in another, for example, and one death might deprive a family of its primary source of support, whereas another has little economic impact. When damages are assessed, differences such as these are likely to be taken into account.[12] The therapeutic style has still another focus: the person.[13] A course of treatment depends on the particular nature of the deviant's condition, not the conduct that is associated with it or the consequences that result from it. In fact, the deviant is not viewed as responsible for what happened; it was not chosen; it could not be avoided. When the person has been helped back to normality, the conduct and its consequences will disappear. The conciliatory style of social control shifts the focus yet again: to the relationship between the parties involved. An effort is made not to become exclusively preoccupied with any one person's or group's conduct, its consequences, or any one of the individuals or groups embroiled in the dispute. A relationship has been disturbed and needs attention; a resolution of the conflict must be found; social harmony must be restored.

Virtually any kind of deviant behavior may be handled with any of the four styles of social control. Moreover, in cross-cultural and historical perspective, there has been enormous variation in when and how each is applied. Consider, for example, the handling of homicide. In modern societies, we tend to assume that intentional homicide, committed with malice, is a crime that should be punished, but over the centuries in many simpler societies, compensation of the victim's family has been a common response to the same behavior (see, e.g., Pollock and Maitland, 1898: Vol. 1, 47–48; Evans-Pritchard, 1940: 150–176; Jones, 1974: 66–69). In other cases, homicide may be regarded therapeutically as the symptomatic behavior of someone possessed by a supernatural

[12]Another variable aspect of social control is the system of liability that specifies who is subject to social control, and when, given the occurrence of an event regarded as deviant. Where compensation is expected, for instance, the system of liability specifies who will be asked to pay, whether this is the party who is deemed responsible or someone else, such as the responsible party's family or organization. (For a discussion of liability in cross-cultural perspective, see Koch, Chapter 4 of this volume; see also Moore, 1972.)

[13]A group as well as a person might be handled therapeutically. Although an organization, for instance, would not ordinarily be regarded as insane or possessed by supernatural spirits, it might nevertheless have its misconduct attributed to a malfunction of some kind, possibly to a matter needing the attention of a management consultant or other specialist in organizational behavior (see Gluckman, 1972: 37–40). Occasionally an even larger collectivity might be described in therapeutic language, as when people speak of a "sick society."

spirit or disabled by a mental illness (see, e.g., Middleton, 1965: 51; Peters, 1967: 272), and in still others it may be taken primarily as an aspect of a conflict in need of resolution, possibly by a ritual of forgiveness or other gesture of reconciliation (see, e.g., Hasluck, 1954: chap. 25; Barth, 1959: 96–98; van den Steenhoven, 1962: 82).[14]

It should be recognized that each style of social control occurs in a wide range of normative settings, from the most formal and legalistic to the most informal and casual. Violent self-help (which, incidentally, may extend to homicide in many cases) is penal in style, for example, as is the modern system of criminal justice, which may be invoked against those who employ self-help. So is banishment. So are most forms of social control in hierarchical relationships, such as those directed against people of lower status by their social superiors—beatings by husbands and parents, evictions by landlords, dismissals by employers—and also those occasionally exerted from below, such as acts of rebellion and retaliation by slaves, servants, and other underlings (see Baumgartner, Chapter 11 of this volume). Compensation also varies in its degree of formality. It is commonly found as a remedy in modern courts of law, for example, but it is sometimes even more developed in simple societies that have no legal institutions of any kind, particularly herding societies, where cattle, camels, or other livestock serve as a standard of value for reckoning damages (see, e.g., Evans-Pritchard, 1940: 150–176; Howell, 1954; Lewis, 1959; Goldschmidt, 1967: 100–106).[15] The therapeutic style is practiced by modern professionals such as psychiatrists, psychologists, and social workers, though it occurs in more communal settings too, as may be seen in the reponse to spirit possession, "soul loss," and witchcraft in many tribal societies, ideological deviation in the People's Republic of China, and, in the case of associations such as Alcoholics Anonymous and Synanon, habitual drunkenness and drug addiction in modern America (Horwitz, 1982: 148–160, 180–181; see also Horwitz, Chapter 8, Volume 2 of the present work). Somewhat more informal are the friends and relatives who might behave therapeutically by withholding blame and showing sympathy for an associate whose misconduct they dislike but attribute to circumstances that the individual did not choose and could not avoid. Conciliation is also found in diverse settings—between intimates or strangers, individuals or organizations, in

[14]For a cross-cultural study of stylistic and other variation in the social control of homicide, see Cooney (forthcoming).

[15]It might seem that compensation would tend to supplant vengeance—"an eye for an eye"—wherever money, livestock, or other means of payment are available, but in some societies only vengeance is believed appropriate and adequate when certain wrongs occur, whereas the acceptance of compensation is viewed as cowardly and dishonorable (e.g., Barth, 1959: 85; Bourdieu, 1966: 216).

all societies and walks of life, wherever quarrels arise, feelings are bruised, or pride and self-respect placed in jeopardy. Perhaps the conciliatory style is most strikingly illustrated by the specialists in human relations who have been observed by anthropologists in tribal societies, such as the "camp clown" among the Mbuti Pygmies of Zaire, the "leopard-skin chief" of the Nuer of the Sudan, the "saint" among the Swat Pathan of Pakistan, or the "crosser" of the Yurok Indians of California (see, respectively, Turnbull, 1965: 182–183; Evans-Pritchard, 1940: 172–176; Greuel, 1971; Barth, 1959: chap. 8; Kroeber, 1926: 514–515), but social control of this kind is no more difficult to find at an international conference, among fellow workers, on a playground, or at a breakfast table.

Before this section concludes, it is important to note that the several styles of social control described here do not exhaust the possible responses to deviant behavior. Thus, whereas the penal style of social control tends to focus on an act, the compensatory style on its consequences, the therapeutic style on a person, and the conciliatory style on a relationship, another strategy focuses on reducing the opportunity to engage in deviant behavior, either by altering the situation of potential deviants or by altering the habits of potential victims. This is the strategy of prevention. Potential deviants might be subjected to greater surveillance (known in modern police work as "preventive patrol"), for example, or they might be deprived of their freedom of movement to some degree (known in modern penology as "preventive detention" and "incapacitation"), and potential victims might be encouraged to decrease their vulnerability (known by modern specialists in crime prevention as "target hardening").[16] Still another strategy focuses on the

[16]The vocabulary employed here should not suggest that prevention is found only in modern societies or where an effort is made to reduce conduct that might be regarded as criminal. Although the technology of prevention is most highly developed in societies such as modern America—where, for instance, it involves diverse methods of surveillance by governmental and private police, electronic devices, and locks of all kinds to make victimization more difficult—earlier and simpler societies have often used the same approach to deviant behavior. In ancient Rome, for example, some slaves were branded on the forehead or required to wear iron collars to make their apprehension easier if they ran away, and they were sometimes placed in chains to eliminate the possibility altogether (see Wiedemann, 1981: 173–174, 193–194). For centuries, vicious dogs have been used to protect herds and dwellings (see, e.g., Hasluck, 1954: 73, 204), and fences have been erected for the same purpose (e.g., Chagnon, 1977: 29). Prevention also seems to be a common strategy for reducing the deviant behavior of children: Prohibited objects may simply be hidden or placed out of reach, for example. Children themselves may prevent a certain amount of deviant behavior by adults as well (such as by wandering freely and exercising surveillance in private places or other situations where adults might not have access). For a discussion of preventive behavior by and toward children in a tribal society, see Maybury-Lewis (1967: 67–72).

causes of deviant behavior. This is the strategy of reform. It acts on environmental conditions, such as poverty and unemployment, that are believed to generate deviant behavior.[17] It may be debatable whether prevention and reform should be understood theoretically as styles of social control in a narrow sense, but clearly both are relevant to the broader study of how people adapt to conduct of which they disapprove. Each may augment, or even provide an alternative to, the handling of individual cases by punishment, compensation, therapy, or conciliation.[18]

[17]Social scientists have developed a number of theories that they and others believe should guide reform of this kind. Some even feel that these theories demonstrate that society itself is responsible for crime and other deviant behavior. In contrast, the penal and compensatory styles of social control suggest that the deviant actor is responsible; the therapeutic style, that an abnormal condition, such as a mental illness, is responsible; and the conciliatory style, that everyone involved in a particular conflict is responsible to some degree.

The two modes of prevention noted earlier may shift the responsibility for deviant behavior in still other directions: If preventive behavior is oriented toward potential deviants, as in surveillance programs, any deviant behavior that occurs may be blamed on those who are charged with preventing it, such as when the police are blamed for a crime or an adult is held responsible for not adequately watching the movements of a troublesome or destructive child. If a prevention program is victim oriented, however, the victim of a deviant act may be held responsible for failing to take the proper precautionary measures, such as when the theft of an automobile is blamed on the owner because he or she left the keys in the ignition, or when a woman is blamed for her own rape because she made herself available by walking alone on the street at night.

[18]Another possible focus of social control is the supernatural. The anthropological literature describes many practices designed to neutralize or otherwise counteract responses to deviant behavior by gods or other spirits. Typically, the standard of conduct involved is a taboo, the violation of which—a sin—automatically creates a condition of spiritual pollution and danger. This condition may result in a misfortune such as a sickness, injury, or unhappy afterlife unless appropriate measures are taken to expiate the sin and placate the supernatural spirits concerned. In most cases, expiation is achieved by a sacrifice, confession, or other ritual (see generally Radcliffe-Brown, 1952; Douglas, 1966). Among the Nuer of the Sudan, for example, it is believed that incest may result in yaws or syphilis for both partners and possibly also for close relatives and that adultery may strike at the lumbar region of the cuckold (Evans-Pritchard, 1956: 183–185). In fact, any sickness at all is taken by the Nuer as evidence that a sin has been committed (Evans-Pritchard, 1956: 191–193), a presumption made by Arctic Eskimos and many others as well (see Hoebel, 1954: 70–73). Among the Cheyenne of the North American Plains, murder is regarded as "putrid" and is believed to bring misfortune on the entire tribe—such as failure in war or hunting—unless the killer is banished and a ritual known as the Sacred Arrow Ceremony is performed (Llewellyn and Hoebel, 1941: 132–135). The Tallensi of Ghana believe that any homicide, regardless of the circumstances, is a sin against the mystical power of the earth and will result in the destruction of the killer's family unless "heavy sacrifices" are made (Fortes, 1945: 176–177).

Such beliefs and practices might arguably be construed as a style of social control in

QUANTITY

The several forms and styles of social control vary in the degree to which they define and respond to deviant conduct. In principle, there-fore, each may be measured as a quantitative variable, or counted. This may be especially apparent in the realm of law, where responses to deviant behavior often have an explicitly numerical character, such as punishments involving a specific period of time in prison or a specific amount of money. Even where law is not dispensed in uniform intervals such as days or dollars, however, it is possible to identify a wide range of phenomena that may be construed as increments in the quantity of law, such as a call to the police, an arrest, the filing of a lawsuit, a prosecution, a conviction, a decision in behalf of a plaintiff, a prison sentence, or an award of damages. Each of these actions constitutes an increase in the degree to which someone's conduct is regarded as de-viant within a governmental framework, and so each may be under-stood as an increase in law itself. (For further remarks on the measure-ment of law, see Black, 1979a.)

More generally, social control of every sort varies in its degree or magnitude, so that we may speak of the quantity of self-help, therapy, expiation, gossip, or whatever. In the case of self-help, this magnitude might be said to increase with the force and violence applied by the aggrieved: A homicide is more self-help than a lesser injury or property destruction, for instance, whereas each of these is more than a mere threat or admonishment. And just as a code of law may specify the quantity of governmental social control that is appropriate in each case—such as the years in prison that must be served—so other codes may specify how much social control should be applied in other set-tings. There is, so to speak, a jurisprudence of self-help and of every other kind of social control. In traditional societies, a "code of honor" may prescribe when and how much violent self-help should occur from one incident to another (see the essays in Peristiany, 1966, especially those by Pitt-Rivers and by Bourdieu). In medieval Europe, handbooks called "penitentials" listed in great detail the many sins that might be committed and the penance appropriate for each, such as a particular period of silence, prayer, singing of psalms, fasting, seclusion, sleeping on nutshells, flagellation, or exile (see McNeill and Gamer, 1938; see also

---

their own right: the expiatory style. On the other hand, perhaps expiation should more properly be viewed as a religious equivalent of the other styles. It might involve a belief in supernatural punishment of the sinner, for example, a demand for compensation to the gods (as in a sacrifice), a curing ritual to cleanse the sinner's soul, or a ceremony of spiritual reconciliation.

Tentler, 1977). In modern societies, prisoners and children—among others—are commonly subject to disciplinary codes (see Foucault, 1975). Where a third party intervenes in a conflict in a largely nonpartisan fashion, we may measure the degree of authoritativeness involved in each case (see Gluckman, 1965: 222), ranging from the friendly peacemaker who merely distracts or separates the principals to the mediator who acts as a broker between them, the arbitrator who gives an opinion but cannot enforce it, the judge who gives an opinion and also is able to enforce it, and, finally, the repressive peacemaker who handles the conflict as a punishable offense in itself (see Black and Baumgartner, 1983, for a detailed explication of these roles).

The quantity of social control has no necessary association with its form or style. Violent self-help, for example, may be just as severe as the most extreme punishments applied by a court of law, in modern as well as in traditional societies. But penal practices are not always more severe than other styles of social control. The enforcement of traffic law is penal in style, for instance, but typically it is less burdensome for the deviant than are most compensation awards and many treatments for mental illness.

In any event, whatever its form or style may be, the quantity of social control in each case should never be taken for granted. It requires explanation. In fact, in most cases people with a grievance against someone else probably do nothing at all. They just "lump it" (see Felstiner, 1974: 81; Galanter, 1974: 124–125). Accordingly, the very existence of social control itself requires explanation. We have long sought to understand why people commit crime and other kinds of deviant behavior, but we have barely begun to investigate why conduct is regarded as criminal or otherwise deviant in the first place.[19] It is time for a new question: Why do people commit social control?

[19]In the early 1960s, a number of sociologists called attention to the processes whereby crime and other deviant behavior are "labeled" as such, or defined as unacceptable (see, e.g., Erikson, 1962; Kitsuse, 1962; Becker, 1963). This movement, known as "labeling theory," constituted a shift away from the more traditional emphasis on the characteristics of deviants and their behavior. Initially it did not lead so much toward a theory of social control, however, as toward a new theory of why people engage in deviant behavior: the theory of "secondary deviation," which holds that the labeling of people as deviant increases the likelihood that they will engage in still more deviant behavior in the future (Lemert, 1967; see also Scheff, 1966; Matza, 1969). For example, a criminal record may make it more difficult for people to find legitimate employment, thereby increasing their motivation to turn to illegal sources of income. Despite the direction in which labeling theory first led, it did encourage research on criminal justice, the treatment of mental illness, and other processes of social control and so helped to lay the foundation for the theory of social control itself.

To approach social control as a dependent variable is to acknowledge that it differs from one situation to another, and to assume that it is possible to predict and explain these differences. As noted earlier, the sociological study of law has yielded a number of formulations about how legal life varies across social settings. It seems that this earlier work might be relevant to an understanding of other kinds of social control. Law apparently varies with its location and direction along every known dimension of social space. It varies with the vertical dimension, or inequality of wealth, for example, increasing and becoming more penal as it is directed downwardly from higher against lower ranks. It varies with the horizontal dimension, or the distribution of people in relation to one another, including their degree of intimacy, specialization, and integration. In a given community, for instance, those who are the most intimate seem to have the least law. Also relevant is the corporate dimension: Groups use more law against individuals than vice versa, and they seem to use proportionately more against one another as well. But groups are not punished so much as are individuals; more often they are asked only to compensate their victims. Law further varies with culture, the symbolic dimension of social space: Homogeneity, like intimacy, apparently retards the growth of law, and unconventionality involves legal disabilities similar to those associated with poverty or a lack of organization. Finally, social control itself describes yet another dimension—the normative—and it too may be related to the incidence of law. Law appears to vary inversely with other social control, for instance, to be stronger when normative life of other kinds is weaker, and vice versa.[20] (For an elaboration of these and other formulations about legal variation, see Black, 1976.)

It seems plausible that not only law but every other kind of social control varies with its location and direction in social space. Surely, for example, inequality is relevant to what happens not only in courtrooms

---

The theory of social control provides a radical alternative to theories of deviant behavior of every kind. Given that deviant behavior is conduct that is subject to social control, every instance of deviant behavior is also an instance of social control. Thus, to say that poor people are more likely to commit crime is also to say, simultaneously, that poor people are more likely to be defined as criminals. Variation in the nature and rate of deviant behavior—across a population, across time, or whatever—necessarily reflects variation in the nature and rate of social control. It is therefore possible to explain deviant behavior with the theory of social control (Black, 1976: 9–10).

[20]This does not imply that the total quantity of social control in a given setting is constant. When law replaces other forms of social control (or vice versa), the extent to which a particular kind of conduct is punished or otherwise regarded as deviant may change considerably.

but also in private homes, in workplaces, in the community, and in international affairs. Surely it is relevant to the occurrence of scolding, gossip, beating, deprivation, desertion, expulsion, destruction, and, considering the behavior of third parties, the occurrence of adjudication, arbitration, mediation, negotiation, and advocacy. Surely the structure of intimacy is also relevant, as well as the division of labor, social participation, corporate action, cultural heterogeneity, and so on. Hence, this should be our point of departure: What predicts and explains the behavior of law may also predict and explain social control in general.[21]

The Quantity of Normative Variation

Even though social control varies enormously from one setting to another in its form, style, and magnitude, and even though the kind of theory contemplated here addresses such variation as its central problem, it should not be assumed that social control always varies to the same degree. In fact, under the right conditions, how people define and respond to deviant behavior may approach perfect uniformity from one instance to the next. For example, a traffic officer checking for expired parking meters will normally write a citation (a "ticket") for virtually every violation discovered, and for every one the fine will be exactly the same. Under other conditions, however, traffic enforcement may be highly selective (see Black, 1980: 32–36). Similarly, the compensation that must be paid for a wrongful injury—say, an accidental death—differs greatly across the many cases handled in a modern society such as the United States, though the circumstances involved, such as drunken driving or medical malpractice of a particular kind, might be exactly the same. But in a tribal society, such as that of the Nuer of the Sudan or

[21]This is not to say that other kinds of social control necessarily behave according to the same principles as law—though this may be true in some cases—but only that the same features of the social environment may be relevant to both. Precisely how these features are relevant, if at all, remains a problem for investigation. In the case of witchcraft accusations, for example, it appears that the patterns resemble legal behavior to a remarkable degree: The social location of witches is significantly similar to that of defendants in legal cases, particularly criminal cases (see Black, 1976: 56–59). Witchcraft accusations may even fall within the jurisdiction of law in some societies. The labeling of people as mentally ill has much in common with law as well (see Horwitz, 1982). In the case of other forms of social control, in contrast, the patterns appear to be quite different: Whereas more law appears to flow downwardly than upwardly in status structures, for instance (Black, 1976: chaps. 2–6), such forms as flight, self-destruction, and covert retaliation by the aggrieved seem to occur primarily in the opposite direction (see Baumgartner, Chapter 11 of this volume). Social status apparently is relevant both to law and to these other normative phenomena, then, but in radically different ways.

the nomads of northern Somalia, compensation for an accidental homicide differs relatively little from one case to the next (see Howell, 1954: 54; Lewis, 1959; 1961: chap. 6).[22] Accordingly, the quantity of normative variation should be understood as a variable in its own right.

It is possible to predict and explain the degree to which social control varies from one setting to another, and to do this with a single formulation that applies wherever comparisons can be made, whether across cases, groups, communities, or societies: *Normative variation is a direct function of social diversity.* Differences in the form, style, and quantity of social control increase and decrease with differences across social settings. Case by case, for example, social control varies with the social characteristics of the principals in conflict and with those of any third parties who become involved. The participants might be high or low in social status, or mixed; they might be more or less intimate, more or less interdependent, more or less homogeneous in culture; they might be groups, individuals, or both. Characteristics of this kind may differ a great deal from one case to the next, or they may not. If they do, to this extent there will be variation in the social control that occurs—in whether a case is taken to an official agency, for example, in whether a winner is declared and, if so, in what consequences befall the loser. Thus, in modern societies, where the social diversity of cases is much greater than in tribal societies, there is more variation in social control from one case to the next. This explains why, as noted earlier, an incident in modern America such as an accidental homicide might have numerous possible consequences, ranging from no reaction at all to imprisonment or huge amounts of money in compensatory damages, whereas in a tribal society the possible variation is far narrower. About the only differences across a simple society such as a tribe are those of age, sex, and intimacy, and so only these are likely to be relevant to the handling of a given grievance (see Note 22).[23]

Even within a modern society, cases are not always so diverse as those arising from accidents, where practically anyone—rich or poor, married or single, employed, educated, conventional, respectable, or

[22]Compensation in tribal settings is not totally indifferent to the social characteristics of the parties involved. The killing of a man may require more compensation than the killing of a woman or a child, for example, and the degree of intimacy or genealogical distance between the parties may be relevant as well. Nevertheless, the life or limb of all people of the same sex, age, and social distance is typically worth approximately the same from one case to the next. This is not true in modern societies such as the United States.

[23]No matter how little social diversity a society or community might have within its population, the handling of grievances may vary greatly with the number of supporters each side of a conflict is able to mobilize (see, e.g., Barth, 1959: chap. 9, especially 119–120; Gulliver, 1963: 297–302; 1969; 1971: chap. 5).

whatever—might be involved with practically anyone else. For instance, a larger number of criminal cases are interchangeable in their social characteristics, and so there is less variation in how they are handled. Prostitutes are likely to be processed by the authorities in much the same fashion from one to the next, and so are "skid row" drunks, burglars, and robbers. In cases such as these, the alleged offenders are nearly always poor and otherwise lacking in social status. They tend to differ among themselves primarily in the nature and length of their criminal records, which in turn appear to be the major source of variation in how they are handled (see, e.g., Spradley, 1970: 176–177; Wiseman, 1970: 89–90; Mileski, 1971: 504–505; Farrell and Swigert, 1978).[24]

Social diversity is variable not only across legal settings but also across normative settings of all kinds, and everywhere the same principle applies: the more diversity, the more differences in social control. The more families vary in their social composition, for example, the more their normative life also varies. For this reason, the manner in which husbands express grievances against their wives, and vice versa, varies greatly across modern America, where some marital relationships are patriarchal in structure, others matriarchal, and still others egalitarian. Wife-beating—as a form of discipline—occurs frequently in some but not others, and the same is true of desertion, avoidance, conciliation, psychotherapy, or whatever. In tribal and peasant societies, by contrast, the structure of each marital relationship is likely to be much the same as the next, and so conflict management is much the same as well. Wife beating is likely to have roughly the same likelihood from one family to the next, and the same redundancy applies to other modes by which grievances might be expressed.

As mentioned earlier, variation in social control depends not only on the degree of social diversity found among people who have conflicts with one another but also on that prevailing among those who might intervene as third parties. Although settlement agents such as police officers and judges have long been quite homogeneous in their social characteristics—for example, judges have nearly always been male, middle-aged or elderly, economically prosperous, and racially, ethnically, and religiously conventional—this homogeneity has begun to decrease during the twentieth century. If the trend toward greater diversification continues, we should expect an increasing degree of variation in judicial dispositions, other things being equal. And this should be all the more

[24]Some kinds of criminal cases differ considerably in their social characteristics, however, and their handling varies accordingly. An example is homicide in modern societies such as the United States (see, e.g., Lundsgaarde, 1977: 90–92, 224–229, 232; Bowers and Pierce, 1980).

pronounced if—as it appears to be—the diversification of third parties is accompanied by a diversification of the cases in other respects. In fact, during the past century or so (at least in the United States), it seems to have become increasingly difficult to predict the disposition of cases with the written law alone. Technically similar cases have increasingly been handled differently. In other words, the rules have been losing their importance. The widely held view that law is essentially an affair of rules (e.g., Hart, 1961; Fuller, 1964) may thus be an historically grounded notion that is becoming obsolete.

Finally, it should be added that the amount of variation in social control does not automatically reflect the amount of social diversity across the cases handled. This relationship depends on the extent to which the social characteristics of the cases are known when and where they are processed. Knowledge of this kind, or social information, cannot be taken for granted; it is itself variable (see Black and Baumgartner, 1980: 204, n. 18). For example, police officers handling parking violations in a large city generally have little or no social information about the diverse owners or drivers of improperly parked automobiles, and, as noted earlier, there is little or no variation in how parking violations are processed. But when the police handle so-called moving violations, such as speeding or disobeying traffic signals, officers encounter the drivers and learn some of their social characteristics. Because these characteristics differ considerably across the population of violators, there is more variation in how violations of this type are handled (see Black, 1980: 32–35). Judges sentencing convicted criminals have still more social information about offenders and their victims, and so there is still more variation in the handling of otherwise identical cases (except, as mentioned earlier, where the parties are largely the same in their social characteristics).

The quantity of social information entering a process of social control is not random, however; it can be predicted and explained with various features of each case. The more intimately related the parties are, for example, the more of their social characteristics will be known among themselves. Hence, social information is abundant in the tribunals of tribal and peasant villages where everyone is well acquainted with everyone else, but it often is sparse in the courtrooms of modern cities. Social information probably varies with the social status of the parties as well, if only because higher-status people may be more likely to advertise their own social superiority. And social information appears to vary with social control itself: The greater the amount of social control that may be applied to each case, for instance, the more people seem to gather information about the social characteristics of those involved. At one extreme is the parking violation, where the owner or driver usually remains socially anonymous and risks only a small monetary fine; at the other extreme is the capital case, where the accused criminal's entire life history is likely to be compiled and presented to the court. Whenever social control is potentially greater, then, any social diversity across the cases is likely to be better known, and this added knowledge in turn increases the degree of variation in how the cases are handled. Accordingly, all else constant—including the social diversity across the cases—the following principle may be proposed: *Normative variation is a direct function of the quantity of social control.* This principle explains why the handling of capital crimes involves so much more variation than the handling of lesser offenses such as traffic violations (compare, e.g., Bowers and Pierce, 1980, with Lundman, 1979).[25] In sum, it appears that uniformity in the application of law and other social control is reserved for two situations: (*a*) those in which the cases are—or seem to be—socially identical; and (*b*) those in which the cases are trivial.

Models of Social Control

When each party has complete knowledge of the social characteristics of the others involved, the social structure of a conflict predicts and explains how it will be handled. Accordingly, the more economically we are able to describe such a configuration—the conflict structure—the more effectively we can predict and explain the social control occurring within it. Insofar as our theoretical formulations imply how various social conditions are associated with each kind of social control, we can construct a model of each, depicting all of these conditions at once. By comparing these models with actual instances of conflict and social control, and by observing how well each corresponds to reality, the validity of the models can be assessed. A model that fits the facts, case after case, provides support for the theoretical formulations from which it is derived and also has uses of its own.

Consider first the place of intimacy in the theory of social control, in particular, the theory of the third party. There is reason to believe that—all else constant—the likelihood that a settlement agent will intervene in

---

[25]It might seem that this pattern would arise naturally from the wider range of responses to deviant behavior that higher levels of social control allow. Where capital punishment is the maximum penalty, for example, a vast range of lesser penalties is theoretically possible, whereas this range is not available when the maximum is lower, as in small monetary fines. But this difference has no logically necessary relationship to how these penalties are applied. Thus, if capital cases were socially identical in every respect, there would be no reason to expect that the application of the death penalty would display any more variability than the levying of two-dollar parking fines.

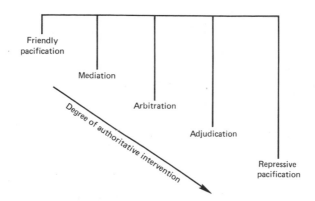

Friendly
pacification

Mediation

Degree of authoritative intervention

Arbitration

Adjudication

Repressive
pacification

FIGURE 1.1. Modes of settlement behavior. (Adapted from Black and Baumgartner, 1983: 87.)

a conflict varies with the degree of intimacy, or relational distance,[26] between the parties in conflict. More specifically, it seems that this likelihood increases with the relational distance between the parties until a point where they are complete strangers (such as members of different societies), when it declines. In other words, *settlement behavior is a curvilinear function of relational distance.*[27] It is also possible to specify the kind of settlement behavior that is likely to occur under varying conditions of intimacy. Recall that five modes of settlement behavior can be distinguished—friendly pacification, mediation, arbitration, adjudication, and repressive pacification—and that these describe the continuum of increasingly authoritative intervention depicted in Figure 1.1.

How do these modes vary with the structure of intimacy? Leaving aside the degree of relational distance between the principals themselves, it might first be observed that settlement behavior seems to occur only when the amount of intimacy is largely equal between the third party and each of the principals (see Simmel, 1908: 149–153). Otherwise, the third party is likely to act as a partisan on behalf of the principal who is closer: Intimacy breeds partisanship.[28] People tend to support their

[26]Relational distance refers to the degree to which people participate in one another's lives; it is measured by such variables as "the scope, frequency, and length of interaction between people, the age of their relationship, and the nature and number of links between them in a social network [Black, 1976: 41]."

[27]This is a more general formulation of a proposition about the behavior of law (see Black, 1976: 40–46, for the original formulation as well as a summary of empirical evidence supporting it).

[28]This proposition derives from research on helping behavior showing that the likelihood that help will be given to a person in distress increases with the intimacy between the potential helper and the potential beneficiary (see Black and Baumgartner, 1980: 200–201).

friends and family members against strangers, for example, and in such cases generally would not be able, or allowed, to claim objectivity about the merits of each side in the manner of an arbitrator or judge. Even to intervene less authoritatively as a friendly peacemaker or mediator would be difficult. Thus, for example, among the Ifugao of the Philippines, the traditional settlement agent known as the *monkalun* (who seemingly may choose to act as a mediator, arbitrator, or judge) cannot be a close relative of either principal: "Were he closely related to the plaintiff, he would have no influence with the defendant, and mutatis mutandis the opposite would be true [Barton, 1919: 87]." Similarly, among the nomads of northern Somalia, elders who arbitrate disputes must be acceptable to both sides, and neither will allow a relative of the other to perform this function: "Kinship ties to either party are regarded as prejudicial to a fair judgment [Lewis, 1961: 229]." In a Druze village of Lebanon, the selection of mediators obeys the same principle: "Anyone nearer to one disputant than the other is not likely to be acknowledged a disinterested party by both [Ayoub, 1965: 13]." In modern societies as well, unequal intimacy with the principals is normally thought to disqualify a judge from hearing a case. Whether in a traditional or a modern setting, then, we might say that *the settlement agent and the principals form an isosceles triangle of relational distance, with the settlement agent at the apex* (Black and Baumgartner, 1983: 113).[29]

We shall now consider how each of the five modes of settlement behavior varies with relational structures of this kind. How does a mediation structure differ from an arbitration or adjudication structure? When is pacification friendly rather than repressive? In short, what predicts and explains the degree of authoritativeness with which a settlement agent intervenes in a conflict?

The pattern seems to be as follows: *The authoritativeness of settlement behavior is a direct function of the relational distance between the settlement*

[29]This does not mean that unequal degrees of intimacy with the principals will always result in the withdrawal or removal of a designated settlement agent from a case. For practical reasons a replacement might be difficult to obtain, for example, or the disadvantaged principal might have social disabilities of other kinds that would undermine an appeal for a replacement. It should also be noted that where the triangle formed by a third party and the principals is radically obtuse—with highly unequal relational distances between the third party and each of the principals—the mode of intervention is not predicted to be settlement behavior at all. Instead, the third party would tend to favor the closer side at the expense of the more distant side, thus acting more as a supporter than a settlement agent. This pattern is illustrated by the manner in which police officers tend to deal with a complaint by a citizen against a fellow officer: Typically they side with their colleague from the beginning and function as supporters in opposition to the citizen (see, e.g., Chevigny, 1969; Black, 1980: 174).

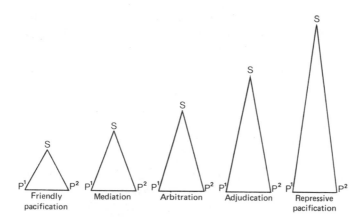

FIGURE 1.2. The relational structure of settlement behavior. (S = settlement agent; P^1 and P^2 = principals; length of sides = relational distance.)

agent and the principals (Black and Baumgartner, 1983: 113). With reference to the continuum of authoritative intervention portrayed earlier, friendly pacification should be most frequent where the settlement agent is highly intimate with the parties in conflict; mediation, where a bit less intimacy is found; arbitration, where there is still less; adjudication, where there is hardly any intimacy, and repressive pacification should be the most frequent where the settlement agent is the most distant of all. Accordingly, each of the five modes of settlement behavior may be represented by an isosceles triangle of intimacy, with each differing from the others in the distance that is found between the settlement agent and the principals, as shown in Figure 1.2.

As implied earlier, another feature that a model of settlement behavior (and, for that matter, any model of social control) should take into account is the structure of social support, if any, that each side of a conflict enjoys. A model should describe the relationship between each supporter and all of the other participants. Because intimacy itself is conducive to partisanship, it may be expected that advisers, advocates, allies, and other supporters will be relationally closer to one side than to the other (for a typology of support roles, see Black and Baumgartner, 1983: 88–98). This pattern is often reported in the scholarly literature on conflict management, such as, for example, among the Kabyles of Algeria, whose support behavior perfectly obeys a principle of differential intimacy:

> A sense of solidarity obliged one to protect a kinsman against a non-kinsman, a
> member of one's own party against a man from another moiety, an inhabitant of the

village—even though of a rival party—against a stranger to the village, a member of
the tribe against a member of another tribe [Bourdieu, 1966: 201].

The same tendency is found everywhere. Moreover, whether closer to
one of the principals or not, some partisans may also have ties to the
other side, or possibly to a settlement agent involved in the conflict.
Configurations such as these surely bear on the kind of settlement behavior that actually occurs and must be comprehended by a maximally
predictive model of each. But it should be emphasized that the relational
structure of a conflict is only one of many factors relevant to its processing. A more powerful model would include a number of variables at
once, such as the status structure of the conflict, the involvement of
groups, the cultural distances between the parties, and the availability of
alternative modes of social control.

Thus, for example, it appears that *settlement behavior is more likely to
occur when a third party is higher than the principals in social status.*[30] It also
seems that the nature of the intervention varies accordingly: *The authoritativeness of settlement behavior is a direct function of the relative status of
the third party* (Black and Baumgartner, 1983: 113; see also Baumgartner,
1984). All else constant, therefore, we would expect friendly peacemakers to be closest in social status to the principals, mediators to be
somewhat higher than those whose conflict they mediate, arbitrators
higher yet, judges still higher, and, finally, repressive peacemakers to be
the highest of all in social status, relative to the principals. Social status
is relevant to support behavior as well, and the status of the supporters
on each side is relevant to how, if at all, a settlement agent might
intervene. Here again, without further elaboration, the point is simply
to illustrate the kind of variation to which theoretical formulations might
be addressed. Ultimately it should be possible to specify every aspect of
a conflict structure that is associated with every kind of settlement behavior and, more generally, every kind of social control that might occur. Models of these structures might then be compared with any given
conflict in the natural world so as to predict and—if successful—explain
how it is handled. The closer a model fits reality in any case, the more
precisely we may apprehend the kind of social control that will actually
occur. If, for instance, a conflict structure includes no one who is equally
close or distant, relationally, to or from the principals and no one who is

[30]The concept of social status refers here to any "location of a person or group in social
space, seen in relation to others [Black, 1979b: 153]." A status might consist in a level of
wealth or a degree of integration in a community (by employment, marriage, or other
kinds of social participation), cultural conventionality, or respectability, among other
characteristics.

superior to both in social status, a model combining the patterns noted earlier would predict no settlement behavior at all. On the other hand, if someone is found in the structure who is equidistant from the principals and also higher than both in social status—increasing the likelihood of settlement behavior[31]—measurements of the relational and status distances involved could further predict how authoritative the intervention would be, whether it would be likely to reach the level of arbitration, adjudication, or whatever. Ideally, a successful model of social control of any kind would show simultaneously how it is situated along every dimension of social space: vertical, horizontal, corporate, symbolic, and normative.

Models of social control such as those proposed earlier may be applied not only microscopically, to predict and explain the handling of a particular conflict, but also macroscopically, to a community, society, or other setting in which numerous conflicts arise routinely from one day to another. Each of these larger settings typically contains one or more recurrent conflict structures that, theoretically speaking, imply a specifiable range of social control. For example, we know that hunters and gatherers, such as the Mbuti Pygmies of Zaire, the Hadza of Tanzania, and the !Kung San Bushmen of Botswana, traditionally live in small bands in which everyone is intimately related and in which status differences among adults are negligible (see, respectively, Turnbull, 1961, 1965; Woodburn, 1979; Lee, 1979). It is therefore structurally impossible for these people to have a conflict among themselves that would fit our proposed models of relatively authoritative intervention, such as adjudication and repressive pacification: There is simply no one in their daily life who is socially distant enough—relationally or hierarchically— to be a judge or repressive peacemaker. In fact, societies of this kind generally do not even have mediators or arbitrators.[32] Their only settlement agents seem to be the least authoritative of all—friendly peace-

---

[31]Settlement agents do not necessarily have both of these characteristics, but when both occur together, settlement behavior is especially likely. For an example of settlement agents who are equidistant from the principals but who appear to be essentially equal to them in social status, see Gulliver's description of mediators among the Ndendeuli of Tanzania (1969; 1971: chap. 5).

[32]More precisely, settlement agents of this kind are not regularly available within their own ranks, though they may recruit people from outside the tribe to intervene more authoritatively in their conflicts. For example, the !Kung San Bushmen have been known to approach members of a neighboring Bantu tribe, the Tswana, for mediation services (Lee, 1979: 393). Mbuti Pygmies reportedly have tried to bring cases to the tribunal of another Bantu people, the Ndaka, but have been turned away (Turnbull, 1961: 234–235). Under colonial rule, European officials were asked to provide the same services, and it seems likely that missionaries and even anthropologists have been approached as well.

makers. For example, the only settlement agent to be found among the Mbuti Pygmies is the so-called camp clown, who handles conflicts primarily by making a fool of himself, thereby distracting the principals from their dispute and possibly making them join together in laughter as well (Turnbull, 1965: 182–183). For our purposes, then, the hunters and gatherers might be regarded as friendly-pacification societies. Another step beyond these in social complexity, including status differentiation, are the herding societies, such as the Nuer of the Sudan and the nomads of Tibet, who are not quite so intimate and egalitarian as those who forage for their livelihood (see Evans-Pritchard, 1940; Ekvall, 1964, 1968). Understandably, therefore, they have mediators but rarely anyone more authoritative, for their conflicts do not—cannot—have the social characteristics associated with modes of intervention further along the continuum of authoritativeness. Herding peoples might thus be classified as mediation societies. Following the same reasoning, we can also identify arbitration societies. Typically these include people who engage in at least some horticulture and have still more social distance and inequality in their local communities, such as the ancient Irish, the Swat Pathan of Pakistan, and various societies in Polynesia (see, respectively, Ginnell, 1894; Barth, 1959; Hogbin, 1934; Sahlins, 1958). And there are, so to speak, adjudication societies, such as the nations of the modern world, where the social structure accommodates a still more authoritative mode of settlement behavior.[33] Perhaps it is even justifiable to speak of repressive-pacification societies, illustrated in recent history by the colonial regimes of Africa, Oceania, and other areas where rulers and ruled are separated by vast distances in social space, and where tribal modes of conflict management such as feuding and fighting are likely to be handled by the authorities as "disturbances of the peace," or crime, and not as the pursuit of justice at all (see, e.g., Evans-Pritchard, 1940: 152; Harner, 1972: 210; Koch, 1974: 223; Reay, 1974: 205, 209). In short, it is possible to construct models of social control with applications across the entire range of social life, from face-to-face encounters to communities and societies.

The Good, the True, and the Beautiful

This chapter has introduced social control as a natural phenomenon that varies with its location and direction in social space. The central

---

[33]Societies such as modern America, where people initiate a relatively large number of legal complaints but then usually settle them without a formal trial, could arguably be described as negotiation societies.

theme has been that it is possible, in principle, to develop a body of sociological theory that will predict and explain how normative life differs from one setting to another or, in other words, to understand social control as a dependent variable. A general theory of law—a single species of social control—has already been initiated, and it now seems feasible to expand our program to include the behavior of virtually anything else that is normative, all of the social practices that define and respond to conduct as good or evil, right or wrong, proper or improper. This undertaking may seem ambitious, but, within a still more general perspective, social control itself proves to be only a limited instance of a larger phenomenon: evaluation.

People everywhere apply standards to everything. Whether the standards pertain to what is good or bad, true or false, beautiful or ugly, or to what is useful, delightful, or disgusting, all of this and more is evaluation. Seen in this context, social control is but one mode of evaluation, known by its normative character, its standards of right and wrong. A second mode of evaluation has an intellectual character: It is concerned with the truth and importance of ideas about the nature of reality, including their application to matters of a practical nature, to what is effective, prudent, and wise. From an intellectual standpoint, people may be regarded as intelligent, insightful, inventive, or smart or as stupid, fatuous, or foolish. Yet a third mode of evaluation has an aesthetic character: It pertains to what is worthy of appreciation, what is graceful, attractive, awesome, exciting, or delicious or ordinary, distasteful, vulgar, or gross. These three modes of evaluation—normative, intellectual, and aesthetic—appear to be the major frameworks in which people make value judgments.[34] Furthermore, it is possible to observe similarities in how they come into play in social life.

It seems, for example, that people of higher status enjoy an advantage whenever they are evaluated, whether normatively, intellectually, or aesthetically. Thus, just as a downward offense by a person of higher status against someone of lower status is less likely to be punished than is an offense in the opposite direction (see generally Black, 1976: chaps. 2–6), so an idea that is presented downwardly, by a person of higher status to someone whose social position is lower, is more likely to suc-

[34]These modes of evaluation roughly correspond to the three "action orientations" delineated by Talcott Parsons—the evaluative, the cognitive, and the cathectic—which he suggests have direct parallels in three "culture patterns," namely, systems of value orientation, systems of belief, and systems of expressive symbols (Parsons, 1951: 12–14, 327). Years ago, Leon Mayhew remarked to a class in which the present author was enrolled that Parsons meant to be classifying three fundamental concerns of human beings: the good, the true, and the beautiful.

ceed—to be viewed as interesting or important—than is an idea presented upwardly (Black, 1979b: 158). Those of higher status are also likely to be regarded as aesthetically superior, with better taste in music, clothing, food, and everything else (see Black, 1979b: 160–161). Even their recreational activities are likely to be considered more sophisticated. And, to mention another pattern, just as people are less likely to invoke law against their intimates (Black, 1976: 40–42), so their intellectual and aesthetic reactions to relatives, friends, and acquaintances are more positive. In general, therefore, the degree of consensus about questions of quality in science, art, or any other field is predictable from the social structure of evaluation in each: What are the social characteristics of the evaluators? How similar are they? What is their relationship to those they evaluate (see Black, 1979b: 161)? It should be possible to formulate propositions that predict and explain evaluations of every kind.

We may also ask why each mode of evaluative behavior occurs at all. Why is something evaluated in the language of right and wrong in one case, in terms of its cleverness or stupidity in another, its attractiveness or vulgarity in still another? The same conduct or object may evoke entirely different standards among different people. A book, speech, or film, for example, may be judged in terms of its truth, its artistic merit, or its morality. Similarly, some might consider a theft as immoral and outrageous, others might regard it as clever or stupid, and still others might relate to it aesthetically as "cool" or "fun."

It seems that the particular mode of evaluation employed depends on the social conditions that prevail in any given case. Each tends to appear in a limited range of locations and directions in social space. Some people are moralistic, constantly asking whether whatever they encounter is proper or not: Does it conform to the rules? Is it legal? Should it be punished? To others, all that matters is efficiency. They intellectualize everything: How smart is this or that? Is it rational? What does it accomplish? Does it work? And still others care only about aesthetics: Is it in good taste? Is it graceful? Pleasurable? Does it feel good? Particular settings are also inclined toward one mode of evaluation more than another. Entire societies may be dominated by a single evaluative mode, so that we might speak of moralistic societies such as Puritan New England or Soviet Russia, intellectual or technocratic societies such as those of modern Scandinavia, and aesthetic societies such as traditional Japan or Bali.

Just as the conduct of people does not by itself predict and explain the social control to which it will be subject, neither can conduct or anything else tell us how people will evaluate it, whether normatively, intellectually, or aesthetically. And just as social control cannot be taken for granted, so ultimately we must ask why value judgments—of any kind—occur at all. Although the scientific study of social control is only now beginning, then, already it is possible to imagine a general theory of evaluation.

ACKNOWLEDGMENTS

I thank M. P. Baumgartner, Marc Clinton, Mark Cooney, John Griffiths, Calvin Morrill, and Trevor Nagel for commenting on an earlier draft.

References

Abel, Richard L.
    1979   "Western courts in non-Western settings: Patterns of court use in colonial and neo-colonial Africa." Pages 167–200 in *The Imposition of Law*, edited by Sandra B. Burman and Barbara E. Harrell-Bond. New York: Academic Press.
Andenaes, Johannes
    1966   "The general preventive effects of punishment." *University of Pennsylvania Law Review* 114: 949–983.
Aubert, Vilhelm (editor)
    1969   *Sociology of Law: Selected Readings*. Baltimore: Penguin Books.
Ayoub, Victor F.
    1965   "Conflict resolution and social reorganization in a Lebanese village." *Human Organization* 24: 11–17.
Barth, Fredrik
    1959   *Political Leadership among Swat Pathans*. London: Athlone Press.
Barton, Roy Franklin
    1919   *Ifugao Law*. Berkeley, Calif.: University of California Press, 1969.
Baumgartner, M. P.
    1978   "Law and social status in colonial New Haven, 1639–1665." Pages 153–174 in *Research in Law and Sociology: An Annual Compilation of Research*, vol. 1, edited by Rita J. Simon. Greenwich, Conn.: JAI Press.
    1984   "Law and the middle class: Evidence from a suburban town." *Law and Human Behavior* 8: forthcoming.
    forth-   *The Moral Order of a Suburb*. New York: Academic Press.
    coming
Becker, Howard S.
    1963   *Outsiders: Studies in the Sociology of Deviance*. New York: Free Press.
Berman, Harold J.
    1978   "The background of the Western legal tradition in the folklaw of the peoples of Europe." *University of Chicago Law Review* 45: 553–597.
Biderman, Albert D.
    1967   "Surveys of population samples for estimating crime incidence." *The Annals of the American Academy of Political and Social Science* 374 (November): 16–33.
Black, Donald
    1972   "The boundaries of legal sociology." *Yale Law Journal* 81: 1086–1100.
    1976   *The Behavior of Law*. New York: Academic Press.

1979a "A note on the measurement of law." *Informationsbrief für Rechtssoziologie*, Sonderheft 2: 92–106. Reprinted in *The Manners and Customs of the Police*. New York: Academic Press, 1980.

1979b "A strategy of pure sociology." Pages 149–168 in *Theoretical Perspectives in Sociology*, edited by Scott G. McNall. New York: St. Martin's Press.

1980 *The Manners and Customs of the Police*. New York: Academic Press.

Black, Donald, and M. P. Baumgartner

1980 "On self-help in modern society." Pages 193–208 in *The Manners and Customs of the Police*, by Donald Black. New York: Academic Press.

1983 "Toward a theory of the third party." Pages 84–114 in *Empirical Theories about Courts*, edited by Keith O. Boyum and Lynn Mather. New York: Longman.

Black, Donald, and Maureen Mileski (editors)

1973 *The Social Organization of Law*. New York: Seminar Press.

Bohannan, Paul (editor)

1967 *Law and Warfare: Studies in the Anthropology of Conflict*. Garden City, N.Y.: Natural History Press.

Bourdieu, Pierre

1966 "The sentiment of honour in Kabyle society." Pages 191–241 in *Honour and Shame: The Values of Mediterranean Society*, edited by J. G. Peristiany. Chicago: University of Chicago Press.

Bowers, William J., and Glenn L. Pierce

1980 "Arbitrariness and discrimination under post-*Furman* capital statutes." *Crime and Delinquency* 26: 563–635.

Chagnon, Napoleon A.

1977 *Yanomamö: The Fierce People*. 2d edition. New York: Holt, Rinehart and Winston (1st edition, 1968).

Chevigny, Paul

1969 *Police Power: Police Abuses in New York City*. New York: Vintage.

Clark, Alexander L., and Jack P. Gibbs

1965 "Social control: A reformulation." *Social Problems* 12: 398–415.

Cohen, Albert K.

1966 *Deviance and Control*. Englewood Cliffs, N.J.: Prentice-Hall.

Cooney, Mark

forth- The Social Control of Homicide: A Cross-Cultural Study. Unpublished doctoral
coming dissertation, Harvard Law School.

Counts, Dorothy Ayers

1980 "Fighting back is not the way: Suicide and the women of Kaliai." *American Ethnologist* 7: 332–351.

Curran, Barbara A.

1977 *The Legal Needs of the Public: The Final Report of a National Survey*. Chicago: American Bar Foundation.

Douglas, Mary

1966 *Purity and Danger: An Analysis of Concepts of Pollution and Taboo*. London: Routledge and Kegan Paul.

Durkheim, Emile

1893 *The Division of Labor in Society*. New York: Free Press, 1964.

Ekvall, Robert B.

1964 "Peace and war among the Tibetan nomads." *American Anthropologist* 66: 1119–1148.

1968 *Fields on the Hoof: Nexus of Tibetan Nomadic Pastoralism*. New York: Holt, Rinehart and Winston.

Erikson, Kai T.
  1962   "Notes on the sociology of deviance." *Social Problems* 9: 307–314.
Evans-Pritchard, E. E.
  1940   *The Nuer: A Description of the Modes of Livelihood and Political Institutions of a Nilotic People.* London: Oxford University Press.
  1956   *Nuer Religion.* Oxford: Clarendon Press.
Farrell, Ronald A., and Victoria Lynn Swigert
  1978   "Prior offense as a self-fulfilling prophecy." *Law and Society Review* 12: 437–453.
Felstiner, William L. F.
  1974   "Influences of social organization on dispute processing." *Law and Society Review* 9: 63–94.
Fortes, Meyer
  1945   *The Dynamics of Clanship among the Tallensi: Being the First Part of an Analysis of the Social Structure of a Trans-Volta Tribe.* London: Oxford University Press.
Foucault, Michel
  1975   *Discipline and Punish: The Birth of the Prison.* New York: Pantheon, 1977.
Friedman, Lawrence M., and Stewart Macaulay (editors)
  1977   *Law and the Behavioral Sciences.* 2d edition. Indianapolis, Ind.: Bobbs-Merrill (1st edition, 1969).
Fuller, Lon L.
  1964   *The Morality of Law.* New Haven, Conn.: Yale University Press.
  1971   "Human interaction and the law." Pages 171–217 in *The Rule of Law,* edited by Robert Paul Wolff. New York: Simon and Schuster.
  1978   "The forms and limits of adjudication." *Harvard Law Review* 92: 353–409.
Fürer-Haimendorf, Christoph von
  1967   *Morals and Merit: A Study of Values and Social Controls in South Asian Societies.* Chicago: University of Chicago Press.
Galanter, Marc
  1974   "Why the 'haves' come out ahead: Speculations on the limits of legal change." *Law and Society Review* 9: 95–160.
  1981   "Justice in many rooms: Courts, private ordering, and indigenous law." *Journal of Legal Pluralism* 19: 1–47.
Gibbs, Jack P.
  1981   *Norms, Deviance, and Social Control: Conceptual Matters.* New York: Elsevier.
Ginnell, Laurence
  1894   *The Brehon Laws: A Legal Handbook.* London: T. Fisher Unwin.
Gluckman, Max
  1965   *Politics, Law and Ritual in Tribal Society.* New York: New American Library.
  1972   "Moral crises: Magical and secular solutions." Pages 1–50 in *The Allocation of Responsibility,* edited by Max Gluckman. Manchester: Manchester University Press.
Goldschmidt, Walter
  1967   *Sebei Law.* Berkeley, Calif.: University of California Press.
Greucl, Peter J.
  1971   "The leopard-skin chief: An examination of political power among the Nuer." *American Anthropologist* 73: 1115–1120.
Gulliver, P. H.
  1963   *Social Control in an African Society: A Study of the Arusha, Agricultural Masai of Northern Tanganyika.* Boston: Boston University Press.
  1969   "Dispute settlement without courts: The Ndendeuli of southern Tanzania."

Pages 24–68 in *Law in Culture and Society*, edited by Laura Nader. Chicago: Aldine Press.

1971   *Neighbours and Networks: The Idiom of Kinship in Social Action among the Ndendeuli of Tanzania*. Berkeley, Calif.: University of California Press.

Harner, Michael J.
1972   *The Jívaro: People of the Sacred Waterfalls*. Garden City, N.Y.: Anchor Books, 1973.

Hart, H.L.A.
1961   *The Concept of Law*. Oxford: Clarendon Press.

Hasluck, Margaret
1954   *The Unwritten Law in Albania*. Cambridge: Cambridge University Press.

Hay, Douglas, Peter Linebaugh, John G. Rule, E. P. Thompson, and Cal Winslow
1975   *Albion's Fatal Tree: Crime and Society in Eighteenth-Century England*. New York: Pantheon.

Hoebel, E. Adamson
1954   *The Law of Primitive Man: A Study in Comparative Legal Dynamics*. Cambridge, Mass.: Harvard University Press.

Hogbin, H. Ian
1934   *Law and Order in Polynesia: A Study of Primitive Legal Institutions*. New York: Harcourt.

Hollingshead, August B.
1941   "The concept of social control." *American Sociological Review* 6: 217–224.

Homans, George C.
1950   *The Human Group*. New York: Harcourt, Brace.

Horwitz, Allan V.
1982   *The Social Control of Mental Illness*. New York: Academic Press.

Howell, P. P.
1954   *A Manual of Nuer Law: Being an Account of Customary Law, Its Evolution and Development in the Courts Established by the Sudan Government*. London: Oxford University Press.

Jeffreys, M.D.W.
1952   "Samsonic suicide or suicide of revenge among Africans." *African Studies* 11: 118–122.

Jones, Schuyler
1974   *Men of Influence in Nuristan: A Study of Social Control and Dispute Settlement in Waigal Valley, Afghanistan*. New York: Seminar Press.

Kagan, Richard L.
1981   *Lawsuits and Litigants in Castile, 1500–1700*. Chapel Hill, N.C.: University of North Carolina Press.

Karsten, Rafael
1923   *Blood Revenge, War, and Victory Feasts among the Jíbaro Indians of Eastern Ecuador*. Smithsonian Institution Bureau of American Ethnology, Bulletin 79. Washington, D.C.: U.S. Government Printing Office.

Kawashima, Takeyoshi
1963   "Dispute resolution in contemporary Japan." Pages 41–72 in *Law in Japan: The Legal Order in a Changing Society*, edited by Arthur T. von Mehren. Cambridge, Mass.: Harvard University Press.

Kitsuse, John I.
1962   "Societal reaction to deviant behavior: Problems of theory and method." *Social Problems* 9: 247–256.

Koch, Klaus-Friedrich
   1974   *War and Peace in Jalémó: The Management of Conflict in Highland New Guinea.* Cambridge, Mass.: Harvard University Press.
Kroeber, A. L.
   1926   "Law of the Yurok Indians." Pages 511–516 in *Proceedings of the 22nd International Congress of Americanists*, vol. 2. Rome: Instituto Christoforo Colombo.
LaPiere, Richard T.
   1954   *A Theory of Social Control.* New York: McGraw-Hill.
Lee, Richard Borshay
   1979   *The !Kung San: Men, Women, and Work in a Foraging Society.* Cambridge: Cambridge University Press.
Lemert, Edwin M.
   1967   "The concept of secondary deviation." Pages 40–64 in *Human Deviance, Social Problems, and Social Control.* Englewood Cliffs, N.J.: Prentice-Hall.
Lewis, I. M.
   1959   "Clanship and contract in northern Somaliland." *Africa* 29: 274–293.
   1961   *A Pastoral Democracy: A Study of Pastoralism and Politics among the Northern Somali of the Horn of Africa.* London: Oxford University Press.
Llewellyn, Karl N., and E. Adamson Hoebel
   1941   *The Cheyenne Way: Conflict and Case Law in Primitive Jurisprudence.* Norman, Okla.: University of Oklahoma Press.
Lowie, Robert H.
   1948   "Some aspects of political organization among the American aborigines." *Journal of the Royal Anthropological Institute of Great Britain and Ireland* 78: 11–24.
Lundman, Richard J.
   1979   "Organizational norms and police discretion: An observational study of police work with traffic law violators. *Criminology* 17: 159–171.
Lundsgaarde, Henry P.
   1977   *Murder in Space City: A Cultural Analysis of Houston Homicide Patterns.* New York: Oxford University Press.
Macaulay, Stewart
   1963   "Non-contractual relations in business: A preliminary study." *American Sociological Review* 28: 55–67.
Macfarlane, Alan
   1970   *Witchcraft in Tudor and Stuart England: A Regional and Comparative Study.* New York: Harper & Row.
MacLeod, William Christie
   1937   "Police and punishment among native Americans of the Plains." *Journal of the American Institute of Criminal Law and Crimonology* 28: 181–201.
McNeill, John T., and Helena M. Gamer (editors)
   1938   *Medieval Handbooks of Penance: A Translation of the Principal Libri Poenitentiales and Selections from Related Documents.* New York: Columbia University Press.
Malinowski, Bronislaw
   1926   *Crime and Custom in Savage Society.* Paterson, N.J.: Littlefield, Adams, 1962.
Mannheim, Karl
   1940   *Man and Society in an Age of Reconstruction: Studies in Modern Social Structure.* Revised edition. New York: Harcourt, Brace and World (1st edition, 1935).
Matza, David
   1969   *Becoming Deviant.* Englewood Cliffs, N.J.: Prentice-Hall.

34   Donald Black

Maybury-Lewis, David
1967   *Akwẽ-Shavante Society*. Oxford: Clarendon Press.
Middleton, John
    1965   *The Lugbara of Uganda*. New York: Holt, Rinehart and Winston.
Mileski, Maureen
    1971   "Courtroom encounters: An observation study of a lower criminal court." *Law and Society Review* 5: 473–538.
Moore, Sally Falk
    1972   "Legal liability and evolutionary interpretation: Some aspects of strict liability, self-help and collective responsibility." Pages 51–107 in *The Allocation of Responsibility*, edited by Max Gluckman. Manchester: Manchester University Press.
    1978   *Law as Process: An Anthropological Approach*. London: Routledge and Kegan Paul.
Nader, Laura (editor)
    1965   *The Ethnography of Law*. Supplement to *American Anthropologist* 67 (December).
Nader, Laura, and Harry F. Todd, Jr. (editors)
    1978   *The Disputing Process—Law in Ten Societies*. New York: Columbia University Press.
Park, Robert E., and Ernest W. Burgess
    1921   *Introduction to the Science of Sociology*. Abridged edition. Chicago: University of Chicago Press, 1969.
Parsons, Talcott
    1951   *The Social System*. New York: Free Press.
Peristiany, J. G. (editor)
    1966   *Honour and Shame: The Values of Mediterranean Society*. Chicago: University of Chicago Press.
Peters, E. L.
    1967   "Some structural aspects of the feud among the camel-herding Bedouin of Cyrenaica." *Africa* 37: 261–282.
Pitt-Rivers, Julian
    1966   "Honour and social status." Pages 19–77 in *Honour and Shame: The Values of Mediterranean Society*, edited by J. G. Peristiany. Chicago: University of Chicago Press.
Pollock, Frederick, and Frederic William Maitland
    1898   *The History of English Law: Before the Time of Edward I*. 2d edition. Cambridge: Cambridge University Press, 1968 (1st edition, 1895).
Pospisil, Leopold
    1958   *Kapauku Papuans and Their Law*. Yale University Publications in Anthropology, Number 54. New Haven, Conn.: Yale University Press.
Radcliffe-Brown, A. R.
    1952   "Taboo." Pages 133–152 in *Structure and Function in Primitive Society: Essays and Addresses*. New York: Free Press (originally presented as the Frazer Lecture in 1939).
Reay, Marie
    1974   "Changing conventions of dispute settlement in the Minj area." Pages 198–239 in *Contention and Dispute: Aspects of Law and Social Control in Melanesia*, edited by A. L. Epstein. Canberra: Australian National University Press.
Reid, John Phillip
    1970   *A Law of Blood: The Primitive Law of the Cherokee Nation*. New York: New York University Press.

1980   *Law for the Elephant: Property and Social Behavior on the Overland Trail.* San Marino, Calif.: Huntington Library.
Roberts, Simon
    1979   *Order and Dispute: An Introduction to Legal Anthropology.* New York: Penguin Books.
Ross, Edward Alsworth
    1901   *Social Control: A Survey of the Foundations of Order.* New York: Macmillan.
Sahlins, Marshall D.
    1958   *Social Stratification in Polynesia.* Seattle: University of Washington Press.
    1965   "On the sociology of primitive exchange." Pages 139–236 in *The Relevance of Models for Social Anthropology,* edited by Michael Banton. London: Tavistock.
Samaha, Joel
    1974   *Law and Order in Historical Perspective: The Case of Elizabethan Essex.* New York: Academic Press.
Sanders, William B., and Howard C. Daudistel (editors)
    1976   *The Criminal Justice Process: A Reader.* New York: Praeger.
Scheff, Thomas J.
    1966   *Being Mentally Ill: A Sociological Theory.* Chicago: Aldine Press.
Simmel, Georg
    1908   *The Sociology of Georg Simmel,* edited by Kurt H. Wolff. New York: Free Press, 1960.
Snyder, Francis G.
    1981   *Capitalism and Legal Change: An African Transformation.* New York: Academic Press.
Spradley, James P.
    1970   *You Owe Yourself a Drunk: An Ethnography of Urban Nomads.* Boston: Little, Brown.
Tentler, Thomas N.
    1977   *Sin and Confession on the Eve of the Reformation.* Princeton, N.J.: Princeton University Press.
Toulmin, Stephen
    1982   "Equity and principles." *Osgoode Hall Law Journal* 20: 1–17.
Turnbull, Colin M.
    1961   *The Forest People.* New York: Simon and Schuster.
    1965   *Wayward Servants: The Two Worlds of the African Pygmies.* Garden City, N.Y.: Natural History Press.
Vago, Steven
    1981   *Law and Society.* Englewood Cliffs, N.J.: Prentice-Hall.
van den Steenhoven, Geert
    1962   Leadership and Law among the Eskimos of the Keewatin District, Northwest Territories. Doctoral dissertation, Faculty of Law, University of Leiden.
Warner, W. Lloyd
    1958   *A Black Civilization: A Social Study of an Australian Tribe.* Revised edition. New York: Harper and Brothers (1st edition, 1937).
Weber, Max
    1925   *Max Weber on Law in Economy and Society,* edited by Max Rheinstein. Cambridge, Mass.: Harvard University Press, 1954 (2d edition; 1st edition, 1922).
Wiedemann, Thomas
    1981   *Greek and Roman Slavery.* Baltimore: Johns Hopkins University Press.

Wiseman, Jacqueline P.
    1970   *Stations of the Lost: The Treatment of Skid Row Alcoholics.* Englewood Cliffs, N.J.:
           Prentice-Hall.
Woodburn, James
    1979   "Minimal politics: The political organization of the Hadza of north Tanzania."
           Pages 244–266 in *Politics in Leadership: A Comparative Perspective,* edited by
           William A. Shack and Perry S. Cohen. Oxford: Clarendon Press.

2

The Division of Labor
in Social Control*

JOHN GRIFFITHS

Insofar as there has up to now been anything like a general explanatory theory of social control, it has tended to develop within the jurisdiction of the sociology and anthropology of law. The various attempts at explanatory theory that have been made in that context derive from a shared descriptive theory. Writers with otherwise little in common have been united in the assumption that there is a category of human experience called "social control" (or something similar), of which "law" is a distinct variety particularly worthy of or susceptible to study. This conception of the relationship between law and other social control as one of species to genus I shall henceforth refer to as the *taxonomic approach* to the concept of law. The purpose of this essay is to show what is wrong with it and to suggest an alternative.

What I want to establish in this essay is that a non-taxonomic descriptive theory is possible, an approach that makes the ancient dilemmas concerning the *differentiae* of "law" irrelevant.[1] "Legal" phenomena do

---

*An earlier version of this chapter was presented at the 1980 Annual Meeting of the Law and Society Association in Madison, Wisconsin.

[1]Intimations of a similar approach are to be found in Pospisil ("phenomena of social control often represent a continuum [1971: 19]"), but he goes on to argue, in seeming contradiction, that "unlike colors phenomena of social control are categorized into law, custom, political decisions, religious taboos, and so on, each on the basis of a different set

TOWARD A GENERAL THEORY OF SOCIAL CONTROL
Volume 1: Fundamentals

not have to be seen as a distinct species of social control requiring its own distinct explanatory theory. Instead, relative "legalness" can be regarded as one dimension of variation in social control, specifically, the *dimension of variation in the degree of division of social control labor*.[2] Social control is then conceived of not as consisting of "legal" and "non-legal" varieties, but as *more or less legal*—as exhibiting a greater or lesser degree of division of labor—wherever it occurs. Such an approach opens the way to the development of a general explanatory theory of social control that explains, among other things, its relative legalness. "Law," from such a vantage point, is revealed as a folk concept, suitable only for use within an internal perspective by the participants in a given system of institutionalized social control, as a means of distinguishing that system from its competitors.

Before we get into the exegesis and defense of such a conception of the relationship between law and social control, a few words are in order concerning the context in which it is to be read. The conception is proposed as a modification of the theory recently developed by Donald Black in *The Behavior of Law* (1976). Once "legalness" is seen as a dimension of variation in social control, it is possible to turn what Black sets forth as a theory of law conceived as one type of social control into a theory of social control in general.

Black's theory rests on three assumptions concerning the nature of the theoretical enterprise in sociology which I share[3] and which therefore underlie the arguments here. First, the subject matter of sociology is variation in social facts—the "behavior" of those facts. Second, the object of sociology is the prediction and explanation of such variation

---

of criteria (rather than on the basis of a quantity of the same criterion, as is the case with different colors)," which seems to put him squarely back into the taxonomic tradition; von Benda-Beckmann (law exists in all semiautonomous social formations, but the "degree to which" it exists—is "institutionalized"—varies greatly [1979: 26–38]); and Galanter (continuous variability in division of social control labor [1981: 19, n. 26]). See also Friedman and Macaulay (1977: 591). Yet so far as I am aware, no one has taken the consequences of such suggestions seriously with respect to the concept of law; that is, no one has seen in them the seed of a reformulation of the empirical concept of law capable of transcending the taxonomic tradition altogether. See von Benda-Beckmann (1981) for a criticism of "norm typologies" which on many points is parallel to the argument in this essay.

[2]Compare Engels, quoted in Stanley Moore (1960: 645): "With the development of civil society . . . the division of labour assigns to a few people the reconciliation of conflicting individual interests, and barbarous methods of protecting rights disappear."

[3]I do not share Black's belief that the phenomena of social control can be described without reference to rules, although I agree with him that the predictive value of rules is often small and that their independent explanatory value is negligible and theoretically problematic.

through the systematic formulation and testing of hypotheses which relate variation in one sort of social fact to variation in others and which are deducible from higher-order propositions (that is, propositions which apply to and are therefore testable on a wider range of sorts of variation than that which they are invoked to explain). And third, variation in social facts is in principle quantifiable. Thus, if concepts such as law, legalness, and social control are to figure in sociological theory, they must be taken as referring to identifiable social facts, and variation in those social facts should ultimately be expressible in quantitative terms.

The first problem for the sociology of law, given the preceding assumptions, is to identify the sort of social fact it takes as its subject matter. Without clarity about that, it either lacks cohesion as a science or simply borrows its conception of its subject matter from the everyday usage of the man in the street, whose use of his folk conception of "law" is as remote from the purposes of social science as his use of his conception of "matter" when he stubs his toe is from the concerns of particle physics.

The traditional approach to this problem of subject matter is the taxonomic one, in which a sociological theory of law must begin by identifying law as a specific sort of thing in the manner of taxonomic biology, by genus and species. However radical his theory of law may be in other respects, Black is altogether conventional so far as the structure of his descriptive theory is concerned. The subject matter of sociology of law is, for him, a certain species of the genus social control, to wit: social control by the state (Black, 1976: 2). As I hope to show, however, any such taxonomic identification of law as a species of social control is impossible. My quarrel with Black is, therefore, that he confines his explanatory theory to an arbitrarily delimited category of social control about which nothing general can be asserted. The sociology of "law" as such is a theoretically misguided undertaking, analogous to a physics of objects that are 75° or warmer. The general explanatory theory to be sought must be a theory of *social control*. Within such a general theory the causes and effects of variation in legalness—the degree of division of social control labor—must, of course, play a central role. A general theory of social control that ignores the dimension of legalness is like a physics that ignores temperature.

The argument in support of the various assertions made so far will proceed as follows. First, I examine the taxonomic approach and show it to be inadequate, largely via discussion of a well-known example of its use: Richard D. Schwartz's (1954) attempt to explain why one of two Israeli agricultural settlements exhibited "legal control" whereas the other exhibited "informal control." Against this background, I derive a reformulated conception of the relationship between law and social control that places the two Israeli settlements on a continuum of greater and lesser legalness in social control. Next, I show how the new conception can incorporate the results of existing research concerning law—that is, how that body of hitherto incommensurable propositions and data can be reduced to a coherent whole and thus form the basis for a general theory of social control. Having thus sought to make the new conception plausible in terms of existing research and theory, I turn to the question of its operationalization and address (in a tentative way) two questions: What is "division of labor" in social control? and What is "social control"? Finally, I take up the question that relates all of the foregoing to the development of a general theory of social control, namely, How is variation in the degree of division of labor in social control to be explained? Here I propose a modification, in light of what has gone before, of Black's theory of law, a modification which makes most of his propositions relevant to variation in social control generally, and one of them relevant to the extent to which social control is relatively legal.

Conceptions of the Relationship between Law and Social Control

The non-taxonomic conception of the relationship between law and social control derives from reflection on anomalies in Schwartz's (1954) study of social control in two Israeli settlements. One had a distinct judicial institution and the other did not, and Schwartz tries to explain why this was the case. For present purposes, it is not his explanatory strategy or the specific content of his explanations that is important, but rather his conceptualization of the variation that is to be explained. He distinguishes between "legal" and "informal" social control, and it is the presence of legal control in the one but not in the other settlement that arouses his curiosity. Legal control he defines as "that which is carried out by specialized functionaries who are socially delegated the task of intra-group control" (compare Homans, 1950: 284). The Judicial Committee of one settlement (the *moshav*), though simple in organization and procedure, was a "specialized agency" of legal control—a "distinctly legal institution"—for which no counterpart existed in the other settlement (the *kvutza*). The *kvutza*'s social control system "must be considered informal rather than legal" because the members of the *kvutza* had "not delegated sanctioning responsibility to any special unit." Public opinion was the major sanction of the *kvutza*'s social system, and "it is an instrument of control which is employed not by any specialized functionaries but by the community as a whole [pp. 907– 912]." His explanatory effort is directed at a discontinuous, binary variability, at the presence or absence of a distinct sort of thing. His conceptual apparatus exemplifies the taxonomic approach to the relationship between law and social control and represents a position in the taxonomic tradition that is quite familiar, especially among anthropologists (see, e.g., Hoebel, 1954; Pospisil, 1971).

One of the many admirable features of Schwartz's study is the richness of the illustrative material it offers to the reader.[4] This material enables one to criticize Schwartz's conceptual apparatus with the very data in terms of which he presents it. It is not true that the *kvutza*, which Schwartz describes as having only an informal social control system, knew no delegation to specialized functionaries of its social control labor. It merely delegated fewer, and to some extent different, aspects of that labor than did the *moshav*. It shared with the *moshav*, for example, a distinct legislative organ—the "General Assembly"—and Schwartz gives several examples of the legislative activity of this body in the *kvutza*.[5] Furthermore, the *kvutza*'s General Assembly as a whole did at least occasionally deal with particular trouble cases and hence functioned as a specialized judicial organ.[6] What can be said, then, against the conclusion that on Schwartz's own definition of legal control it was present in *both* settlements?

Two sorts of counterarguments could be made. It might be argued that the qualification "legal" is restricted to the delegation of *adjudicatory* labor to specialized organs and that only the *moshav*, with its Judicial

---

[4]Schwartz's data and his interpretation of them are confirmed in most important respects in a follow-up study by Shapiro (1976).

[5]The teakettle incident (1954: 476), which Schwartz himself refers to as involving "legislative work" by the General Assembly, led to a decision that members could not receive as personal property a gift of an expensive, electricity-consuming, and socially divisive apparatus such as an electric teakettle. The General Assembly also "modified the norm" on spending money, from a subjectively experienced need standard to a fixed annual amount, in reaction to the difficulty of exercising social control over spending behavior with the former sort of norm (1954: 490).

[6]The teakettle incident described in Note 5 is in part an example. So also is the case of the obstinate misfit, who was denied membership but ultimately had to be driven out of the *kvutza* by stronger measures (an action that Schwartz himself says could be considered "legal") (1954: 490). This case, and another involving someone who declined to dig trenches during Israel's war of independence and suffered for it later on, illustrate as well the specialized social control role of the work-assignment authorities, who in each case made assignments on punitive rather than on economic grounds. Finally, there is the case in which the Children's Assembly dealt with a banana theft (by abrogating the movie privileges of *all* the children) (1954: 482).

Committee, did this. There are two objections to this counterargument. First, it does not fit Schwartz's facts (since the General Assembly of the *kvutza* did do some adjudication). More importantly, it is a purely arbitrary restriction of the concept of law. There is no apparent reason why specialization in other aspects of social control should not be put on a equivalent theoretical footing with specialization in adjudication, especially since it is often difficult to recognize on the ground the tripartite separation of powers supposed by political theory. Neither settlement seems to have had specialized enforcement (despite Schwartz's at times rather loose reference to delegated "sanctioning"), but if they had had, I would still see no reason not to recognize this also as representing some degree of formality in social control. On the other hand, both settlements had specialized legislating, making them distinctly more formal than other societies that lack this aspect of division of social control labor. Restricting the concept of law to one arbitrarily selected aspect of the division of social control labor has nothing to recommend it.

A second counterargument could be made against the conclusion that according to Schwartz's own definition legal control was present in the *kvutza* as well as in the *moshav*. It could be argued that the *kvutza* lacked "specialization" in the required sense. Schwartz may have implicitly rejected the idea that a group can be said to have "delegated" part of its social control work to a "specialized" organ if that organ consists of all the group's members. But however plausible such an argument seems on first impression, it would be wrong; it ignores the distinction between acting in a personal and in an official capacity. When the *kvutza*'s General Assembly legislated or adjudicated, its members acted in their official capacity—they acted in a way in which they were quite incapable of acting when not sitting as members of the General Assembly. Voting for a new rule and participating in its judicial application are fundamentally different from exercising direct, unspecialized, everyday social control. The difference is one between a situation in which there are and one in which there are not "secondary" rules which institutionalize social control alongside "primary" rules of a substantive nature (see Hart, 1961; see also Fallers, 1969: 11; Richards, 1971: 2). The fact is that Schwartz's "informal" settlement is nowhere near the bottom end of the specialization spectrum. There are well-known instances of societies in which almost no specialized legislative and almost no specialized judicial role exists, not even one lodged in all of the society's members together—societies, that is, in which the specialized *functions* of legislation and adjudication are practically unknown (see, e.g., Marshall, 1960; Goody, 1967). In short, there was specialization of social control labor in the *kvutza* in the sense that its General Assembly did things—legislation and adjudication—that no individuals, acting individually, could do themselves; and the *kvutza* was relatively formal in its social control in the sense that there are other societies that lack institutions capable of such specialized behavior.[7]

It follows that according to Schwartz's own criteria both settlements had "formal" control, which leaves him without any variation to explain. And yet there obviously was a difference. But Schwartz's formal/informal dichotomy—his version of the traditional legal/non-legal taxonomic dichotomy—is inadequate to capture the difference that existed. Although the *kvutza* did not lack formal control, it did have it in lesser degree than the *moshav*. The latter settlement had all of the specialized organs the former had, plus one additional level of adjudicatory specialization, the Judicial Committee. Schwartz's analysis would not be subject to the objections I have raised if he had made what seems an almost trivial change: that is, had he sought to explain why one society had more of something than the other, instead of trying to explain why the one had that thing and the other did not.

What is wrong with the taxonomic approach to the relationship between law and social control? I believe the question once asked scarcely needs extensive argumentation, so I shall merely note some of the more important considerations:

1. The taxonomic approach has proved to be a hopeless dead end. No one has ever been able to secure agreement about where the line between "law" and "no-law" should be drawn. Reflection on the lessons to be drawn from the taxonomic literature leads to the conclusion that every taxonomic answer to the question, What are the empirical attributes of law as a distinct type of social control? is doomed to a frustrating and unproductive failure. Lack of a common definition of its central concept stands in the way of cumulative research and theory construction in the sociology and anthropology of law.

---

[7]See, for example, Gulliver's (1963) description of the Arusha of Tanzania. But it would be equally wrong to say that the Arusha lacked "legal" control altogether—their control was merely *less* "legal" than that of the *kvutza*. Arusha processes involved distinct roles for elected and removable "spokesmen" who had well-understood duties and even the power (rarely used) of executing sanctions.

If the frequently heard association between the role of a third party in dispute processes and the relative "legalism" characteristic of the application of rules in such processes is correct (see, e.g., Aubert, 1963; Fallers, 1969; Abel, 1973: 280–282), then the apparently greater "legalism" of *kvutza* social control processes than of those among the Arusha can be explained in terms of the role of the General Assembly—the community as a whole in institutionalized form—as a third party in *kvutza* social control processes. The community is present as a factor in Arusha social control processes, of course, but only as a diffuse background entity not institutionalized by means of secondary rules.

2. Even if a dividing line could be agreed on, the essential arbitrariness of any such dichotomization of a continuous variability impedes the development of powerful explanatory propositions concerning either law or social control. Situations close to either side of *any* arbitrarily selected line will have more in common with each other than either will have with situations further removed from it although within its own classification. The *moshav*'s "legal" control, for example, is far closer to the *kvutza*'s "non-legal" control than either is to the "legal" control of the state. No proposition is likely to be true of all "legal" states of affairs by contrast with all "non-legal" ones, any more than anything would be likely to be true of all "hot" things by contrast with all "cold" ones. All theories of law, taxonomically conceived, are at the same time under- and over-inclusive, and the same is true for all theories of non-legal social control.

Black tries to escape this problem in an ingenious and revealing way. One of his propositions is that legal social control varies inversely with non-legal social control (1976: 107). And all of his other propositions concerning variation in law also apply to variation in non-legal social control. To the extent that any predicted variation in law does not take place because of the under- or over-inclusiveness of his propositions— that is, because the predicted variation did take place, but just over the law/no-law divide—his theory automatically adjusts and explains the non-occurrence of the predicted variation in law in terms of some counterbalancing non-predicted variation in non-legal social control. It thus explains variation in *all social control*, the legal and the non-legal together. It is a theory of social control and offers in the end no explanation at all for the form—legal or non-legal—that social control exhibits. This inner logic does rescue Black's theory from the dilemma of under- and over-inclusiveness built into the taxonomic approach to the concept of law, but it does so at the cost of cutting the heart out of his theory. His book is entitled, after all, *The Behavior of Law*. I shall return to this problem with Black's approach, and what can be done about it, at the end of this essay.

3. The preceding paragraphs take it as given that the variability in social control, of which some range is designated "law" on the taxonomic approach, is continuous, so that *any* line between "law" and "no-law" will be arbitrary. The taxonomic approach requires that those who adopt it justify the dividing line they choose. The nature of the justifications proffered is itself sufficient reason to incline one toward the judgment that the line must be an arbitrary one (at least for empirical purposes). Such justifications are nearly always, explicitly or implicitly, in terms of the ideal essence of law or of some moral *desiderata* that

anything to be dubbed law ought to exhibit. The popularity over the past couple of centuries, for example, of the identification of law with the nation-state plainly derives from liberal ideas concerning the essential qualities and moral values inherent in law—uniformity, formal equality, predictability, and the like, which the liberal tradition associates with the modern nation-state (see, e.g., Austin, 1832; Radcliffe-Brown, 1933; see also generally M. Smith, 1974: 114–121). An empirical theory of law and of social control generally cannot be erected on the foundation of such a conception because it is not empirically operationalizable (see Black, 1972).

Of course, there is nothing in the taxonomic approach which makes specification of the line between law and other social control in nonempirical terms inescapable. But there seems to be only one other possibility: One can concede the essential arbitrariness of the criterion selected and defend it either on strictly practical grounds (e.g., the state assembles statistics concerning the social control work done by its agencies) or not at all. By conceding that the location of the line is arbitrary, however, one necessarily concedes that the taxonomic division of social control into law and other social control is, empirically considered, arbitrary. It follows that the sociology of law has no distinct empirical object to study, that is, that it cannot exist as a discipline. One can hardly imagine a "sociology of the topics on which the state maintains official statistics" as a scientific enterprise. It also follows that the idea of "the legal," taxonomically conceived, cannot figure in a general theory of social control. The taxonomic approach hence leads inexorably, via the impossibility of drawing the line it requires in a satisfactory way, to a kind of conceptual nihilism (as seen, e.g., in Llewellyn, 1939: 431; Frank, 1963: viii; Abel, 1973: 221–224). But the intuition most of us have that there actually is something in the world that more of less corresponds to our everyday commonsensical experiences with legal phenomena refuses to die on command. A general theory of social control which, because of the taxonomic approach to the concept of law, is robbed of any capacity to address such everyday experience of the "legal" is an impoverished theory. The problem lies not with the empirical content of our experiences of law but rather with the failure of sociology and philosophy to capture the object of that experience with a suitable conception.[8]

[8]Given the specifically empirical concerns of my argument, it is striking that an analysis of the concept of law from a rather different perspective, and dealing with a different body of intellectual experience, has come to a closely parallel conclusion. In *Taking Rights Seriously*, Ronald Dworkin mounts a "general attack on [legal] positivism [1977: 22]." Legal positivism is a collection of taxonomic approaches to the question What is a rule of law?—

4. The taxonomic approach leads either to the conclusion that some social fields have no law or to selection of a criterion for distinguishing "law" from "no-law" that treats practically all instances of social control as instances of law. Both options are unsatisfactory because they make it impossible for a general theory of social control to address its propositions concerning variability in the legal dimension of social control to all social fields: A theory of social control that adopts the taxonomic approach will in this sense be not a general but only a particular one. Anthropologists, especially, have long struggled against definitions of law, in terms of the state or of courts, which have as an implication that many societies have no law. This struggle seems to derive partly from moral and political concerns that have nothing to do with science and so need not concern us here. But it seems also to rest on the implicit judgment that sociological theories which employ variables not present in a good many societies are poor sociological theories: They are theories applicable only to some classes of social fields, not to social life as a whole (see Black, 1972: 1096–1097; Abel, 1973: 221).

It seems impossible to define law in taxonomic terms as a universal social fact. One can pick a very abstract criterion such as "authority" to distinguish law from the rest of social control, but to ensure that law is universally observable, one must then stretch the concept of authority until it is almost unrecognizable and, in any event, unusable for empirical purposes (e.g., Llewellyn and Hoebel, 1941: 283–284; Pospisil, 1971). Or one can pick "obligation"—"the rules of law stand out from the rest in that they are felt and regarded as the obligations of one person and the rightful claims of another [Malinowski, 1926: 55]"—but this suffers from the simultaneous defects of being subjective and including vir-

---

approaches, that is, which seek to answer that question by identifying legal rules as a particular species of a genus, usually, as Dworkin puts it, by means of their "pedigree" (e.g., commands of a sovereign). As with taxonomic approaches generally, "different versions of legal positivism differ chiefly in their description of the fundamental test of pedigree a rule must meet to count as a rule of law [p. 17]." The conclusion of Dworkin's argument is that legal standards cannot be taxonomically identified, that they cannot be "distinguished in principle and as a group from moral or political standards [p. 60]." "Moral or political standards" in this context refers to the standards of *positive* morality (see Griffiths, 1978a: 1139–1142). Because the standards of positive morality are simply those of social control, we can translate Dworkin's conclusion into the terms of my argument as follows: The rules of law cannot be distinguished in principle and as a group from the rules of social control.

That the taxonomic approach should thus appear incapable of supporting a philosophical analysis of the concept of law, whereas it is also incapable, as I argue here, of supporting an empirical theory of law, seem to be two good and mutually reinforcing reasons to look for a better approach.

tually all of social control within the concept of law. If one turns to more concrete criteria—courts, physical sanctions, and so on—one is confronted by the twin objections that none of them is universally present in all social fields and that even some of what is generally regarded as "legal" in our own society is not captured by them. In short, the trouble with concrete, empirically usable criteria is that they are all under-inclusive, and the trouble with all criteria that are universally present is that because they include all or practically all of social control within the concept of law, they are vague and unusable.

If we choose to study *legalness* as a kind of variability in social control instead of *law* as a species of social control all these difficulties disappear:

1. The sociology of law and of social control is out of the taxonomic cul-de-sac altogether. The legal aspect of social control is no longer sought in a variety of social control but rather in a kind of variation in social control. The tiresome and quarrelsome chase after a criterion for distinguishing law from social control generally is irrelevant. Not only will abandoning the taxonomic approach permit cumulative research in the future, but we can apply a non-taxonomic approach retroactively to bring hitherto incommensurable research results into a common scale. The theory of law can be integrated into the general theory of social control as that aspect of the more general theory which specifically addresses one dimension of variation, the division of labor.

2. Since we are no longer trying to distinguish between two sorts of social control, the over- and under-inclusiveness of any dividing line is no longer a problem for the development of a theory of law and of a general theory of social control.

3. For the same reason, the tendency toward essentialistic or moralistic criteria for distinguishing law from no-law is no longer a problem, and the nihilism that says that any definition of law is impossible loses its appeal.

4. Finally, although it is difficult to define law in a way which makes it universally present in human societies, every society can be located on a dimension of variation in the division of social control labor. The question is no longer whether a given society has law, but to what degree its social control is legal.

By making it possible to avoid altogether the incommensurable taxonomic criteria which have so far stood in the way of cumulative research and theory, by overcoming the difficulties of over- and under-inclusiveness built into the taxonomic approach, by eliminating the appeal of non-empirical conceptions of law and of nihilistic arbitrariness concerning the nature of the legal as an aspect of variability in social control, and by providing a universally applicable but also empirically usable conception of that variability, a successful non-taxonomic approach to the relationship between law and social control provides an essential condition for a general theory of social control. But a conviction that the taxonomic approach should be abandoned is not yet a persuasive argument for any given proposed alternative. Although the usefulness of a conception of legalness as variability in the division of social control labor seems plausible—given the way we derived it from Schwartz's comparison of the *kvutza* and the *moshav*—we must now squarely confront the question of whether a reformulation of the relationship between law and social control in terms of a conception of continuously variable legalness can be made to do empirical work. There are two aspects to that question: Will such a change require us to jettison whatever accumulation of understanding we have acquired within the taxonomic tradition? And can some apparent difficulties with this conception of legalness be overcome? The next two sections of this essay take up those questions in turn.

The New Conception and the Old Sociologies of Law and Social Control

Would adopting a conception of the "legal" as the degree of division of social control labor preclude further use of the fruits of work within the taxonomic tradition? Far from it. The new conception affords a common scale for research results which have hitherto appeared to concern different things and which have therefore been recalcitrant to subsumption under any general theory. Whatever position a given researcher has adopted in the taxonomic debate, we can take his or her references to "law" not as indications of the presence of a distinct type of social control in his or her data, but as an indication of the general level of division of social control labor with which his or her data are concerned. The conception of legalness as the degree of division of social control labor permits us to reread the fruits of research in the taxonomic tradition in the following way: A taxonomic definition of law determines a point on the continuum of increasing division of social control labor, and the data reported concern variation in social control behavior holding constant the extent to which social control labor is divided. Black's (1976) theory of law concerns the explanation of variation of just this sort.

The continuum of variation in the division of social control labor (DSCL) begins at absolute zero and extends outward indefinitely:

LEGALNESS

No DSCL   Increasing DSCL

•——>

To the extent that a distinction between law and social control is made in terms of specialization—or can be translated into such terms—that distinction can be located at least ordinally on this scale. It can be regarded as the identification of a point on the continuum beyond which the author concerned chooses to regard social control phenomena as "legal," and below which they are regarded as something else ("other social control," "custom," etc., even—sometimes and yet more confusingly—"morality"):

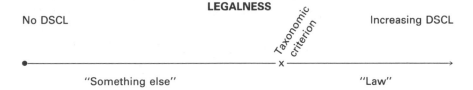

To the extent that existing conceptions of law can be located on such a scale, then, despite the bewildering variety of definitions, which make it look as if the authors concerned are writing about radically different things, it will turn out that they have really only been differing over points on a common line. It is as if people had quarrelled for years about whether the difference between "hot" and "cold" lay at the freezing point of water, at body temperature, or at the boiling point and then realized that a single dimension of continuous variation underlies the contending positions. Hitherto incommensurable research results concerning the causes and effects of temperature differences could then be unified and made cumulative on the basis of the common scale underlying the various dichotomies.

This brings me to the crux of the matter: Can we in fact locate most or all of the important empirical conceptions of law as points on a scale of variability in the division of social control labor? This can be done in a rough and ready way with a few simple annotations on the scale of increasing legalness:

Authority   *Institutions*   **LEGALNESS**   *State*

No DSCL   Increasing DSCL

•——>

0   a   b   c

The annotations are given here for their heuristic value only. However crude, such subdivisions of the continuum are more or less sufficient to deal with the existing literature. (I shall ignore in what follows the various "manifestations" of law [Pospisil, 1971: 18]—rules, decisions, official behavior, and so on—that the writers with whom I shall deal had in mind, for the qualification "more or less legal" for which I am arguing can be applied to any such "manifestation.")

RANGE 0–a: FROM NO DIVISION OF SOCIAL
CONTROL LABOR TO SOCIAL ARRANGEMENTS
SHORT OF DISTINCT "AUTHORITIES"

Malinowski's is the most inclusive conception of law as a category of social control phenomena. He treats it as equivalent to obligatory social rules sanctioned by "a purely social binding force [1926: 51]"—in short, as equivalent to social control in general. Malinowski explicitly rejects the idea that law entails "independent institutions [p. 59]." He regards it as "one well-defined category within the body of custom [p. 54]," a conception which excludes only those categories of regular behavior from which a normative element is wholly absent, such as "patterns of pottery making, flint flaking, tooth filing, toilet training, and all the other social habits of a people," to quote Hoebel's (1954: 20) characterization of pre-Malinowskian conceptions which had treated law as equivalent to custom in general. (In fact, Malinowski's conception *does* encompass tooth filing if it is made obligatory—enforced by means of social rules.) Malinowski's treatment of Trobriand law is, to translate into the conception of the relationship between law and social control for which I am arguing, an account of social control at a very low level of division of labor. His analysis of the relatively non-legal social control (which he calls "law") among the Trobrianders is strikingly similar to Schwartz's account of similar social control (which Schwartz calls "informal") on the Israeli *kvutza,* although the precise mechanisms of interdependence in the two societies are rather different (see also Homans, 1950: chap. 11; Macaulay, 1963). Like Schwartz, Malinowski is trapped by the taxonomic approach to the concept of law into ignoring instances of specialization in his own data, and Trobriand society was probably somewhat more legal than his discussion suggests.[9]

[9]The role of "sorcerer," for example, seems to have been a specialized one, and Malinowski himself describes the "black magic" a sorcerer uses as "a genuinely legal force, for it is used in carrying out the rules of tribal law." The role appears, from his brief discussion, to have encompassed judicial and executory elements (1926: 86). For other examples of social control specialists in circumstances of very little division of social control labor,

A more recent example of a taxonomic approach to law as obligatory social rules, explicitly Malinowskian in inspiration, is Sally Falk Moore's conception of the "semi-autonomous social field" which has "rule-making capacities, and the means to induce or coerce compliance [1973: 720]." But limited as she is by the traditional taxonomic approach to the concept of law, Moore seems not to be able to make up her mind whether she is analyzing the interaction in a semi-autonomous social field of that field's law with external law which challenges the field's autonomy or whether she is describing the interaction of law (of the state) with another sort of binding rule ("non-legal and illegal [1973: 729]"). In subsequent writing Moore has suggested that we abandon the term *law* altogether for the term *reglementation*, referring to phenomena which (by definition) are present in every semi-autonomous social field (1978: 17–19, 30). She thereby recognizes the existence of social control activity pursuant to social rules as a universal feature of all semi-autonomous social fields and apparently abandons her earlier inclination to divide that activity taxonomically into legal and non-legal sorts, depending on the "sources" of rules and of coercion. The "reglementation" she has in mind varies from almost entirely unspecialized social control to the highly specialized social control of the state.

RANGE a–b: FROM "AUTHORITIES"
TO "INSTITUTIONS"

Pospisil is the most insistent proponent within the taxonomic tradition of a conception of law as social control which exhibits all degrees of division of social control labor above the point at which the specialization of "authority" can be identified. He defines law (so far as the purposes of my present argument are concerned) as those rules of "institutionalized social control" which are applied in decisions of a "legal authority [1971: 95]," and a "legal authority" as "an individual or group of individuals . . . whose decisions are followed by the majority of the group's members [p. 57]" (see also Llewellyn and Hoebel, 1941: 23–29, 283–285). His "comparative theory" of law is, thus, a theory concerning those social rules applied in social control at and above a certain level of division of social control labor. Variation in the degree of specialization above the level of "authority" is not held constant. Once one draws the line at "authority," a rule inferred from the settlement that a Kapauku

---

see Roberts, 1979: 89 (clowns), 95–96 (priests); Evans-Pritchard, 1940 (leopard-skin chiefs); and Gulliver, 1963 (counselors). See generally Black and Baumgartner (1983) for a typology of specialized third parties in social control settings.

elder begs the parties to accept is just as "legal" as a rule formulated by a
court of last resort in the hierarchy of a modern state. Insisting that
"law" is present in both cases seems just as unilluminating as the older
tradition of insisting that the "law" of the state is radically different from
the "social control" of the Kapauku.

RANGE b–c: FROM "INSTITUTIONS" TO THE "STATE"

We come here to what seems nowadays the commonest conception of
law among anthropologists: Social control is considered "legal" if it is
institutionalized. The type of institution generally contemplated is an
adjudicative one—a tribunal or a court (e.g., Schapera, 1938: 38; Gluckman, 1967: 164; see also Stanley Moore, 1960, discussing the views of
Marx and Engels). The jurisprudential foundation for the conception of
law as institutionalized social control is laid in H. L. A. Hart's *The Concept of Law* (1961). Hart argues that law is characterized by the union of
two kinds of rules: "primary rules" of behavior (which in themselves do
not differ from the "social rules" of non-legal social control) and "secondary rules" which provide for the identification, application, and
change of primary rules. These secondary rules constitute and regulate
the legal institutions which distinguish law from other forms of social
control. To put the matter in terms of Bohannan's notion of "double
institutionalization": "Law is . . . 'a body of binding obligations regarded as right by one party and acknowledged as the duty by the other'
[quoting Malinowski, 1926: 58] *which has been reinstitutionalized within the
legal institution. . . .* [1965: 36]." Like Hart, Bohannan observes that "it is
one of the most characteristic attributes of legal institutions that some of
these laws [i.e., *re*institutionalized customs] are about the legal institutions themselves [p. 36]" (compare Fallers's use of Hart's analysis, 1969:
11).[10]

Within the range of variation just described, one important group of

---

[10]For reasons which have been extensively argued by Dworkin (1977), the idea that
"legal standards can be distinguished in principle and as a group from moral or political
standards [p. 60]," in the way that Hart and Bohannon explicitly and the rest of the
institutionalized-social-control school of thought implicitly suppose, is mistaken. See Note
8. The secondary rules constitutive of institutions cannot be distinguished in principle
from the secondary rules entailed in all specialized social control, from the most rudimen-
tary forms of "authority" (in a Pospisilian sense) on up. Institutionalization is, like law, a
matter of degree, not of kind, and the institutions contemplated by Hart and Bohannon
cannot be taxonomically distinguished from all other situations of division of social control
labor. It can never be a useful exercise to worry about whether the *kvutza*'s General
Assembly, for example, was or was not an "institition," or to try to settle the question by
definition.

writers has emphasized adjudicatory institutions. There is, however, nothing essential to the conception of law as institutionalized social control that requires such an interpretation. Thus, Max Weber defined law as an "order [that is] externally guaranteed by the probability that coercion (physical or psychological), to bring about conformity or avenge violation, will be applied by a *staff* of people holding themselves specially ready for that purpose [1925: 5]." It is not coercion in itself that is essential, for law shares that aspect with social control generally: What is "lacking [from non-legal social control is] the staff which could hold itself specifically ready for action meant to guarantee obedience [p. 6]." For Weber, the required division of labor—its specialization in an enforcement "staff"—need not entail "any judicial organ"; and he refers inclusively to agents of social control "such as judges, prosecutors, policemen, or sheriffs," and includes even "blood vengeance and feud," provided that they are institutionalized in "some kind of regulatory order [p. 6]." Specialization more or less confined to the execution of social control has received little attention in the ethnographic literature but is by no means an unheard-of state of affairs (see, e.g., Griffiths, 1983).

Hoebel's conception is similar to Weber's: "A social norm is legal if its neglect or infraction is regularly met, in threat or in fact, by the application of physical force by an individual or group possessing the socially recognized privilege of so acting [1954: 28]" (compare Schapera, 1957: 153–154). From the structure of Hoebel's argument, however, it appears that he may regard both specialized adjudication and specialized enforcement as essential to the concept of law. If so, his conception of law belongs at a slightly higher point along the continuum of increasing specialization of social control labor, where the coexistence of more than one sort of specialized institution is required before social control is deemed to qualify as law. Evan is an explicit exponent of such a conception. He identifies "three normative functions . . . [which] are performed by the occupants of specialized statuses: legislative, judicial, and executive," and rejects what he takes to be Ehrlich's conception of law as primary social rules of conduct because it does not limit the legal to situations in which "statuses are . . . functionally specific relative to the three analytically distinguishable normative processes [1962: 168]."

RANGE c- › : POLITICALLY ORGANIZED SOCIETY
AND HIGHER DEGREES OF DIVISION OF SOCIAL
CONTROL LABOR

Taxonomic conceptions of law as an aspect of a politically organized society, or the state, are legion. For lawyers, the ancestral Austinian definition of law as commands of a sovereign (Austin, 1832, discussed in Hart, 1961: chap. 2) will suffice as a representative.[11] For anthropologists, the classic example is Radcliffe-Brown (1933: 212, quoting Roscoe Pound): Law is "social control through the systematic application of the force of politically organized society." And for sociologists, the most recent and uncompromising representative is Black, who defines law as "governmental social control [1976: 2]."[12]

There are many objections to the identification of law with the state for purposes of empirical work, but only a few are of interest here. The first is that it is not possible to distinguish taxonomically the social control activities of the state from the rest of social control.[13] A second objection is that the identification is arbitrary. I do not mean to invoke the hoary old canard that defining law in terms of the state is ethnocentric, that it is offensive because it entails the conclusion that some societies have no law (see, e.g., Pospisil, 1971: 13–14). This seems to me about as persuasive as an objection to the definition of a mammal in terms of warm blood and the rest on the grounds that it is mammalocentric and offensive to reptiles and fish. There is no empirical reason why all societies must be definitionally guaranteed to have law. Rather, the objection is that such a criterion for law is arbitrary in the sense that no case has been made for its scientific value and that it seems rather unlikely that such a case could be made. Those who restrict the concept of law to social control by the state are in a position similar to that of someone who would restrict the concept of a mammal to those warm-blooded, and so on, species *which can be found in zoos:* The short-term practical advantage of the limitation is obvious, but its scientific value— its special potential for contributing to biological theory—is rather obscure. They seem to be good reasons for treating social control on both sides of the "state" line within the same general theory and therefore for avoiding a conception of the object of explanation which does not en-

---

[11]Legal realist definitions of law in terms of (predictions of) court behavior usually belong in this range as well, since the "courts" contemplated are agencies of the state. But compare Radin (1938: 1145, n. 11), quoted with apparent approval by Hoebel (1954: 23) and Llewellyn and Hoebel (1941: 23–49).

[12]Black himself anticipates the argument of this essay, namely, that the taxonomic approach is an obstacle to the development of a general theory of social control, in the following footnote to his taxonomic definition of law as "governmental social control":

> For me the choice of a particular sociological concept of law is not at all critical to my larger aim, since my ultimate interest goes beyond law per se to all forms of social control. For me, the study of law is preliminary and subordinate to the more general study of social control systems of all kinds. Therefore, if my concept of law is too narrow or too broad it does not matter theoretically, since it will in any case be relevant to a sociology of social control [1972: 1096, n. 35].

[13]See Note 11.

compass all sorts of specialized behavior that (*a*) exhibit similar distinctive characteristics (legal reasoning, specialized production and administration of norms, conflict prevention and regulation, etc.); (*b*) take place in response to similar sorts of triggering circumstances and seem to be more or less interchangeable social responses to such circumstances; and (*c*) have the same genesis and a common history.

Many sociologists and anthropologists of law in recent years have been persuaded by one or another of the just-mentioned arguments to reject the identification of law with the state, and as already noted, most of these have accepted some version of the conception of law as institutionalized social control. Even those whose definition of law commits them to the requirement of a state often slip into referring to other specialized social control as "law" (see, e.g., Black, 1976: 109).

It is not necessary to reject any of the interesting work done by those who have treated law as "governmental social control," despite the reservations set forth earlier concerning that conception of law. The state can, for our purposes, be regarded as reflecting merely a higher degree of division of social control labor than the non-state institutionalization that comes just below it on the scale of increasing specialization. At a minimum, the notion of the state entails not only specialization of *function* for adjudication, execution, and legislation but also specialization of *persons:* These social control tasks must be carried out by a more or less permanent staff which is more or less exclusively devoted to them and which is more or less distinct from the population at large. Specialization of the whole enterprise of government and, within that enterprise, social control is characteristic of what we call the state; the state is, so far as social control is concerned, merely one step further in the direction of increasing specialization. What Black calls a "theory of law [1976: 6]" is thus a theory of social control with the degree of division of labor held fairly constant and rather high.

We are now at the end of a long argument, the purpose of which has been to support the contention that legalness should be conceived as the division of labor in social control, and that doing so, far from requiring the rejection of all earlier empirical work, for the first time puts that work onto a common scale, makes its results commensurable and potentially cumulative, and hence offers some hope for the development of an empirical theory of social control in general.

The Concept of Division of Social Control Labor

Up to this point I have taken it for granted that it is clear what is meant by the expression "division of social control labor." Specialization in social control, after all, plays an important implicit or explicit part in all of the taxonomic conceptions of law we have been considering. But its application to observable phenomena is certainly not unproblematic. It is therefore appropriate to address some attention to questions of operationalization. It would be fatuous, however, to try to settle such questions even provisionally at this point. My intention is merely to raise them and to say just enough about them to lend some plausibility to the assumption that the problems entailed in operationalization can be overcome.

WHAT IS THE DIVISION OF LABOR IN
SOCIAL CONTROL?

The first problem is, To what, precisely, does "division of labor" refer? We have to be satisfied that at least an ordinal measure can be constructed before we can attribute much practical significance to the proposition that legalness is a continuous variable. Given the central role that the idea of division of labor has played in both economics and sociology, and the familiar way in which it is commonly bandied about, one might feel entitled to expect some accumulated precision in its operationalization. One would be disappointed. Beginning with Durkheim, there has been an irregular trickle of complaints at the fact that "the theory of the division of labor has made such little progress since Adam Smith [Durkheim 1893: 46]." Marx (1887: chap. 14) and Weber (1922: 218ff.) have made some tentative distinctions between types of division of labor, but neither attempted to apply these distinctions in empirical work, let alone to reduce them to a quantifiable variable that could figure in a theoretical proposition such as Adam Smith's association of market size with the extent of the division of labor (1776: 17–21).

A small flurry of recent work has busied itself with quantifiability, dealing with the number of roles in a productive unit and the distribution of the relevant population over these roles (see, e.g., Kemper, 1972; Gibbs and Poston, 1975; D. Smith and Snow, 1976). The basic idea is that the division of labor is a function of the number of roles in relation to population and of the equality of the distribution of actors over the available roles. The key trouble with such an approach, for our purposes, is that it deals with overall occupational *differentiation*, not with the degree of *specialization* in the performance of one particular task. It permits comparisons of social fields in terms of their overall level of division of labor, but it does not permit comparisons of such fields in terms of the degree to which any given task, such as social control, is specialized.

There is another important objection to the various measures of differentiation just mentioned: They take no account of several aspects of the division of labor which feature prominently in social control. Thus, they ignore the relative permanence with which an actor is assigned to a role, although it seems that a social field in which social control roles can be filled on a rotation basis by various different actors exhibits less specialization than one in which such roles are occupied on a relatively permanent basis. A related objection is that they ignore the problem of part-time occupancy of roles. They ignore, in short, the distinction between role-specialization and actor-specialization. This distinction is essential in social control: The existence of a specialized legislative role is important, for example, even if everyone fills it at the same (officially appointed) time. Without an adequate treatment of the variables of impermanent and part-time role-occupancy, such central features of many legal systems as lay judges and juries cannot be dealt with. In short, the measures in their present form are simply inapplicable to many legal systems which have no permanent, full-time occupants of legal roles, and are inapplicable to important aspects of most of the rest.

In this essay the *division of social control labor* refers to the extent to which the various activities comprising social control are "delegated" (in Schwartz's expression) to specialists. The extent of such delegation is a function of two main factors: the proportion of total social control labor which is so delegated, and the degree of specialization which obtains.[14] At least rough ordinal measurement of the proportion of delegated social control labor seems to have presented researchers with no insuperable difficulties. Various researchers have shown, for example, that the ratio of specialized to total social control labor in the case of distinct sorts of behavior between family members is lower than in the case of persons not so related (see Black, 1976: 107–109).

The degree of specialization would seem to be a function of at least the following elements: the degree of differentiation within a social control institution; the degree to which social control roles are performed full time, to the exclusion of other tasks, by the incumbents; the degree of permanence with which incumbents occupy such roles; and the proportion of the population engaged in such tasks (see Abel, 1973: 253–255). Thus Schwartz (1954) considered that the *moshav* exhibited a higher level of specialization because it had at least one distinct social control role which the *kvutza* lacked. If the Judicial Committee of the *moshav* had exhibited internal specialization (e.g., by having a jury together with the

---

[14]In all but the simplest social situation one will have to deal with aggregates based on delegation to a number of different sorts of institutions.

judges, or an appeals body above them) he would presumably have regarded social control in the *moshav* as still more specialized. Similarly, a Judicial Committee whose members were permanently appointed (hence not interchangeable with the rest of the population) would have been considered more specialized than one whose membership fluctuated, while on the other hand the less of his working time each member spent on Judicial Committee work, the less specialized social control labor would have been regarded. And a Judicial Committee consisting of many or all of the *moshav*'s members would have been less specialized than one to which only a few members were appointed.

Operationalization of the concept of division of social control labor along the lines suggested will permit comparisons of social control in different social fields, as long as all but one of the component elements can be held fairly constant (so that an increase in the number of roles does not have to be weighed against a decrease in the permanence of assignment, for example). It should ultimately be possible to reduce the variable to a single dimension.

The concept can likewise be operationalized for comparisons of tribunals or processes within a single social field as, for example, when one is concerned with differences in the "legalness" of the institutions available for dealing with a given sort of conflict. In that case, only the degree of specialization and not the relative frequency of delegation is relevant.

THE NATURE OF SOCIAL CONTROL LABOR

What is "social control"? The place to begin is, I believe, Hoebel's observation that the variability exhibited by human behavior in any given setting is but a fraction of what could in principle occur (1954: 10ff.; see also von Benda-Beckmann, 1979: 25, 28). The infinite imaginable variability of behavior is limited by the biological and psychological nature of human beings, by external constraints (of which some are natural and some are the results of prior human endeavors, such as technology), and by social constraints. Social constraints on behavior include all those reductions in the variability of behavior beyond what human nature and the external circumstances with which it is confronted can account for, or to put the matter in its positive form, all those reductions in the variability of behavior for which a set of specific social arrangements is responsible.

If this were what was meant by "social control" by those who use that concept in the sociology of law, then it would be a difficult but in principle reasonably distinct idea. It seems clear, however, that when Black (1976) and Pospisil (1971), for example, contrast law with other social control, and when Schwartz (1954) contrasts control not delegated to specialized functionaries with control which is so delegated, none of them is contemplating education, propaganda, and the like, as forms of social control. On the other hand, no one doubts that these social activities do tend to reduce the variability of behavior. We must therefore distinguish socialization (all those processes which work on the value that individuals attach to potential sorts of behavior) from social control: those processes which take individuals as they are and manipulate the relative eligibility—to invoke a traditional Utilitarian term (see Hart, 1968: 165)—of the choices available to them.

It may be that societies have other ways of manipulating the eligibility of individual choice, but the method we refer to as social control does so by means of *rules of behavior*.[15] Such rules alter the eligibility of potentially available choices by attaching negative or positive *sanctions* to particular sorts of behavior, by providing social *institutions* within which those who wish to accomplish certain ends can do so only in a limited number of ways (testate succession being the archetypal example), or by offering *prefabricated social arrangements* that provide security and efficiency by reducing the need for individual choice from among what otherwise would be an infinite variety of behavioral arrangements (marriage being an example of this sort of social amenity).

"Social control" is an aspect of social organization, a social function, an analytic concept. In this essay, however, we are concerned with a kind of human activity—it is, after all, only behavior and not social functions which can exhibit division of labor. Although for reasons of style I occasionally refer to this activity as "social control," it is essential

---

[15]"Rules of behavior" is in several respects a rather unhappy expression, and I use it throughout this essay without intending the various restrictions it may suggest. See Fallers (1969: 11ff.) for a discussion of some of these. *Rule* is merely shorthand for all of the various sorts of standards of a system of norms, including those which are not strictly speaking "rules" (see Dworkin, 1977: 22ff.), and also (if it is felt necessary to treat them as independent entities in such a system) "categorizing concepts" (Fallers, 1969) or "cognitive conceptions" (von Benda-Beckmann, 1979: 28–29). Nor should *rules* be read to suggest a necessary connection with sanctions, let alone a direct one: This is an empirical question, not a matter of definition. Cf. F. & K. von Benda-Beckmann (1981) on the facilitative aspect of rules. Finally, *behavior* ought not to suggest the exclusion of liability rules, for example (see generally Freeley, 1976).

to be clear that it is *social control labor* with which we are concerned. In particular, one must not slip into the error of supposing that social control is always (by definition) effective—that is, that actual "control" takes place. The social control labor with which we are concerned may or may not produce actual "control" and it must be defined in a way which entails no assumptions about its consequences.

"Social control labor" is all of the human activity entailed by the maintenance and operation of a system of rules of behavior. It can be conceived, for heuristic purposes, as consisting of legislative, adjudicative, and executive labor: Rules must come into being, be ascertained, interpreted, and applied, and be carried out. Division of social control labor can therefore be encountered in a social field with respect to any one, or all, of these three aspects of social control.[16]

The concept of the division of social control labor requires that we face on additional problem: the idea of a social control *role*. As we have seen, division of labor is to be operationalized in terms of such specialized roles and the distribution of actors over them. In part, we have here a problem common to all operationalizations of the idea of division of labor: The scope of a given category of specialization is essentially arbitrary even within a productive unit, and specialization can take place between as well as within productive units (hence, whether production of a pin entails 10 or 30 steps depends on how you look at it, and also on whether you take account of the steps involved in manufacturing a pin-making machine). The differentiation measures referred to earlier, for example, are only applicable to situations in which the definitions of roles are given in the empirical object of study itself, since the authors concerned do not themselves attempt to provide one. Various branches of a single firm or bureaucracy operating with identical job descriptions can be compared with one another, but nothing more (see, e.g., Blau, 1970).

For purposes of measuring specialization in social control labor, the role distinctions formally recognized in a social field itself cannot be used uncritically. Not every role distinction made in a social control system for internal purposes counts as an additional element of specialization. If we choose to regard the classification "member of the Judicial Committee of the *moshav*" as designating a distinct category of special-

---

[16]Many points of agreement with the foregoing discussion can be found, albeit set forth in rather different terms, in LaPiere (1954).

ization in social control, for example, we must do so on analytic grounds and not merely because the folk system concerned recognizes the classification. The question, so far as empirical theory is concerned, must always be, Does this folk distinction correspond to a distinct function in the production of social control?

It is the task of theoretical analysis to determine which sorts of role distinctions are empirically important. The degree to which folk distinctions are relevant for empirical purposes will depend on what those purposes are. Schwartz and Miller (1964), for example, used very crude categories (legal counsel, mediation, police) in their study of the relationship between societal complexity and specialization in social control. (See also Wimberley, 1973.) For their purposes, more refined categories were unnecessary. Black and Baumgartner (1983), by contrast, attempt a far more detailed typology of the sorts of "third party" social control specialists that are institutionalized by secondary rules, without, however, according theoretical status to every available folk distinction.

Explaining the Division of Social Control Labor

The elements of an explanatory theory concerning variation in the extent to which social control labor is specialized are to be found in Black's *The Behavior of Law* (1976). But Black's theory in its present formulation does not address itself to the question. The required reformulation can best be approached through an analysis of the reasons why Black's theory of law as it stands cannot account for variation in the legalness of social control. First, however, an indication of the direction in which I am heading: The explanation for the relative legalness of a given quantum of social control labor lies in the degree of intimacy and multiplexity of the relationships involved and the extent to which they cross-cut one another in the social field with which one is concerned.[17] In other words, it is Black's concept of "relational distance" that provides the basis for an explanation of the degree of division of social control labor.

---

[17]The general idea is not a novel one (see, e.g., Gulliver, 1963; Macaulay, 1963; Gluckman, 1967).

Black's theory of law consists of a number of independent variables—"dimensions of social space," as he calls them—each of which "predicts and explains" variation in the "quantity of law." As we have seen, his conception of law is a traditionally taxonomic one in which "law" is that sort of social control which occurs under the aegis of the state—"governmental social control." Law can be a quantitative variable in his theory because he conceives of it not as a set of normative propositions but as a kind of behavior, as social control by agents of the state. It is the amount of that particular sort of labor that he proposes to explain.

The trouble is that Black's independent variables predict not only the quantity of "law" but simultaneously also that of "other social control," without fixing the ratio of the one to the other. Stratification, for example, is positively associated with both of them. This multiple prediction would not matter if the two dependent variables were independent of one another. His theory would in such a case simply predict the quantity of two different things; its usefulness for predicting the quantity of "law" would not be affected by the fact that it also predicted something else. But "law" and "other social control" are not independent of each other. As a matter of (taxonomic) definition, "law" is a *type* of social control. It follows that, given any total quantity of social control, whatever is not "law" must by definition be "other social control." Seen in this light, Black's well-known proposition that the quantity of "law" varies inversely with that of "other social control" is a tautology, not an explanatory proposition.

Because of the taxonomic relationship of the two dependent variables—law and other social control—to each other, any proposition that purports to explain both of them at the same time in fact explains neither of them separately. It explains their sum. If the sum total of social control is constant, for example, stratification (which is positively associated with both) cannot explain the distribution of social control over legal and non-legal varieties: If the one goes up, the other must by definition go down. The positive association of stratification with each of them derives simply from the fact that stratification predicts and explains variation in the sum total of social control. Black's "theory of law" is, thus, a theory of the total quantity of social control (to which is added the seemingly powerful but in fact empty observation that "law varies inversely with other social control"). The question I want to pose is whether we can reformulate the theory in such a way that it explains not only the total quantity of social control but also the division of labor—the degree of legalness—which that total quantity exhibits.

Without here considering the question, let us assume that in general terms Black's theory of law is a provisionally adequate explanatory theory concerning the total quantity of social control.[18] That quantity varies with the stratification, morphology, culture, and organization of a social field. There is, however, one independent variable in the theory that— considered in relation to the explanation of the quantity of total social control labor—is problematic: "relational distance."[19] According to Black, both law and other social control vary positively with relational distance.[20] The proposition seems plausible so far as law is concerned: Little law penetrates the innards of intimate relationships—familial, communal, or commercial.[21] But the proposition is downright false so far as non-legal social control is concerned: It is precisely in intimate relationships that such social control is at its most intense.[22] Black him-

[18]A major weakness of the theory is that it can predict the quantity of social control on a given "legal level" (to invoke Pospisil, 1971)—that is, as between comparable social fields—but not the distribution of the quantity of social control over the various legal levels of a more encompassing social field. Without such a restriction to a given legal level, Black's theory would lead one to expect less social control on the level of the family than on that of the state, for example (all of the variables other than "organization" pointing in such a direction). But the opposite is obviously the case. The theory permits comparisons at the family level or at the state level, but not between the two. As far as the quantity of social control is concerned, this weakness also infects the revised version of Black's theory here presented; but the revised version does permit interlevel comparisons of the relative legalness of social control.

[19]The independent variables named in the text comprise all of the variables in Black's theory which explain the quantity of social control with one exception: "cultural distance." As in the case of the variable "relational distance," I am not happy with its role in his theory. See Notes 24 and 25 for further discussion.

[20]Black's proposition actually is that law and other social control exhibit a "curvilinear" relationship to relational distance: Their quantities increase at first with increasing relational distance but "after a point" decline again. The simplification in the text to a "linear" relationship will be justified on empirical and theoretical grounds in Notes 24 and 25.

[21]For familial, see Gulliver (1963) and Black (1970, 1971, 1980: chap. 5); for communal, see Schwartz (1954), Gulliver (1963), and Doo (1973); for commercial and economic, see Macaulay (1963) and Sally Falk Moore (1973).

[22]Black gives but one example of the application of the proposition to non-legal social control: "Conduct otherwise defined as deviant is more likely to be accepted, or 'normalized,' when it occurs between intimates [as, for example, within a family] [1976: 56]." The "normalization" here contemplated seems to entail either that deviant behavior is not treated as "delinquent"—that is, in a "legal" way—but rather informally or, on the other hand, that different rules of behavior obtain. In neither case does the example stand for the proposition that social control as such is low in intimate relationships; rather, it stands for the proposition that *external* social control (that is, relatively *legal* social control) is low. See also Black's discussion of witchcraft, which asserts that "the relationship between the naming of witches and relational distance is curvilinear [1976: 56–58]," but which in fact establishes nothing whatever concerning a relationship between intimacy and the total quantity of social control that might be brought to bear on the sort of persons likely to be formally accused of witchcraft.

The contrary proposition, that social control is higher in more intimate relationships, is

self, elsewhere in *The Behavior of Law*, associates law positively but other social control negatively with relational distance.[23]

Rethinking the explanatory potential of relational distance leads one also to doubt whether it actually even explains the quantity of legal social control. There seem to be many examples of social fields characterized by relatively high relational distance but little law. In fact, these fields exhibit little social control of any sort. What relational distance seems to explain is not the quantity of "legal" social control, let alone other social control, but rather the ratio of the one to the other. Whatever social control there may be (and that is explained in terms of Black's other variables), it is likely to be more legal the greater the relational distance characteristic of the social field or relationship in question. In non-taxonomic terms: Not the quantity of social control but the degree of division of social control labor varies with relational distance.[24]

Such a modification has a number of attractive features for Black's "theory of law."[25] More to the point for present purposes, it gives us an

---

widely accepted and supported by a wealth of evidence of various sorts (see Homans, 1950: chap. 11).

[23]See Black (1976: 107–109), in particular his use of the comparison between the *kvutza* and the *moshav* as an instance of the proposition that where non-legal social control is greater (in the more intimate *kvutza*), legal social control is less (that is, than in the less intimate *moshav*). Black also observes that "in nearly all societies the family has more social control of its own than other groups and relationships"—surely this is because of, not despite, the greater intimacy of family relations.

[24]The question remains whether this relationship is essentially "linear" or "curvilinear," to use Black's terminology. Is there a point beyond which a further increase in relational distance, given a constant quantity of social control, leads to lesser rather than greater division of social control labor? I can think of no empirical support for the idea that the relationship is not essentially linear. The apparent counterexamples illustrate a low level of total social control, not a relatively low level of legalness therein. Examples from the level of international relations are especially slippery: The relevant actors there (hence also the relevant social control and the relevant relational distance) are states, not individuals.

[25]In particular, it permits the elimination of two "curvilinear" relationships which seriously spoil the predictive and explanatory power of Black's theory: that between law and differentiation, and that between law and relational distance (see Note 24).

It seems likely that the relationship of differentiation to total social control is linear. Black may be led to suppose that it is curvilinear because he is trying to explain two different things with one proposition—the quantity of social control and the relative legalness thereof. But it is relational distance, not differentiation, which explains the degree of legalness. What Black calls variation in the quantity of law is often variation not in the quantity but in the legalness of social control, and the examples he cites (1976: 39–40, 58) do not show that the quantity of social control declines after a certain level of differentiation is reached, but only that the relative legalness of social control declines. And it is equally clear from his examples that the explanation for such a decline in legalness with further increases in differentiation lies not in differentiation as such, but in relational explanatory proposition with respect to the division of social control labor. Within the context of Black's theory, and holding the other elements of that theory constant (i.e., given a certain quantum of total social control labor):

The division of social control labor varies directly with relational distance.

Thus, the relatively greater specialization of social control on the Israeli *moshav*, by contrast with the *kvutza*, is explained not by the lesser quantity of non-specialized social control labor on the *moshav*[26] but by the greater relational distance there resulting from a non-collective economic organization. The proposition similarly predicts Schwartz's and Miller's (1964) finding that what they call "legal evolution" (a progres-

---

distance: "There is less law [that is, less legalness in whatever social control there may be] where people are undifferentiated by function, *with little or no exchange among themselves*, and, at the other extreme, where each is *completely dependent upon the next* [1976: 39, italics added]." Because relational distance is low in the two cited circumstances, they merely illustrate the proposition that legalness varies with relational distance; differentiation has nothing to do with it.

The proposed revision of Black's theory makes it possible to eliminate two curvilinear relationships and thereby to increase its predictive and explanatory power. In the revised version, differentiation has a linear relation to the quantity of social control, and relational distance a linear relation to the extent of division of labor therein. (It might also be suggested, without pursuing the matter here, that the variable "cultural distance" is merely one aspect of relational distance, that like the latter it explains the legalness rather than the quantity of a body of social control, and thus that its relation to legalness is a linear one. If sound, this suggestion would permit the elimination of the last vestige of curvilinearity from Black's theory.)

The revision also eliminates a latent functionalism in Black (which in Schwartz [1954] is explicit): the notion that every society needs a given quantity of social control, so that whatever it does not get "informally" it will arrange to get by means of "law." This notion of the total quantity of social control as a sort of balloon which, if squeezed on one end, bulges out on the other has long seemed to me a central weakness in both Schwartz's and Black's analysis, since there is no apparent reason why the total quantity of social control should be constant at all. There is no reason, for instance, why the *moshav* could not simply have had less social control (instead of more formal social control), or why a decline in "other social control" could not entail merely less social control altogether instead of a compensating increase in "law."

[26]Black's theory, as here revised, would explain this difference (if it existed) in terms of the greater differentiation and organization of the *kvutza*, somewhat offset by the greater stratification of the *moshav*.

Ideas similar to the proposition stated in the text are sometimes put forth in terms of the conditions under which non-legal social control is "effective" (see, e.g., Homans, 1950: chap. 11; Schwartz, 1954). It should be clear, however, that an account of how nonlegal social control works is no explanation for the presence or absence of legal control, since "ineffective" non-legal control could just as well entail a low quantity of social control as a shift to more specialized social control.

sion from mediation to mediation plus police to both of those plus counsel) goes hand in hand with increased "societal complexity." And it
explains the relationship, discussed by Merry (1982), between social
organization and the presence and use of mediation for handling disputes. Finally, in a study of the rates of appeals from adverse grading
decisions in Dutch law faculties, we found that the increasing intimacy
of the instructor–student relationship as the student progresses in his or
her study corresponds with a diminished use of the possibility of specialized social control against grading decisions (Griffiths, 1978b: 10–11).
One could go on multiplying illustrations of the proposition (see, e.g.,
the studies cited in Note 17)—indeed, many examples are to be found in
The Behavior of Law—but perhaps enough has been said to justify a claim
to plausibility on its behalf.[27] The thing now is to test it.[28]

ACKNOWLEDGMENTS

This chapter bears the imprint at various places of the critical reception it has received
from a number of people, among others Franz von Benda-Beckmann, Marius Heijen,
Donald Black, and Nico Roos.

[27]It should be noted that the proposition applies both to comparisons on one "legal
level" and to comparisons across "legal levels" (see Note 18), and also to the intragroup
social control experiences of individuals.

[28]In connection with the operationalization necessary for testing, a few words should
be added concerning the concept of relational distance. This concept addresses the sorts of
interpersonal bonds which exist in a given social field (compare Black, 1976: 40–41). Bonds
are complexes of predictable behavior between persons, whose predictability derives from
a combination of past behavior between the persons concerned (or others to whom they
are themselves in relevant respects bonded, in which case, the bond is "indirect") and of
the social norms applicable to their relationship. The more, the stronger, and the more
various the bonds to which a person is subject, the more predictable is his or her social
behavior.

Relational distance can be decomposed into a number of elements: The *strength* of a
bond will depend on the investment (e.g., in time and services) that has been made in it
and its continued value to the people concerned—as to which, the importance of the
reciprocity of the bond has often been emphasized (e.g., Durkheim, 1893; Malinowski,
1926; Homans, 1950: chap. 11). The *closeness* of a bond depends on the frequency with
which the interpersonal behavior concerned occurs and the directness (lack of intermediary persons) of the bond. The *rate* of bonding is the likelihood that any two given people
who come into contact with one another in a social field will have social bonds with each
other. The *multiplexity* of bonding is the likelihood that people joined by a bond of one sort
are also joined by bonds of other sorts (see Gluckman, 1967). And the *crisscrossing* of bonds
is the extent to which bonds of one sort (e.g., kinship) unite different persons in a social
field from bonds of another sort (e.g., economic relations) (see Colson, 1953; Granovetter,
1973; Boissevain, 1974; Flap, 1978). Accordingly, relational distance in a social field is a
function of the strength, closeness, rate, multiplexity, and crisscrossing of the interpersonal bonds that occur there.

References

Abel, Richard L.
   1973 "A comparative theory of dispute institutions in society." *Law and Society Review* 8: 217–347.
Aubert, Vilhelm
   1963 "Competition and dissensus: Two types of conflict and conflict resolution." *Journal of Conflict Resolution* 7: 26–44.
Austin, John
   1832 *The Province of Jurisprudence Determined.* London: Weidenfeld and Nicolson, 1954.
Benda-Beckmann, Franz von
   1979 *Property in Social Continuity.* The Hague: Martinus Nijhoff.
   1981 "Ethnologie und Rechtsvergleichung." *Archiv für Rechts- und Sozialphilosophie* 67: 310–329.
Benda-Beckmann, Franz and Keebet von
   1981 "Transformations and change in Indonesian adat." Paper delivered at the Minangkabau Symposium, IUAES Intercongress, Amsterdam, April, 1981. Forthcoming in *Minangkabau Social, Cultural and Political Forms: Perspectives on Continuity and Change,* edited by L. L. Thomas and F. von Benda-Beckmann. Athens, Ohio: Ohio University Press.
Black, Donald
   1970 "Production of crime rates." *American Sociological Review* 35: 733–748.
   1971 "The social organization of arrest." *Stanford Law Review* 23: 1087–1111.
   1972 "The boundaries of legal sociology." *Yale Law Journal* 81: 1086–1100.
   1976 *The Behavior of Law.* New York: Academic Press.
   1980 *The Manners and Customs of the Police.* New York: Academic Press.
Black, Donald, and M. P. Baumgartner
   1983 "Toward a theory of the third party." Pages 84–114 in *Empirical Theories about Courts,* edited by Keith O. Boyum and Lynn Mather. New York: Longman.
Blau, Peter
   1970 "A formal theory of differentiation in organizations." *American Sociological Review* 35: 210–218.
Bohannan, Paul
   1965 "The differing realms of the law." Pages 33–42 in *The Ethnography of Law,* edited by Laura Nader. Supplement to *American Anthropologist* 67 (December).
Boissevain, Jeremy
   1974 *Friends of Friends: Networks, Manipulators and Coalitions.* Oxford: Basil Blackwell.
Colson, Elizabeth
   1953 "Social control and vengeance in Plateau Tonga society." *Africa* 23: 199–212.
Doo, Leigh-Wai
   1973 "Dispute settlement in Chinese-American communities." *American Journal of Comparative Law* 21: 627–663.
Durkheim, Emile
   1893 *The Division of Labor in Society.* New York: Free Press, 1938.
Dworkin, Ronald
   1977 *Taking Rights Seriously.* London, Duckworth.
Evan, William M.
   1962 "Public and private legal systems." Pages 165–184 in *Law and Sociology,* edited by William M. Evan. New York: Free Press.

Evans-Pritchard, E. E.
    1940   *The Nuer: A Description of the Modes of Livelihood and Political Institutions of a Nilotic People.* New York: Oxford University Press.
Fallers, Lloyd A.
    1969   *Law without Precedent.* Chicago: University of Chicago Press.
Feeley, Malcolm M.
    1976   "The concept of laws in social science." *Law and Society Review* 10: 497–523.
Flap, H. D.
    1978   "Geordende anarchie, sociale netwerken in statenloze samenlevingen." *Amsterdams Sociologisch Tijdschrift* 5: 443–483.
Frank, Jerome
    1963   *Law and the Modern Mind.* 2d edition. New York: Anchor Books (1st edition, 1930).
Friedman, Lawrence H., and Stewart Macaulay
    1977   *Law and the Behavioral Sciences.* 2d edition. Indianapolis, Ind.: Bobbs-Merrill (1st edition, 1969).
Galanter, Marc
    1981   "Justice in many rooms: Courts, private ordering, and indigenous law." *Journal of Legal Pluralism* 19: 1–48.
Gibbs, Jack P., and Dudley L. Poston
    1975   "The division of labor: Conceptualization and related measures." *Social Forces* 53: 468–476.
Gluckman, Max
    1967   *The Judicial Process among the Barotse of Northern Rhodesia.* 2d edition. Manchester: Manchester University Press. (1st edition, 1955).
Goody, Jack
    1967   *The Social Organization of the LoWilli.* 2d edition. Oxford: Oxford University Press (1st edition, 1956).
Granovetter, Mark S.
    1973   "The strength of weak ties." *American Journal of Sociology* 78: 1360–1380.
Griffiths, John
    1978a "Legal reasoning from the external and the internal perspectives." (Review of Dworkin, 1977.) *New York University Law Review* 533: 1124–1149.
    1978b "Some aspects of the distribution of grading appeals in three Dutch law faculties." *New York University Review of Law and Social Change* 7: 1–13.
    1983   "Village justice in the Netherlands." (Review of G. van den Bergh, *Staphorst en zijn Gerichten.* Amsterdam: Boom Meppel, 1980.) *Journal of Legal Pluralism* 22: forthcoming.
Gulliver, Philip H.
    1963   *Social Control in an African Society.* Boston: Boston University Press.
Hart, Herbert L. A.
    1961   *The Concept of Law.* Oxford: Oxford University Press.
    1968   *Punishment and Responsibility.* Oxford: Oxford University Press.
Hoebel, E. Adamson
    1954   *The Law of Primitive Man.* Cambridge, Mass.: Harvard University Press.
Homans, George C.
    1950   *The Human Group.* New York: Harcourt, Brace.
Kemper, Theodore D.
    1972   "The division of labor: A post-Durkheimian analytical view." *American Sociological Review* 37: 739–753.

LaPiere, Richard T.
1954 *A Theory of Social Control*. New York: McGraw-Hill.
Llewellyn, Karl N.
1939 "A realistic jurisprudence—the next step." *Columbia Law Review* 30: 431–465.
Llewellyn, Karl N., and E. Adamson Hoebel
1941 *The Cheyenne Way: Conflict and Case Law in Primitive Jurisprudence*. Norman, Okla.: University of Oklahoma Press.
Macaulay, Stewart
1963 "Non-contractual relations in business: A preliminary study." *American Sociological Review* 28: 55–67.
Malinowski, Bronislaw
1926 *Crime and Custom in Savage Society*. Paterson, N.J.: Littlefield, Adams, 1962.
Marshall, Lorna
1960 "!Kung Bushman bands." *Africa* 30: 325–354.
Marx, Karl
1887 *Capital*. 3d edition. Vol. 1: *A Critical Analysis of Capitalist Production*. Moscow: Foreign Language Publishing House, 1961 (1st edition, 1867).
Merry, Sally Engle
1982 "The social organization of mediation in non-industrial societies: Implications for informal community justice in America." Pages 17–45 in *The Politics of Informal Justice*, vol. 2: *Comparative Studies*, edited by Richard L. Abel. New York: Academic Press.
Moore, Sally Falk
1973 "Law and social change: The semi-autonomous social field as an appropriate subject of study." *Law and Society Review* 7: 719–746.
1978 *Law as Process: An Anthropological Approach*. London: Routledge and Kegan Paul.
Moore, Stanley
1960 "Marxian theories of law in primitive society." Pages 642–662 in *Culture in History*, edited by Stanley Diamond. New York: Columbia University Press.
Pospisil, Leopold
1971 *Anthropology of Law*. New York: Harper & Row.
Radcliffe-Brown, A. R.
1933 "Primitive law." Pages 212–219 in *Structure and Function in Primitive Society*. New York: Free Press, 1965.
Radin, Max
1938 "A restatement of Hohfeld." *Harvard Law Review* 51: 1141–1164.
Richards, Audrey
1971 "Introduction: The nature of the problem." Pages 1–12 in *Councils in Action*, edited by Audrey Richards and Adam Kuper. Cambridge: Cambridge University Press.
Roberts, Simon
1979 *Order and Dispute: An Introduction to Legal Anthropology*. Harmondsworth: Penguin Books.
Schapera, Isaac
1938 *A Handbook of Tswana Law and Custom*. Oxford: Oxford University Press.
1957 "Malinowski's theories of law." Pages 139–155 in *Man and Culture*, edited by Raymond Firth. London: Routledge and Kegan Paul.
Schwartz, Richard D.
1954 "Social factors in the development of legal control: A case study of two Israeli settlements." *Yale Law Journal* 63: 471–491.

Schwartz, Richard D., and James C. Miller
    1964   "Legal evolution and societal complexity." *American Journal of Sociology* 70:
        159–169.
Shapiro, Allen E.
    1976   "Law in the kibbutz: A reappraisal." *Law and Society Review* 10: 415–438.
Smith, Adam
    1776   *The Wealth of Nations.* New York: Random House, 1937.
Smith, David L., and Robert E. Snow
    1976   "The division of labor: Conceptual and methodological issues." *Social Forces* 55:
        520–528.
Smith, M. G.
    1974   "The sociological framework of law." Pages 107–131 in *Corporations and Society:*
        The Social Anthropology of Collective Action. Chicago: Aldine Press.
Weber, Max
    1922   *The Theory of Social and Economic Organization.* Oxford: Oxford University Press,
        1947.
    1925   *Law in Economy and Society.* New York: Simon and Schuster, 1967.
Wimberley, Howard
    1973   "Legal evolution: One further step." *American Journal of Sociology* 79: 78–83.

3

From Disputing to Complaining

LAURA NADER

Anthropological studies of disputing and complaining have been conducted within a historical and cross-cultural framework and have consequently contributed to the development of evolutionary and correlational theories of social control. These studies had both a static and a dynamic dimension from the very beginning. In 1861, Maine argued that changing relations in law (from status to contract) were a result of shifts from kin-based to territorially organized societies. In 1915, Hobhouse contended that in accordance with their dominant modes of subsistence, human societies were scaled along a progressive sequence of legal systems that developed gradually from self-help to sanctions of a penal or compensatory nature. And Durkheim (1893) believed that sanctioning patterns were associated with societal integration.

In this chapter, I shall pursue the notion that systems of social control evolve in relation to one another (see Black, 1976). Drawing on the more recent work of anthropologists and legal historians, I hope to delineate from an evolutionary perspective the aspects of disputing and complaining that have been emerging in the literature. Underlying my thinking is the concept of *legal drift*, which, following a related usage in linguistics (see Sapir, 1921), lays emphasis on the use and users of public forums. The concept of drift draws attention to the unconscious selection of specific complaining and disputing mechanisms by individuals par-

TOWARD A GENERAL THEORY OF SOCIAL CONTROL
Volume 1: Fundamentals

ticipating in legal procedures. The consequence of their selection is the cumulation of certain disputing or complaint processes in a particular evolutionary direction. These unconsciously generated cumulative movements may be considered as separate from and yet equally as important as any consciously created ones that might be attributed to legal engineering or legal development schemes.

The users of social control mechanisms make the litigation process either marginal (Hurst, 1981) or central (Kagan, 1981; Nader, forthcoming) in a society. It appears that *when the litigation process is marginal for whatever reason* (i.e., when the process deals only with a limited part of the potential litigating activity), *and when the array of litigating parties is also marginal* (i.e., when it touches the lives of only a few members of the society), *complaining or unilateral activity of another sort will increase in importance and disputing will decrease.* In the United States, the marginality of the process indicates that the activity of interest has necessarily moved from the judicial to the extrajudicial forum, and from disputing to complaining. In other countries the patterns have been similar.

A sequence in the development of American courts was suggested by Friedman and Percival (1976), who trace a movement from preindustrial courts with an emphasis on mediation and conciliation, to trial courts that followed the legalistic model whereby disputes were adjudicated, to the relative disappearance of the dispute-settlement function from the courts and its replacement by routine administration. A similar shift was described for Norway (Aubert, 1969), where legislation steered specific conflicts outside the courts as the function of law underwent a change from conflict resolution to conflict prevention. In Spain, Kagan (1981) examines shifts from increased litigation to reduced use of the courts over a 300-year period from 1500–1700. In the developing countries, other scholars (Colson, 1976; Abel, 1979) describe the change in courts from their traditional function in maintaining law and order to "development," leading to a decline in tribal litigation.

In some countries these shifts moved the users of law from one mechanism to another, as in Norway, where users were moved from courts to administrative agencies. In other places, users were shuttled out of the system entirely, as in formerly colonial African societies. Materials in the United States, however, indicate that although courts might have been changing their function, users may not have changed a great deal. Hurst (1981) points out that *what* people were litigating about was changing from the nineteenth to the twentieth centuries, as was procedural style. Yet in another sense there was no significant change at all. Hurst argues that state court business showed an important continuity in the second half of the twentieth century: "Nineteenth-century litigation involved only limited sectors of the society in any bulk. This relative marginality of the litigation process also characterized the years after 1950. . . . Lawsuits touched only limited parts of the dense, diverse activity of the business world [1981: 420]." Furthermore, the array of litigating parties after 1950 differed little from those of earlier decades. Hurst thus notes that in the nineteenth-century United States there were no more merchants suing fellow merchants than there were in the twentieth-century dockets, and people of small means were not often plaintiffs except in tort or family matters (1981: 421).

Hurst describes the continuing marginality of litigating parties, which needs explanation because during conditions of such rapid social change in the United States, an increase in demand for disputing mechanisms was inevitable. It is the change in the environment that has accentuated the observation Hurst makes, and it is the changes in the social and political conditions that have turned potential users of disputing mechanisms into complainers. The demand for disputing mechanisms increases with an expanding society. In the United States, moreover, this demand was met through an expansion of extrajudicial mechanisms rather than through an expansion of courts or a massive effort at prevention.

A better understanding of the distribution and use of various procedures—unilateral (complaining), bilateral (negotiation), and trilateral (mediation, arbitration, and adjudication)—is crucial for comprehending the evolutionary direction in law from disputing to complaining as dealings with strangers increased. This direction was the consequence of the selection by users of processes that were subject to the specific choices and constraints they encountered. In discussing the work of other scholars, I am interested in tracing findings that elaborate the general observations that the use of law varies in accordance with the other forms of social control within societies and that the existence and usage of particular legal processes vary with specific social and political dimensions (Black, 1976; Nader and Todd, 1978). I am also interested in the paradigms used by these scholars, whether a complaining paradigm (a unilateral approach that focuses on a predispute stage) or a disputing paradigm (which focuses on bilateral or trilateral procedures).

In organizing this chapter, I have chosen to combine a "history of ideas" approach with the ethnographic realities: Ideas about ethnographic materials are as much data as are ethnographic facts. An examination of anthropological ideas about law points to the power of an eclectic approach to understanding and to the weaknesses of a dispute paradigm refined to improve our understanding of the disputing process. The focus on dispute, I shall argue, has had the added consequences of giving inadequate attention to power differentials in society and of assuming that the micro picture is but the macro miniaturized. Although the anthropological study of law began with a consideration of both micro and macro processes over time, the firsthand discovery of ethnographic diversities shifted attention to particular societies, and to the correlational approach. With the shrinking universe before us, with the continuing diffusion of Western legal ideas to former colonies, it may now be the time to look for larger patterns of change resulting from many of the very structural changes noticed by earlier scholars such as Sir Henry Maine (1861) and Emile Durkheim (1893). Accordingly, in the following pages I shall deal with the manner in which anthropologists have organized ethnographic diversity in societies where people are both producers and consumers and contrast the disputing paradigm with the complaining paradigm, which developed in the context of ethnography in societies where producers are separated from consumers. The contrast will illuminate the drawbacks of the dispute-resolution model for understanding power differentials as they affect disputing or complaining along an evolutionary scale.

Organizing Ethnographic Diversity

The field ethnographies of the first six decades of the twentieth century made a number of contributions to the understanding of legal systems in particular societies, and of these societies themselves within a comparative framework. In describing specific societies, anthropologists often characterized them by their dominant or most eye-catching procedures. Their reports were thus punctuated with terms encapsulating the procedures of the societies they studied. "Crossers" were found among the Yurok of California to function as a double negotiating team (Kroeber, 1925); "go-betweens" among the Ifugao of northern Luzon mediated problems between families for a fee (Barton, 1919). "Song duels" among the Eskimos comprised the means by which serious disputes were brought before a public jury (Hoebel, 1954); violent "self-help" characterized the Australian aborigines' disputing patterns (Radcliffe-Brown, 1933); "reasonableness" was an important principle for African Barotse judges (Gluckman, 1955); and so on.

At the same time, however, anthropologists were describing the substantive aspects of law within the framework of Western legal categories. For example, Radcliffe-Brown (1933) wrestled with the confusion resulting from the attempt to apply the modern distinction between criminal and civil law to preliterate societies. But as the ethnographic detail improved in quality, the description became less a matter of contrast with Western notions and more one of understanding indigenous systems of social control in their entirety, or of understanding the legal process at least as a form of social control. Malinowski's work (1926) was important in the development of this holistic perspective on law.

But this ethnographic tradition that encouraged a functional and diachronic examination of data was accompanied by a comparative tradition, one that contributed to a cross-cultural understanding of what goes together and what never does, by coupling and decoupling behavior in specific ways. I find the combination of both these traditions useful in comprehending how societies may shift from unilateral to bilateral or trilateral mechanisms for handling grievances.

For purposes of comparison, the earlier ethnographers classified societies along several dimensions that we still find important: economic, relational, procedural, and political. The classifications that resulted were based on recognized distinctions. Thus, in the economic domain, distinctions between hunters and gatherers, nomads, horticulturalists, agriculturalists, and industrial societies were used. In the relational field, distinctions were made between simplex and multiplex relations (single-stranded versus multistranded) and between continuing and noncontinuing relations. In the procedural field, distinctions were based on the presence or absence of a third party (negotiations between two parties contrasted with mediation, arbitration, and adjudication) and by the way unilateral behaviors such as complaining were usually excluded. In the political realm, stateless societies were contrasted with states that had centralized authority.

The relation between economic modes of production and the organization of social control mechanisms yielded generalizations of a very broad nature. For example, hunters and gatherers do not develop adjudicatory mechanisms, and would rather use avoidance as a means of dealing with trouble. We know that economically simple societies do not develop a hierarchy of courts, and yet some forms of dispute processing such as mediation, negotiation, or self-help occur universally in economically simple as well as in economically complex societies. We also know that in all societies, whatever their subsistence needs and no matter how simple their level of social organization, there are socially accepted forms of behavior that people are expected to follow. In other words, there are rules.

Because the generalizations about economic systems and social control mechanisms were so broad, the variations within categories of subsistence began to receive attention, and the economic variable was diminished in importance. For example, some hunting and gathering groups like the !Kung San of the Kalihari Desert deal with disputes in a relatively peaceful way, whereas others like the Eskimos seem to regulate violence with violence. Some agricultural groups like the Mexican Zapotec have developed courts, whereas others like the Shia Moslem of southern Lebanon have not developed third parties to handle village-wide problems (Nader, 1965). Some structural variables were used to explain the variation. The otherwise notable work of E. A. Hoebel (1954), which linked legal complexity to livelihood patterns, proved to be of limited use in explaining these differences: for example, the variations in dispute processing found between agricultural societies like the Jalé of New Guinea and the Zapotec of Mexico, which were characterized, respectively, by fighting and talk-directed settlement. If not economics, then what? The social and political structure and the culture of societies needed to be considered.

Attempts to explore the connection between political forms and dispute resolution were more creative in explaining variation and helped dispel the notion that order in society was directly connected with the presence of centralized political organs such as courts, police, and the like. It was because we found order in state and stateless societies alike that we were led to examine the question of how disputing is managed in stateless, acephalous societies without the aid of organs of government. In the process of doing so we were to discover a wide range of checks on human conduct that are functional equivalents of enforcement agencies in state societies and are often equivalent to the basic structuring of society as a whole (see, e.g., Kroeber, 1925; Colson, 1953). The study of how social control mechanisms operate could no longer be limited to strictly legal institutions, although an understanding of dispute management and methods of handling trouble cases could well be reached within this narrower framework.

The shift of focus from systems of social control to systems of dispute management, from positive inducement to handling norm violation after the fact, was a predictable result of specialization and narrowing of the subject matter. *The Cheyenne Way* by Llewellyn and Hoebel (1941) marked the beginning of many years of concentration on the "trouble case" approach. Malinowski (1926) in *Crime and Custom in Savage Society* had deliberately formulated a wide-angle framework for understanding law in society; Llewellyn and Hoebel shifted the focus to public forums. The unit of analysis was henceforth the case, and more often than not the case as handled through a public means, such as council hearings, judicial proceedings, or professional negotiation. Anthropological theories became more static, more correlational, less concerned with change even though we were often studying societies in a state of rapid change. The dispute paradigm took over.

In his monograph on *The Judicial Process among the Barotse of Northern Rhodesia* (1955), Max Gluckman extended earlier notions in an effort to develop a relational theory of decision making. Making use of the case method, he generalized that if one could determine the nature of the social relationships between the parties to a dispute, one could predict the procedure that would be employed in the decision-making process. In Gluckman's terms, "The fact that the parties (and often the judges too) are normally involved in complex or multiplex relations outside the court-forum, relations which existed before and continue after the actual appearance in court, . . . largely determine[s] the form that a judicial hearing takes [1969: 22]." The idea is that the nature of relationships imposes restraints on the settlement process. The hypothesis is usually formulated as follows: Relationships that are multiplex and involve many interests demand certain kinds of settlement such as compromise, which will enable the relations to continue. Disputants in simplex relationships, however, will rely on adjudication or arbitration, which will lead to win-or-lose decisions. This model of dispute processing is based on the rationale of preventing the breakup of long-term and important relationships. The crucial component probably has less to do with the nature of crosscutting or multiplex ties than it does with the need or desire to maintain continuing relations. Gluckman's use of the "reasonable man" idea fits well into his understanding of what knowledge was used to create a compromise settlement, and his interest in judicial decision making rather than any other kind stemmed from what he found operating in the public forum of the African Lozi, the court. Others who worked in noncourt societies have pursued decision making of a different sort, still, however, using the dispute paradigm.

In his book *Disputes and Negotiations*, P. H. Gulliver (1979) examined negotiation or joint decision making in cases of dispute. As he said himself, his interest in negotiations originated as a result of his research in a number of African societies in which judicial institutions were little developed and where the principal disputing process was negotiation. In the aforementioned book he attempts to show that "patterns of interactive behavior in negotiations are essentially similar despite marked differences in interests, ideas, values, rules, and assumptions among negotiators in different societies [p. xv]." His intent is to contribute to the explanation of "what happens in negotiations, how it happens, and why [p. xvi]." He is interested in the internal dynamics of negotiations as well. Whereas Gluckman was interested in adjudication as a decision by a third party, Gulliver sees joint, interdependent decision making by the parties themselves as the result of an interactive process. In comparing the features of negotiation and adjudication, Gulliver noted that negotiation occurs in all kinds of disputes, whatever the relationship between the disputants. He makes the observation that he is describing essentially culture-free interactive processes and that despite differences in detail and sociocultural context the processual patterns in negotiations were essentially the same (1979: 261). Antagonism resulted from the conflict, but coordination was essential for joint action. Gulliver certainly contributed to an understanding of small-group dynamics and particularly to dyadic interaction, but how can we use his work if we are interested in understanding the evolutionary change from disputing to complaining? Or has narrowing the question to decision-making processes in cases of trouble necessarily directed research away from general theory or from understanding whole systems of social and cultural control and how they evolve?

The focus on the trouble case does not, however, always lead into the refinements of decision making. The use of the extended case method has also led us into the realm of social organization of control and order. Although both Gluckman and Gulliver have contributed as well to the literature on order and social structure, I shall use the work of Elizabeth Colson to illustrate this focus. In her work on the Plateau Tonga of Zambia (1953), Colson illustrates the operation of crosscutting loyalties, a phenomenon previously recorded by A. L. Kroeber in his study of the Zuñi Indians (1917). Conflicting ties of loyalty, in addition to ties based on reciprocal exchange, function in many groups to pressure quarreling parties to terminate a dispute. Colson skillfully describes the way in which membership in plural groupings functions to integrate social groups in times of conflict, or at least how a complex network of cross-linkages in social relations serves to hold in check a potentially escalatory situation. She also touches on considerations of strategy, pointing to the choices open to the parties involved. Colson's emphases on the processes of control, the relation of these processes to structural considerations, and the importance of litigants' strategies for manipulating the structure, together with her use of detailed case materials, constitute an important contribution to the developing theory of complaining. Her work is centered not so much on law as on other processes of social control, not so much on decision-making actors as on the entire system of control in which actors (or users) are operating in roles of primary, secondary, or tertiary importance. That the Tongans are acephalous politically has less bearing on the manner in which they handle conflict than do the cross-linking features of their social organization. Again, this fact will be important to remember as we approach the discussion of complaining in modern society. Suffice it to say here that the extended case method in both formal and informal settings was central to ethnographic research on law and social control during the 1960s and served to highlight the activity of different mechanisms within the same society. Shame, ridicule, conflicting loyalties, fighting, in addition to negotiation, mediation, arbitration, and adjudication were accorded equal weight in field studies. The distribution of power and the variety of motives for pursuing a grievance ensure that alternative mechanisms are available for complaints. But such a sophisticated notion appears late in the anthropological research, much of which had dealt with dominant patterns of dispute management rather than with the variation of patterns that exist in all societies.

The Berkeley Village Law Project

My own work—and that of my students at the University of California at Berkeley—utilized the ideas of the aforementioned scholars and a number of others such as Barth (1966), Bailey (1960; 1969), and Turner (1957). Many of the earlier scholars represented the structural-functionalist school of anthropology, and many were studying peoples who, at least in theory, were operating as indigenous communities not yet enveloped in the nation-state. *The Disputing Process* (Nader and Todd, 1978) and other publications of the Berkeley Village Law Project describe the process of disputing in 10 societies. Their descriptions are not limited to official legal procedures available to litigants but are delimited by the avenues chosen or developed by litigants in search of a remedy to their grievances. The focus is on users, the paradigm still of dispute. The material in *The Disputing Process* comprises a wide variety of worldly (rather than supernatural) mechanisms used by disputing individuals, ranging from mechanisms of avoidance to judicial compromise, from fighting to talk-directed settlement. Within each one of these societies there was a good deal of variation in social control patterns, in types of relationships, in cases, and in types of remedy agencies. Within the same society, we saw differences in disputing style; cases between intimates might be treated in one way, those between acquaintances in another, and those between strangers in yet another style.

The Disputing Process contains a series of intrasocietal rather than intersocietal comparisons. That is, the intent was to describe and explain the considerable variation found within a society and to avoid the caricaturing of societies by using only the most salient or accessible means of settlement. For example, chapters on a Sunni Muslim village in Lebanon and a small Turkish village show how patterns of social control vary according to the social status of the parties involved. Among the Jalé of New Guinea, although the description is of a system of social control based on self-help where the social distance between the parties is a predictor of the extent of this self-help, the variety of behaviors range from dyadic conflict to war. Particular disputing processes were explained in terms of their culture and their relationship to the wider social forces that determine the number of options in disputing behavior that people have in any society. In elaborating on Gluckman's (1969) idea that the nature of people's relationships imposes restraints on their settlement processes, some of the researchers noticed that persons in multiplex relations adjudicated more than might have been expected. In disputes involving scarce resources, individuals may rank the resource higher than they rank the relationship, and they may be willing to sacrifice social relationships with their opponents in order to gain access to the resource (Starr and Yngvesson, 1975). The disputants are active makers of the disputing process as different issues determine the strategies they employ, often regardless of the type of relationship they have. Noncompromise outcomes commonly involved land and other important property and prestige or access to power and influence within the community—all of which are scarce resources or are perceived as scarce. Thus, in situations in which the object of the dispute is most highly valued and in limited supply, the social relationship will be sacrificed. A cost–benefit accounting forces one to view the justice motive from the perspective of all the parties involved in a case. The users, the players in a dispute drama, are an interesting unit. The concept of strategy is added to third-party decision making, thus enlarging the interactive elements in dispute processing.

In addition, the ordering of the societies depicted in *The Disputing Process* reflected a certain line of thinking. The volume was ordered by the degree of incorporation of each society into the nation-state, from least to greatest degree of integration. This ordering was not in terms of any evolutionary scheme ranging from primitive to civilized, nor was it in terms of subsistence forms such as hunting and gathering, fishing, horticultural, or industrial economies, nor was it established in relation to descent systems such as matrilineal, patrilineal, or bilateral. Instead, presentation of the 10 societies was based on the fact that one among them, the Jalé community, was the most free from the influence of the nation-state and thus placed first, and those that followed ranged on a continuum from the Atlantic fishermen, who were located well within a state but who preferred to avoid it, to others who ignored or circumvented the state, to those who, like the Lebanese, manipulated the state system in order to maintain or enlarge their village power base, to those who were forced to operate within the appellate structure of a state whose constitution claimed that the law should, out of fairness, ignore the pluralistic component of its constituency. In other words, the organization of *The Disputing Process* was political in nature. It recognized that government law was a law of a magnitude other than customary law. The role of both relative and absolute power in disputing becomes clear in situations of legal pluralism (as when two or more legal systems operate within a single political system) or class stratification. Power as a concept central to disputing and complaining could not be ignored, especially as we moved into situations where social and physical distance between litigants was increasing, and at the same time where the social structure played a diminished role in conflict resolution.

Although the book was ordered by degree of political incorporation, many variables entered into the analysis of each society: reciprocity, cross-linking structures, dual and antagonistic structures, politics, and economics in relation to scarcity and degrees of dependency on production and consumption units beyond the control of villagers. The broader intent was an understanding of the disputing process (and the actors in that process) as part of a social control system rather than simply as part of a law-centered system. Variables entered into the picture that were not the concern of Malinowski (1926) or even of Llewellyn and Hoebel (1941) and Hoebel (1954): the presence of a nation that claimed a monopoly of law, the development of people's increasing dependence in their consumption patterns on the production of others, their increasing stratification and inequality, and the centralization of power. In such settings prevailing in Western societies and those influenced by the West, the mechanisms in *The Disputing Process* are described as "extrajudicial processes." The closer we come to societies where law or government social control reigns, the greater is the intellectual segmentation: Some people study extrajudicial processes, others study the judicial. We have learned of the pitfalls of such segmented thinking from the findings of holistic studies of smaller societies; it is impossible to assess the social control function of a single institution, such as a court, without an understanding of the role it plays in larger systems. As Black has formulated it: "Law varies inversely with other social control [1976: 108–109]." As law increases in power and influence, other forms of social control may indeed decrease in importance. In societies where people share common social and political linkages, a kind of generalized social control results. In such contexts, gossip and public opinion help deter socially harmful behavior and serve to settle disputes.

By the 1970s there were no favored typologies, but there was a favored paradigm and there was a shift in research strategies as anthropologists moved their field sites back into their own societies. The ethnographic studies of particular isolated societies no longer provided a model of reality, if they ever did, although the anthropologist's heart might indeed be set on understanding face-to-face village relations. The findings and refinements that resulted from the earlier studies of particular face-to-face societies could, however, be applied to a dynamic understanding of law and its function as social control in complex societies. Two options might be taken: (a) to use the holistic approach to understand law as social control in the context of a broader historical model, as, for example, in the study of how Americans complain about goods and services when they feel for whatever reason that they do not have access to courts (Nader, 1980); or (b) to use the holistic approach to replicate pieces of village studies in parts of complex societies, as is reflected in Gulliver's work mentioned earlier or the more recent work of Witty (1980), in which she attempts to understand the principles of mediation using the United States and Lebanon as contrasting examples. In other words, when anthropologists began to work on disputing in the complex, modern context, they did one of two things: Either they looked for functionally equivalent contexts in the sense that Gulliver or Witty sought to compare principles of negotiation or mediation in two or more strikingly different societies that shared similar interaction patterns, or they looked for differences in traditional and modern settings that had implications for an evolutionary theory.

Although I was aware that procedures such as negotiation might have universal characteristics, as a strategy I chose to look at the differences. Although studies of the Trobrianders (Malinowski, 1926), the Barotse (Gluckman, 1955) or the Zapotec (Nader, 1964; 1969) took account of the operation of law and order in face-to-face societies, I began to notice in my work on how Americans complain that the unexamined relations were those that were face to faceless, between people who did not know one another and who never would, who were strangers and, in the American case, unequal in power (Nader, 1976), who could not often get close to a disputing process. The theoretical search becomes more akin to a historical ethnography, and a combination of vertical and horizontal models, across time and space, is needed. As we shall see, the principles that have emerged from what is essentially the study of small-group dynamics as they impinge on negotiation, mediation, or adjudication are important to any understanding of the evolution of legal relations. In addition, however, power constitutes a very important factor, particularly in its distribution over time.

Important insights are derived from treating all the participants in the disputing process as deserving of sociological attention. The interaction between all the users, not only people in third-party positions, as implied by theories of relationship discussed earlier (see pages 71, 77), is a key factor in any theory of complaining, and social distance is an important facet of this interaction. In situations of unequal power between potential litigants, however, we stop speaking so much about disputing, which implies a dyadic relationship between equals and access to a disputing mechanism, and begin to speak about complaining. We speak no longer about the plaintiff but rather about the victim. In short, a theory of disputing begins to evolve toward a theory of complaining.

Complaining and the Direction of Law

In an industrialized nation such as the United States, there has been an increase over time in the contact between strangers of unequal power, for example, between a buyer in Iowa and a seller in Detroit. This situation had not been experienced by human beings before the communications revolution. It appears that when most of the actual and potential disputes are between strangers rather than between parties who know one another, certain structural changes occur in law and other social control patterns in the society. For example, we observe that courts decline in personnel relative to population growth and need (Nader, 1978); their function shifts from dispute settlement to facilitating economic transactions (Friedman, 1973; Colson, 1976; Friedman and Percival, 1976; Hurst, 1981); access to public-complaint institutions decreases (see Nader, 1980: 3); the true plaintiff becomes the victim, and the state becomes the plaintiff. In addition, the function of law as a power equalizer diminishes, and the role and use of law (rather than the amount of law), as compared with other forms of social control, may be reduced relative to issues that affect the quality of life. When this happens, it has been postulated that extrajudicial processes will develop (Black, 1976; Nader, 1978), along with self-help procedures, in direct response to these trends. Such conditions will produce different kinds of aggrieved people: those who believe in the system and are willing to pursue their complaints within that system, and those who do not believe in the system about which they are complaining. Albert Hirschman has written (1970) about those complainers who "voice" (believers in the system) and those who "exit" (cynics). For our purposes here, I shall distinguish between voicers and nonvoicers. The nonvoicers may be intimidated, cynical, or people who express their complaints against the system through forms of self-help that are destructive to the system.

In my research on extrajudicial alternatives in the United States (Nader, 1977; 1978; 1979; 1980), I was interested in a certain type of complainer, the voicer, and in the ways in which Americans voiced their complaints about products and services either directly or indirectly through third-party mechanisms operating to handle product and service complaints. At the most general level, the research was concerned with a series of questions: Is there something about the way an industrial society handles so-called minor disputes that is organizationally and structurally different from the handling of similar problems in the small, face-to-face societies that anthropologists have traditionally studied? Are the differences linked to variables such as the number of stranger relations, stratification, the movement from status to contract, economic development, and industrialization? Are the similarities linked by type of relationship (equal or unequal, consumer or producer, face to face or faceless) or to the limits inherent in certain modes of complaint handling? Finally, do the conditions of state law, growing industrialization, and changing production and consumption patterns have durable effects on dispute resolution?

The findings of this research on complaining is relevant for testing propositions generated by earlier cross-cultural research, and also for formulating ideas about the evolution of law in what may be a kind of social system generically different from that described by most anthropological literature. For example, in our cross-cultural work we observed that mediation works most effectively for disputants who hold relatively equal power, are involved in a broadly defined, multipurpose continuing relationship, and have something to gain from a resolution of the dispute. In the American data, complaint mechanisms based on negotiation or mediation are unlikely to benefit the aggrieved when power is unequal. Also, when complaint handling occurs within a context in which there is a conflict of interest (as when the party being complained against is the one hearing the case) and when this is done in the absence of public scrutiny (as when companies or trade associations keep consumer cases confidential), the complainant is at a disadvantage. From the point of view of the party being complained against, however, such mechanisms are advantageous.

Complaint-handling organizations, like any organizations, favor the people who provide for their funding and continued survival, and monopolizing complainants is a common strategy they adopt to insulate complainers from dissatisfaction about the way in which the complaint mechanism itself operates. The relative power of purchasers and providers is a key variable determining the ability of extrajudicial complaint mechanisms to resolve economic disputes independently. It is producers, not consumers and not the government, that determine and support the majority of complaint alternatives in the United States. The status of the consumer has been lowered by the disintegration of a market system of exchange between parties having equal power and equal access to information. A final observation places our specific findings in context: When state law is organized by means of costly mechanisms for case-by-case processing, legal relief will not be easily available for a range of problems arising from complaints about the defects in purchased items and public service. This lack of law brings individual dispute settlement into the governmental process through ward heeling, which often impedes prevention measures through government and encourages sellers to violate the law within the area where access to law is unavailable.

The extrajudicial dispute-handling mechanisms we studied exist in systems of complaint management dominated by producers and successfully protective of their interests. Keeping in mind that complainants and complainees have different motives, let me formulate a simple set of rules that govern the performance of complaint mechanisms from the point of view of the aggrieved complainant. First, complaint organizations such as trade association consumer panels, which operate under the constraints imposed by conflicts of interest, cannot act as neutral third parties in complaints voiced by the aggrieved. Second, if the party settling the case is also the one being complained against, as is usually the case in automotive complaints, the complaint has little chance of success. Third, voluntary organizations operating from a consumer perspective are alert to the advantages of centralized or aggregate complaint processing for dispersed and aggrieved consumers. And, lastly, without the intervention of the judicial system to enforce settlements as a last resort, third-party complaint handlers will be of limited use to consumer complainants. In other words, the system of hearing consumer complaints in the United States, regardless of its manifest form, is at best a system of negotiation between parties of dramatically unequal status and power and at worst a system that receives unilateral complaints. Most extrajudicial complaint mechanisms are based on a model designed to serve producers' needs in several ways: First, it aids producers in meeting their short-term goals, which are essentially to increase profits as measured quarterly, and, second, it enables producers to maintain and legitimize their position of power, with its associated rank and prestige, because it permits them to circumvent complainants' requests if they so wish without fear of sanction (Nader, 1979). The absence of true dispute-handling systems has widespread social repercussions and renders the dispute paradigm useless for analysis.

Let me return to my previous observations that producers, not consumers, create and determine the shape of extrajudicial complaint mechanisms in a way that affects the use of dispute mechanisms more generally. In working with the American complaint materials, I noticed that various controlling concepts curtail the development of bilateral or consumer-structured complaint mechanisms (Nader, 1980: 57–110). For example, the idea of *caveat emptor* (let the buyer beware), which first appeared in law reports at the beginning of the seventeenth century, meant that the sale of goods was to be a private affair between the parties. If the product had a hidden defect, the buyer had very little chance of remedy. But a great many legal systems recognize at least in some situations what lawyers call an "implied warranty"—let the seller beware. The concept of *caveat emptor* is based on the assumption that a buyer and seller have equal bargaining power.

The ideology that expresses the value that everyone is equal before the law contradicts a position that argues that the consumer is occupying a role with inherently weaker bargaining power. Recognition of this contradiction by the contemporary consumer movement has moved law governing consumer transactions away from pure contract, where the two parties are treated as abstract entities, A and B, to a conception that recognizes one party as inherently weaker. There are, for example, provisions in new California laws that award attorney fees only to the winning consumer, not to the winning business—an example of a kind of inequality of treatment before the law intended to compensate for real inequality of an economic nature. Most aspects of the present complaint process, however, reflect a treatment of the consumer and the business as basically equal, with the result that business is given an advantage.

The idea that confidentiality protects us all is also part of a producer-oriented complaint system. The control of information is an important basis of power. Confidentiality of complaints, known only to the producer, in a market where it is impossible for consumers to be adequately informed through word of mouth, prevents them from learning from the experience of others and also prevents them from seeing themselves as part of an offended group.

A producer ideology includes a view of the complainant as a malcontent and deviant and a conception of the state and only the state as the guardian of public rights, with a mandate to bring legal action to protect the welfare of the general public. In this way of thinking, private citizens are not viewed as the appropriate parties to bring legal action to protect the general welfare, as, for example, suing a drug company for selling harmful drugs. The same mentality resulted in defining the corporation as a legal "person," which, among other things, crippled the use of sanctions because corporations cannot go to jail (Stone, 1976: 87). Individuals within a corporation are shielded from the stigma that may be attached to the corporate entity and from ways of determining which individuals are responsible for violating the law (Elkins, 1976: 83; Stone, 1976: 87).

The ideologies that we have barely begun to sketch seem to interrelate in various ways. Together, they help reinforce the self-image of the complainant as a rule breaker rather than as a disputant. For purposes of analysis the dispute paradigm gives way to a complaint paradigm. Differences between consumer realities and producer ideals that might characterize a complaint system can then be charted as follows:

Producer Model	Consumer Model
1. Buyer and seller have equal bargaining power.	1. Seller is more powerful than dispersed buyers.
2. Complaints should be handled one by one.	2. Complaints should be prevented or handled preferably by block solutions.
3. Complaints should be dealt with confidentially.	3. The complaint system should be public.
4. Product information belongs to the company.	4. Product information belongs to the user public.
5. Corporate responsibility is diffuse.	5. Actors within corporations are responsible.
6. Complainant is seen as a malcontent.	6. The complainant is exercising the rights of a buyer.

To reiterate in more traditional terms: *Relations* between consumers and producers are simplex (i.e., single stranded), distanced (i.e., between strangers along an elongated global distribution line), and dramatically unbalanced in power; in the *economic* realm, the salient characteristic is dependency—some produce for others to consume—in the *procedural* field, the existence of diverse procedures ranging from negotiation to adjudication is undermined by the reality of negotiation as a predominant use pattern; *politically*, the presence of nation-state law is less important to the complaining process (as it is beyond the reach of most complainants) than is the consequence of a state monopoly on social control that has resulted in the atrophying of an independent public opinion. The crucial relation is between economic modes of production and consumption and the organization of social control mechanisms.

A Choice of Two Models

There seems to be a disinclination to treat power as a central variable in the study of disputing processes. First, as Gulliver (1979: 186–194) has

observed, there is a widespread assumption in dispute-resolution studies that power is equally distributed among contestants until the outcome is decided. Although we can recognize that in the analysis of any
one case one party may be of higher rank and power than another, we
might ignore that some parties are so powerless in terms of political and
economic resources and procedural access that their grievances are not
recognized and consequently are not settled, processed, resolved, or
managed. Our preoccupation with modes of dispute resolution may be
only marginally productive in terms of theory building unless the dispute-resolution structures are seen as a subset of a larger system of
controlling processes.

A second assumption that stems from a dispute-resolution model is
the notion that social conditions determine forms of dispute processing
for reasons of good fit (Felstiner, 1974): Anthropologists have found
mediation operating in settings where disputing parties share common
experiences and their power relations are relatively symmetrical. Although such an assumption might hold where social conditions have
been stable for a long period of time, I would hesitate to accept the view
that it reflects the realities of a fast-changing, highly stratified, and di-
versified society. Our American data, in contrast, show a corresponding
lack of fit. That is, we find negotiation, compromise, and mediation
operating in contexts in which current understanding of social organization tells us we should not find them (Witty, 1980; Abel, 1982). If consumer complaint mechanisms meet producer needs and not consumer
needs, we need to explain why it is that consumers use them. Consumer
use patterns may be a result of their having "false" perceptions or
"shared" ones with producers. Their use patterns may also be explained
by the notion of limited options. For Americans who complain, alternative mechanisms such as courts require knowledge and cost money.
Whatever the reason, the salient finding is a lack of fit between social
conditions and modes of dispute resolution.

It may be useful here to introduce an alternative model, one that
focuses more generally on controlling processes than on dispute processing. It is from history that the model of controlling processes is best
illustrated. The historical events that have resulted in the present economic grievance process in the United States are a necessary part of any
contextual descriptive theory of complaining (Samson, 1980). Three
hundred years ago most people living in what is now the United States
were both consumers and producers; dependency was not a critical
variable. As the country's primary economic activity changed from subsistence agriculture to industrialization and the roles of consumer and
producer became separated, the balance of power shifted. The absolute

power that consumers had previously enjoyed diminished with this separation of roles. By the latter part of the nineteenth century, the greater power of producers over consumers could be measured by their organization of personnel and resources, effective political lobbying, numbers of complaints received and left unsettled, and the numbers of social movements created to remedy this power shift, such as the small-claims courts, the regulatory agencies, and legal aid. In the evolution of legal relations concerning the expression of grievances about products and services, there was a movement from dyadic to unilateral procedures, from disputing to actions of voicing complaints or resorting to avoidance or self-help strategies instead. As the social gap between parties to economic grievances has widened, the aggrieved are compelled to seek out their adversaries and, when they find them, to do battle using weapons designed by the latter (Best, 1981).

Finally, how does the dispute-resolution model take into account the role of the state? By the twentieth century, the absolute power positions of consumers, producers, and government have changed. Now, both organized producers and organized government have considerably more power than dispersed consumers, and the strength of each of these parties varies with access to legal services. Although the battle between producers and consumers was well under way in the nineteenth century, with many of the consumers being connected with the women's movement, the state did not become an active participant in mediating issues raised by consumers until the latter part of that century. Not surprisingly, the state took an interest in basic needs. The Hatch Act of 1887 was aimed toward the "maximum contribution by agriculture to the welfare of the consumer." Food and dairy commissions emerged in order to control the quality and price of agricultural produce. The Food and Drugs Act of 1906 created the Food and Drug Administration. The precipitous rise in prices during the first decade of the twentieth century incurred government investigation, as did the issues of distribution and truth in advertising. These issues were viewed by the government as a set of concerns common to a class of people, the consumers. They were addressed not as individual problems but as class problems to be remedied by legislative and regulatory means. By 1958, however, economist John Kenneth Galbraith noted, "As more goods are produced and owned, the greater the opportunities for fraud and the more property that must be protected. If the provision of public law enforcement services do not keep pace, the counterpart of increased well-being will, we may be certain, be increased crime [1958: 256]." Presumably, the consumer movement of the 1960s developed because public law-enforcement services were not keeping pace. Procedures set up by the political government were not structured to handle minor economic complaints (which involved major economic crime); procedures set up by what we might call the economic government were based on an ideology and structure designed to minimize long-term gains for the complainant.

With the increased erosion of the consumers' status and influence occurring alongside further government bureaucratization, the one-by-one approach to complaints gained widespread favor in the popular culture. The question was no longer class justice but individual justice, for as producers became distanced from consumers, so too consumers became distanced from one another. It is no accident that the dispute-resolution model came to be used by social scientists at a time when concerns of microjustice superseded the interests of macrojustice (Conrad, 1971).

The building-block approach to disputing and complaining has produced findings that are analytically useful. A complementary approach to the subject may be achieved by means of a historical perspective on the shifts in the distribution of power that affect the evolution of legal relations and the overall rank and status of the major actors—these in this example being business, government, and consumers. In the United States, a crisis was caused by the departure of producers from the immediate social field of consumers, destroying the latter's informal social control system. The precipitous rise in prices, the problems of adulterated food, and the almost total dependency of consumers on producers that accompanied this crisis created a new role for government. In this sense, modern industrial nations are generically different from the face-to-face societies we have studied in the past.

The presence of unilateral procedures forces us to think about the distribution and use of power. This is made quite clear in Black and Baumgartner's (1981) essay on self-help that questions the modern assumption that citizens must forever depend on the state to handle their grievances. The lack of fit between mechanisms used for complaining and the needs of the complainant is also leading the complainant to question the legitimacy of both the economic government with its extra-judicial mechanisms and the political government with its judiciary ones—both of which are increasingly inadequate to handle the everyday justice problems associated with products and services in a consumer society. We might wonder how social order can be maintained in a society in which economic and political governments present complainants with yet another lack of fit: Most complaints about goods and services have no place in the judicial system. The so-called minor injustices are the very stuff that is moving the potential user population in the direction of increased complaining. The informal justice mechanisms have not worked in any grand way for complainers; that is, complaints have not moved into disputing, which would indicate increased status for the complainant. Rather, in the contemporary situation, complaining is an indication of the relative power of purchaser and producer or seller.

Concluding Remarks

Law varies with its social context. As consumers have become distanced from the producer, both informal and social control (community pressures by means of public opinion and alternative consumption options) and formal social control (that is, government law that would include many of the so-called informal justice procedures as well) have escaped their grasp. The result is increased unilateral behavior—complaining or exiting. In state systems of law the plaintiff role atrophies because of use monopoly by the state. The law drifts in the direction of its dominant users. In modern societies the use of law becomes marginal. Cumulative, directional changes occur when social pressures repeatedly make a once-acceptable option unacceptable.

In this chapter, I have given some indication of the process by which anthropologists have come to know something about the dynamics of law in context by means of contrasting and making more controlled comparisons between societies. At the same time, I indicated that an analysis of the evolutionary direction of law cannot come from a narrow focus on particular disputing processes or from a specific disciplinary framework. Macrounderstanding will be both eclectic and integrative, if unwieldy. But today the interesting questions are in the macroscopic picture. If we work with a user model of law, we see law as a creation of the social conditions that shape the activity of potential litigants. Law is not only an instrument of state engineering. Nor is social control primarily the function of the state as exercised through law. The time has come for a closer examination of the movement from disputing to complaining and its meaning for the future of nation-state law.

ACKNOWLEDGMENTS

I am especially grateful to Donald Black, Cathie Jane Witty, Suzanne Bowler, and JoAnn Martin for their critical comments and readings of earlier drafts of this chapter.

References

Abel, Richard L.
   1979 "Western courts in non-Western settings: Patterns of court use in colonial and

neo-colonial Africa." Pages 167–200 in *The Imposition of Law,* edited by Sandra B. Burman and Barbara E. Harrell-Bond. New York: Academic Press.

1982   "The contradictions of informal justice." Pages 267–320 in *The Politics of Informal Justice,* vol. 1, edited by Richard L. Abel. New York: Academic Press.

Aubert, V.

1969   "Law as a way of resolving conflicts: The case of a small industrial society." Pages 282–303 in *Law in Culture and Society,* edited by Laura Nader. Chicago: Aldine Press.

Bailey, F. G.

1960   *Tribe, Case and Nation.* Manchester: Manchester University Press.

1969   *Strategems and Spoils: A Social Anthropology of Politics.* Oxford: Basil Blackwell.

Barth, F.

1966   *Models of Social Organization.* Occasional Paper No. 23. London: Royal Anthropological Institute of Great Britain and Ireland.

Barton, R. F.

1919   *Ifugao Law.* Berkeley, Calif.: University of California Press, 1969.

Best, A.

1981   *When Consumers Complain.* New York: Columbia University Press.

Black, Donald

1976   *The Behavior of Law.* New York: Academic Press.

Black, Donald, and M. P. Baumgartner

1981   "On self-help in modern society." Pages 193–208 in *The Manners and Customs of the Police,* Donald Black. New York: Academic Press.

Colson, Elizabeth

1953   "Social control and vengeance in Plateau Tonga society." *Africa* 23: 199–212.

1976   "From Chief's court to local court." In *Freedom and Constraint A Memorial Tribute to Max Gluckman,* edited by Myron Aronott. Amsterdam, The Netherlands: Van Gorcum.

Conrad, Alfred F.

1971   "Macrojustice: A systematic approach to conflict resolution." *Georgia Law Review* 5: 415–428.

Durkheim, Emile

1893   *The Division of Labor in Society.* Glencoe, Ill.: Free Press, 1960.

Elkins, James R.

1976   "Corporations and the criminal law: An uneasy alliance." *Kentucky Law Journal* 65: 73–129.

Felstiner, W.L.F.

1974   "Influences of social organization on dispute processing." *Law and Society Review* 9: 63–94.

Friedman, M.

1973   *Some Historical Aspects of Law and Social Change in the United States.* Berkeley, Calif.: Center for the Study of Law and Society.

Friedman, L. M., and R. V. Percival

1976   "A tale of two courts: Litigation in Alameda and San Benito counties." *Law and Society Review* 10: 267–301.

Galbraith, John K.

1958   *The Affluent Society.* Cambridge, Mass.: The Riverside Press.

Gluckman, Max

1955   *The Judicial Process among the Barotse of Northern Rhodesia.* Manchester: Manchester University Press.

Gluckman, Max (editor)
1969 *Ideas and Procedures in African Customary Law*. London: Oxford University Press, for the International African Institute.
Gulliver, P. H.
1979 *Disputes and Negotiations*. New York: Academic Press.
Hirschman, Albert
1970 *Exit, Voice and Loyalty: Responses to Decline in Firms, Organizations and States*. Cambridge, Mass.: Harvard University Press.
Hobhouse, L. T.
1915 *Morals in Evolution: A Study in Comparative Ethics*. London: Chapman and Hall.
Hoebel, E. A.
1954 *The Law of Primitive Man: A Study in Comparative Legal Dynamics*. Cambridge, Mass.: Harvard University Press.
Hurst, James W.
1981 "The functions of courts in the United States: 1950–1980." *Law and Society Review* 15: 401–472.
Kagan, R. L.
1981 *Lawsuits and Litigants in Castile*. Chapel Hill: University of North Carolina Press.
Kroeber, A. L.
1917 "Zuñi kin and clan." *Anthropological Papers*, No. 18. New York: American Museum of Natural History.
1925 "Principles of Yurok law." In *Handbook of the Indians of California*. Smithsonian Institution Bureau of American Ethnology, Bulletin 78. Washington, D.C.: U.S. Government Printing Office.
Llewellyn, K. N., and E. A. Hoebel
1941 *The Cheyenne Way: Conflict and Case Law in Primitive Jurisprudence*. Norman, Okla.: University of Oklahoma Press.
Maine, Sir Henry Sumner
1861 *Ancient Law: Its Connection with the Early History of Society and Its Relation to Modern Ideas*. London: John Murray.
Malinowski, Bronislaw
1926 *Crime and Custom in Savage Society*. London: Kegan Paul, Trench, Trubner & Co.
Nader, Laura
1964 *Talea and Juquila: A Comparison of Zapotec Social Organization*. University of California Publications in American Archaeology and Ethnography, No. 48 (3). Berkeley, Calif.: University of California Press.
1965 "Choices in legal procedure: Shia Moslem and Mexican Zapotec." *American Anthropologist* 67(2): 394–399.
1969 "Styles of court procedure: To make the balance." Pages 69–91 in *Law in Culture and Society*, edited by Laura Nader. Chicago: Aldine Press.
1976 "The Problem of Order in a Faceless Society," in *American Courts and Justice*, American Judicature Society.
1977 "Powerlessness in Zapotec and U.S. societies." Pages 309–325 in *Anthropological Studies of Power*, edited by R. Fogelson and R. Adams. New York: Academic Press.
1978 "The direction of law and the development of extra-judicial processes in nation state societies." Pages 78–95 in *Cross-Examinations: Essays in Memory of Max Gluckman*, edited by P. H. Gulliver. Leiden: E. J. Brill.
1979 "Disputing without the force of law." *Yale Law Journal* 88 (special issue on dispute resolution).

forthcoming *To Make the Balance: A Study of Zapotec Law and Order.*

Nader, Laura (editor)

    1980   *No Access to Law.* New York: Academic Press.

Nader, Laura, and Harry F. Todd, Jr. (editors)

    1978   *The Disputing Process—Law in Ten Societies.* New York: Columbia University Press.

Radcliffe-Brown, A. R.

    1933   "Primitive law." Pages 202–206 in *Encyclopedia of the Social Sciences,* vol. 9. New York: Macmillan.

Samson, P.

    1980   *The Emergence of Consumer Interests in America.* Ph.D. Dissertation. University of Chicago.

Sapir, E.

    1921   *Language.* New York: Harcourt, Brace.

Starr, J. O., and B. Yngvesson

    1975   "Scarcity and disputing: Zeroing-in on compromise decisions." *American Ethnologist* 2: 553–566.

Stone, Christopher

    1976   "Stalking the wild corporation." *Working Papers for a New Society* 4: 17–21; 87–89; 92–93.

Turner, V.

    1957   *Schism and Continuity in an African Society: A Study of Ndembu Village Life.* Manchester: Manchester University Press.

Witty, Cathie J.

    1980   *Mediation and Society: Conflict Management in Lebanon.* New York: Academic Press.

4

Liability and Social Structure*

KLAUS-FRIEDRICH KOCH

Liability and Conflict Management

This chapter sketches the outline and describes some preliminary results of an unfinished research project aimed at developing a comparative ethnological theory of liability.[1] This theory subsumes the following ideas: All societies must deal with conflicts involving a claim by one party for redress against another party alleged to have caused the harm or injury that precipitated the conflict. Therefore, all societies must, first, provide procedures to deal with conflicts that arise among its members; second, establish rules that define responsibility and determine liability; and third, prescribe the conditions under which these rules may be invoked.

MODES OF PROCEDURE

We know that the institutional form of procedures for conflict management depends on the nature of a society's sociopolitical organization.

---

*This chapter is a revision of Working Paper No. 2 from the Research Program in Legal Anthropology, Northwestern University.

[1] The term *ethnological* emphasizes the broad, cross-cultural approach taken in this study, in which the exploration of liability in Anglo-American jurisprudence and legal practice is a marginal but not insignificant concern.

TOWARD A GENERAL THEORY OF SOCIAL CONTROL
Volume 1: Fundamentals

In particular, we know that the greater the degree of a society's political integration and the greater the degree of centralization in the administration of public affairs, the more regulated, predictable, and controlled are its procedures (if only because the management of conflict is part, and an important part at that, of administering public affairs).[2] The scale of institutional formalization, conceived in terms of ideal types along a continuum, ranges from mere private self-help to judicial review by legal specialists whose decisions can be enforced through formally legislated means of coercion. Unmitigated self-help in the fashion of Thomas Hobbes's "war of all against all" does not exist anywhere in pure form. Even where violent self-help is the approved course of action in seeking redress for a wrong, existing kin bonds and neighborly ties always influence what a person does if he has been wronged.

Nevertheless, the cross-cultural ethnographic record shows that societies with little or no government tend to rely on self-help or, at best, informal mediation as their dominant mode of conflict management.[3] The term *government* as used here denotes the institutionalization of authority positions whose incumbents control—alone or together with subsidiary bodies such as councils—the behavior of individuals in the public interest, however that maybe defined in a particular culture. The exercise of this type of authority differs from leadership in that it devolves at least in part from an *official* capacity rather than exclusively from the *personal* capacity that characterizes a leader's influence and power. When government extends beyond the confines of local communities *and* its authority is not defined, though possibly legitimated, by kinship, we are dealing with a political organization called a "state."[4]

Two basic processes of conflict management that include six distinct modes of procedure can be distinguished: the triadic modes of adjudication, arbitration, and mediation, and the dyadic modes of negotiation, coercion, and avoidance (see Koch, 1977). The last three represent self-help procedures in which third parties, other than partisan representatives and supporters, do not participate. Coercion and avoidance are the

[2]Numerous studies in early European legal history as well as comparative research on indigenous African law have shown that a centralization of political power regularly entails the recognition and punishment of injuries as "public" wrongs (see, e.g., Schapera, 1956; Milner, 1965).

[3]The problem of identifying a dominant mode of conflict management is discussed in a cross-cultural study in which this variable has been used to explore the relationship between types of procedure and forms of political organization on the community level (Koch and Sodergren, 1976).

[4]So-called city-states are, of course, on a level of political organization where they are no longer communities. For the definition of *community* implied here, see Murdock and Wilson (1972: 255).

obverse of each other. By using coercion, a party seeks to impose the outcome of a dispute on its adversary by force, which often involves physical violence but may also entail resort to psychological pressure or metaphysical means such as witchcraft. By using avoidance, the aggrieved party takes no direct action to obtain redress, although its physical withdrawal or suspension of normal communication and exchange may induce the opponent to make amends (see Koch, Altorki, Arno, and Hickson, 1977).

A special mode of conflict management, ostracism, combines attributes from several of the six ideal types of this model. Ostracism is the practice of communal shunning of an offender by which the members of the community demonstrate public support for the aggrieved party. At the same time, their action carries an element of adjudication, for it reflects a judgment—in this case by public rather than by judicial opinion. In societies where ostracism is a common practice, this procedure of handling conflicts also entails a measure of coercion, for it abrogates at least some of the offender's customary rights and privileges.[5] Whether the "community" should be regarded as a third party in this situation can be left to one's conceptual preference. Be that as it may, in most cases the nature of the wrong committed determines the reaction of the community. It will act as a constituency in support of the aggrieved party if the offense violated the rights of an individual; it will act as the aggrieved party itself if the offense endangered the spiritual or physical welfare of the whole group.[6] On the other hand, it must be expected that ethnographic reality will blur this conceptual distinction. For example, ostracism of a repeated offender and known troublemaker, although demonstrating support for the individuals whose rights he has violated, also sanctions his conduct because it has impaired the cohesion and social harmony of the group.[7] In any case, as Redfield has noted,

[5]See the case studies by Smith (1961) and Hostetler (1964) on the legal functions of ostracism and the discussion of the sanction of expulsion by Moore (1972: 89–93).

[6]See Fürer-Haimendorf (1967) for ethnographic documentation of this difference.

[7]I suspect that the use of either avoidance or ostracism ultimately depends on a specific combination of political and economic conditions. Avoidance appears to be most adapted to the need of containing conflict in societies with a minimal degree of political integration *and* a subsistence economy that allows individuals to change their place of residence freely. As the Jalé case (described later) suggests, in a society where a change of residence is restricted by its sociopolitical structure (localized agnatic descent groups forming corporate units) and by its economy (horticulture), resort to avoidance will be an extreme measure. Ostracism, on the other hand, appears to be an effective sanction only if the shunned (or, in extreme cases, banished) person suffers considerable hardship as a consequence of his expulsion. In societies where people have multiple options of group affiliation, ostracism happens only when a chronic troublemaker has exhausted all options, which seems to be the case with the Chenchu (described later).

"In not a few . . . societies general disapproval is expressed not merely diffusely and casually, but in a sort of standardized collective gesture of disapproval. These modes of conduct we must recognize as closely related to law in that they are specific secular sanctions that have a public character and that assume a formal nature [1964: 13]."

PRINCIPLES OF LIABILITY

The following analysis will show how the procedures by which societies manage conflict determine the culturally recognized conditions that establish liability, that is, a party's obligation to render restitution or compensation and/or to suffer punishment or vengeance. These conditions are circumscribed by principles that distinguish absolute and relative liability, on a formal dimension, and individual and collective liability, on a social dimension. Liability may be absolute (or strict)[8] in the sense that if bare causation, however defined, is shown, personal responsibility or culpability and the circumstances under which the injury occurred are irrelevant; or it may be relative (or contingent) and thus depend on the recognition of culpability and the circumstances surrounding the injury. Furthermore, liability may be either an individual obligation and lie only with the person who is held to have caused an injury—however "cause" is construed in a given case—or a collective obligation and fall on that person and/or other people by virtue of their association with one another. The term *collective* entails a set of ideas that permit an analytical distinction between corporate, joint, and vicarious liability. Liability is corporate when it attaches to a defined group, organization, or agency as such; for example, to a kin group, a firm, or the state, each representing a constituency in which membership is either ascribed (members of a patrilineage), elected (shareholders of a company), or circumstantial (residents of England). Joint liability is an obligation to render compensation or to suffer punishment that is shared by the liable party and other individual members from among his group, whether the group is a relatively permanent social unit or a more temporary association. The Nazi use of *Sippenhaft*, which subjected family members of a person charged with political offense to punitive measures, is a fairly recent European example of coercing compliance with

---

[8]Legal scholars have found reasons why the terms *strict* and *absolute* should denote different kinds of liability (see, e.g., Gross, 1979: 342–371). This question is ignored here. The distinction between *liability* and *responsibility* here adopted is made by Allott, Epstein, and Gluckman (1969: 66), and it appears to be the prevailing one in legal anthropology. In general, I do not assume a semantic identity of the concepts as used in this study and in Anglo-American jurisprudence.

FIGURE 4.1. Types of liability.

government decrees by imposing a form of joint liability. Vicarious liability devolves on persons by virtue of their particular relationship to the party who caused the injury in dispute, whether or not the latter is held responsible for it. A case in point is the obligation of parents to make good for certain harm caused by their minor child.

In combination, the formal principles, absolute (A) and relative (R), and the social principles, individual (I) and collective (C), yield the four composite ideal types of liability diagrammed in Figure 4.1.

From the ethnographic record it appears that types of liability vary with given modes of conflict management as well as with the efficiency of these modes to review evidence, that is, the circumstances under which the injury in question occurred such as by intent, mistake, negligence, or accident.[9] A society's dominent mode of conflict management, in turn, appears to depend on its sociopolitical organization and on its subsistence economy.[10] The efficiency to review evidence is generally found to increase with the degree to which procedures are regulated through the institutionalization of formal forums in which cases can be heard, debated, and decided on their "merits." A review may be irrelevant, however, in establishing liability for different, if not opposite, reasons. In societies where conflicts are usually managed by peaceful discussion through negotiation or mediation, an emphasis on reconcilia-

[9]Complex legal systems may use the notions of provocation, mistake, inadvertence, "acts of God," and mental capacity to make more refined distinctions of circumstances, but ideas corresponding to "temporary insanity" and "acts of God" appear also in tribal jurisprudence. For African examples, see the study by Seidman (1966).

[10]Describing the practice of negotiating an indemnity payment for homicide retaliation among the pastoral Humr of the Sudan, Cunnison explains:

> For the Humr it appears that there is no level at which relationships are of such little consequence that they can be dominated by feuding. Ecological factors at least partially account for this. The terrain is such that it is possible for Humr to spread out in the dry season, but the rains quarters are cramped, and especially in the early weeks of the rains, the pools fill irregularly and herders from all [groups] are compelled to concentrate where the water happens to be. The situation demands great forbearance in dry years. This same need to intermingle is recognized also in the absence of sectional land rights, tribesmen being free to set up camp in any part of the whole tribal land, no matter to what section of the tribe they belong [1972: 117].

tion may outweigh any need to distinguish between possible causes of an injury. This appears to be the case, for example, among the Arusha of Tanzania (Gulliver, 1963).[11] On the other hand, in societies where conflicts tend to be managed by coercive self-help, the absence of any forum in which evidence can be reviewed precludes an inquiry into the circumstances surrounding an injury. The Jalé of New Guinea described in this essay are typical of such societies. In segmentary societies where homicide often initiates a feud and the relationship between the parties rather than the circumstances of the killing defines liability, and where procedures for reviewing evidence exist, "guilt . . . may be rebutted to establish mitigation, but still not then avoid liability. When mitigation is established, even though it does not discharge liability, the injured party is readier to accept compensation and not insist on blood for blood [Gluckman, 1965b: 133]." In any case, defining principles of liability—and applying or obviating them in a given dispute—is a crucial problem for all societies because ordered and predictable social relations are impossible without a shared knowledge of the rules under which a person (and/or his kin or local group, for example) may be held liable for his action or inaction.

Corporate kin-group liability is generally found in societies with a low degree of political integration, if kin groups hold vital resources (land or herds) in common ownership. On the other hand, societies with a hunting-and-gathering economy that allows people to associate freely with different local groups lack the structural basis for corporate liability to exist. Furthermore, the effect of corporate liability seems to vary with a society's dominant mode of conflict management. If people must rely on coercive self-help, and redress is by retaliation, collective liability may restrain a person tempted to commit a wrong and deter an aggrieved party from exacting vengeance because both actions jeopardize the safety of the members of their respective groups and their resources.[12] If, on

---

[11]Moore interprets strict liability in similar cases "as a means of assuaging the resentment of those who have been injured or damaged in a social situation in which injurer and injured must go on in a continuing social relationship . . . whether or not the injurer was apparently at fault [1972: 62, 66]."

[12]The peacekeeping effect of collective liability has been asserted for many societies. Chadwick, for example, writes of Gaelic society: "There was no personal payment. The 'kindred' stood or fell together. In this way they were responsible for one another and would obviously keep a close eye on one another's doings. In this way too every 'kindred' group would see to it that the kindred did duty as both police and judges. There could have been no better way in such a society of keeping justice on an even keel [quoted in Stein and Shand, 1974: 115]." It seems only logical that under these circumstances a group must protect itself against members by whose reckless actions it incurs collective liability. Reviewing the handling of this problem in some African societies, Moore concludes,

the other hand, people can rely on procedures of negotiation and mediation, and redress is by compensation and fines, the allocation of liability to a group may facilitate a settlement because it divides the payment required among its members.

These considerations suggest the following two propositions:

Proposition I   *The distinction between individual and collective liability is determined by three interdependent variables: the political status of the group that owns principal subsistence resources, the nature of these resources, and the society's dominant mode of conflict management.*

Proposition II   *The recognition of personal responsibility as culpability in determining liability as an obligation depends on the efficiency of existing legal procedures to review evidence.*

Given the obvious significance of liability in the jural ideology of a society, it is surprising to realize that even the best documented works in legal anthropology generally fail to explicate how the societies studied assign responsibility and assess liability. Certainly throughout the history of Western jurisprudence, going back to ancient Greek and Roman law and philosophy, this problem has been a central concern, whether it has been treated under the rubric of contract, crime, tort, or justice.[13] Although, as Epstein (1969: 292) has already remarked, we cannot really understand how societies settle disputes without knowing how they define liability, anthropologists have, in fact, only lately explored the whole idea in any systematic and comparative fashion (Gluckman, 1965a, 1972; Fürer-Haimendorf, 1967; Moore, 1972; Nader and Combs-Schilling, n.d.). We know so little about this fundamental legal concept because it can be fully elucidated only through the study of a people's moral, psychological, nosological, eschatological, and cosmological beliefs. So far, only the classical study of this belief complex among the Azande of the Sudan by Evans-Pritchard (1937) has explored the logic of

---

"Where every member of a corporate group has the power to commit it in this way to a collective liability, a corollary rule always exists whereby the corporation may discipline, expel or yield up to enemies members who abuse this power or whom the corporation does not choose to support in the situation in which he has placed them [1972: 89]."

[13]See, for example, the collection of essays in Morris (1961). For a treatment of this problem in Anglo-American law, see Hart (1968) and Hart and Honoré (1969). Within the scope of this exploratory study the relationship between the type of claim (e.g., compensation for homicide or repayment of a loan) and the form of liability applicable to the case in any given society will not be considered, although it is critical to a more refined analysis than that attempted in this essay.

its jural implications in some detail, but his work has inspired several recent studies on the idiom of responsibility in other societies.[14]

An important caveat needs to be stated. As Allot, Epstein, and Gluckman (1969: 69–70) have emphasized in their discussion of liability in African customary law, a valid distinction between individual and collective liability (corporate or joint) can be made only by specifying the social context in which a wrong has been committed. Individual liability may be enforced within a particular kin or residence group whose members may be collectively liable for an offense by one of them against a member of another group even though their individual shares in the payment of damages may differ. The difference between the two liabilities may also relate to the nature of the offense and to the presence or absence of intent to cause harm, as it does, for example, in the legal systems of the Berti (Holý, 1967) and the Humr (Cunnison, 1972) in the Sudan and as it is formulated in the *shari'a*, the orthodox Islamic law that derives from both Koranic legislation and the *sunna*, the deeds and sayings of the Prophet Muhammad (see Anderson, 1951; Muhammad, 1967). Furthermore, the recognition of a person's responsibility for harm caused, in the sense of his culpability, may be legally irrelevant in fixing liability on his group, whereas the treatment of that person by his collectivity of kinsmen or neighbors may very much depend on that recognition.[15]

This exploratory essay does not systematically examine these contextual variations of liability. Moreover, many of the preceding considerations are speculative and can only partially be examined with the ethnographic data used in this limited cross-cultural study. Nevertheless, my preliminary analysis of these data shows how the comparative study of liability in stateless societies can elucidate patterns of covariation in a people's jural ideology, legal procedure, social structure, and economic organization.

The Idiom of Liability in Stateless Societies

The following four case studies describe only a few of these patterns. The seminomadic Chenchu of India represent a type of society where

[14]It is noteworthy in this context that Gluckman, whose book on the Barotse courts (1955) is one of the most insightful studies in legal anthropology, had to rely on data from other societies in his subsequent analysis of liability (1965a: chap. 7). The idea of witchcraft in assigning liability is explored in Koch (n.d.).

[15]Compare Moore (1972: 86–93), who does not make the analytical distinction between responsibility and liability used in this cross-cultural analysis.

group harmony in conflict situations is maintained with avoidance as the dominant procedure of conflict management. The Jalé people, horticulturalists in the mountains of New Guinea, exemplify the fragmentary political organization and a mode of subsistence that entails the management of conflict by coercive self-help. And both the Ifugao of Luzon, who subsist on rice irrigation agriculture, and the Yurok, a fishing and hunting tribe of California Indians, demonstrate the effect of crosscutting affiliations that favor the management of conflicts by mediation. These four societies were chosen for two reasons: They have four distinct types of subsistence economy, and their published ethnographic records include relatively detailed data on liability. Moreover, each of these societies has developed a distinct way of allocating liability that appears to be adapted to its particular socioeconomic organization.

LIABILITY AMONG HUNTERS AND GATHERERS: THE CHENCHU

The Chenchu, described by Fürer-Haimendorf (1943, 1967), are a seminomadic tribal people living in the forest of the Nallamalai Hills in Andhra Pradesh, India, where they extract their subsistence by hunting and gathering wild-growing roots, tubers, and berries.[16] Among the Chenchu the principal local group consists of a camp of a small number of families whose members share joint usufructory rights, that is, rights to exploit the resources of their common territory for procuring food. During seasonal scarcity this small group may further subdivide so that at times its individual families camp at different localities. A married man may choose to live on and derive his family's subsistence from at least three different tracts of land: his father's, his mother's, or his wife's natal territory. Both economic necessity and usufructory rights in different tracts of land favor the flexible residence pattern that results in an ever-changing and fluctuating composition of local groups.

Their common predicament of gaining a livelihood solely by collecting prevents the formation of rank distinctions. Nobody can accumulate wealth that could serve as a basis of superior status and political influence. Only a person's age confers some moral authority. In the absence of any government, this authority of the old men may have legal consequences when members of different local groups are involved in a conflict. The informal council of elders from both groups may then discuss the case and seek to mediate a settlement in the interest of social harmony and public peace.

[16]The "ethnographic present" refers to the time before the British colonial administration disturbed their traditional way of life.

In disputes occurring within the local group, the intervention of elders is even less formal. If their attempt to mediate in the conflict fails, one of the parties usually leaves the group, and avoidance characterizes their future relationship. Avoidance functions as an effective mode of conflict management in Chenchu society because liability is an individual obligation. Each person is liable only for a wrong he himself has committed. Thus, on leaving his group, an offender does not jeopardize the welfare of relatives and neighbors who stay behind. A man who repeatedly causes trouble, however, jeopardizes his own welfare in the long run. Although the social and economic organization of the Chenchu allows the troublemaker to evade the unpleasant consequences of his conduct, the options of joining a different group are limited. Therefore, the sanction of public opinion and the ultimate threat of finding himself unwelcome everywhere induces conformity with the norms of communal cooperation and curbs behavior that damages the harmony of a group.

The paramount importance of avoidance as a mode of conflict management among the Chenchu became evident when, at the beginning of this century, the colonial government sedentarized the people in large settlements. Violent offenses such as homicide, assault, and rape increased in dramatic proportions. This development resulted simply because "Chenchu society, adjusted to lessen and remove friction by placing distance between potential opponents, had no other machinery to restrain violence, and as men who had quarreled or were rivals were prevented from getting out of each others' way, the traditional means of avoiding clashes could not operate [Fürer-Haimendorf, 1967: 22]."

Although the ethnographer's account unfortunately is silent on how the Chenchu evaluate evidence,[17] it nonetheless suggests a few inferences regarding the relationship between principles of liability, social structure, and economic organization in certain foraging societies. *If a subsistence economy based on hunting and gathering requires considerable spatial mobility and provides an individual with several options for joining a particular camp, flexible group affiliations facilitate the management of conflict by avoidance, which, in turn, derives its peacekeeping function from the absence of any principle of collective liability.*

LIABILITY AMONG HORTICULTURALISTS: THE JALÉ

The Jalé, whose legal system and violent patterns of conflict management have been described in Koch (1974a), provide a stunning contrast

[17]Perhaps the very ease with which the Chenchu seem to resolve trouble obviates the need to inquire into motive and circumstance.

to the peaceful Chenchu.[18] Living in concentrated settlements along the slopes of steep valleys in the Central Mountains of West New Guinea (Irian Jaya), the Jalé subsist largely on tubers, such as the sweet potato and taro grown by swidden cultivation, and supplement this vegetable diet with pig husbandry and some very limited hunting of forest animals.[19] Each village consists of several wards, residential compounds containing a men's house and a number of family huts. These family huts are the domicile of married or widowed women and their unmarried daughters and young sons. When a boy is between 11 and 13 years of age, he takes up residence in the men's house of his agnatic lineage, a kin group whose members can trace their descent through the male line to a known common ancestor. Most men's houses are the home of several named lineages who, together with other lineages of the same name living in neighboring wards or in other villages, compose sibs, named patrilineal segments of the society that recognize common but genealogically nontraceable descent. Every sib belongs to either of two exogamous sections of the population, that is, to a moiety whose members must marry someone from the other moiety. A lineage holds its garden lands as a corporate estate, and sons obtain their usufructory rights directly from their fathers by continual inheritance as they grow up.[20]

No government exists either on the village level or within the ward, but so-called *big men*, usually the senior, nonsenile members of the largest lineage in their wards, are recognized as the leaders of their men's-house groups. Their influence depends on personal attributes such as physical strength, eloquence, and generosity, and it has some limited effect on controlling conflict among the residents of their men's houses. But no big man either alone or together with other big men commands the authority to arbitrate disputes between neighbors, although their voice and opinion may carry more weight than that of other men. Consequently, conflicts in Jalé society tend to be managed by the threat and use of coercive self-help. Although negotiated settlements occasionally occur as well, each settlement so effected depends entirely on the perceived need of the parties involved in the conflict to continue

[18]The data in this section derive from fieldwork conducted by the author between 1964 and 1966.

[19]Swidden cultivation entails the intermittent replanting of crops on a tract of land that has been cleared of overgrowth by a primitive method known as "slash-and-burn" following a long fallow period.

[20]A woman may receive a small part of her father's land on her marriage, and her husband in cultivating her share merely acts as her trustee. He cannot become its "owner," although his male descendents, with time and after several replantings, will regard these gardens as part of their own land.

or resume a cooperative relationship. Pigs are the only medium by which compensation can be made. At the same time, pig debts or offenses that can be translated into pig debts, such as adultery, encroachment on land, physical injury, and killing, are the main causes of conflict. Pig debts are a prominent issue in disputes because every occasion that changes a person's status (for example, initiation, marriage, parenthood, old age) as well as the peaceful settlement of many disputes requires the payment or exchange of pigs.

The process of conflict management typically varies with the nature of the relationship existing between the parties. Kinship and residence and the political situation in which disputes arise determine to a decisive degree the procedures of their resolution. In disputes among agnatic kinsmen and in quarrels between spouses and affines, shared political and economic interests amongst the parties and their relatives favor a mediated or negotiated settlement. If the parties have temporarily severed their relationship, reconciliation rituals can repair the solidarity of a lineage, and gifts offered within the context of existing exchange cycles can reconcile estranged affines. Disputes between nonkin members of a ward can be managed peacefully as long as the parties actually live together in the same place and, especially, if hostilities with other groups demand concerted military action, but—as in conflicts within a lineage that has moved apart—a spatial separation of the parties impedes negotiations and may promote violent vengeance. Finally, in disputes between unrelated members of neighboring wards, two factors may restrain the parties from resorting to forceful retaliation: the mediating effort of a principal's coresidents with affinal links to the opponent (or to members of the opponent's men's-house group) and the recognition that undisturbed garden work and effective defense against an outside enemy require amity among neighbors. Unless a person has suffered bodily injury, a dispute between neighbors remains amenable to a compromise settlement through negotiation. Altercations, usually after dusk, bring a grievance to public attention and serve to express hostile sentiments in nonviolent fashion. Bodily injury in a retaliatory action, however, tends to elicit a revenge attack, which often initiates a war.

Although parties belonging to different villages may succeed in settling a dispute by peaceful negotiation, an unsuccessful verbal confrontation in these cases often leads to forceful retaliation. An unresolved intervillage conflict affects the political relationship between whole communities and often prevents any negotiation when a new dispute arises between different persons. Generally, the probability that a confrontation results in armed combat increases with geographical distance and paucity of affinal relationships between the local groups involved in the conflict. The same conditions also impede an early settlement when villages in different valleys participate in the war. In this situation, alliances are created by default rather than by considerations of affinity and traditional amity, and unsatisfied claims to compensatory pigs for injuries and deaths among allied wards greatly inhibit the conclusion of a peace treaty that all men's houses honor.

In Jalé society we find the specific combination of sociopolitical and economic variables expected to be associated with a jural ideology that stipulates both absolute and collective liability: coresident agnatic descent groups with corporate and exclusive ownership of settlement sites and agricultural lands, a minimal degree of political integration, and a concomitant absence of standard procedures of mediation that would facilitate a review of evidence. Jalé reasoning deduces liability from a jural principle that might be called the "doctrine of effective action." This doctrine does not distinguish between intent, mistake, negligence, and accident as aggravating or extenuating circumstances. In evaluating only the consequences of an act, the Jalé do not question a person's culpability when they establish his formal liability, that is, his obligation to indemnify the injured party, which in the case of a killing is the dead person's lineage. A few actual cases may serve to illustrate the irrelevance of personal responsibility in assigning liability.

> **Case 1.** A young man was buried by a landslide along with his maternal uncle, whom he was helping to build a fence in his garden when the accident occurred. The uncle's son promptly delivered a "guilt" pig to the young man's eldest living agnate, the son of his elder brother. The young man's agnates would have claimed a "lung" pig, the customary condolence gift, if he had worked on land that his uncle had given him for his own seasonal use. The payment of a "guilt" pig, however, signified that the uncle's kinsmen held the uncle responsible for his nephew's death and accepted the obligation to indemnify the victim's agnates.

The next cases accentuate the irrelevance of intent and negligence:

> **Case 2.** A man became liable for the death of a woman and her child despite his efforts to prevent the fatal accident. He was cutting down a large branch of a tree that grew close to a path when the woman approached. Disregarding both the markings that he had placed across the path to warn people of the danger and his furious shouts, the woman hurried on. As she passed the tree, the branch broke and killed her and the child she was carrying on her shoul-

ders. The woman's kinsmen were entitled to indemnification because "the branch fell down by his hands," even though the accident occurred "through the woman's own fault."

Case 3. When a man's wife dies in childbirth, he is liable to indemnify his affine for the loss of their agnate, a conspicuous example of
absolute liability. The rationalization that the woman died "by his
penis" substantiates particularly well the doctrine of effective action, for had the man not impregnated his wife, she would not have
died in childbirth.

What the Jalé consider an effective action need not be the cause of a
person's injury or death. In a purely logical sense one can see some,
albeit remote, causal connection between death in childbirth and im-
pregnation and a more proximate connection of action and effect in the
case of the falling branch. But the Jalé extend the notion of causation
even further. For example, if someone invites a neighbor to join him on
a trading trip across the Central Range and this man suffers a fatal fall
from a cliff, the initiator of the trip must pay a "guilt" pig to the deceased's agnates. Refusal to comply with this obligation creates a grievance that may lead to forceful retaliation.

It is clear, then, that *in Jalé society, where no procedures for reviewing
evidence exist, to be liable means to be guilty.* The recognition of personal
responsibility may, however, influence the procedure by which an injured party seeks to obtain redress, but that procedure depends on the
particular kin and residence relationships between the parties. For example, in cases similar to those just described, the kinsmen of the woman who died in childbirth will be most lenient with the husband and give
him time to furnish the required pig, especially if they want to continue
their affinal gift exchanges. The kinsmen of the man who fell from a cliff
will insist on immediate compensation from their neighbor, with whom
they share less tangible interests. If their claim remains unsatisfied, they
will attempt to seize a pig from their neighbor by stealth. On the other
hand, if a man is killed in a fight, his kinsmen may not even claim any
indemnity and instead may contemplate blood revenge. Which course
of action they choose will depend entirely on their relations with the
liable party and his kin group. If they are ward or village neighbors,
vengeance is far less likely to occur than it is if they live in different
villages. And in both situations, existing affinal links between members
of their men's houses will reduce the chances of violent retaliation.

The case involving the accidental death by a landslide has already
brought up the principle of extending liability to a person's kin group.

Among the Jalé, an individual's obligation to render compensation is shared by his lineage. If the nature of the relationship between the parties makes it impossible to arrange a payment of compensation, the range of people subject to retaliation generally increases with the residential distance between the parties and the magnitude of the conflict. In any case, there are numerous occasions in which the corporate liability of a lineage to pay compensation extends into a joint liability of the culprit's neighbors to suffer retaliation. For example, if an aggrieved party has a claim against a fellow villager such as the abductor of his wife, he will, if no negotiated settlement can be achieved, attempt to seize the pig or pigs to which he is entitled only from the abductor himself or his agnates. If, on the other hand, the abductor is from a different village, he will try to seize a pig from anyone of the abductor's ward and, possibly, from any of his fellow villagers.

The same pattern applies to conflicts involving blood revenge. The range of potential victims increases with the residential distance between the parties, although in every case of forceful self-help, either by pig seizure or by revenge killing, the aggrieved party and his supporters, relatives, or neighbors prefer to retaliate against the liable person and his agnatic kinsmen. Other members of his men's house are next in line as potential victims, and only in a state of war would any of his fellow villagers be subject to their vengeance.

Although physical injury, death, and wife abduction are the main occasions where liability has to be established, a person may suffer loss or damage in many different ways. Somebody's pig may destroy one's fence and uproot one's crops, another's disregard of pollution taboos may endanger one's health, and malicious or careless gossip may harm one's reputation. The extent and enforcement of collective liability in these cases is largely unknown. It appears, however, that property damage—including the wounding of dogs and pigs—initially calls for repair or restitution by the responsible party. If such claims remain unsatisfied, the grievance can precipitate a confrontation that may lead to injuries and even killings. As the scope of a conflict enlarges, support and alliance structures determine the involvement of more people in the dispute including the parties' kinsmen, men's-house groups, neighbors, and affines from other villages.

The corporate liability of a lineage for an offense committed by one of its members does not cease if the injured party has obtained redress by retaliation that victimized an unrelated neighbor of the offender. It merely shifts their liability to the person who suffered retaliation on their account, say, by having his pig stolen in a retaliatory action. Regardless of the formal assignation of liability in this case, however,

whether the owner of the pig seeks restitution by negotiation or counter-
seizure from the liable or from the aggrieved party in the original dispute again depends on his relationship with either side. A hypothetical
case, described by Koch, may serve to clarify this point:

> Let us assume two cases where A and B are the principals in a dispute and B
> steals a pig from C in a retaliatory action against A. If all three parties belong to the
> same village, C tries to negotiate restitution from B. If, on the other hand, A and C
> belong to the same village and B to a different village, C demands restitution from
> A. A man follows the same strategy in his attempt to obtain the customary compen-
> sation from the abductor of his wife. He will demand a pig from the woman's
> agnates if they live in a neighboring ward and if a state of hostility with the abduc-
> tor's village or an expected violent confrontation makes direct negotiations with the
> abductor a perilous endeavor.
>
> The Jalé view any inter-village confrontation as a precarious enterprise for the
> person claiming restitution because of his residential association with one of the
> parties to the original dispute. In contrast, they regard inter-ward negotiations
> following the seizure of a pig from a man of the wrong ward as entailing little
> danger for the claimant because he can expect sympathy from both parties to the
> original dispute.
>
> There is a peculiar difficulty with a settlement in which C receives compensation
> from A. While A would be liable to compensate any injury suffered by his support-
> ers, he is not responsible for the loss of a pig incurred by a nonpartisan resident of
> his village in the course of his conflict with B. However, according to Jalé notions of
> liability, C nevertheless blames A for the seizure and resorts to retaliation if he is
> unable or unwilling to claim restitution from B. If A accedes to C's demand for
> compensation, this arrangement merely serves to eliminate the imminent danger of
> a new conflict. A pig paid in this fashion represents little more than a gift that
> should be reciprocated at a future occasion. The uncertain nature of a settlement of
> this kind then creates a new grievance that may aggravate any future dispute
> between A and C over an issue entirely unrelated to the original problem [1974a:
> 130–131].

Although in Jalé society a person and his lineage always incur liability
toward a specific person and his kin group, the people distinguish one
type of offense from all other forms of injurious behavior: sexual intercourse between a man and a woman who belong to the same moiety.
They view such incestuous copulation as an odious infamy and believe
that the evil consequences endanger the very survival of the people. The
offenders are held to be responsible for a catastrophic crop failure and
the deterioration or death of humans and pigs. Their liability thus extends to everybody. Ideally, both culprits should be put to death—
because their lives constitute the only kind of restitution that can avert
the disaster—and their own agnates should execute them. Case histories

show, however, that other men may kill the offenders and that one of them may even escape death by submitting to a scatophagous rite.[21]

Incest is the only delict that the Jalé consider an offense "against society." Other wrongs may impair or even permanently sever relationships between kinsmen and local groups, but incest alone undermines and negates the foundation of the social order. Consequently, the principle of corporate liability of the agnatic group has special legal consequences in incest cases. Unless the kinsmen of the offender succeed in persuading the community at large to accept the scatophagous rite in lieu of the culprit's death, they must either kill him themselves or solicit, or at least publicly approve, his execution by other members of the community. The effect of this rule on limiting conflict is clear: If nonagnates killed the perpetrator, they would have put their own lives in jeopardy should the victim's kinsmen one day doubt the truth of the allegations that preceded the execution. Indeed, in a society where all disputes over life and death are commonly settled by violent confrontation, and blood revenge is both virtuous and just, this rule eliminates a potential cause for further killings.

The corporate liability of Jalé lineages for disputes among agnates requires that the solidarity of its members is protected at all times. Therefore, when serious disputes arise among agnates, one of the parties—usually the aggrieved—often initiates a state of avoidance between himself and his opponent. Avoidance suspends all modes of normal communication. The antagonists no longer speak with each other, cease to share food even when eating in the men's house at the same time, and avoid sitting or sleeping close to each other. Often the aggrieved party leaves the men's house and moves to a neighboring ward or takes up residence with an affinal relative in a different village. Continuation of common residence allows the members of their men's house to mediate their dispute through friendly exhortations, and a verbal apology sometimes coupled with the presentation of a small gift usually suffices to restore amicable relations. If one of the parties has left the men's house, however, a move usually accompanied by a ritual curse against his adversary, the chances of an early, informal reconciliation diminish, and only a special ceremony conducted by a curer can repair their solidarity.[22]

In view of the significance of avoidance in Chenchu society, the Jalé

[21]For a description of this rite, see Koch (1974b) and Zöllner (1977: 87–91). Incest is the only wrong where doubt about an alleged culprit's guilt calls for an oracular review of evidence through the performance of an ordeal.

[22]For a comparative analysis of such ceremonies, see Koch et al. (1977).

case indicates that avoidance can function as an effective mode of conflict management only if an offense does not entail liability of people other than the offender. Because in Jalé society liability is corporate and lies with the lineage, only agnatic kinsmen can resort to avoidance to contain a conflict.[23] Their relationship voids the notion of liability altogether. Therefore, if a person renders compensation to an agnate whom he was wounded by giving him a pig, the name or category of the pig is always one that denotes an offering within the exchange cycle to which both parties are tied.

In summary, the Jalé case suggests that *the principles of corporate and absolute liability appear jointly in societies where defined, landowning, unilineal descent groups constitute the basic social units and a low degree of political integration is associated with the absence or extreme weakness of institutionalized third-party intervention.* The next case study will show that if the composition of a society's basic social unit favors the creation of crosscutting group affiliations, procedures of mediation emerge even in the absence of government and facilitate at least a review of evidence regarding personal responsibility and the circumstances under which an injury occurred.

LIABILITY AMONG IRRIGATION FARMERS:
THE IFUGAO

The Ifugao inhabit the rugged mountains of the interior of northern Luzon in the Philippines, where they practice intensive rice agriculture by a highly sophisticated method of terrace irrigation. Ifugao ideas of responsibility and liability were analyzed by Barton in his classic monograph, *Ifugao Law* (1919).

Three principles structure all social relations in Ifugaoland: kinship, class, and residence. Kinship links are of overriding importance. A person's family, composed of the relatives of both his parents to the third ascending and descending degrees, constitute a corporation holding rice and forest land and heirlooms in joint ownership. This corporate nature of the Ifugao family has significant implications for conflict management. The family, as a bilateral kin group, shares a collective right to obtain redress for an injury against any of its members inflicted by a member of another family and a collective liability to suffer the consequences of a wrong committed by any one of its members against another family. Actual practice, however, assigns different degrees of lia-

[23]Although among the Jalé it is usually the aggrieved person who leaves the ward, among the Chenchu the person leaving the camp appears in most cases to be the offender—a difference deserving further analysis.

bility to the members of a party's family depending on their relative genealogical nearness as well as according to that party's personal standing and reputation within his kin group. The principle of corporate family liability means that no person can legally proceed against another member of his kin group (except in cases of intrafamily witchcraft), with the inevitable consequence that wrongs committed within this group remain without formal redress, though symbolic and material prestations may be proffered to atone for an intrafamily offense.

Rank or class distinctions derive from wealth that accrues through possession and control of the main local resource, rice land. Upper-class standing requires the possession or accumulation of more produce than a man and his own family can consume, allowing him to sell or loan rice to the needy. Formal recogntion of his rank requires a show of ostentatious generosity at feasts that people of a whole district attend. Men who grow enough rice to feed their families throughout the year but produce no surplus belong to the middle class, and families who must supplement their rice diet with sweet potatoes, grown on the higher slopes, make up the lower class. This incipient capitalist stratification of Ifugao society has interesting jural implications. The more elevated a person's rank, the greater is the amount both of the damages he can demand in compensation for an injury suffered and of the indemnity for which he is liable if he has committed a wrong. Obviously, as Barton explains, this system can work best in cases where both parties belong to the same class. If, on the other hand, the disputants are of unequal rank, a compromise that fixes the damages somewhere in between the amount demanded by the aggrieved party and that deemed applicable by his opponent is the usual solution if a peaceful settlement of their dispute is arranged. Ultimately, the relative fighting strength as measured in terms of successful head hunts of the two families involved in the conflict determines the point at which a compromise appears acceptable to both kin groups. In every case, however, it is only the amount of damages, not liability itself, that is negotiable.

The third principle structuring social relations among the Ifugao, residence, is of least jural importance. Villages, scattered settlements as they are in most valleys of Ifugaoland, do not form political units in the sense that coresidence prescribes defined common activities on the village level. At the very least, their role as a base for recruiting support in conflicts is vastly subordinate to that of the dispersed family group, which organizes joint military ventures such as head-hunting expeditions. Barton probably underestimated the *political* importance of the local community, however, for his data clearly show that residential contiguity mitigates the range and severity of sanctions demanded and meted out in disputes between neighbors and thus promotes their peaceful settlement.

Barton's account of the Ifugao legal system is unique in the ethnographic literature in that it describes a highly complex code of substantive law for a people lacking any formal institutions of government. The approved procedure by which infractions of the rules regulating economic, social, and religious activities are sanctioned is mediation by a go-between, the *monkalun*. The person selected as the intermediary in a given dispute cannot be a close relative of one of the parties because the Ifugao ethos of family loyalty would necessarily mark him as a partisan supporter of the party to whom he stands in the closest consanguineal or affinal relationship. He may be a distant relative to both disputants if they acknowledge that his intervention is motivated by his interests to achieve a settlement acceptable to both. Although the very existence of codified indemnities promotes a negotiated settlement of disputes through the brokerage and, sometimes, pressure of the *monkalun*, the absence of governmental institutions and public enforcement mechanisms relegates the management of some disputes to violent retaliation, which may escalate the conflict into a feud.

In every dispute the Ifugao carefully distinguish between principals and their accomplices and accessories in assigning responsibility for a wrong and hold each liable in varying degrees for its commission. The person who conceives and plans a homicide, for example, suffers the greatest punishment, whether or not he actually participates in the slaying. Other people on his side share in their common liability according to their role in the episode. These roles, which are codified and carry, in decreasing degrees, both part of the overall responsibility for the death and its equivalent share of their joint liability, include the following: the principal who planned the killing, the "thrower" who cast the spear, the "companions" of the principal who helped in various ways in the planning or execution of the plan, including the "shower" who supplied information that facilitated its success.

The following hypothetical case constructed by Barton (1919: 57; here abridged) illustrates the meaning of these distinctions:

> A (the principal) decides to avenge the death of a relative and recruits B and a number of his other kinsmen for a revenge expedition into the village of the killer and intended victim, D. Before the day set for their trip, A dies. His kinsmen (his companions) are not deterred and proceed with their plan. In D's village they meet C (the "shower" to be), who informs them of D's whereabouts. The revenge party finds D in his garden, and B (the "thrower") kills him

with his spear. D's kinsmen, in turn, decide to avenge his death by killing both A and B and, given the opportunity, one or two of the other companions, as any debt, civil or punitive, among the Ifugao has to be requited with interest. If A were still alive and D's kinsmen succeeded in killing him, they may settle for this minimal score if further expeditions were to endanger their own safety. However, because A had died, B, as the "thrower," will be their preferred victim, with C, as the "shower," next in line along with any of the other companions. Should B also die before they succeed in their vengeance, all companions including C, the "shower," are in equal jeopardy. Their jeopardy would also increase if B were still alive but D's kinsmen failed in repeated expeditions to take his life, in which case the principle of at least one life for a life outweighs customary considerations of graded responsibility and liability.

This seemingly mechanical correspondence between responsibility and liability does not mean that the Ifugao ignore the question of intent altogether in assessing liability. On the contrary, they differentiate very clearly between injuries involving intent (*gulad*) from those that happened by accident (*nakolat*), provided, however, absence of intent can be proven. In the case described, the "shower" is regarded as one of the companions because he is presumed to have known of the intent of A's kinsmen; he certainly has no way of proving that he did not. The avengers whom he informed of his neighbor's whereabouts did plan to kill him; therefore, his liability is vicariously linked to their intent.

In order to void any claim against himself as companion, a person whom some circumstances have linked to an offence must demand a special payment (*tokom*) from the offender to demonstrate his non-complicity (Barton, 1919: 76–77). Cases in which such payments were demanded involve the owner of a field in which a woman was kidnapped, a man who loaned a basket to a boy who was kidnapped while carrying the basket, and a trader whose companion was seized to be sold as a slave (Barton, 1949: 141). Simply demanding the *tokom*, however, does not always exculpate a person. Unless and until he actually enforces the payment, he may be considered an accomplice, and he may thus have to share the liability for the wrong committed.[24] Whether an absence of responsibility implies an absolution from liability, however, depends on both the nature of the offense and its circumstances. Gener-

[24]Because a member of the aristocratic class must in all circumstances demand the *tokom* and a poor person may use discretion in the matter, Barton believes that this obligatory intervention by the upper class "is a faint malodorous beginning of the police power of the state [and] reflects an incipient territorial principle in society [1949: 142]."

ally, neither drunkenness nor insanity obviates liability for homicide. But state of mind does mitigate the consequences of any other offense in that the offender's apologies and voluntary contributions to sacrifices and feasts to express his sorrow for the injury substitute for damages. Such leniency is even extended in cases of death resulting "every year in the free-for-all scrambles over sacrificed [water buffaloes] [Barton, 1919: 58]."[25]

Not only do the Ifugao differentiate between intent and accident in establishing liability, but also they distinguish between accident, negligence, and mistake. In order to void the notion of intent and instead recognize an accident as the cause of a person's death, the fatal injury must have been witnessed. An example of such a situation is cited by Barton (1919: 58–59) in the killing of a participant in a hunt. If a hunting party has surrounded a wild boar, and the beast charges one of the hunters who, intending to kill it, stabs one of his companions with the shod point of his spear handle, no blame for the death lies with him as long as the others of the party bear witness to his innocence.[26]

Negligence is distinguished from mistake in that mistake still entails intent. For example, if a spear thrown in target practice kills a child who ran in the way, the thrower is liable for paying only a fraction of the indemnity usually demanded for homicide, the amount depending on the degree of his carelessness. On the other hand, a man who kills a neighbor in the darkness of night in the belief that he is an enemy bent on taking his life must pay higher damages because his negligence in identifying his neighbor was compounded by his intent to kill the man presumed to be his enemy.

Apart from such situational factors that decide the amount of damages due, social and political factors further complicate Ifugao jural ideas and impinge on the settlement of claims for indemnity. Thus, inhabitants of foreign villages are treated less leniently than are neighbors, who in turn are treated less leniently than are members of one's family, against whom no claims may be made at all if the parties are closely related, such as in a case involving a person and his own or his parents' siblings. In addition, as already explained, in any given dispute the relative rank or standing of the parties vis-à-vis each other determines the amount of damages required for its settlement.

How family links modify the extent of damages for which a man who

[25]I suspect that in this case the difficulty of identifying the person(s) responsible for the death explains its treatment as a tragic accident.

[26]It is of interest to note here that the earliest compilation of Roman law, the Twelve Tables, refers to injuries caused by a spear in discriminating between intentional and accidental wrongs; the Nuer of the Sudan make the same distinction (see Howell, 1954).

killed somebody by mistake becomes liable is evident in the following case:

> Dumauwat of Baay was irrigating his fields at night. Some of his companions told him that there were head-hunters from an enemy village near. In the darkness, Dumauwat encountered another man, Likyayu, the betrothed of his daughter. He asked him who was there. On account of the noise of water falling from the rice fields, Likyayu did not hear the inquiry, and said nothing. Dumauwat speared him. Likyayu cried out. Dumauwat recognized his voice, and carried him home. He furnished animals for sacrifice to secure Likyayu's recovery. Likyayu recovered. Had he died, Dumauwat would have been called on for the full amount of the fine; but had Likyayu been *firmly* engaged to Dumauwat's daughter, that is, had the [secondary] ceremony been performed the full amount of the . . . fine would not have been demanded, since the relationship would have been an extenuating circumstance [Barton, 1919: 71].

Even when someone fatally injures a person in a brawl or in a state of insanity or drunkenness, in themselves mitigating circumstances except for homicide, the relationship between killer and victim determines the consequences of the death. "In case the slain died before his slayer could agree to provide animals for sacrifice," Barton explains, "the latter would probably be killed by the kin of the slain if he were of a foreign district. He might be killed if a non-related co-villager. He would be fined [the customary indemnity] if a kinsman. He would probably go scot free if a brother or uncle [1919: 71]."

The general rule that any Ifugao must beware of being implicated in the commission of a wrong has its corollary in the rule that anybody who implicates a person in a wrong committed—thus impairing his reputation and endangering his safety—is held liable to indemnify him regardless of whether the claimant had any knowledge of the offender's intent. For example, if a visitor from another village is slain by a neighbor of his host, the latter has a right to claim damages from the killer. But the slain man's host not only has a right to demand compensation but also must seek to enforce his claim lest the victim's kinsmen consider him an accomplice and contemplate his death along with that of the killer.

The principal ideas and procedures relating to liability in the Ifugao legal system can now be summarized. In the absence of any government, even on the village level, the need to preserve the economic viability of the family as a corporation with joint ownership in vital resources is reflected in its legal status. This bilateral kin group is the most inclusive political unit in Ifugao society, and its members cannot proceed against one another. Together they share a collective liability assigned to each member in varying degrees as determined by his relative genealogical proximity to the principal in a given dispute with another kin group. Unlike among the Jalé, collective liability among the Ifugao cannot be defined by residence, because the Ifugao family constitutes a kin group whose members live in different localities.

The primacy of family loyalty, however, does not entirely ignore the necessity of keeping relations between covillagers in harmonious order. Not only does the irrigation system demand neighborly cooperation, but also "neighbors and co-villagers do not want to see their neighborhood torn by internal dissension and thus weakened as to the conduct of warfare against enemies [Barton, 1919: 88]." Consequently, as one would expect on the evidence cited in studies explaining the effect of crosscutting affiliations,[27] the Ifugao have developed a system of mediation that, supported by a formal code of indemnities, favors the peaceful settlement of disputes by go-betweens. In this case, a family's obligation to share the liability for damages arising from a wrong committed by one of its members exerts just the sort of pressure that mitigates, though does not eliminate, resort to violent retaliation. Furthermore, *the use of mediation as an institutionalized procedure by which parties to a dispute and their witnesses can voice their views of the circumstances of an injury as to intent, accident, mistake, and negligence permits the recognition of responsibility (as culpability) in assigning liability.*

LIABILITY IN A FISHING SOCIETY: THE YUROK

The relationships between a society's subsistence economy, kinship system, political organization, mode of conflict management, and liability observed among the Chenchu, the Jalé, and the Ifugao suggest that in a stateless society where members of dispersed kin groups have individual title to vital resources, the allocation of liability should also be individualized. If the Yurok Indians of California are representative of this type of society, their way of defining liability indeed exemplifies this pattern.

The Yurok derive their livelihood from fishing the rivers and from gathering and hunting in the forest surrounding their villages.[28] Like the Ifugao, the Yurok settle disputes by mediation (see Kroeber, 1925, 1926), and their case further supports the view that societies without corporate unilineal descent groups of the Jalé type rarely resort to the management of conflict by coercive self-help, even in the absence of government.[29] Although a patrilineal focus on descent reckoning exists,

[27]See, for example, Colson (1953) and Murphy (1957).
[28]The "ethnographic present," again, refers to the time before European intrusion.
[29]The intrinsic parallels in jural ideology and legal procedure among the Yurok and the Ifugao have been recognized before (see Lowie, 1963).

it does not constitute a structural principle in Yurok society. Lineal and affinal links are of equal importance and disperse a person's loyalties among a large number of relatives with whom he can trace connections through either of his parents or his own in-laws. This wide diffusion of kin relationships has its legal consequence in a system of highly individualized, strictly reciprocal, right–duty relationships. "All rights, claims, possessions, and privileges are individual and personal, and all wrongs are against individuals. There is no offense against the community, no right or power of any sort inhering in it [Kroeber, 1925: 20]." Joint ownership in resources, where it exists, is by fixed shares, so that, for example, if several men own a fishing place "they [use] it in rotation for one or more days according to their share, relieving each other about the middle of the afternoon for 24-hour periods [Kroeber, 1925: 33]."

All Yurok of equal rank regardless of their age and sex have identical civil rights, even though it is usually men who, acting as guardians or trustees on behalf of women and children, protect their rights and press their claims if these rights have been violated. Claims are settled by several go-betweens, each party selecting his own. Although individual go-betweens act as partisan supporters, as a group they are nevertheless expected to reach an equitable decision. "Apparently they inquired into the fact of liability plus the presence of intent [Kroeber, 1926: 515]." The aggrieved party seeks the full amount of compensation fixed for the injury in question under customary law from the offender, who in turn attempts to beat down the demand until a point is reached when both sides agree to the compromise that usually ends a dispute in Yurok society.

A sophisticated monetary system of valuation allows the Yurok to scale the amount of indemnity for any type of injury and aids the disputants and their go-betweens in their quarrels and deliberations over the size of compensation claimed and offered.[30] The severity of certain injuries such as killing, sexual affronts, and insults is determined by the relative rank or wealth of the aggrieved party. Thus the amount of indemnification for the death of a man of high rank is greater than that demanded for the death of a poor man. Blood revenge, which sometimes occurs, does not cancel the original debt. In this case both sides have claims for indemnity arising from their separate offenses against each other.

Although Kroeber's report is meager, even contradictory,[31] on Yurok

[30]Yurok money consists of dentalium shells whose size measures their exact value, one of five named currency units. Depending on their length, 11–15 shells of the same grade are placed on strings, the worth of each representing the sum value of the shells it holds.

[31]Kroeber states, for example, "Every invasion of privilege or property must be exactly compensated" and then reports on a rather curious practice: "If one man used another's

ideas of liability it is clear that liability is absolute. For example, in the case of a house burning down while its owner ferries someone across a river, the passenger is liable for the damage because the ferryman might have extinguished the fire and saved his house had he not provided the service (Kroeber, 1925: 35). Because under Yurok law a traveler has the rights to command this service from anybody able to provide transport with his boat, and may even claim a fine from a person who refuses him ferriage, this case indicates the strictness of the Yurok concept of absolute liability.

Absolute liability does not imply that culpability is irrelevant to the settlement of a dispute. On the contrary, intent and malice call for a payment in addition to the sum assessed for the injury itself. The Yurok regard intent as a separate wrong.[32] The distinction between a claim as determined by absolute liability and a claim for punitive damages is particularly evident in case a man has killed his wife willfully or in drunkenness. Her kin then have no claim against him for blood money (provided he has taken unencumbered possession of the woman by full payment of the bride-price), but they are entitled to receive a fine. Had the woman's death been accidental, no claim against her husband could be made.

Kroeber did not perceive the structural advantage for the peaceful settlement of disputes by mediation that is provided by the crosscutting loyalties entailed in a person's kin and residential relationships. This network of multiple linkages, by preventing the formation of localized descent groups with corporate liability, facilitates the intervention of go-betweens in Yurok disputes. Their intervention in turn includes a review of evidence that permits a legal distinction between culpability and liability of a special kind. Liability for an injury is absolute and cannot be

---

fishing place, even without explicit permission of the owner, and fell and slipped there and cut his leg or was bruised, he would at once lay claim to the fishing place as damages [Kroeber, 1925: 20, 34]." If this were viable practice, one would have to expect Yuroks getting bruised very often at other people's fishing places.

[32]So did some European tribes. According to Gluckman, "The standard payment of blood money was due in all circumstances to the kindreds (differently constituted) of the deceased in both Anglo-Saxon and Welsh law, but if killing was intentional an additional payment was due to the nearest blood relatives [1965b: 131–132]." The *shari'a* also prescribed an increment in the value of *diya* ('blood money') to be paid to the victim's kinsmen in the case of premeditated murder; but only as late as 1840 did Ottoman legislation add the penal sanction of imprisonment to the payment of customary *diya* indemnity (Hardy, 1963: 38, 49). It is further noteworthy that a conceptual elaboration of individual responsibility in the *shari'a* followed from the Prophet Muhammad's original insistence on recognizing intent and thus on distinguishing between sanctions for premeditated and other killings (Hardy, 1963: 30–34).

mitigated or diminished in consideration of the liable party's personal responsibility for an injury. On the other hand, intent and, probably, negligence constitute separate offenses and subject a person found liable for an injury in an absolute sense to an additional but negotiable liability. One may assume that under these circumstances *the definition of intent as a wrong in itself carries a deterrent effect similar to that of collective liability, which works as a brake on retaliation by coercive self-help in societies where no reliable procedures of mediation exist.*

COMPARATIVE ANALYSIS

Some specific inferences that have emerged from the analysis of liability in four stateless societies can now be summarized in terms that appear plausible within the theoretical framework of a comparative legal ethnology. The Chenchu case indicates that in a society whose subsistence economy and social structure ensure a high degree of residential mobility, the principle of collective liability cannot exist if avoidance, a procedure particularly well adapted to these socioeconomic conditions, is to function as an effective mode of conflict management. Although the Chenchu data are inconclusive on this point, it can be assumed that the very ease with which conflicts are managed under these conditions obviates the need for a review of evidence relating to the distinction between absolute and relative liability, that is, an inquiry into culpability and circumstances. As the Jalé case illustrates, however, if people who are tied to a particular locality by virtue of their vital dependence on garden land held in joint tenancy with other members of an agnatic descent group must manage conflict by coercive self-help, the concepts of both corporate and absolute liability appear as a cultural response to the need to maintain a viable social order. If under these conditions an offender's abscondence were to leave the injured party without redress and if, in the absence of procedures to review evidence, the assertion that an injury happened by accident were to confer immunity, the maintenance of public peace would be impossible. Consequently, in societies such as that of the Ifugao, where the bilateral, dispersed kin group constitutes the basic socioeconomic unit sharing ownership of agricultural land, a different ideology of liability appears. In this case crosscutting group affiliations to family and neighborhood facilitate the intervention in a conflict of a mediator and thus permit a review of evidence, and, therefore, a jural distinction between personal responsibility and liability. The efficiency of this mode of conflict management, however, seems to depend on the ultimate assignation of corporate liability to an offender's family, even though this liability is distributed in unequal shares among the family members.

TABLE 4.1.
Variables Associated with Types of Liability

Society	Economy	Unit owning principal resources	Dominant mode of conflict management	Liability[a]			
				C	I	A	R
Chenchu	Hunting and gathering	Camp of individual families	Avoidance	−	+	?	?
Jalé	Swidden agriculture	Coresident agnatic descent group	Coercion	+	−	+[b]	−
Ifugao	Irrigation farming	Dispersed bilateral extended family	Mediation	+[c]	−	−	+
Yurok	Fishing and hunting	Individual person	Mediation	−	+	+[d]	−

[a] C = collective; I = individual; A = absolute; R = relative.

[b] Relative liability influences procedures for settlement.

[c] Genealogical position determines an individual's share of his family's collective liability.

[d] Absolute liability for injury exists together with relative liability for intent.

The case of the Yurok indicates that for the jural ideology of a stateless society to entail the concept of strictly individual liability and to distinguish, in this case, separate, absolute, and relative liability, two conditions must exist. There must be a division of vital resources on an individual basis and an institutionalized procedure of mediation through which evidence can be reviewed.

Table 4.1 summarizes the observed relationships between a society's subsistence economy, principal social unit owning vital resources, dominant mode of conflict management, and types of liability. Although four societies do not constitute a sample that would permit bold theoretical generalizations, the structure of the observed covariations nevertheless suggest two broader propositions: First, it appears that *in stateless societies, collective liability is linked to the group owning vital resources if an individual's share in the group's corporate estate is exclusively ascribed by descent. If, on the other hand, an individual's membership in a group is flexible and negotiable, that is, contingent on consanguineal as well as multiple affinal links, the principle of collective liability does not emerge.* This situation, exemplified by the Chenchu, is probably typical for societies with a foraging economy, in which the procurement of food depends not on long-term, localized, investment of labor (as it does with cultivation), but on a purely extractive and migratory mode of resource exploitation.

Second, *in the absence of any form of governmental social control, the interrelated variables of subsistence economy, ownership of resources, and kinship structure determine the dominant mode of conflict management.* Because a review of evidence is necessary for the parties to a dispute to recognize and acknowledge the circumstances under which an injury occurred, a jural distinction between absolute and relative liability depends on the availability and the efficiency of procedures, such as mediation, to facilitate this review.[33]

Implications for a General Theory of Liability

I consider these propositions to reflect uncertain insights into one of the most complicated and, at the same time and perhaps for this reason, most neglected problems in legal anthropology. It is evident that a change from collective to individual and from absolute to relative liability does not imply evolutionary steps on the order of the Mainean shift from status to contract (Maine, 1861). The matter is much more complex, as the analysis of the case studies reviewed in this essay has shown—mainly, by suggesting questions for further inquiry, including an anthropological look at our own modern ideology of liability.

For example, it is theoretically important to know whether, and if so, how, the categorical separation of civil and criminal law contributed to the initial jural recognition of *mens rea*, and its subsequent elaboration beginning with the famous M'Naghten case of 1843, as a cardinal principle of criminal justice.[34] The available ethnographic evidence indicates

[33]A more comprehensive cross-cultural analysis of the conditions leading to the emergence of collective liability would require a substantial elaboration of the notions of "corporate ownership" and "resource." The concept of "shared rights in the use and control of *any* resource considered the domain of a group as a whole" is probably more suitable, because it would allow, for example, a comparison of the idea of collective liability as it exists in tribal societies and among gangs and Mafia families in contemporary America. In recent feuds between street gangs in modern Chicago, the consequences of gang membership appear to be rather similar to those linked to membership in a Jalé lineage.

[34]The principle of *mens rea* ('guilty mind') achieved jurisprudential prominence with the so-called M'Naghten Rules of 1843. These rules were formulated by the judges of the House of Lords in response to widespread popular resentment and scholarly criticism of a jury verdict that found Daniel M'Naghten (who meant to murder Sir Robert Peel, prime minister, but mistakenly killed his private secretary) not guilty because medical testimony had declared him insane. The original doctrine enunciated in the rules stipulates "that to establish a defence on the ground of insanity it must be clearly proved that, at the time of committing the act, the accused was labouring under . . . a defect of reason, from disease of the mind, as not to know the nature and quality of the act he was doing, or, if he did know it, that he did not know he was doing what was wrong [cited from a reprinted excerpt in Morris, 1961: 395]." A critical review of recent reforms of the doctrine appears in Hart (1968: 186–209).

that this separation in European law could not have occurred without fundamental changes in the material basis, social structure, and political status of kin groups; but an anthropological analysis of this process still needs to be done.[35]

Seen in a cross-cultural perspective, the distinction at common law between criminal guilt and civil liability has produced a most unusual situation, one in which the interest of the state in punishing an offender takes absolute precedence over the interest of the victim of the offense, so that the incarceration of a convicted assailant or burglar, and concomitant deprivation of gainful employment, is deemed more important than the right of the victim to compensation or restitution, which the offender might be able to make were he or she to continue employment (or be given a job if he or she had none).[36] Recent legislation to enable victims of crime to claim indemnification from the state reflects, however, a new view of the relationship between a citizen and the government. If the victim must relinquish his or her right to first remedy to the state, then, indeed, the state could reasonably be held liable to the victim, on the assumption that it had failed to protect his or her welfare. More than 4000 years ago, Hammurabi, king of Babylon, promulgated such a law to protect people who had suffered loss from brigandage (Harper, 1904).[37]

It is also important to discover why, apart from the reasons supplied by juristic rhetoric, liability in tort—the civil law of wrongs such as negligence—no longer requires proof of culpability in all cases. For example, does the continuing extension of strict liability relate to a judicial difficulty of securing the technological evidence needed to determine whom to blame for injuries caused by an unsafe or defective product when it reaches the consumer through a long chain of intermediate commercial transactions, and the product itself is manufactured from materials obtained from numerous suppliers, who, in turn, use processing techniques developed and installed by yet other parties? Ethnologi-

[35]Given the nature of available records, this is an extremely difficult task. For one attempt in this direction, see Green (1972).

[36]In proposing a radical return to a deprofessionalized, popular system of conflict management in industrialized societies, Christie (1977) pleads emphatically for victim-centered justice.

[37]The problem of restitutive justice is, of course, much more complex, and its issues are controversial. Barnett, who reviews some important recent studies, advocates a radical change in the U.S. legal system aimed at substituting restitution to the victim for punishment of the offender as the principal purpose of criminal justice, so that "equality of justice means equal treatment of victims [1977: 298]." In England, the Criminal Justice Act of 1972 has empowered the courts to order a convicted offender to indemnify a person for any injury or loss suffered as a result of the offense.

cal theory at least suggests that the existing impediments to procure such evidence might explain this extension. And it suggests, furthermore, that the parallel but opposite trends of extending strict liability in tort, on the one hand, and of restricting the notion of criminal responsibility (after M'Naghten), on the other, originate with different epistemological problems concerning the nature of evidence. It is probably more difficult for technicians to *prove* causation in tort cases where chain transactions may involve a number of parties connected with the manufacture, transportation, storage, sale, installation, maintenance, and use of a product than it is for physicians to *assert* an accused's mental incapacity in a particular past instance.[38]

The social and economic factors that have produced the form and content of liability insurance also invite a new look. Whether such insurance is elective or compulsory, it may be regarded as a modern scheme to administer a collective liability, one that is adapted to an industrial economy and which the subscribers share in making their premium payments. There is, however, a hidden moral dimension in this scheme, and it deserves careful scrutiny.[39] In his description of feuding in pre-Islamic Arabia, Hardy suggests that collective liability was an "obstacle to the growth of a sense of individual responsibility for the wrong done [1963: 23]." Although the relationship between liability and responsibility is rather more complex, Hardy's hypothesis, in reverse, would link the spread of liability insurance to a decline of that sense of individual responsibility.

The ethical implications of this thought are as vast as they may be

---

[38]Because in terms of scientific "proof" psychiatric testimony about a person's mental capacity at the time he or she committed a felony has no greater validity than a tribal medicine man's diagnosis of witchcraft, its incorporation into our judicial folklore invites critical sociological inquiry.

[39]The functional similarity between a liability insurance policy by subscription and the tribal custom of collective liability by ascription is exceptionally well illustrated in a ruling of the Supreme Court of the Somali Republic. In upholding an appellate decision in a traffic accident case that ordered a motorist and his kin group to make an indemnity payment to the injured party, the court quoted with approval the opinion of the lower court:

> Under the British . . . legal system, the driver and owner of a vehicle causing an accident would be liable to compensate the victim, but this liability would normally be covered by compulsory car insurance. There is no compulsory insurance here and under the existing circumstances it would be impracticable to introduce it. Somali [customary law] provides a form of insurance. In natural justice the victim of a traffic accident should be entitled to compensation where the accident is due to the other party's negligence. Obviously if his only claim is against the driver, the victim will have little hope of recovering compensation awarded, as in most cases the driver would be unable to pay. In the circumstances, [the court] cannot agree with the defence submission that [customary law] should not apply to such cases [quoted in Muhammad, 1967: 111].

ominous. The issue is certainly not so simple as Harper and James, for example, make it appear when they write that even if insurance were to "dilute the deterrent effect of liability upon the individual [and] foster irresponsibility [1961: 271]," there are still great benefits to be gained: The aggregation of capital in the hands of insurance companies enables them to carry out research and development programs in the area of accident prevention and so to promote industrial safety for the benefit of the general public on a scale impossible to achieve in other ways. In view of the continuing battle of "public-interest" advocacy for better regulatory control of industrial hazards and product-safety standards, the conclusion that "the benefits . . . of liability insurance are not offset by any encouragement of irresponsibility [Harper and James, 1961: 273]" betrays a naive opinion of big business's concern for the welfare of the general public. It is necessary to realize, as Stein and Shand (1974: 127–128) have argued, that the regulation of civil liability by a system of compulsory insurance would not eliminate the element of deterrence so long as a victim's access to compensation does not confer immunity from prosecution on the liable party.[40] In any case, that the idea of strict liability in tort coexists with a generalized conception of justice that links liability to personal culpability, as in criminal law, indicates a need to extend the comparative study of liability to an analysis of variables ignored in this exploratory essay.[41]

References

Allott, A. N., A. L. Epstein, and M. Gluckman
    1969   "Introduction." Pages 1–81 in *Ideas and Procedures in African Customary Law*, edited by Max Gluckman. London: Oxford University Press.
Anderson, J. N. D.
    1951   "Homicide in Islamic law." *Bulletin of the School of Oriental and African Studies* 13: 811–828.
Barnett, Randy E.
    1977   "Restitution: A new paradigm of criminal justice." *Ethics* 87: 279–301.
Barton, R. F.
    1919   *Ifugao Law*. Berkeley, Calif.: University of California Press, 1969.

[40]It would indeed be questionable policy if a judicial review into the insured party's criminal responsibility for harm caused were routinely obviated by a compensatory payment to the victim, because the costs of such payments under any general insurance plan are ultimately always borne by the public.

[41]Further exploration of liability also needs to include an examination of statutory strict liability in the criminal law where, its application being akin to the consequences of verdicts of criminal negligence, this idea exists somewhat as an anomaly in that it conflicts with the solidly entrenched concept of *mens rea* (see the critical discussions by Hart, 1968: 136–157, and Wasserstrom, 1960).

1949   *The Kalingas: Their Institutions and Custom Law.* Chicago: University of Chicago Press.
Christie, Nils
1977   "Conflicts as property." *British Journal of Criminology* 17: 1–15.
Colson, Elizabeth
1953   "Social control and vengeance in Plateau Tonga society." *Africa* 23: 199–212.
Cunnison, Ian
1972   "Blood money, vengeance and joint responsibility: The Baggara case." Pages 105–125 in *Essays in Sudan Ethnography Presented to Sir Edward Evans-Pritchard,* edited by Ian Cunnison and Wendy James. London: C. Hurst.
Epstein, A. L.
1969   "Injury and liability in African customary law in Zambia." Pages 292–304 in *Ideas and Procedures in African Customary Law,* edited by Max Gluckman. London: Oxford University Press.
Evans-Pritchard, E. E.
1937   *Witchcraft, Oracles and Magic among the Azande.* Oxford: Clarendon Press.
Fürer-Haimendorf, Christoph von
1943   *The Chenchus: Jungle Folk of the Decan.* London: Macmillan.
1967   *Morals and Merit: A Study of Values and Social Controls in South Asian Societies.* Chicago: University of Chicago Press.
Gluckman, Max
1955   *The Judicial Process among the Barotse of Northern Rhodesia.* Manchester: Manchester University Press.
1965a   *The Ideas of Barotse Jurisprudence.* New Haven, Conn.: Yale University Press.
1965b   "Reasonableness and responsibility in the laws of segmentary societies." Pages 120–146 in *African Law: Adaptation and Development,* edited by Hilda Kuper and Leo Kuper. Berkeley, Calif.: University of California Press.
Gluckman, Max (editor)
1972   *The Allocation of Responsibility.* Manchester: Manchester University Press.
Green, Thomas A.
1972   "Societal concepts of criminal liability for homicide in mediaeval England." *Speculum* 47: 669–694.
Gross, Hyman
1979   *A Theory of Criminal Justice.* New York: Oxford University Press.
Gulliver, P. H.
1963   *Social Control in an African Society: A Study of the Arusha, Agricultural Masai of Northern Tanganyika.* Boston: Boston University Press.
Hardy, M. J. L.
1963   *Blood Feuds and the Payment of Blood Money in the Middle East.* Leiden: E. J. Brill.
Harper, Fowler V., and Fleming James, Jr.
1961   "Accidents, faults, and social insurance." Pages 267–273 in *Freedom and Responsibility: Readings in Philosophy and Law,* edited by Herbert Morris. Stanford, Calif.: Stanford University Press.
Harper, Robert Francis
1904   *The Code of Hammurabi, King of Babylon. About 2250 B.C.* Chicago: University of Chicago Press.
Hart, H. L. A.
1968   *Punishment and Responsibility: Essays in the Philosophy of Law.* London: Oxford University Press.
Hart, H. L. A., and A. M. Honoré
1969   *Causation in the Law.* Oxford: Clarendon Press.

Holý, Ladislav
    1967   "Social consequences of diya among the Berti." *Africa* 37: 466–479.
Hostetler, John A.
    1964   "Persistence and change patterns in Amish society." *Ethnology* 3: 185–198.
Howell, P. P.
    1954   *A Manual of Nuer Law: Being an Account of Customary Law, Its Evolution and Development in the Courts Established by the Sudan Government.* London: Oxford University Press.
Koch, Klaus-Friedrich
    1974a *War and Peace in Jalémó: The Management of Conflict in Highland New Guinea.* Cambridge, Mass.: Harvard University Press.
    1974b "Incest and its punishment in Jalé society." *Journal of the Polynesian Society* 83: 84–91.
    1977   "The anthropology of law and order." Pages 300–318 in *Horizons of Anthropology*, edited by Sol Tax and Leslie G. Freeman. 2d edition. Chicago: Aldine Press.
    n.d.   "Law as magic: The function of witchcraft in conflict management." Unpublished paper, Department of Anthropology, Northwestern University.
Koch, Klaus-Friedrich, Soraya Altorki, Andrew Arno, and Letitia Hickson
    1977   "Ritual reconciliation and the obviation of grievances: A comparative study in the ethnography of law." *Ethnology* 16: 269–284.
Koch, Klaus-Friedrich, and John A. Sodergren
    1976   "Political and psychological correlates of conflict management: A cross-cultural study." *Law and Society Review* 10: 443–466.
Kroeber, A. L.
    1925   "The Yurok: Law and custom." Pages 20–52 in *Handbook of the Indians of California.* Smithsonian Institution Bureau of American Ethnology, Bulletin 78. Washington, D.C.: U.S. Government Printing Office.
    1926   "Law of the Yurok Indians." Pages 511–516 in *Proceedings of the Twenty-second International Congress of Americanists*, vol. 2. Rome: Instituto Christoforo Colombo.
Lowie, Robert H.
    1963   "Compromise in primitive society." *International Social Science Journal* 25: 182–229.
Maine, Henry Sumner
    1861   *Ancient Law: Its Connection with the Early History of Society and Its Relation to Modern Ideas.* Boston: Beacon Press, 1963.
Milner, Alan
    1965   "The sanctions of customary criminal law: A study in social control." *Nigerian Law Journal* 1: 173–193.
Moore, Sally F.
    1972   "Legal liability and evolutionary interpretation: Some aspects of strict liability, self-help and collective responsibility." Pages 51–107 in *The Allocation of Responsibility*, edited by Max Gluckman. Manchester: Manchester University Press.
Morris, Herbert (editor)
    1961   *Freedom and Responsibility: Readings in Philosophy and Law.* Stanford, Calif.: Stanford University Press.
Muhammad, N. A. Noor
    1967   "Civil wrongs under customary law in the northern regions of the Somali Republic." *Journal of African Law* 11: 99–118.

Murdock, George P., and Suzanne F. Wilson
    1972 "Settlement patterns and community organization: Cross-cultural codes." *Ethnology* 11: 254–295.
Murphy, Robert F.
    1957 "Intergroup hostility and social cohesion." *American Anthropologist* 59: 1018–1035.
Nader, Laura, and Elaine Combs-Schilling
    n.d.   "Restitution in cross-cultural perspective." Pages 13–33 in *Restitution in Criminal Justice,* edited by Joe Hudson. St. Paul: Minnesota Department of Corrections.
Redfield, Robert
    1964 "Primitive law." *University of Cincinnati Law Review* 22: 1–22.
Schapera, I.
    1956 *Government and Politics in Tribal Societies.* London: C. A. Watts.
Seidman, Robert B.
    1966 "*Mens rea* and the reasonable African: The pre-scientific world-view and mistake of fact." *International and Comparative Law Quarterly* 15: 1135–1164.
Smith, Robert J.
    1961 "The Japanese rural community: Norms, sanctions, and ostracism." *American Anthropologist* 63: 522–533.
Stein, Peter, and John Shand
    1974 *Legal Values in Western Society.* Edinburgh: University Press.
Wasserstrom, Richard A.
    1960 "Strict liability in the criminal law." *Stanford Law Review* 12: 730–745.
Zöllner, Siegfried
    1977 *Lebensbaum und Schweinekult: Die Religion der Jalî im Bergland von Irian-Jaya (West-Neu-Guinea).* [N.p.] Theologischer Verlag Rolf Brockhaus.

5

The Social Organization
of Vengeance

JONATHAN RIEDER

"If you prick us, do we not bleed? if you tickle us, do we not laugh? if you poison us, do we not die? and if you wrong us, shall we not revenge?"[1] With these words from the mouth of Shylock, Shakespeare evokes the instinctive, human quality of vengeance. Revenge is on a par with primal experiences like dying, bleeding, and laughing, the sharing of which fashions a badge of common humanity. Striking back expresses the wisdom of the natural body. Adam Smith, writing in *The Theory of Moral Sentiments*, employed a similarly naturalistic idiom to describe the dynamic of retribution: "As every man doth, so shall it be done to him, and retaliation seems to be the great law that is dictated to us by nature [1759: 117]."

Yet it is equally the bent of human societies to surround natural processes with complex rules and mythologies, turning the raw, unformed possibilities of nature into a distinctively social artifact. These symbolic mediations embody the capacity of men and women to master nature, to stand outside of and above it. One ethnographer of Latin America writes that the Tarahumara does not "avail himself of meat torn from a scarcely dead animal and eaten raw. The Tarahumara interposes between his meat and his hunger a cultural system of cooking [Zingg,

[1]William Shakespeare, *The Merchant of Venice*, act 3, scene 1, lines 65–68.

131

1942: 82]." It is vengeance as a social fact, not as a natural fact, that forms the subject of the discussion to follow. After a brief look at the moral basis of revenge, I shall explore the relationship between the state and vengeance, the impact of stratification on revenge, and the effects of ties to allies and enemies on cycles of revenge. Although the general principles to emerge from the analysis apply to sexual, political, and organizational vengeance in advanced societies, I shall confine many of my remarks to vengeance as a form of social control in more simple societies, where the majesty of the state and the dominion of law have not yet driven vengeance underground or to the margins of society or forced it to assume disguised and backhand forms.

The Justice of Vengeance

Social science and popular culture alike have often treated revenge as an irresistible impulse. In this telling, vengeance induces an emotional state akin to demonic possession that consumes its perpetrator as well as its victim. The person in its grip is a slave to passion. Echoing the hopeful evolutionism that has recurrently marked writing about ferocious justice, Durkheim thought: "The need of vengeance is better directed today than heretofore. The spirit of foresight which has been aroused no longer leaves the field so free for the blind action of passion. It contains it within certain limits; it is opposed to absurd violence, to unreasonable ravaging [1893: 90]."

Whatever the merits of the popular view of revenge as an irresistible impulse, a number of drawbacks detract from its analytic worthiness, but only one of them need concern us now: the tendency to psychological reductionism. The stress on the demonic aspect of revenge neglects its essentially moral character. First, in countless societies, the force of communal duty impels an injured party to perform violent self-help, and cultural ideals glorify vendetta and celebrate its most heroic practitioners. In contrast to exhortations to turn the other cheek, the failure of a Comanche to cleanse affronts to his honor was a grave disgrace, not an act of grace (Hoebel, 1940: 188). The Bedouin who fails to carry out his vengeance obligations elicits anxiety among his kinsmen. "The wisest among them consult together, and one of them is asked to remind their defaulting kinsman of his duty, summoning him to act, and calling upon him to avenge himself [Bourdieu, 1966: 208]." One errs by too strictly dividing the world into psychic states and social norms. There is a kind of emotional learning, part of every society's process of cultural reproduction, which converts the affective into the ethical.

Revenge has a moral quality in a second sense. In his treatise on
Ressentiment, Max Scheler took pains to distinguish revenge from spite,
malice, vindictiveness, envy, and rage. "It is of the essence of revenge
that it always contains the consciousness of 'tit-for-tat,' so that it is never
a mere emotional reaction [1915: 46]." Incidental to an outburst of rage,
the conviction of being in the right is vital to vengeance (Homans, 1961).
Revenge is one of the moral emotions, as different from rage as indignation is from simple frustration. In reflecting on peasant rebellions, James
Scott observes that "it is this moral heritage that, in peasant revolts,
selects certain targets rather than others . . . and that makes possible a
collective . . . action born of moral outrage." As Scott concludes, "To
speak of righteous anger is, in the same breath, to speak of standards of
justice, or moral values [1976: 167]."

The third aspect of the moral quality of vengeance consists of its
implicit wish to restore symmetry to imbalanced social exchange. It is
the other side of the coin of reciprocity. Cicero noted that "there is no
duty more indispensable than that of returning a kindness," adding "all
men distrust one forgetful of a benefit [quoted in Gouldner, 1960: 161]."
Vengeance is equally mindful of the principle of equivalence: not the
one of a reward returned for one received, but rather a punishment
meted out for one absorbed. Alvin Gouldner's equation of revenge with
"negative reciprocity" finds literal application in the talionic justice of an
eye for an eye, a tooth for a tooth.

The moral quality of revenge commends Robert Redfield's insight
that "custom restrains an injured party from unlimited revenge. Retalia-
tive force is stylized by custom into a sort of ritualistic revenge, and
something like legal process results [1964: 12]." Although the propensity
in much anthropology and sociology to view vengeance as "private
law" has a number of drawbacks, it rightly underlines the normative
status of revenge as a form of social control that is implicit in Francis
Bacon's aperçu, "revenge is a kind of wild justice [1625: 18]."

The desire to requite one evil for another embodies an embryonic
form of law. Yet that wish is not satisfied in every society, on every
occasion, or in every dispute. To speak of a universal norm of retribution, on the same plane as a universal norm of reciprocity, does not
account for the vast diversity of attitudes toward vengeance throughout
history or across societies. Nor does it clarify why mediation, restitution,
and expiation surface as compelling ways to settle disputes in one society and not another, or under certain conditions in a society that at other
times practices vengeful self-help. The Comanche ridicule a man
fainthearted in the arts of blood revenge, but a simile in the Talmud
avers, "He who avenges himself, or bears a grudge, acts as one who has

had one hand cut by a knife and now sticks it into the other hand for revenge [Baeck, 1961: 214]."

The Civilization of Vengeance

Rather than positing the generality of vengeance, the task remains to specify the conditions that elicit mercy or retribution. Although that ambitious project cannot be completed here, from the moment one begins the endeavor, the rationality of vengeance as a method of social control, not its unreasoning ravaging, emerges as one of its striking signatures. Before that discussion can be started, a few words about the relationship between state development and revenge are needed to place it in its proper context.

In many sociological accounts, private vengeance and formal law are entwined in a relationship of mutual exclusion. The movement of history, it is said, tends to replace the former with the latter. The versatile household sheds its many functions and yields retaliatory force to specialists in detection, adjudication, and punishment. Seen from the retrospective vantage point of modernity, revenge is a compensatory adjustment to a lack. Paula Brown's analysis of dispute settlement among a New Guinea people depicts the functional quality of self-help: "Without an overriding authority to maintain peace and keep order in any group, fighting was the accepted means of dealing with disputes [1964: 349]." To borrow from the language of human ecology, an unfilled niche selects out an institutional adaptation to disorder. Revenge offers an inexpensive solution to a pressing need in a lean environment that cannot sustain the formal apparatus, the legal specialists, and the police force that societies in more lush environments can afford. With greater societal complexity and productive wealth, the political community, Max Weber argued, engenders "a form of permanent public peace, with the compulsory submission of all disputes to the arbitration of the judge, who transforms blood vengeance into rationally ordered punishment, and feuds and expiatory actions into rationally ordered legal procedures [1922: 908]."

Weber's formulation of the state as a monopoly of the means of coercion has exerted a powerful influence on subsequent discussions of vengeance. It seems as if there exists a finite amount of legitimate coercion in a society, so that the expansion of one system of social control obliges the trimming of the dominion of the other. If the state and vengeance are both jealous of each other's prerogatives, the two are not equal combatants, and in many versions of legal development, the state gradually crowds out all other forms of dispute settlement. Norbert Elias (1939) and Michel Foucault (1975) have identified the cultural process of rationalization that justifies the institutional expropriation of the private means of violence. At the midpoint of Western development, Foucault argues, the state replaces the private vengeance of kin groups with its own more majestic vengeance, but the zest for retribution endures as a vital part of the spectacle of the scaffold:

> The condemned man, carried in procession, exhibited, humiliated, with the horror of his crime recalled in innumerable ways, was offered to the insults, sometimes to the attacks of the spectators. The vengeance of the people was called upon to become an unobtrusive part of the vengeance of the sovereign. Not that it was in any way fundamental, or that the king had to express in his own way the people's revenge; it was rather than the people had to bring its assistance to the king when the king undertook "to be avenged on his enemies," especially when those enemies were to be found among the people. It was rather like a "scaffold service" that the people owed the king's vengeance [1975: 58–59].

Eventually, ferocity undergoes the same process of disenchantment that transforms every other aspect of modern culture, and a more dispassionate rationale comes to support punishment. "Instead of taking revenge, criminal justice should simply punish [Foucault, 1975: 74]."

Having granted a broad evolutionary momentum to the growth of the apparatus of formal law, one must note four kinds of departure from the simple law of "crowding out" that radically delimit its applicability. First, the subjection of revenge to formal process is not smooth. It proceeds in a jerky, convoluted fashion. Patrimonial elements endure and flourish in the heart of bureaucratic organizations, creating a kind of legal *bricolage*. "Medieval laws even accept the acts of defiance, or *reptos*, and challenges between nobles as a valid formula for settling their differences in affairs of honour," writes Juan Caro Baroja. "'If a noble brings dishonor, or wrong, or harm upon another, he may be challenged for it in this way, by saying: I reject your friendship, and I challenge you, . . . for I have the right to exact repayment for it' [1966: 92]."

Secondly, the teleology of evolutionists tends to be mechanistic in the extreme. The image of state expansion as inexorable process or virtual necessity clouds the political struggles and complex motives that sustain what Elias calls "the civilizing process." The simple inverse relation between political complexity and feuding in preindustrial societies founders on the complicating factor of intertribal warfare. Jural or political authorities in societies with robust state institutions have particular motives to "intervene to prevent the development of feuding when the

society was threatened by war [Otterbein and Otterbein, 1965: 1478]."
Weber invoked the same specificity of state intentions in the French
monarchy's suspension in the thirteenth century of the feuds of royal
vassals during foreign war. Although he was aware that the supression
of revenge "rises with the development of the coercive apparatus into a
permanent structure," Weber emphasized that "initially it is directed
only against those forms of private violence which would injure directly
the military interests of the political community [1922: 908]." This selectivity of abstention or intrusion by the state is not limited to preindustrial societies or the transitional stage at which formal law first arises.
Police and judicial authorities in contemporary America refrain from
intervention in or prosecution of technically felonious acts when the
offender and victim have strong ties with each other, when an element
of self-help in settling a grievance is involved, as in the collection of a
gambling debt, and when the offenses involve lower-status people,
whether grievances among themselves or against upper-status individuals (Black, Chapter 1, Volume 2 of the present work).

Third, patrimonial survivals, the diverse motives underlying state
intrusion, and the fusion of the king's and people's vengeance indicate
that the formal law itself may become an instrument of private or of
public vengeance. State-sponsored violence, racist crusading, political
trials and defamation, and lynchings form part of the repertoire of regime attempts at social control (Raper, 1933; Kirchheimer, 1961). The
concentration of state power, the available technology of coercion, and
the conduits of judicial and police institutions expand the capacity to
prosecute vengeance. Incumbents in formally democratic as well as authoritarian regimes have meted out vengeance against members of their
enemies lists by taking advantage of the official apparatus of power. The
police develop informal standards of "doing justice" when "deference is
violated, when outcomes violate their sense of justice, when they are
degraded in status, and when their efforts to control are subverted by
other organizations in the subsystem [Reiss, 1971: 140]." One paradoxi-
cal consequence of systems of secret informing is to create opportunities
to use the public system for private ends. Informers in Nazi Germany,
during the Spanish civil war, and in occupied Poland have found de-
nunciation a handy way to cloak the settling of personal grudges in the
high-flown purposes of the totalitarian state (Gross, Chapter 3, Volume
2 of the present work).

Fourth, the tangible presence of a state does not suffice to ensure an
acceptance of the official machinery of justice. Sectors of the population
may withhold trust from it and retain the option of self-help. Gaia Servadio underlines the insight of that keen observer of the Sicilian Mafia at

the turn of the century, Giovanni Lorenzoni: "The Mafia came into being from the lack of trust in justice, from which followed the principles of private revenge and omerta." "It was," she quotes Lorenzoni, "'an exaggeration of the feeling of the self and had become a modus vivendi' [1976: 69]."

The same *modus vivendi* continues to flourish in the midst of advanced industrial societies. Self-help endures as a vital part of traditions of dispute settlement in certain regions of the white working class in contemporary America (Suttles, 1972: chap. 8; Rieder, 1984: chap. 6). Thus, in one racially tense community, violent reprisals were meted out against a white homeowner who sold his house to a black family and violated informal norms of a segregated housing market. A realtor described the normative dimension involved in the retaliatory strike. "You see, in the Italian areas, they do it themselves. They burn the house down. They do it to the white who sells, not the black who moves in. It's really a form of retaliation. The white who sells is the betrayer of the community." Working-class youngsters in the same community participate in a form of dispute settlement that bears striking resemblance to blood feuding in stateless societies. One white boy involved with blacks in a drawn-out cycle of attack and reprisal defined the superiority of self-help to the law. "We can't fight back legally, because we tried that, and it doesn't get us anywhere. . . . I mean if somebody comes up to me and hits me, I know I'm going to hit back, I know I'm not going to take it." Such efforts to take back from the state a share of vengeful resources transcended youthful passion but received cultural permission from adults who urged the boys onward with cries of "Do what you gotta do," "If you see an invasion, you gotta cut it off," and "It's our right to dissent." Moreover, police officers from the local precinct transmitted their approval of the resort to physical means of reprisal. A civic leader with many friends in the station house relayed the support she received from official agents of justice. "A lot of the cops are saying, 'Good luck, do what you gotta do' [Rieder, 1984: chap. 6]."

The Functions of Vengeance

The presence of institutions for resolving conflict, then, does not ensure their amicable resolution; conversely, their absence does not produce disputes in the absence of sources of conflict themselves. Three additional factors may be identified as catalysts of private violence: precarious habitats that encourage the war of each against all, fragmented social relations, where no encompassing social principle or corporate solidarity submits the interest of the one to the interest of the many, and the presence of masculine warrior groups. The satisfaction of these conditions inaugurates a system of private violence. No central authority accumulates all disposable resources of coercion at its center, and each man, kin group, or village captures a share of vengeful capacity. A consideration of horizontal revenge between relative equals in such societies and vertical revenge between relative unequals clarifies the effect of stratification on the organization of vengeance.

The peoples of the Levantine basin have pronounced cults of masculine vengeance (Schneider, 1971). As a result, the societies encircling the Mediterranean provide a reservoir of episodes of riposte and challenge that illuminate the dynamic logic of horizontal vengeance between relative equals in anarchic settings. The casual attitude toward self-help in such settings encourages the exploitation of hints of weakness. Impressions thus count in such deterrent systems of social control as much as does the substance of reality. Cunning arises here in a sense above and beyond the self-regulating wisdom of violence but as each individual's attempt to size up competitors. In the hair-trigger setting, bluff, sleight of hand, and dramaturgic skill in ceremonial displays of resolve become weapons. What Baroja describes as the "hypersensitive, punctilious posture" of the Spanish male "convinces others to exercise restraint, not so much to avoid physical retaliation as to avoid the consequences of continuing rancor [Schneider, 1971: 17]." The bullfight affirms the logic of manly reprisal within the ceremonial context of the game. It is "the ritual revindication of masculinity and if this value is debased then the whole human species is defiled [Pitt-Rivers, 1954: 90]." Fights over resources outside the arena provide a less symbolic occasion for preventing desecration. Thus does an Andalusian cultivator complain of his blocked right to access to the water he shares with another peasant; he threatens to take what is his if the other does not yield at the proper time, assuming the ready posture of the toreador: "Try to stop me if you dare," in Spanish, literally, "if thou hast testicles, come! [Pitt-Rivers, 1954: 90]."

All the symbolic plumage of the Mediterranean male cannot be reduced to gratuitous psychological display. In social systems that rely on private vengeance as a key method of settling disputes, a failure to stand up to provocation indicates the challenged lacks the full social personality of a man. The man is a weakling who can be overriden with impunity. The injured party in the Balkans who is slow to avenge an indignity finds that local men come to sleep with his wife (Hasluck, 1954: 391). There is a homology between sexual property, the property of honor, and economic property, and conduct in one sphere is taken as a pledge of conduct in the others. Will a man who does not physically vindicate his honor defend his female property? Or his land and live-stock? The control of female sexuality through norms of virginity and chastity provides a silent metaphor for power (Schneider, 1971: 17). The woman's comportment conveys to a vigilant, witnessing public her def-erence to or defiance of her protector's power. A Balkan herder says, "It is important for the unfaithfulness of a wife to remain a secret. If the husband catches the wife in the act, he is considered a coward if he does not kill the adulterer and will be despised [Denich, 1974: 255]." Similar-ly, "adultery attacks the moral integrity and honor of the family and makes a laughingstock of its leader and head [Campbell, 1964: 152]."

The clarity of the likely reprisal, the cult of male honor, and female subordination form a language of the body, composed from the mate-rials of gesture and etiquette, that helps organize an uncertain social environment. They fashion a system of warning against the temptations of seizing another's resources, whether land or women, by sending signals of likely vengeful sanctions. As Bette Denich has described this functional logic: "Each man is obligated to defend his group against both physical and symbolic attack. The latter category includes a wide range of acts that diminish a group's reputation for honor. Response in kind is required for the sullied group to retain its 'honor,' which is really a symbolic screen for its power [1974: 248–249]." The stability of sanc-tions, the certainty that honor will be vindicated as utterly as the bull-fighter fearlessly stands before a charge, creates in a sense not quite intended by the author of the phrase "the peace in the feud."

Systems of self-help scatter vengeful capacity widely over the constit-uent units rather than gather social control at an administrative center. Like other decentralized systems, they suffer from strains that press for resolution in different ways. First, an unstable system emerges in which challenge, riposte, and recoil are a constant menace to public order. The war of each against all erupts into ruthless struggle at the point of competition. This special case of vengeance gives rise to the generalized image of the inherent tendency of revenge to "snowball." Lorenzoni argued that the private revenge of mafiosi "increased murders because, if the offence is remedied by the State, the cycle closes; but if it is remedied by the individual, a new cycle is opened [Servadio, 1976: 69]."

Secondly, a delicate balance of retaliatory force may relegate actual violence to the symbolic plane. Theatrical hints and symbolic displays of bravado keep everybody in check at the equilibrium point where the costs of each disputant's vengeance offset the potential gain of predato-ry conduct. Even in the most anarchic, bellicose settings, standoffs occur as fleeting adjustments if not as habitual strategy. The costs of continuing revenge are often high enough to threaten group survival. Bailey describes the process of reversing cascades of vengeance: Noting that at a certain threshold of success, desertions to the winning side cascade, he asks, "Why does not one leader wipe out all the other leaders, his last successful contest putting an end to the game?" The terse answer defines the actuarial pressures toward arresting the cycle: "Forty-one murders notched on his gun butt would make a man a bad life-insurance risk in any culture. Murder makes a man an object of revenge, and the more murders he commits, the more enemies wait for the chance to cut him down in a revenge killing [1969: 93]." A similar rationality governs the emergence of institutionalized forms of climbing down from the brink, so that a series of challenge and counterchallenge may permit reappraisal and withdrawal.

The third resolution of decentralized systems of coercion involves a shift from an open competition of relatively equal avengers toward oligopolistic control by powerful avengers, flanked by retainers loyal to their rule and dependent on their umbrella. Weaker parties search for strong benefactors to right wrongs and "big men" emerge out of the crowded field of challengers. In this final case, equilibrium moves toward inequality based on rule of the strong rather than toward the equality of balanced force. Hierarchy provides one answer to the problem of order. The resources on which big men's status depend may be symbolic, like reputation for fierceness, or physical, like the number of brothers, strength and elaboration of a lineage, or the holding of land. The *campieri*, or field guards, hired by the overseers of Sicilian estates had a reputation for toughness, which they "advertised by their arrogant airs and their carrying of arms." Their very demeanor encoded into gesture a seriousness about violence. "The ways in which some of them dressed, moved around, and squinted symbolized toughness. Their reticence and the opaque ambiguity of phrases, gestures, and mimic signs they used among their peers set them apart from ordinary people." The dramaturgy "expressed a capacity and willingness to coerce with physical violence. . . . What earned these men 'respect' (*rispettu*) was, first, their capacity to coerce with physical violence and thus invoke fear in others [Blok, 1974: 61–62]."

Games of Vengeance

Hierarchy provides one contingent answer to the instabilities of horizontal revenge between relative equals. A consideration of vertical revenge between relative unequals highlights quite different organizational imperatives. Slavery represents the end point of the spectrum of inequality: It stands as an ideal typical case of all relations of sexual, political, and organizational inequality. In contrast to the lateral flow of punishment between equals, punishment flows vertically in relations of dominance and dependency. The asymmetry of power alters the calculus of coercion.

A dilemma affects the weak. Vulnerability leaves the dependent open to wrong, yet incapable of avenging it. The two are inextricably related. Freedom from fear of retaliation emboldens the powerful, who are tempted to abandon a strategy of reciprocal exchange in favor of coercive plunder. Max Scheler explained the origins of *ressentiment* in this inability of the weak to take revenge on superordinates or to enforce the claims of justice. "Revenge tends to be transformed into *ressentiment,*" he argued, "the more it is directed against lasting situations which are felt to be 'injurious' but beyond one's control—in other words, the more the injury is experienced as a destiny [1915: 50]." Much of Scheler's statement of the problem of thwarted vengeance derives from Nietzsche's dictum that "a little revenge is more human than no revenge," identifying the complex psychic confidence game involved in slavishness. As Walter Kaufmann writes: "To be kindly when one is merely too weak and timid to act otherwise, to be humble when any other course would have unpleasant repercussions and to be obliging when a less amiable gesture would provoke the master's kick or switch—that is the slave's morality, making a virtue out of necessity [1950: 371–372]."

The abstract model of master and slave distorts the full understanding of the ambiguities of inequality and exaggerates the ease of achieving "hegemony." Domination rarely achieves perfection. It involves a constant struggle to make the dominated comply with their fate, to define dependency as proper and just. Slavishness depends on a psychic capture, in which the slaves come to embrace the values of meekness, turn the other cheek, and defer the realization of justice to an otherworldly time or place. Yet not all slaves are slavish. Slavishness is one tendency, but not a destiny, of domination. Slaves in the American plantation South often refrained from retaliation for an injustice, not because they had internalized the values of their rulers, but because they shrewdly understood the cost of striking back to outweigh the wound of dignity involved in pacifism or patience. "It took enormous strength for a woman to keep her man from avenging an insult or a beating she had suffered," Eugene Genovese writes, "and to convince him that the test of his masculinity was self-restraint, not some action that would deprive her of a husband and her children of a father [1974: 501]." A slave's investment in revenge sometimes collided with the collective interests of all slaves in supressing revenge. When a slave burned a building with little economic significance, the slave community might empathize with the act of vendetta, but the destruction of assets like the storehouse or the cotton created a situation of collective liability: "This furious vengeance also threatened the sale of one or more members of the slave community or, worse, bankruptcy and the breakup of the community altogether [Genovese, 1974: 615]."

The allusions to slave resistance demonstrate that the weak do not lack all means of getting even. If we take a few, modest liberties with Randall Collins's principles of explanation of strategies of control in formal organizations, they may be applied to illuminating the breakdown of control in organized power relations of any sort. Starting from the premise that coercion produces measures to escape the painful feeling of being coerced, he offers the proposition that "the greater the coercion that is applied, the more counter-aggression is called forth [1975: 298]." Yet this proposition holds true even when subordinates have meager resources of fighting back. The disparity in power may prompt the weak to devise ingenious methods of reprisal in order to exert even a modicum of social control on their superordinates. The wish to retaliate for an injustice, Peter Blau writes, "may well become an end-in-itself in the pursuit of which people ignore other considerations [1964: 229]." On those occasions, revenge becomes a supreme value. Blau hardly depicts this transformation of value as an all-consuming folly. "No more irrational than the pursuit of any other objective that is intrinsically valued," he argues, "retaliation against the oppressors may be more gratifying to them than securing the continuation of their meagre rewards [1964: 229, 231]."

The social organization of relations of domination and dependency commends the style and form of vengeance, as well as the likelihood of its deployment or suppression. The weak have great incentives to right wrongs anonymously rather than flagrantly. Like peasant and labor violence more generally, a great deal of day-to-day resistance to slavery was expressed furtively—through lying, stealing, slowdowns, and dissembling. The resort of the weak to defamation through rumor, poison-pen letters, and backhand compliments conforms to the same requirements of avoiding detection, which encourages depersonalized forms of vengeance. In slave regimes, arson especially satisfied the claims of justice on the cheap, for it "required no great physical strength or financial resources and could easily be concealed [Thomas, 1971: 531]." Poisoning was a favorite weapon of the American slaves. Proficiency in African herbal technology compensated for lack of access to more advanced means of retaliation.

The secret and symbolic nature of much peasant and slave revenge points to the different organizational imperatives that shape vertical and horizontal vengeance. When punitive sanctions are distributed un-equally, the weak may counter the fear of detection by cloaking retaliation in mysterious anonymity. In contrast, vengeance in much of the Mediter-ranean is unthinkable without publicity. The Bedouins, jubilant when vengeance was taken, shot off their rifles and the woman uttered "you-you" cries "so that all should be aware how a family of honour was capable of obtaining reparation for an offence and of restoring its own prestige promptly"; moreover, "it was also meant to let the enemy family know the cause of its misfortune as well as to issue it with a challenge. What is the good of revenge if it remains anonymous [Bourdieu, 1966: 205]?"

Even the most lambent flicker of rebelliousness opens up possibilities that alter the routines of domination. It means compliance cannot be taken for granted. A number of strategic adjustments follow from this awareness. "There were just enough instances of masters who had been killed by a slave in this way to lend a certain amount of justification to the whites' perpetual sense of insecurity [Thad Tate, quoted in Gen-ovese, 1974: 615]." Living in the shadow of fear, the slaveholders be-came fearless people. Genovese depicts the powerful psychic effects of this stance. "Their slaves could not help noticing, and to the extent they did, the hegemonic position of the master class became the more secure [1974: 616]." Encapsulation and surveillance provide other weapons to surround power relations with an aura of immutability. Rulers have incentives to control the flow of information and thereby to prevent the transmission of new conceptions of fairness or knowledge of vengeful incidents that might spark retaliation. "The newspapers sometimes ad-vertised the murder of a master widely in order to warn others, but at all other times they preferred restraint in reporting so as not to put ideas in the heads of imitative slaves [1974: 616]." The anticipation of the ven-geance of the weak serves to temper harshness of rule. Rather than playing out the irrevocable logic of domination to its more sanguinary denouement, slaveholders engaged in a kind of preemptive, friendly strike to foreclose the development of a cycle of vengeance: adopting a benign posture, pulling their punches, and trying to win the allegiance of their charges.

The logic of preemption is vital to all forms of paternalistic benev-olence that strive to convert exploitation into an amicable domination based on reconciling underlings to the inevitability of their fate. As in other feedback systems, the participants may be only dimly aware of their tacit, but effective coordination. Equity theorists have given this short-circuiting of vengeful cycles some experimental proof. "A harm-doer will derogate a victim who is powerless to retaliate, but will not derogate a victim from whom he anticipates retaliation [Berscheid, Boye, and Walster, 1968: 370]." One's place in a web of group ties may bestow resources of protection that immunize the holder against accusations or may expose peripheral members to contumely. Centrality in a work group, for example, repells accusations of rate busting and displaces them onto the person with the least resources of retaliation (Kapferer, 1969: 181–245; Boissevain, 1974: 53–66). Patrimonial sentiment in the secretary–boss relationship shields the boss from potential reprisals. By virtue of the ecology of power that falls on the secretary from her place at a node in the chain of communication, she develops resources of counterattack, especially the power to savage rather than to save the face of a boss whose backstage persona is graphically accessible to her. Such collusion in the boss's presentation and access to secrets "made it important that she not be in direct competition for the boss's job, for she would have a potent set of weapons to use in the struggle for the position [Kanter, 1977: 82]." Kanter draws the more general point from the vignette. "Whenever there are relationships of such unequal and non-reciprocal authority, both systemic and social psychological pressures arise that attempt to prevent the parties at the receiving end from ever gaining authority on their own. For the system, the threat of retaliation is what must be guarded against [1977: 83]."

The relationship between master and slave discloses many of the properties of a game in which the dominated and the dependent alike calculate strategy and envision the likely response of opponents to their maneuvers. The willingness of the weak to absorb punishment is not infinitely elastic. Gaps in the structure of rule, the temptations of anonymous revenge, and shared expectations of justice even among unequals define the limits of obedience and place a ceiling on coercion. Few masters, however, could have been farsighted enough to calculate the full consequences of this landlord's predation: "Nor do we know how many children reacted like the Mexican peasant boy who saw his father collapse helplessly in tears when a treacherous landowner expropriated his land. Emiliano Zapata did not despise his father. He swore vengeance [Genovese, 1974: 494]." Precisely his mindfulness of these intricacies of domination prompted Machiavelli to advise rulers to choose between paternalism or ferocity, for he deemed the muddy, middle course an open invitation to rebellion: "Men ought either to be caressed or destroyed, since they will seek revenge for minor hurts but will not be able to revenge major ones. Any harm you do to a man should be done in such a way that you need not fear his revenge [1513: 7]."

The Design of Vengeance

A quality of calculation marks the theatrics of pride, the wily sizing up of a rival's mettle, the furtive revenge of the weak. Before launching a retaliatory strike, the aggrieved first reckon the cost of pacifism and the dividends of reprisal. Or, seen from a more ethereal slant, an omniscient society fashions a rough-hewn, adaptive order, substituting the hidden hand of violence for the heavy hand of the state.

The fate of a quarrel, however, is shaped by more than weighing the potential gain or loss of retaliation against injury. The problem of the model of the game as formulated earlier is that it operates with too narrow a conception of cost and constraint. It fails to enter into the ledger the cost of disrupting a complex network of social relationships that may be sundered by the dispute of a dyad, two collectivities, or two organizations. Every disputant lives at the coordinates of a field of social ties to friends, enemies, and bystanders. Some fights branch out to involve friends, kin, allies, clients, authorities, mystical agents, third parties, bystanders, the state, and referees. Other fights coil around themselves in a tight circle. Whether a fight moving toward feud actually crosses the brink of self-help, or turns back toward reconciliation, whether it recruits allies who inflame the grievance and demand satisfaction or third parties who dampen the flames of anger, depends on the configuration of alliance and attachment. In order to show the effects of ties to allies and adversaries on the fate of a dispute, I shall discuss three kinds of design: disputes that take the form of a cascade of reprisals, disputes in which the definition of liability is problematic, and disputes in which third parties choke off the resort to self-help. The intimate dependence of forms of social organization on their environments characterizes dispute settlement in all three instances.

The fight between strangers, distant tribes, or nations with little intercourse spreads involvement differently from a fight between relatives, people linked by common residence or history, or those who break bread together. All things being equal, the likelihood of a vengeful settlement varies inversely with the relational intimacy of the disputants (Gulliver, 1963: 240–267; Peters, 1967). Including scope, frequency, and length of interaction, age of relationship, and the nature and number of links between disputants as the measure of relational intimacy, Donald Black defines the far ends of the spectrum of intimacy as abstention from mutual involvement and total interpenetration (Black, 1976: 41). Cannibalistic revenge among the Jalémó of New Guinea is a feature of *soli* wars, which pit distant villages against one another, but beyond the pale in *wim* wars, which involve intraward squabbles within a single territorial unit. The general rule in Jalémó is expressed by the charming adage "People whose face is known should not be eaten [Koch, 1974: 80]," which means that the specific history of the relationship between two disputants from distant villages modifies the strictly territorial basis of relational status. "In practice," Koch writes, "immunity from anthropophagic vengeance derives from the nature and relative frequency of affinal links between two villages [1974: 80]."

Distance between adversaries up to the point of total avoidance amplifies the chance to ignite a vengeful sequence, yet the bonds between disputants do not alone determine the fate of a dispute, the likelihood of its containment, or the rate and scope of its enlargement. The nature of the links between each disputant and their respective allies equally affects the course of revenge. The great chain of obligation, whether frayed or robust, multistranded or single stranded, sparse or dense, expands the involvement of affected interests along preset channels. Some disputes between individuals remain confined to the dyad. A variety of mechanisms limit the breadth of feud and its impact on watchful audiences. In other settings, the dispute of two individuals comes to symbolize cleavages based on larger social principles. A great deal of ambiguity may attend the definition of the proper scope of enlargement. A quarrel in a New York City high school eventually developed into a full-fledged racial feud, but the white participants originally defined the dispute as a "one-on-one," not a racial incident. The fight began as a dispute between a white and a black youth, but, as one participant in the feud put it, "they were 'fair ones.' That's what got me. The colored kid had beat this white kid, see, but the colored kid said he was coming back with 'his boys' 'cause everybody broke up the fight.'" The interruption of the fight by the white boy's friends seemed a breach of racial equivalence to the black youth. "He was saying, 'why you break it up man? I was kicking his ass.'" What struck the whites to violate the normative character of violence struck the blacks as the rightful completion of a natural cycle of reprisal. The ambiguity did not stop there, for some whites and blacks viewed the incident in terms of collective racial liability, and other whites and blacks saw the fight as a dispute between the two networks of the original disputants (Rieder, 1984: chap. 6).

Vengeance spreads rapidly when strong ties extend liability and responsibility to a wide circle of third parties. Such robust bonds may entail an obligation to avenge a wrong suffered by another or the capacity to stand in as a substitute object of retaliation for a wrong committed by someone else. The reach of vengeance varies a good deal across societies and situations. The duty to retaliate may fall onto an entire tribe, a men's house, the lineage, an organization, the minimal nuclear household, a brother, the clan, a blood brother, a nation, or a race.

The extent of corporate vengeance ties tends to be isomorphic with the scope of corporate relations in other realms of social life, although unique circumstances always qualify the basic law. The ruthless struggle of each against all in much of southern Italy limits effective organization to the nuclear family, and the reach of vengeance ties is correspondingly short. In Greece, the Saratkatsan herders exempt collateral relatives from the duty to retaliate, and after marriage, the sibling group no longer forms "a unity against the outsider nor are they socially equivalent: they have become differentiated by their marriages and young families [Campbell, 1964: 54]." Although a man is obliged to take the side of kinsmen in quarrels, "he must not put his own life in jeopardy lest he risk depriving his family of its head [Schneider, 1971: 8]." The needs of other collectivities expand the radius of collective responsibility. An attack on a Balkan herding unit mobilizes the retaliatory wrath of all the others. Liability does not quit at the borders of the nuclear family, and marriage does not suspend the sibling duty of revenge. Corporate norms make good organizational sense. The nuclear family is embedded in embracing structures of patrilineality and patrilocality. The economic, the residential, and the defensive interests of all are coterminous and virtually indistinguishable. The division of military, productive, and communicative labor joins the brothers and blurs the lines of the self. They own the flocks together, inherit together. The same interpenetration of work, kinship, residence, ritual, and defense knits together the members of men's houses in many corners of the globe. In these cases, the high-flown sentiments of the corporate body, one for all and all for one, faithfully reflect the underlying mutuality of its members' ties, which dissolves self-regard in the quick of corporate life.

The practical requirements of group formation expand and contract the scope of responsibility, but internal exigencies of the group only partly explain the complexity of ties of revenge. The nature of the environment in which the group finds itself also shapes obligation and organization. Social milieus vary a good deal in their homogeneity, carrying capacity, and stability, as well as on a range of other characteristics. Unstable or resource-lean environments tend to encourage flexibility, loose coupling, and weak ties. All things being equal, the tight coupling that is the essence of strong vengeance ties emerges in "beneficent" environments that permit complex rather than shallow forms of social organization. Put another way, rich environments can afford strong vengeance ties, whereas groups in vulnerable environments must be free to cut loose from larger units to take advantage of local windfalls. Conversely, the larger collectivity, to limit shocks to its survival, must be free to shed weak, costly segments (Aldrich, 1979: chap. 4).

Jane Schneider (1971) has identified an individualistic-corporate gradient of vengeful responsibility in pastoral societies around the Levantine basin. Each jump in the level of societal complexity expands the orbit of vengeance ties. The individualistic extreme arises in the pressured habitats of historic southwestern Europe, where agriculture greatly encroached on the pastoral way of life. Vulnerability encourages a selfish ethic of "going for yourself," as every family jockeys for its own sustenance in an infelicitous environment. Vengeance undergoes a corresponding confinement to the nuclear family. The corporatist extreme surfaces among Central Asian pastoralists. A more beneficent environment permits greater social complexity, which is embodied in tribal and clan organizations sharing vengeance obligations. North African and Middle Eastern pastoralists form an ambiguous midpoint on the spectrum of vulnerability, complexity, and responsibility. Unlike that of southwestern European pastoralists and agriculturalists, the nuclear family is embedded in polygenous or patrilineal bodies, yet they lack the corporate organization and political complexity of Asian tribes and khanates, as well as the collective vengeance ties that accompany them. Camel-herding nomads in the Middle East, although owners of their own flocks, often contribute stock to the blood money fund of the agnatic vengeance group, share in any indemnities that accrue to members of the group, and avenge any injuries they suffer. In more vulnerable habitats in the pastoral Middle East, formally recognized vengeance ties may mask their actual weakness.

Conduits of Vengeance

Variation in the scope of responsibility suggests that cultural norms closely follow organizational needs. The obligatory is keyed to the practical. The environment lays down criteria that permit or thwart the selection of cultural meanings. Whatever their origins, however, strong vengeance bonds have powerful consequences. Environments that concentrate men together in clusters rather than scatter them about enjoy clear-cut advantages in prosecuting vengeance. Holding the motivation to avenge constant, the presence or absence of networks of vengeance, or what may be deemed vengeful capacity, makes retaliatory action more or less likely. Anthropologists have established the direct association between frequency of feuding and the presence of fraternal solidarity groups (Otterbein and Otterbein, 1965).

The warlike conditions that societies with male corporate groups generate stem from their military advantages over societies that disperse their men. Institutionalized vengeance groups are combat-ready, to use William Gamson's (1975) concept. The start-up costs of recruitment for sexual networks in place are low. Strong ties mean that loyalty erects barriers to easy exit during times of difficulty. Primordial bonds define an automatic universe of what may be called "natural avengers" similar to the pool of "natural lenders" created by the ascriptive ties of the dense ethnic networks of Asian-American businessmen (Light, 1972).

Given the vital tasks with which organized vengeance groups are charged, the rapturous celebration of the feats of warriors appears as something more than braggadocio or the effusions of "overstrained masculinity." Mock battles, an oral tradition of vengeance transmitted by clan poets or other ritual specialists, and the affirmation of revenge through song and chanting expand the cultural capital that facilitates group formation. More than a reflection of underlying social forms or the passive evolutionary survival of symbolic products, the culture of vengeance plays an active role in perpetuating the recourse to violence. Symbolic action rekindles the fierce spirit of vengeful obligation, marks off the borders of the avenging community, and reminds individuals of their commitment to retaliation.

The cultural reproduction of vengeance may take mimetic, supernatural, or literary forms. For participants in medieval high culture, literature provided a written variant of moral exhortation. "Vengeance is the basis of an infinity of epic poems," Baroja observes of Hispanic works like the Poema del Cid: "The avenging of an insult brings as much pressure to bear upon the protagonist as that exerted in Greek tragedy by the idea of Nemesis [1966: 92]." The reluctant Jibaro must contend with the displeasure of dead kin and the fear of ghostly sanctions. The errant spirit of the murdered Indian "visits his sons, his brothers, his father, in the dream, and, weeping, conjures them not to let the slayer escape but to wreak vengeance upon him for the life he has taken [Karsten, 1923: 11]." The warlike leagues of the Bedouins engaged in mock battles that dramatically consecrated the values of manly vengeance through a ritualized exchange of blows and insults (Bourdieu, 1966: 201).

The Contingency of Vengeance

The combat-ready status of fraternal solidarity groups provides a graphic reminder of the costs and benefits of coercive deployment. Organized vengeance groups permit a functional adjustment to uncertain or bellicose environments. Simultaneously, they add to instability by creating a primitive version of the doctrine of "launch on warning." An act of wrong easily touches off a virtually automatic chain reaction of riposte to challenge, which spreads involvemment link by link along the chain of strong-tie vengeance. Yet the strength of those bonds should not obscure the forces at work that modify obligation. A look at the conditions leading to the suspension of the vengeance duty underlines a variety of counterforces beyond the presence of the state that restrain bloody settlement. Many things intrude to limit the seamless fit between a model of society and the actual conduct of its members, but only one of them need concern us here. Obligation bestows jeopardy as well as provides insurance. It subtracts from personal discretion even as it adds to pooled resources of protection.

Collective liability raises into bold relief all the dilemmas in theories of justice associated with innocent bystanders whose relationship with a guilty party or ecological proximity makes them available for gratuitous harm. For example, the kin of a murdered victim plot revenge. They are not stupid. They can envision the likely blood vengeance that will be meted out to them in turn by the kin of the killer they are about to do away with. A solution beckons: They simply jump a few steps in the cycle of vengeance, indulge in a bit of preemptive striking, and eradicate the entire family as a precaution against their own future eradication. Guilt by association attains a kind of ultimate, virtually perfect realization. Or take the case of a homicidal recidivist in a small society. The Eskimo who kills several people at once in a single episode adds to the halo of his prestige, but a chronic offender becomes a public enemy liable at any time to strike down another victim (Hoebel, 1954: 88). The community's bestowal of that invidious status transforms a dispute between individuals into a public matter and brings into play a set of affected interests who shall take vengeance, but this time in the name of the commonwealth. Removal of the offender becomes a legal execution performed by an avenger who serves as an agent for the collective body. The fusion of two separate interests lends force to such acts of communal retribution. On the one hand, the chronic offender threatens the minimal requisites for social survival of a community. His private vengeance passes the threshold below which it can be safely ignored. On the other hand, the offender threatens his network by constantly making them potential victims of his victims' kins' vengeance. The blurring of the line between private and public is symbolized by the request of the community that the father or brother of the offender destroy their wayward relation as an act of civic duty (Hoebel, 1954: 89).

Theory, then, yields to reality, and the kin group trims the sails of its obligation. A collectivity can bear only so much misfortune, which defines a de facto ceiling on liability that members can impose on their networks. The threshold is needed because communal resources are limited, because constant claims by one member deprive others of a sufficient margin of survival, and because outsiders tend to hold the entire group responsible for the misdeeds of a perpetrator. Whatever the justice of guilt by association, individuals come to personify for outsiders the character of their associates. A miscreant contaminates the reputation of the collectivity and exposes it to accusations. Such borrowed liability, which creates collective responsibility by default, generates incentives for a collectivity to monitor the conduct of its members.

A similar logic governs the punishment of doctors and lawyers by their colleagues, internal review procedures of formal organizations, and efforts by immigrant groups to discipline their colleagues. Sally Falk Moore has given us a lucid treatment of the conditions under which liability becomes limited, conditional, and privatized. The central organizational problem is that "a group bearing corporate liability may be committed to potential liability by any member, acting on his own, without authorization or sanction of the group for his particular acts." The organizational solution is simple. "A corrollary rule always exists whereby the corporation may discipline, expel or yield up to enemies members who abuse this power [1972: 89]." Moore thus reverses the distortions introduced by an overly formalistic reading of obligation. Liability varies not simply from society to society but from situation to situation, and only a diachronic analysis can capture the complex modifications of the grammar of obligation. By showing the contingency of what appears in a society's blueprints as an eternal verity, Moore discloses how the alleged givens are deprived of their immutability by organizational imperatives.

The circumstances of social life sometimes effect a reverse transformation of the vengeance tie. The disgraced Chinese-American, banished from his or her strong clan affiliations, faced an infelicitious environment. Ascribed ties of kinship and region exhausted the criteria for participation in all aspects of living. Social life was a thicket of closed corporations with impenetrable barriers to entrée, not a market of open associations. The high-binder tongs arose as a functional resolution of the problem of the pariah, recruiting its members from the ranks of the banished and providing an achieved method of forming strong vengeance ties. An elaborate ritual procedure, a quasi-sacred oath of vengeance, offered psychological replacements for "natural" ascribed loyalties:

> Underworld gangs did not tolerate dual allegiances so that service as a hatchetman involved a clean break with ascribed loyalties to clan, district, and village. Initiation into a tong emphasized the hatchetman's inexorable commitment to the organization. For the veteran tong "soldier," expulsion from the tong was tantamount to a

sentence of death. If the tong itself did not kill an offending member, the relatives of his murdered victims could freely avenge themselves on an expelled hatchetman no longer under the military protection of the tong [Light, 1972: 95].

Contractual specifications hardened the newly acquired status into a strong tie that transcended simple quid pro quo. The tong initiate swore to the injunction "You shall always work to the interest of the tong and never make your office a means of private revenge [Light, 1972: 96]."

An exaggeration of the suppleness of social life does not follow from the reversibility of status. A status is retracted or forgone for good, practical reasons. Before the pleasures and duties of membership are forfeited, a miscreant must impose much "trouble" on the collectivity. More than a cavalier mental exercise or a capricious display of the individual's power to invent social reality, the act of retraction is rooted in concrete organizational imperatives, and once more we run up against the ingenious ways in which society forces the desire for revenge to bow to its will.

If the strongest of ties, a kinsman's duty of blood revenge, is not made of stone, formally weak ties of revenge possess even greater volatility. Where corporate relations are weak or frayed and the circle of natural avengers obliged to retaliate is confined to the core links of the nuclear family, weak-tie relations such as friendship, the purchase of avengers in the marketplace, or patron–client relations extend the reach of the vengeance network. In weak-tie vengeance, contractual and voluntaristic sentiments prevail over primordial obligations.

Delegated vengeance, or vengeance for hire, provides the pure form of weak-tie vengeance. Among the Bedouins, for example, a man of *nif*, or honor, does not deign to reply to an affront in some situations. Ignoring an infamy, he proclaims his moral superiority over the offender. "Non-reply may also be a refusal to reply, an explicit decision not to riposte." As a result, "the offended person refuses to recognize that he has been offended; and by his disdain and scorn, he makes the offense recoil on its perpetrator, who is dishonored [Bourdieu, 1966: 205–206]." Condescension may leave the haughty injured party liable to incursion, but a functional resolution of that double bind is at hand: the professional avenger or killer for money. The hiring out of a proxy "scoundrel" to insult an enemy serves a slightly different function: It leaves open the possibility of mending the breach by later disavowing responsibility.

Weak-tie vengeance flourishes in societies with weak state institutions, highly competitive habitats, and fragmented social organization. Clientalistic relations compensate for the sparseness of corporate organization. The gangs, caciques, and padroni relations prevalent throughout insecure peasant societies attest to the urgent need to add to the strength of acephalous bands or autonomous households. The Mafia emerged in southern Italy and Sicily as entrepreneurs of violence under such anarchic conditions. The ceiling on liability in weak-tie vengeance is a good deal lower than it is in strong-tie vengeance. The lesser requirements for exit from the relationship mean that weak ties have an inherently greater volatility. The cultural obsession with "shrewdness," betrayal, and jealousies in such competitive societies reflects the dearth of strong corporate ties that hold the clientele when the patron's fortunes change. Such environments are especially susceptible to snowballs. Thus, big men on a run build allies in an exponential progression, as clients willing to serve as allies in vengeance flock to a successful leader. Barth's (1959) description of the Pathan shows the fragility of the commitment to avenge, as followers swing wildly from a stance of ally to one of adversary when the going gets tough. The very dynamic that attracts clients to strong men explains the force of reverse cascades, with spirals of desertion following hard on the heels of a leader's humiliation in revenge.

Revenge among Intimates

A quarrel between adversaires who lack rich, complex, and multiple ties with one another has a remarkable clarity rarely achieved in other disputes. Each disputant peeks out at their antagonist with a jaundiced eye, from across a gulf of interest, emotion, and imagination. Randall Collins has well described the "logic of emotions" that affects the social range of identification with others and the chastening force of sympathy: "It is the group boundaries that determine the extent of human sympathy . . . with the extension of the mutual links of an elaborate division of labor, the moral sense expands, becomes more abstract and universal, less concrete and particular [1974: 417]." Without mutual ties and entanglements, the single-minded sense of right on each side of the breach concentrates moral passion and gives it a fierce absolutism. The case of snowballing defections, however, points to the possibility of switches in loyalty. They remind us that one's enemy in a present dispute may be a onetime friend or future relative. Quite a different pattern of revenge surfaces in conflicts between intimates.

A fight between clansmen, inside an organization, or among neighbors envelops the participants in a vengeance game of immeasurably greater complexity, and often multiplexity. The analysis of revenge in such close encounters again points to the complex influences that speed or impede the enlargement of a quarrel. The greater the intimacy, the greater tends to be the taboos on revenge and the greater the chance of conciliation. In their folk taxonomies of disputing, countless societies translate the distinction that the Maring of New Guinea voice as the difference between "inside," or brother, fights and "outside" fights between more distant relations (Rappaport, 1967: 110). Lewis's account of the principle of centrifugal vengeance—"dia-paying groups of different clans are more ready to seek retaliation than closely linked lineages, even when the latter are in keen competition for the same natural resources [1961: 244]"—finds ultimate expression among the Somali in the quarrels of father and son: "Where a father kills his son, or a son his father, vengeance is impossible and compensation cannot be paid, for as Somali put it, 'who would pay and who would receive damages?' [1961: 257]."

The resolution of quarrels between intimates in societies otherwise given to vengeful prosecution offers a rough-hewn way of controlling for the effect of a disposition toward bellicose settlement so that the force of the particular situation can be seen in all its clarity. The momentary pacific impulses of the head-hunting Jalémó of New Guinea suggest the way intimacy tends to squelch vengeance, if only by the rarity of the departure from the customary violence that punctuates life among them. The basic unit of living among the Jalémó is the core of agnates who live in the men's house. Occasionally, all the frictions of everyday living combine to spark a fight between those linked by vengeance obligations. In one of the disputes recorded by Koch (1974: 93–95), a father reprimanded a son for plucking hibiscus from his bush. The son, in turn, hit the father with a stone. The father's brother's son then attacked the son. Yet, in contrast to the model of the natural cascade, fellow members of the men's house, rarely gentlemen in their daily affairs, broke up the fight. In a society without formal arbitration or legal authorities, spontaneous mechanisms of settlement provided substitutes for both vengeance and law. Spontaneous avoidance permitted social life to carry on, without forcing others in the men's house to choose sides. Characteristically, in such moments of charged yet repressed tension, supernatural sanctions assuaged the tension. The injured party hurled a curse, calling on the bones of a deceased ancestor, and mystical retribution replaced actual revenge.

A variety of factors produce multicentric affiliation, crosscutting loyalties, and countervailing pressures. They include patterns of residence, warfare, kinship, inheritance, migration, and demography. Yet a number of more general points that concern the relationship between social organization and environment emerge from the variousness of the particular situations.

The exchange positions of the disputants explain the inverse relation between intimacy and bloodshed. Gulliver remarks of fights among the Arusha of Africa: "Where the disputants have been in some mutually valuable relationship, then they both have an interest in maintaining or restoring it. Each is inclined to accept compromise for the sake of the relationship; but at the same time each has a measure of bargaining power to use against the other [1963: 240]." Yet the motives of the disputants may pale in significance to those of significant others, for the disputants' community of intimates often shares corporate interests in solidarity that offset the antagonistic interests of the disputants. The community of the men's house computes the interest of an entire vengeance group, whose unity is sundered by quarreling. "Residents of a men's house succeed in preventing agnates from resorting to violence as long as both live together in the same men's house," observes Koch, because "agnatic solidarity constitutes a prerequisite for concerted defensive and retaliatory actions against outsiders [1974: 96, 92]." The same principle explains the motivation of neighbors in a contemporary American setting to intervene to arrest a quarrel between two members of the same block:

> Such intercessions by civic groups ranged from passive reaction to complaints generated by residents who came to them as patrons to more proactive conduct initiated on their own behalf. A leader of a homeowners group described how the role of third party created networks through which reminders of obligation might flow. "This guy has an argument with his neighbor, he wants to get back, so he says, 'I have no second thoughts about selling to a black,' he says, 'I'll fix your ass when the time comes to sell. I know who I'm going to sell to,' so we watch these quarrels and convince them that they're not just hurting the one individual but friends and neighbors of fifteen years [Rieder, 1984: chap. 6]."

Beyond creating incentives to intervene, the links of each disputant to every member of a corporate body creates or expands the capacity through which suasion and exhortation can be transmitted to the disputants. Among the Maring of New Guinea, the great number of affinal and cognative ties between two disputing villages provide strong incentives to local neutrals, but they also "provided a set of relationships through which composition might be attempted [Rappaport, 1967: 111]." The same situation obtains among the Plateau Tonga of Africa, when the wives of group A marry men from group B and go off to live in the village of the Bs. But a man from group A has killed a man from group B, and revenge is in the air. The women anxiously send messages to their kin's village through the lines of their strong, primordial ties. "The people here are despising us. They refuse to greet us. They remind us all the time that we and our children are members of group A and we have killed their men. What are you going to do? [Colson, 1953: 208]."

Another point touches on the impact of space, or what Stinchcombe (1968) calls "areal variables," on obligation. Spatial as well as relational closeness has a powerful informal effect on the actual strength of formal ties. Spatial deployment includes the pattern of scatter, dispersal, and density, as well as simple distance from one's formal allies. The problem of an isolated migrant, or a sojourning minority, who is separated from his vengeance group and finds himself living among a kin group that becomes embroiled with his own kin group in a nasty quarrel is subject to a range of contingencies that inhere in his spatial position. By contrast, the closely woven, multistranded ties of Jalémó men who live together in the same men's house permit the spatial concentration of the moral suasion of the corporate group on a single weak point in the group. Within the tertiary portion of the Bedouin lineage, no vengeance can be exacted for homicide because "flowing blood, they are wont to say, can only be staunched by blood (i.e., a vengeance killing), but if a man kills within a close agnatic range the corporate body continues to bleed [Peters, 1967: 264]." Between tertiary segments, feuding is the order of the day. But collateral tertiary segments exist in that betwixt-and-between penumbra dividing the two statuses. Although they are discrete political units, they share grain stores, camp near one another at large watering holes, and attend each others' ceremonial events. Although a single vengeance killing may form an appropriate reply to a homicide, no cycle of prolonged vengeance can develop. "Permanent hostility which characterizes the feud would seriously disrupt everyday economic activities, limit the pastoral movements of the Bedouin beyond endurance, and sever lines of communication which they always strive to keep open [1967: 265]."

The final aspect of the relationship between organization and environment involves the unique perspectives, liabilities, and opportunities that devolve on personnel who span the boundaries of two systems at odds. Consider the case of crosscutting loyalties involved when a man of group A is married to a woman from group B and a member of his in-law group murders someone from his own kin group. Unlike the case of relational intimacy in the men's house, where all members of the corporate group save the two disputants have equal motivation and capacity to stave off vengeance, in the case of cross-pressure, a few interlinked individuals must confront two disputing corporate groups, and disposition to settle in a nonvengeful manner is distributed quite unequally. The husband with an affinal link to the injuring party is compromised, for he has an immense stake in mending the rift and convincing the kin to accept restitution in lieu of retaliation. They must point out, as one of the protagonists in the classical dispute described by Colson does, "[they] have killed our man, but if they agree to settle, we must settle. . . . Will it bring that man back to life for us to lose our wives and children? If you despise them for what one man has done, how can they live among us? [1953: 208]."

The straddler symbolizes the larger category of persons of dual loyalties. The growing doubts about loyalty, the need to exhort the straddler to declare, renders the loyalty fickle and suspect. But the suspicion is less a moral taint than a structural effect of bridging two worlds. A number of things follow from this placement in a field of shifting demands. Ambivalence or faintheartedness are shadow psychological reflections of the underlying pattern of positive and negative ties. Those who are "compromised" by a dispute are caught at the nodes of fused, but loosely coupled, networks. They are relay personnel, well positioned to exhort and communicate, as well as vulnerable linchpins in a system of warfare with great incentives to break the hold of corporate responsibility. The design of social life subverts Talionic justice.

Participation in multiple spheres of attachment, Max Gluckman noted, "strikes into the unity of each vengeance group [1959: 14]." But the causal force pushing toward conciliation consists not of individual motive or private whim but the configuration of the bonds between individuals. The pulls of different principles of affiliation create a structural disposition toward mediation, reconciliation, and compensation. Although sociologists have made great progress in graphing and representing these vectors of social life, they have not detracted from the elegant simplicity of the wisdom of Gluckman's portrait of the peace in the feud. The same analysis equally applies to the pattern of revenge in an organization, in a class structure, or in international politics. Complex forces of density, spread, and dispersion shape the fate of individual quarrels and communal disputes. The chains of association forge mazes through which suasion, vengeance, and meaning flow in predictable fashion. The design of ambivalence creates an order-building mechanism less vindictive than the bloody hand of violence.

Conclusion

Divided loyalties have an effect comparable to the state, relational intimacy, hierarchy, and balanced forces. All work against the enlargement of a dispute into a full-fledged cycle of revenge. The conditional nature of the assertion is critical, for the ability of these forces to thwart a snowball of retaliation is not absolute. Whenever revenge is denied or deferred, the wish for just deserts does not necessarily vanish; whenever its fulfillment in action is blocked, vengeance finds indirect expression through art, religion, and imagination. The seemingly inexhaustible ability of revenge to twist itself into new shapes, to camouflage its true intentions, or to content itself with substitute satisfaction attests to the stubbornness of the revengeful wish. The penchant for disguises is evident in a range of indirect forms of vengeance, which include ghostly revenge, revenge by suicide, poetic justice, otherworldly retribution, ritual or ceremonial vengeance, and, perhaps in the ultimate case, an ethic of mercy. Ultimately, a theory of vengeance is at one and the same time an explanation of the conditions for its renunciation. Because the displacement of revenge often takes culturally expressive forms, its analysis demonstrates the utility of a social-organizational theory of culture creation. A brief sketch of two categories of indirect vengeance hints at some of the elements of such an analysis.

A first order of disguise involves the translation of the vengeful impulse into ritual, ceremonial, or literary form. In one sense, the aesthetic sublimation of revenge obeys the same logic as furtive vengeance. What the body shrinks from translating into physical deed finds expression in words, proffered either with delicacy or gusto. For example, the Eskimo occasionally resort to song duels or ceremonies of insult to ridicule an opponent and caricature his foibles. In one of them, the injured party sings, "Now shall I split off words—little, sharp words like the wooden splinters which I hack offwith my ax [Hoebel, 1954: 94]." The image of words as splinters is not far from the spirit of Shakespeare's line in *Hamlet* "I will speak daggers to her, but use none."[2]

A second order of sublimation removes the blatant admission of a wish for revenge from everyday life, where it might prove dangerous or impossible. As is common in religions of the oppressed, vengeance against the wicked is often reserved for an otherworldly or utopian time, when mystical or religious agents shall requite evil for evil, the last shall be first, and the first shall be last. The lower-class concern with heaven has often been interpreted as a sign of fatalistic acceptance, but the other side of the vision of heaven is the vision of hell—"the afterlife appropriate to the oppressor [Genovese, 1974: 251]"—which reestablishes the moral meritocracy. E. P. Thompson has written of the Methodist influence on the British working class that "faith in a life to come served not only as a consolation to the poor but also as some emotional compensation for present sufferings and grievances: it was possible not only to

2Act 1, scene 2, line 421.

imagine the 'reward' of the humble but also to enjoy some revenge upon their oppressors, by imagining their torments to come [Thompson, 1963: 34]." Weber evoked the fusion of the worldly and otherworldly elements that characterizes the cult of the vengeful messiah that appeared at some stages of Judaism: "Hope of a day of Yahwe as the day of consolation for Israel, of misfortunes for the enemy; and frightful thirst for revenge against the enemy dwells in the grandiose image of the God who like a vintager reddened with the blood of the Edomites bestrides the mountains [1921: 368]."

Revenge obeys basic social laws, conforms to ethical mandates, considers its usage with cunning, consults the calculus of power, flows through well-worn channels, pays homage to cultural etiquette. That law of social determination holds equally true for the renunciation of vengeance, the embrace of an ethic of gracious forgiving, and the rise of messiahs of peace. The ferocity of sentiment yields to an implacable society. But the agility of the dominated, who seek justice if only in veiled form, should warn against a determinism that heralds the power of society at the expense of appreciating the inner life.

ACKNOWLEDGMENTS

I thank Donald Black, Paul DiMaggio, and James Scott for their helpful comments on an earlier draft of this chapter.

References

Aldrich, Howard E.
 1979 *Organizations and Environments*. Englewood Cliffs, N.J.: Prentice-Hall.
Bacon, Francis
 1625 *Essays*. London: Oxford, 1975.
Baeck, Leo
 1936 *The Essence of Judaism*. New York: Schocken, 1961.
Bailey, F. G.
 1969 *Strategems and Spoils: A Social Anthropology of Politics*. New York: Schocken.
Barth, Fredrik
 1959 *Political Leadership among Swat Pathans*. London: Athlone Press.
Baroja, Julio Caro
 1966 "Honour and shame: A historical account of several conflicts." Pages 79–139 in *Honour and Shame: The Values of Mediterranean Society*, edited by J. G. Peristiany. Chicago: University of Chicago Press.
Berscheid, E., D. Boye, and E. Walster
 1968 "Retaliation as a means of restoring equity." *Journal of Personality and Social Psychology* 10: 370–376.

Black, Donald
    1976   *The Behavior of Law*. New York: Academic Press.
Blau, Peter
    1964   *Exchange and Power in Social Life*. New York: Wiley.
Blok, Anton
    1974   *The Mafia of a Sicilian Village, 1860–1960: A Study of Violent Peasant Entrepreneurs*.
           New York: Harper & Row.
Boissevain, Jeremy
    1974   *Friends of Friends*. Oxford: Basil Blackwell.
Bourdieu, Pierre
    1966   "The sentiment of honour in Kabyle society." Pages 191–243 in *Honour and
           Shame: The Values of Mediterranean Society*, edited by J. G. Peristiany. Chicago:
           University of Chicago Press.
Brown, Paula
    1964   "Enemies and affines." *Ethnology* 3: 335–356.
Campbell, J. K.
    1964   *Honour, Family and Patronage: A Study of Institutions and Moral Values in a Greek
           Mountain Community*. Oxford: Clarendon Press.
Collins, Randall
    1974   "Three faces of cruelty: Towards a comparative sociology of violence." *Theory
           and Society* 1: 415–441.
    1975   *Conflict Sociology: Toward an Explanatory Science*. New York: Academic Press.
Colson, Elizabeth
    1953   "Social control and vengeance in Plateau Tonga society." *Africa* 23: 199–212.
Denich, Bette S.
    1974   "Sex and power in the Balkans." Pages 243–263 in *Woman, Culture, and Society*,
           edited by Michelle Zimbalist Rosaldo and Louise Lamphere. Stanford, Calif.:
           Stanford University Press.
Durkheim, Emile
    1893   *The Division of Labor in Society*. New York: Free Press, 1964.
Elias, Norbert
    1939   *The Civilizing Process: The Development of Manners*. Vol. 1. New York: Urizen
           Books, 1978.
Foucault, Michel
    1975   *Discipline and Punish*. New York: Vintage, 1979.
Gamson, William
    1975   *The Strategy of Social Protest*. Homewood, Ill.: Dorsey Press.
Genovese, Eugene
    1974   *Roll, Jordan, Roll: The World the Slaves Made*. New York: Pantheon.
Gluckman, Max
    1959   *Custom and Conflict in Africa*. Glencoe, Ill.: Free Press.
Gouldner, Alvin
    1960   "The norm of reciprocity: A preliminary statement." *American Sociological Re-
           view* 25: 161–179.
Granovetter, Mark S.
    1973   "The strength of weak ties." *American Journal of Sociology* 78: 1360–1380.
Gulliver, P. H.
    1963   *Social Control in an African Society: A Study of the Arusha, Agricultural Masai of
           Northern Tanganyika*. Boston: Boston University Press.

Hasluck, Margaret
  1954 "The Albanian blood feud." Pages 381–408 in *Law and Warfare: Studies in the Anthropology of Conflict,* edited by Paul Bohannan. Garden City, N.Y.: Natural History Press, 1967.
Hoebel, E. Adamson
  1940 "Law-ways of the Comanche Indians." Pages 183–203 in *Law and Warfare: Studies in the Anthropology of Conflict,* edited by Paul Bohannan. Garden City, N.Y.: Natural History Press, 1967.
  1954 *The Law of Primitive Man: A Study in Comparative Legal Dynamics.* New York: Atheneum, 1973.
Homans, George
  1961 *Social Behavior: Its Elementary Forms.* New York: Harcourt, Brace & World.
Kanter, Rosabeth
  1977 *Men and Women of the Corporation.* New York: Basic.
Kapferer, B.
  1969 "Norms and the manipulation of relationships in a work context." Pages 181–245 in *Social Networks in Urban Situations: Analyses of Personal Relationships in Central African Towns,* edited by J. Clyde Mitchell. Manchester: Manchester University Press.
Karsten, Rafael
  1923 *Blood Revenge, War, and Victory Feasts among the Jíbaro Indians of Eastern Equador.* Smithsonian Institution Bureau of American Ethnology, Bulletin 79. Washington, D.C.: U.S. Government Printing Office.
Kaufmann, Walter
  1950 *Nietzsche.* New York: Vintage, 1968.
Kirchheimer, Otto
  1961 *Political Justice: The Use of Legal Procedure for Political Ends.* Princeton, N.J.: Princeton University Press, 1968.
Koch, Klaus-Friedrich
  1974 *War and Peace in Jalémó: The Management of Conflict in Highland New Guinea.* Cambridge, Mass.: Harvard University Press.
Lewis, I. M.
  1961 *A Pastoral Democracy: A Study of Pastoralism and Politics among the Northern Somali of the Horn of Africa.* London: Oxford University Press.
Light, Ivan
  1972 *Ethnic Enterprise in America: Business and Welfare among Chinese, Japanese, and Blacks.* Berkeley, Calif.: University of California Press.
Machiavelli, Nicollo
  1513 *The Prince.* New York: Norton, 1977.
Moore, Sally Falk
  1972 "Legal liability and evolutionary interpretation: Some aspects of strict liability, self-help and collective responsibility." Pages 51–107 in *The Allocation of Responsibility,* edited by Max Gluckman. Manchester: Manchester University Press.
Otterbein, Keith F., and Charlotte Swanson Otterbein
  1965 "An eye for an eye, a tooth for a tooth: A cross-cultural study of feuding." *American Anthropologist* 67: 1470–1482.
Peters, E. L.
  1967 "Some structural aspects of the feud among the camel-herding Bedouin of Cyrenaica." *Africa* 37: 261–282.

Pitt-Rivers, Julian A.
    1954   *The People of the Sierra.* Chicago: University of Chicago Press, 1971.
Raper, Arthur F.
    1933   *The Tragedy of Lynching.* Chapel Hill, N.C.: University of North Carolina Press.
Rappaport, Roy A.
    1967   *Pigs for the Ancestors: Ritual in the Ecology of a New Guinea People.* New Haven,
           Conn.: Yale University Press.
Redfield, Robert
    1964   "Primitive law." Pages 3–25 in *Law and Warfare: Studies in the Anthropology of
           Conflict,* edited by Paul Bohannan. Garden City, N.Y.: Natural History Press,
           1967.
Reiss, Albert J., Jr.
    1971   *The Police and the Public.* New Haven, Conn.: Yale University Press.
Rieder, Jonathan
    1984   *The Trials of Liberalism: The Making of Middle America in Canarsie, 1960–1980.*
           Cambridge, Mass.: Harvard University Press.
Scheler, Max
    1915   *Ressentiment.* New York: Schocken, 1972.
Schneider, Jane
    1971   "Of vigilance and virgins: Honor, shame, and access to resources in Mediterra-
           nean society." *Ethnology* 10: 1–24.
Scott, James
    1976   *The Moral Economy of the Peasant: Rebellion and Subsistence in Southeast Asia.* New
           Haven, Conn.: Yale University Press.
Servadio, Gaia
    1976   *Mafioso: A History of the Mafia from Its Origins to the Present Day.* New York: Dell.
Smith, Adam
    1759   *The Theory of Moral Sentiments.* New Rochelle, N.Y.: Arlington House, 1969.
Stinchcombe, A. L.
    1968   *Constructing Social Theories.* New York: Harcourt, Brace & World.
Suttles, Gerald
    1972   *The Social Construction of Communities.* Chicago: University of Chicago Press.
Thomas, Keith
    1971   *Religion and the Decline of Magic: Studies in Popular Beliefs in Sixteenth and Seven-
           teenth Century England.* London: Weidenfeld & Nicolson.
Thompson, E. P.
    1963   *The Making of the English Working Class.* New York: Pantheon, 1964.
Weber, Max
    1921   *Ancient Judaism.* New York: Free Press, 1967.
    1922   *Economy and Society.* New York: Bedminister Press, 1968.
Zingg, Robert M.
    1942   "The genuine and spurious values in Tarahumara culture." *American An-
           thropologist* 44: 78–92.

6

The Variability of Punishment*

PETER N. GRABOSKY

The Concept of Punishment

It is not entirely unfortunate that the concept of punishment remains loosely delineated and, consequently, poorly measured, for
efforts at developing a general theory of punishment must necessarily
proceed at a high level of abstraction. Nevertheless, a minimal degree of
conceptual clarification is essential. For purposes of the present essay,
we shall regard punishment as the authoritative, deliberate imposition
of pain or deprivation in response to the transgression of some norm.

This definition is sufficiently broad that it encompasses a wide range
of punitive phenomena, from the spanking of an insubordinate child to
the disbarment of an attorney or the incarceration of a convicted burglar.
It incorporates wide variations in the legitimacy of the punishing authority and in the formality of the punishment process.

In modern states, the imposition of punishment tends to be the formal responsibility of specialized institutions or individuals, commonly

*This essay was written while the author was a Russell Sage Fellow in Law and Social
Science at Yale Law School. He is indebted to the Russell Sage Foundation and to Yale
University for financial and institutional support, respectively, during that period. The
author is solely responsible for any opinions and for all errors of fact or interpretation
herein.

TOWARD A GENERAL THEORY OF SOCIAL CONTROL
Volume 1: Fundamentals

referred to collectively as a criminal justice system. The system's component institutions are themselves specialized, with some performing the function of delineating the boundaries of permissible behavior and specifying the sanctions appropriate to the various forms of transgression, and others, in sequence, identifying and apprehending transgressors, adjudicating responsibility, and administering the sanctions prescribed. Smaller collectivities may themselves have specialized sanctioning institutions that may operate in conjunction with or apart from processes of governmental or legal punishment. Thus, a bar association may reprimand or disbar a member for unethical albeit lawful conduct, as well as for having been convicted of a felony.

On the other hand, some social units have no formal sanctioning institutions or procedures at all. A casual "talking-to" often constitutes the sole response to deviance within certain group settings (Freidson and Rhea, 1972), whereas the basic patterns of contemporary parental response to the transgressions of their young offspring exemplify perhaps the most familiar form of informal punishment.

Such rich variation in forms of deprivation and in the processes by which they are imposed raises a troublesome question. Any discussion of the behavior of punishment must take into account the essentially subjective nature of suffering and deprivation. This is hardly a modern insight, and is suggested by the contention of Grotius that a fine weighs more heavily on a poor man than on his affluent counterpart (1853, volume 2: 20–33). More recently, the criminologist Nils Christie has noted that "the experience of incarceration is more grievous in a society in which life at large is easy and enjoyable than in one in which it is difficult and dangerous [1975: 293]."

The development of general theory, however, is best served by focusing on the objective properties of punishment and ignoring the subjective aspects of the punishment process. Such a concept as wealth has been employed extensively and fruitfully in social theory without undue preoccupation with questions of subjective utility; so too can the concept of punishment be employed. We are still left, however, with the vexing problem of comparing qualitatively different forms of punishment. A task sufficiently difficult when undertaken from the vantage point of objectivism thus becomes even more problematic in light of subjective cultural differences. Pospisil (1971: 95), for example, relates that the Nunamiut Eskimo regard ostracism with much more dread than they would a severe beating. One doubts that members of an intensely individualistic advanced industrial society would share this preference.

Our temporary solution to this problem once again may be based on a resort to objectivity. And the monetary analogy remains useful: That different societies (and, indeed, different social units within societies) have different media of exchange has not precluded the formulation of macroeconomic theory. Tasks of measurement and conceptualization are ultimately crucial but will be left to another and later stage of inquiry.

Existing Theories of Punishment

Of those theorists who have undertaken explanations of punishment, the most prominent is Emile Durkheim. His main contributions (1893; 1900) have been justly celebrated for their originality as well as for their scope; the explanations extend from stateless societies to twentieth-century political systems (for critiques and interpretations of Durkheim, see, e.g., Schwartz and Miller, 1964; Lukes, 1973; Schwartz, 1974; Spitzer, 1975a; Clarke, 1976; Cotterrell, 1977).

Durkheim regarded punishment as linked with and representative of the prevailing form of social organization. The pattern of evolution from a simple, undifferentiated social structure to one characterized by an increasingly concentrated population, complexity, and functional specialization tended, in Durkheim's view, to be accompanied by a transformation in collective values. He referred to the form of social solidarity characteristic of simple societies as "mechanical." In such settings, collective values tend to be intensely held and predominant; those individuals who transgress against them evoke strong punitive response. Punishment thus serves as the symbolic reaffirmation of a violated *conscience collective*. As a society develops, however, its collective conscience weakens, and its characteristic solidarity becomes what Durkheim described as "organic." Shared values in these differentiated societies are less salient, and their infringement less prevalent. Increasingly, normative violations take the form of transgressions against individuals; sanctions in general become more restitutive and less repressive, and punishment tends to diminish in severity.

Durkheim recognized the possibility of deviation from the trend toward diminution of punishment, having observed that short-term increases in penal severity had punctuated the histories of modern Europe and of some ancient societies. To explain these deviations, he contended that societies characterized by a high concentration of authority were more punitive than those in which power was more widely shared. The centralization of political power served as the functional equivalent of those collective values so strongly embraced in simple societies. Violations of norms embraced by an absolutist regime thus tend to evoke a more severe punitive response (1900: 33–36).

Durkheim stated as well that deprivation of liberty tends to become the dominant sanction in complex societies. He viewed incarceration as a more lenient response than the aggravated afflictive punishments of primitive societies and saw the rise of specialized institutions of social control as indicative of the movement away from clan and kinship as sanctioning agents (1900: 44–50).

Durkheim also dealt, somewhat more briefly and implicitly, with a theory of the *scope* of penal sanctions. One of his more provocative contentions, set forth in *The Rules of Sociological Method*, held crime to be a "normal" phenomenon, an inevitable condition in any society (1895: 47–75). Maintenance and periodic reaffirmation of a society's central values demand that it identify its marginal members and sanction them appropriately. As a consequence, the boundaries of permissible behavior will be broadened or contracted over time to ensure the presence of a relatively stable number of individuals beyond the margins.

Durkheim's work stimulated much subsequent research. Many of the studies he inspired, however, have cast doubt on his interpretations. Although research on the stability of punishment has provided some basis for acceptance of Durkheim's theory, subsequent inquiry on penal evolution has yielded findings that tend to be flatly contradictory. The first study to cast doubt on the truth value of Durkheim's theories was that of Sorokin (1937, vol. 2: 523–632), discussed at greater length later in the chapter. His analysis of the criminal codes of five European nations over eight centuries showed that simple, homogeneous societies tended to be the *least* punitive. Although Sorokin presented some evidence to support Durkheim's contention that the centralization of political power tended to be accompanied by an increase in the intensity of punishment, he attributed the increase to value conflict rather than to a change in political structure.

Subsequent studies of penal evolution have been consistently unsupportive of Durkheim's work. In their systematic analysis of 51 preindustrial societies from the Human Relations Area Files, Schwartz and Miller (1964) found that restitutive sanctions were present in a number of societies characterized by a minimal division of labor. These ostensibly more lenient sanctions often tended to precede the development of a central system of repressive control. A subsequent study of 48 societies from the same files showed that offenses against the collectivity were more prevalent and sanctions more severe in complex, differentiated societies (Spitzer, 1975a).

Defenders of Durkheim have challenged the Schwartz and Miller study on a number of conceptual and methodological grounds (Baxi, 1974; Cotterrell, 1977; Turkel, 1979). Among the more compelling arguments is the contention that the theory of legal evolution applies not merely to penal systems *in vacuo* but to legal systems in their entirety. In this broader context, the increasing salience of restitutive law is beyond dispute. It must be noted, however, that in the essay "Two Laws of Penal Evolution" Durkheim referred explicitly to variations in the intensity of criminal punishment per se (1900: 32). It may be premature to dismiss Durkheim out of hand; the fact remains, however, that at least across political systems, this hypothesis remains sorely lacking in empirical corroboration.

The proposition that society's reliance on the penal sanction tends toward a state of equilibrium has been tested in a number of diverse settings and has received some support. Erikson's (1966) study of deviance and social control in a Puritan community showed a remarkably stable rate of individuals subjected to the sanctioning process, despite considerable instability in the varieties of crime. More recently, time series analyses of rates of imprisonment in the United States, Norway, and Canada reveal that these rates have also manifested considerable stability (Blumstein and Cohen, 1973; Blumstein, Cohen, and Nagin, 1976; Blumstein and Moitra, 1979). Nevertheless, these findings are far from definitive. The earlier Blumstein studies have been criticized for neglecting variations in the population at risk and for ignoring numerous alternative custodial facilities (Waller and Chan, 1974). The authors themselves suggest that rates of imprisonment tend to fluctuate markedly during periods of drastic social dislocation such as wars and depressions, indicating a relationship more consistent with some of the contending explanations discussed later. And, finally, subsequent studies have revealed substantial declines in rates of imprisonment in Western industrial societies during the mid-twentieth century (Gurr, 1976: 60; Scull, 1977).

These findings also cast some doubt on Durkheim's proposition that deprivation of liberty tends to become the dominant mode of penal sanction in complex societies (1900: 44). Whether he was influenced primarily by patterns characteristic of earlier stages of social development, or by the unique historical moment of early nineteenth-century Western societies when imprisonment rose to prominence (Rothman, 1971; Foucault, 1977; Ignatieff, 1978), it is clear that Durkheim did not anticipate the trend toward noncustodial penal sanctions that has characterized the past half century.

The successor to Durkheim as a major theorist of penal severity, and the scholar who posed the first significant challenge to his predecessor's explanations, was Pitirim Sorokin. His "Fluctuation of Ethicojuridical Mentality in Criminal Law" (1937, vol. 2: 523–632) was the first systematic attempt to measure penal severity and to explain its variation over time and across nations. Sorokin's comparison of the penal codes of five

European societies over a millenium was as innovative as it was monumental. He developed a standardized scheme for equating previously incommensurable punishments and mapped changes in the prescribed severity of the codes with unprecedented rigor. As noted earlier, his findings soundly contradicted Durkheim's theory of penal evolution. Sorokin found no long-term trend in the severity of punishment, but rather a pattern of erratic fluctuations throughout history. Contrary to Durkheim's prediction, the earliest and least complex societies under investigation were characterized by the mildest sanctioning systems. Penal severity increased during the Middle Ages, but the height of absolute monarchy at the end of the seventeenth century coincided with a distinct downward trend in the intensity of prescribed punishment. In direct challenge to Durkheim's hypothesized link between political absolutism and penal severity, Sorokin observed many republics whose prescribed punishments were more severe than those of absolute monarchies. Cross-sectional comparison revealed very little difference between societies at any given point in time, suggesting that variations in penal severity were largely attributable to macrohistorical forces, particularly to lasting changes in the network of political and social relationships.

Sorokin's explanation for the observed variations was expressed in the rather awkward term *ethicojuridical heterogeneity*. By which he meant the extent of disagreement on fundamental values within a society at a given time. Sorokin referred explicitly to value conflict, as opposed to social heterogeneity or stratification, noting that a rigidly stratified society wherein both master and slave embraced prevailing rights and duties would be characterized by relative leniency in the treatment of transgressors. He suggested a number of social phenomena that are indicative of value dissensus, noting that each is consistently accompanied by a wider and more intense application of punishment. Thus, the periods immediately prior to and subsequent to revolutions, eras of imperial expansion and immigration, and, indeed, any period that might be regarded as one of rapid social change, has been marked by an increase in penal severity.

One review that lends support to the theories of both Durkheim and Sorokin is that of Ben Yehuda (1980). In his suggestion that the intensity of witch-hunts in Europe was greatest precisely at those times of dramatic social change, the relationship between penal severity and ethicojuridical heterogeneity is implicit. At the same time, persecution of witches served to reaffirm the *conscience collective*. A number of other studies also support the idea of a positive relationship between heterogeneity and penal severity. Spitzer (1975a: 630) revealed that societies characterized by gross disparities in wealth and social rank were the most punitive. Dye (1969) reported a strong relationship between economic inequality, racial heterogeneity, and rates of imprisonment in the United States. The remaining studies that deal with the relationship between heterogeneity and penal severity do so within the context of an explicit theme: class conflict.

Although it is clear that there is no explicit Marxian theory of penal severity (Hirst, 1972; Cain and Hunt, 1979: chap. 5), the works of Marx contain at least two discussions of penal policy in the service of those individuals in society who control the means of production. An early essay (Marx, 1842) notes the imposition of new penalties for the gathering of fallen wood, whereas *Capital* contains a brief treatment of the emergence of vagrancy law as a means of controlling the large numbers of itinerants who had been displaced by the decline of the feudal system. Marx went on to suggest that the capitalist process of production, once fully developed, would itself break down the workers' resistance and would require only an occasional application of direct force to repress challenges from below (Marx, 1867: chap. 28). Engels (1845: 567–568) observed that penal sanctions are imposed with disproportionate severity on the proletariat.

A number of neo-Marxian writers, both scholarly and polemical, have sought to develop these themes (e.g., Jessop, 1980; Sparks, 1980). Their studies vary widely in terms of insight and rigor, some being highly speculative, whereas others are anchored solidly in empirical reality. The basic assumptions of neo-Marxian penology hold that those members of a society who control the means of production and who dominate productive relations within that society rely on a legal and political superstructure in order to maintain their control. The penal system is an integral part of that superstructure. Changes in penal policy, then, will be implemented in response to threats to the dominant order, or will otherwise be influenced by changes in economic conditions.

The foremost neo-Marxian theorists of penal severity are Georg Rusche and Otto Kirchheimer. The basic theme of their *Punishment and Social Structure* (1939) contends that penal practices reflect the economic imperatives of their respective political systems. With supporting data drawn selectively from modern European history, Rusche and Kirchheimer cannot claim the methodological rigor of Sorokin, but they contributed insights into qualitative changes and small-scale fluctuations that the latter in his sweeping analysis had overlooked. The main theme of their work, one quite consistent with Sorokin's more general interpretation, is their finding of an inverse relationship between economic prosperity and penal severity. During periods of economic expansion, when labor shortages normally exist, fewer and milder punishments tend to be inflicted. Conversely, during periods of economic contraction, punishments tend to be more numerous and more intense. Although severe punishments would be economically unproductive in a full-employment economy, they are much less so under conditions of a glutted labor market. Moreover, harsher sanctions may serve as a deterrent threat to those who might otherwise be driven by desperation to illegal activity. Evidence of this general relationship has also emerged from the more recent and systematically rigorous research of Brenner (1976), Greenberg (1977), Jankovic (1977), and Yeager (1979).

Rusche and Kirchheimer also attribute qualitative changes in penal policy to economic imperatives. When sentences of death were commuted to terms at forced labor or transportation, the commutations reflected not the ascendancy of humanitarian reform, but the need for manpower on public works or for colonial development. The replacement of capital punishment by galley slavery in a number of Mediterranean states was conditioned not by the spirit of forgiveness and brotherly love, but by the demands of technology and military policy. Whether these replacements for capital punishment can be interpreted as manifestations of leniency is problematic, for they were often viewed with as great a dread as were the gallows, garrote, or guillotine.

The idea of the penal system as an instrument of class warfare has become popular. It is eminently compatible with Sorokin's theory of penal severity, as well as with Donald Black's more general theory of law (Black, 1976). Recent years have seen a growing number of studies illustrative of variations in the severity of penal sanctions apparently generated by the rise or decline of challenging subordinates. William Chambliss (1964) undertook a thorough discussion of the origins of vagrancy law, whereas the classic work of Jerome Hall (1935) remained the definitive statement on the development of the law of theft. E. P. Thompson (1975) discussed the role of the notorious "Black Act" in reinforcing existing class relations in eighteenth-century British society. Thorsten Sellin's study (1976) of punishment and slavery showed how the penal system reinforced the institution of slavery in the United States. Ted Gurr (1976) reviewed how penal law was influenced by the rise and eventual accommodation of labor movements in Great Britain, Sweden, and New South Wales. More recently, Andrew Scull (1977) has argued that the growing emphasis on noncustodial sanctions in Western industrial societies primarily attributable to a growing fiscal crisis. A number of other studies illustrate the use of penal law to control subordinate, marginal, and subcultural groups (see Black, 1976: 17, 23–29, 51–52). Although a neo-Marxian theory of penal severity has yet to be fully developed, these studies provide substantial raw material.

Another category of theories of penal severity consists of varied attempts to generalize from individual psychodynamics to the behavior of political systems. Although handicapped by their obvious reductionism—the tendency to attribute personal characteristics to collectivities—these psychosocial interpretations deserve review here; although weak as explanations, they have yet to be thoroughly discredited.

Perhaps the most prominent of the psychosocial theorists was Svend Ranulf, who contended that a disinterested disposition to punish was a distinctive characteristic of the lower-middle class (Ranulf, 1938). The punitive disposition, according to Ranulf, was engendered by the frustrations attending the extraordinarily high degree of repressive self-restraint demanded by lower-middle-class life. Aside from his failure to delineate the concept of lower-middle class, Ranulf was less than systematic in marshaling evidence in support of his thesis. Unable to dismiss those demonstrably punitive societies in which lower-middle class elements were insignificantly represented among sanctioning agents, he contended that the observed punitive tendencies were not disinterested, but rather explicitly defensive or affirmative of some closely shared collective value (Ranulf, 1938: 131, 145). Unfortunately, Ranulf failed to subject his supportive examples to the same exacting scrutiny. Ranulf seized on the increase in punitiveness that followed the rise to power of Fascist and Nazi parties, but took insufficient notice of the emerging influence of social democratic movements in numerous Western societies. For these reasons, Ranulf is less noted for his contributions to a theory of penal severity than for his research technique. His simple content analyses of literary and journalistic sources were among the first undertaken by a European social scientist.

Although Ranulf has thus far failed to inspire any significant subsequent research, there have been other attempts at psychosocial explanations of penal severity. These tend to view the punitive orientation as linked with the repression and frustration of libidinal or aggressive urges. Kann (1941), for example, predicted that penal severity would be greater in societies characterized by a high degree of interpersonal aggression and a low degree of self-directed aggression. Berg (1945) predicted that penal severity would vary with the extent to which a society imposes social prohibitions against sexual behavior. Two other studies suggest that societies in wartime, having ample targets in the enemy for the expression of aggressive instincts, are more lenient with their domestic offenders (Alexander and Staub, 1931: 207–225; Riewald, 1950: 235).

None of these predictions has been subjected to rigorous empirical evaluation; requisite tests would begin by eliminating plausible rival interpretations of observed variations in severity. It stands to reason that one would observe more sanctions imposed in a jurisdiction characterized by more sanctionable behavior, whether aggressive or sexual. For example, economic pressures and manpower needs during periods of war, combined with the absence of a significant percentage of the young male population, would tend to depress rates of sanctioning and of sanctionable behavior, respectively (Archer and Gartner, 1976).

A potentially more fruitful interpretation, and one consistent with Sorokin's and the neo-Marxian theories, suggests that penal severity may be explained in terms of the social distance between social control agents and the targets of their punishment (Robertson and Taylor, 1973; Sutherland and Cressey, 1974: 324–325; Black 1976: chap. 3). Minority group members appear consistently subject to more severe sanctions, a phenomenon that has obvious implications for aggregate relationships between heterogeneity and severity.

An additional explanation of penal severity—derived from Black's general theory—rests on the relative salience of a society's penal system vis-à-vis its alternative institutions of social control. Briefly stated, penal severity will vary *inversely* with the degree to which other institutions of social control are available to cope with deviant behavior (Black, 1976: 107). Two studies (Penrose, 1939; Biles and Mulligan, 1973) have reported on inverse relationship between rates of imprisonment and the availability of mental hospital facilities in western Europe and Australia, but further research on this relationship is warranted. The issue, moreover, is cimplicated by the tendency on the part of social control agents in some societies to employ ostensibly therapeutic facilities as prisons.

The idea of an inverse relationship between alternative social control systems conflicts rather sharply with the cultural consistency theory of punishment. As originally presented by Sutherland (Sutherland and Cressey, 1974: 337), this theory maintains that penal severity within a society will be consistent with other ways of behaving in a society. Thus, the formal sanctioning of deviants can be expected to mirror the degree of punitive response encountered by deviants in the family or the school. Also akin to this theory is Christie's (1968) notion that penal severity will be somewhat indicative of the relative harshness of life at large within a society.

The Theories Extended

SOCIAL DIFFERENTIATION

As was suggested earlier, Durkheim's first law of penal evolution, holding that sanctions will be less severe as society becomes increasingly differentiated, was contradicted by a subsequent study of stateless societies (Spitzer, 1975a). Indeed, systems of extreme penal severity, such as that which formed the basis of social control in nineteenth-century Zulu society, were based on a high degree of functional specialization (Walter, 1969: 80). The same can be said of the organization of killing centers during the Third Reich (Hilberg, 1961). It seems fairly clear, moreover, that Durkheim's theory has not been successful in explaining the punishment practices of collectivities other than societies.

The literature on complex organizations, for example, lends little support to Durkheim's idea: The sanctioning processes of these collectivities appear much more responsive to structural variables such as those to be discussed later in the chapter. On the other hand, the history of science suggests that the diversification and subsequent differentiation of scientific enterprise has been accompanied after a time by a diminution of sanctioning activity.

CENTRALIZATION OF AUTHORITY

Durkheim's major qualification of the differentiation hypothesis, that penal severity will vary directly with the centralization of authority within and between societies, seems to fare somewhat better. Despite Sorokin's partial refutation, cited earlier, some of the gentlest societies are marked by a wide sharing of power, whereas extreme centralization often characterizes the most ferocious (Gillin, 1934; Walter, 1969: 188; Bergesen, 1977; Fabbro, 1978). Changes observed over time in the political organization of the Plains Indians are further supportive. Increases in the severity of sanctioning corresponded with periodic increases in centralization (Walter, 1969: 74).

Evidence from studies of nonpolitical collectivities is also consistent with this general pattern (Udy, 1965: 699; Black, 1976: 101–103). The concentration of power in most professions is minimal, and their sanctioning practices predictably lenient; the scientific community reflects this relationship to an extreme extent (Moore, 1970; Black, 1976: 80–81).

HETEROGENEITY

Although Sorokin made passing reference to the generalizability of his theory of punishment to all collectivities (Sorokin, 1937: vol. 2, 603–605), he made no explicit observations and undertook no rigorous tests beyond the societal context. Accumulating evidence from vastly different social settings, however, suggests that his general explanation has broad applicability.

Ethicojuridical heterogeneity, it may be recalled, refers explicitly to value conflict within a collectivity. Sorokin contended that such conflict characterizes social entities undergoing some form of stress, whether generated by processes within the group or by external forces. Value conflict, however, is often a function of the inherent composition of the collectivity in question. Granted, some demographically or structurally heterogeneous collectivities are characterized by widespread value consensus, but such harmony tends to be an exception rather than the rule. It is thus possible to predict variations in penal severity from structural or demographic variations within and between social groups.

A review of evidence from seven stateless societies reknowned for an absence of violence (Fabbro, 1978) is generally illustrative. The groups in question may be characterized as small, egalitarian, band societies, having economies where exchange is based on generalized reciprocity. Deviant behavior on the part of adult members tends to be met with ostracism or with appeals to the need for mutual cooperation rather than with physical punishment. Child-rearing practices are correspondingly gentle. Thus the small size, social homogeneity, and absence of material inequality in these societies serve to minimize the kind of value conflict that gives rise to both sanctionable behavior and punitive response.

Ethicojuridically homogeneous social units need not be limited to natural settings, but, rather, may be self-consciously engineered. The contemporary American medical profession again provides one illustrative example, and scientific communities provide others (Ravetz, 1971). Among those collectivities whose members are recruited, selectivity of recruitment and the salience (duration and intensity) of the socialization process will serve to minimize value conflict. Sociologists of the professions refer to such collectivities as "self-regulating companies of equals" and suggest that their sanctioning procedures are almost exclusively limited to friendly persuasion (Freidson and Rhea, 1972). This inverse relationship between selectivity of recruitment and reliance on punitive sanctions extends well beyond the professions. As an axiom of organization theory, it has been noted by Etzioni (1968) and Scudder (1954), among many others.

That marginal members of a collectivity tend to be sanctioned with greater frequency and severity than are representatives of the "mainstream" has been proposed by Donald Black and supported with considerable evidence (Black, 1976: chaps. 2–3). For example, Lieberman (1970) reviews how the disciplinary machinery of numerous professions has been used against racial and political minorities, and a similar pattern is alleged to have characterized the history of the American Bar Association (Auerbach, 1976). Hart (1978) showed that black soldiers in the United States Army are punished more frequently than would be predicted by their rate of offending, and Poole and Regoli (1980) found that black prison inmates also experience disproportionate punishment. Robin (1967: 691–693) studied the decisions of department store managers to invoke the criminal sanction against employees discovered stealing from the firm. Holding constant the amount stolen, he found that a significantly higher percentage of lower-status employees (cleaners, servicemen) than higher-status ones (executives, salespersons) are prosecuted. Although these observations pertain to the sanctioning of discrete individuals, one need adopt only a simple logic of aggregation to generalize to social units. As Black's work indicates, the larger or the more stratified a collectivity, or the more numerous its marginal members (i.e., the greater the aggregate of relational distances within the collectivity), the greater its sanctioning severity will be (Black, 1976: 13, 40).

Families differ drastically from professions as social entities, but the link between relational distance and punitive severity is strikingly visible in both. Most instances of child abuse may be regarded as punishment carried to an extreme, and so it is significant that a higher incidence of abuse has been observed among deformed, premature, adopted, foster, and step children than among normal and natural offspring (Caffey, 1972). One assumes that the ability of the punitive parent to identify or to empathize with the child is inhibited by these stigmata. More recent research has revealed that the amount of physical separation between mother and neonate, even after normal pregnancy and delivery, has a negative effect on the mother–infant relationship as well. It might be added that, according to Berkowitz and Frodi (1979), unattractive or handicapped participants in psychological experiments are subjected to more severe punishment than are participants of normal appearance. Milgram (1974) also noted a link between relational distance and punishment in the laboratory setting.

The size of a collectivity tends to bear on the relational distance between its members, for it becomes difficult to develop close, intense bonds with all of one's colleagues as their number increases. Thus, it is hardly coincidental that the peaceful societies discussed earlier (Fabbro, 1978) are all small, or that the severity of punishment tends to vary directly with the size of stateless societies (Scott, 1976). Even more striking is the direct relationship between size and the observed severity of punishment in contemporary American families (Gil, 1971; Goode, 1971), a relationship that is not significantly weakened when race and income are held constant (Maden and Wrench, 1977: 207).

VALUE CONFLICT INTRODUCED BY SITUATIONAL STRESS

The rapidly growing literature on violence in the family (Maden and Wrench, 1977) provides further support for Sorokin's general theory.

Situational stress, generally induced by adverse changes in economic conditions, is regarded as a common antecedent of both child abuse and wife abuse (Straus, 1977b: 219). This relationship between stress and intrafamilial punitive behavior is by no means unique to Western industrial societies, having been observed among the Eskimo (Riches, 1974) and among family units in other foraging societies (Straus, 1977a: 724). It has been suggested that the nuclear family undergoes major changes in structure as a result of processes inherent in the family life cycle and that these changes are often stressful. Combined with the structural asymmetries that tend to characterize most families, these stressful circumstances contribute significantly to the kinds of conflict in question (Gelles and Straus, 1979).

Additional insights may be derived from the literature on social control in science. Collectivities of scientists are not renowned for their punitive activity, and their sanctioning tends to be informal (Hagstrom, 1965: chap. 1; Black, 1976: 81–83). Although this informality is in part traceable to the structure and socialization of scientific communities (to be discussed later), there remain discernible variations in severity that are directly attributable to value conflict. Those periods marked by disagreement with regard to the fundamental premises of scientific inquiry are times when punishment, such as it is, becomes significantly more severe (Kuhn, 1962). Ostracism, denial of resources, withholding recognition, or public criticism tend to be the main forms of response to the challengers of scientific consensus. One of the more celebrated examples of repression in science was the scientific community's reaction to Immanuel Velikovsky's radical explanation of the origins of the universe. It is alleged that members of the scientific community at the time sought to pressure publishers to refrain from publishing Velikovsky's work and also undertook to deny employment to defenders of his theories (*American Behavioral Scientist*, 1963; Hagstrom, 1965: 272). Sorokin's general explanation can suggest hypotheses about variation in sanctioning activity across scientific organizations as well as within scientific disciplines over time. It suggests, for instance, that the discipline in which there is consensus on the proper subjects of inquiry and modes of analysis will be a gentle one, whereas its counterpart in a preparadigm stage, to employ the Kuhnian terminology, will be much less lenient with its deviant practitioners.

The history of the American medical profession illustrates a similar pattern. Far from monopolizing the practice of medicine during the first half of the nineteenth century, licensed physicians faced stiff competition from so-called quacks, purveyors of patent medicines, and other people without formal medical training. Traditional medical science was still in a preparadigm stage, and medical societies frequently disciplined physicians who ignored restrictions on consultations with irregular practitioners (Konold, 1962: 22). Contrast these circumstances with the almost nonexistent sanctioning activity within the contemporary American medical profession (American Medical Association Judicial Council, 1964; Lieberman, 1970: 104), largely unthreatened by alternative modes of practice and free of significant internal disagreements on the form and focus of medical science. Sanctioning levels in the contemporary American legal profession are similarly low (Steele and Nimmer, 1976; American Bar Association Center for Professional Discipline, 1978).

ECONOMIC CONDITIONS: RESOURCE CONSTRAINTS

Rusche and Kirchheimer (1939) made no effort to generalize beyond political systems, and there have been no self-conscious attempts by subsequent scholars to extend their explanations to other kinds of collectivities. There exist nevertheless a number of disparate studies whose findings are quite consistent with Rusche's and Kirchheimer's dominant theme.

The study of industrial discipline, for example, although still relatively undeveloped, has produced some interesting findings. Typical punishments imposed in the workplace include, in decreasing order of severity, termination of employment, temporary suspension, and reprimand (Phelps, 1959: 4). The inverse relationship between economic conditions and the severity of sanctions in the workplace has long been recognized (Slichter, Healy, and Livernash, 1960: 644–645). In capitalist systems, the fate of the employee has always tended to be precarious during periods of economic contraction; it is not mysterious that as economic circumstances render an employee more expendable, he or she is liable to be sanctioned more severely. This general relationship is not limited to the context of large-scale cyclical fluctuations, however. It may also be seen within and between firms, depending on the organizations's market position and production goals. Production under a cost-plus government contract usually permits greater tolerance of employee deviance and more lenient sanctioning of employee transgressions. Similarly, production pressures at the onset of a new model year in the automobile industry are said to be accompanied by greater tolerance of employee misbehavior (Slichter et al., 1960: 644–646). Similar factors explain why violations of assembly specifications can occur with impunity in the aircraft manufacturing industry during wartime (Bensman and Gerver, 1963: 592). On a more general level, the sanctioning of organizations may also depend on resource constraints. If a substandard hospital is the only facility available to a community, for instance, it is less likely to lose its accreditation (Zald, 1978: 83). This relationship presumes, of course, that the deviance in question does not itself jeopardize production goals. Thus, offenses against time discipline will evoke relatively harsh responses, whereas those such as gambling will tend to be overlooked (Gersuny, 1973: 65).

The relationship between resource constraint and sanctioning severity need not be limited to institutions and collectivities in capitalist society. A study of the Chinese Communist treatment of counterrevolutionaries during the decades preceding the establishment of the People's Republic is nicely illustrative. Economic imperatives, particularly the prohibitive cost of feeding prisoners, underlay the policies of early release from incarceration during much of the Yenan period. And prisoners were often released from custody if they expressed a willingness to participate in labor projects (Griffin, 1976: 80, 119–123).

Although the circumstances of the Chinese revolution were fundamentally different from the economic fluctuations that beset capitalist societies, the similar effect of resource constraint and manpower needs on sanctioning practices is undeniable. Thus, factories and revolutionary movements tend to respond in a manner similar to governments when faced with changing economic circumstances.

ECONOMIC CONDITIONS: DEPENDENCE ON EXTERNAL SUPPORT

Evidence from a widely diverse set of collectivities suggests a variation on the preceding economic theme. In particular, the severity of sanctions within a collectivity will be significantly affected by that collectivity's dependence on external support.

The support an organization receives from various sources in its environment often depends on the appearance of internal control (Katz, 1977: 5). Thus, many organizations tend to shield members from outsiders' perceptions of internal deviance and, in doing so, protect the collectivity itself from embarrassment. When the social unit is unsuccessful in minimizing the external visibility of its internal deviance, however, it often undertakes to reassert its claim to legitimacy by responding with marked punitive force. Protection of a social group's public image (and often its political and economic foundation) may explain sharp fluctuations and other apparent inconsistencies in its sanctioning practices. The same act of deviance that might be tolerated when visible only to members of the collectivity will therefore evoke a significantly more punitive response if it attracts wider public attention. A classic illustration of such processes may be drawn from punitive practices of the United States Congress. Members are often aware of their colleagues' misconduct but tend to overlook these transgressions until they reach public attention through independent law enforcement or journalistic investigation. Only then are internal sanctions likely to be invoked.

Literature on the professions yields similar findings. Systematic study of disciplinary proceedings in the Association of the Bar of the City of New York revealed that the most severe sanctions were reserved for those transgressions that happened to have been the most widely publicized (Carlin, 1962: 157–162). Moreover, the publicity accorded the deviant act was significantly more important than the severity of the act itself or the status of the offending attorney in explaining the intensity of the association's response. Similarly, although much employee theft is either overlooked or dealt with informally, public visibility of such transgressions has been found to explain the decision of management to seek prosecution in many cases (Robin, 1967: 691–692).

Throughout most of the present century, medical societies have rarely censured physicians except in those cases that threaten to bring the entire profession into disrepute (Konold, 1962: 75). In an earlier time, when there was much less public trust and professional autonomy than there is now, sanctioning appears to have been more frequent (Konold, 1962: 22). On the other hand, the steadily rising number of states providing immunity from civil liability (for libel and slander) to persons reporting errant physicians was accompanied by a significant increase in the number of physicians disciplined by state medical boards in the United States during the 1970s, and the visibility of professional transgressions has been noticably enhanced as well (Associated Press, 1978). It has also been suggested that the increasing costs of malpractice insurance and the growing threat of government intervention have encouraged a greater use of punitive sanctions within the medical profession (Barber, 1978: 605).

Science yields yet another example. It appears that scientific nonconformity evokes particularly harsh sanctioning when its practitioners direct appeals to the lay public. These overtures to nonscientists seem to jeopardize the autonomy of science by threatening its public support (Hagstrom, 1965: 272). Scientific reaction to the radical cosmogonic theories of Velikovsky are cited by Hagstrom as an example, and a more recent analogue may be seen in the controversy over the effectiveness of laetrile—an apricot derivative—as a cure for cancer.

Sanctioning practices of juvenile gangs appear to fit this general pattern as well. In one instance, a gang member who robbed an old woman in front of the gang's clubhouse was punished not for the mugging but for having committed it so close to the club's headquarters as to risk police retaliation against the entire membership (Fraser, 1978).

Punishment practices in organized athletic competition reflect a similar sensitivity to external support. In some of the more popular spectator sports, such as basketball and ice hockey, strict enforcement of rules would slow the game to the extent that the audience would lose interest. On the other hand, insufficient implementation of penalties could lead to increasing violence, posing great danger to participants and ultimately alienating all but the most bloodthirsty spectators (Lueschen, 1976; Bradley, 1977: 199). This relationship is even more salient in professional sports, where dependence on public support is greatest. In professional settings it may be appropriate to refer to an optimizing process of punishment, significantly conditioned by economic imperatives.

Bronislaw Malinowski's observations of the Trobriand Islanders suggest that dependence on external support is sufficient but not necessary to explain a group's sanctioning activity.

> The breach of exogamy—as regards intercourse and not marriage—is by no means a rare occurrence, and public opinion is lenient, though decidedly hypocritical. If the affair is carried on *sub rosa* with a certain amount of decorum, and if no one in particular stirs up trouble—"public opinion" will gossip, but not demand any harsh punishment. If, on the contrary, scandal breaks out—everyone turns against the guilty pair and by ostracism or insults one or the other may be driven to suicide [Malinowski, 1926: 80].

Just as public perception of sanctioning practices as excessively lenient can jeopardize the legitimacy of a group, so too can perceived excesses of severity. For example, a severe form of ostracism, referred to as "silencing," had a long history at the United States Military Academy, and when a recent case attracted massive publicity, the practice was allegedly discontinued (Ellis and Moore, 1974: 168–73). Mitigation of severity has characterized other visible settings as well. When broadening the base of the Chinese Communist movement became imperative, treatment of counterrevolutionary activity and lesser deviance grew more lenient (Griffin, 1976: 81). Evidence from studies of intrafamily violence is also consistent with this pattern: Domestic violence appears more characteristic of family units that are insulated from neighbors and other kin (Straus, 1977a: 720).

Political systems are likewise sensitive to public scrutiny, particularly when they are dependent on external support. Widespread public attention to human rights violations appears to have brought about a slight mitigation of penal severity in Brazil and Chile, for instance, whereas it seemingly has had little impact in such settings as the Republic of South

Africa and the old Pol Pot regime in Kampuchea, the latter, until its demise, quite self-consciously independent of the international system.

In general, the relationship between the visibility of transgressions and the severity with which they are sanctioned appears to have at least an implicit economic foundation. Only where external support is not crucial to the continued functioning of the collectivity would the general explanation be inapplicable, and such settings seem to be quite rare.

RESIDUAL EXPLANATIONS

Of the remaining theories of penal severity, the one with the most widespread support is that which posits a direct relationship between sexual repression and the severity of sanctions in general. Evidence from stateless societies suggests a positive relationship between the punishment of premarital and extramarital sex and the severity of response to other transgressions (Cohen, 1969; Prescott, 1975). Similarly, nineteenth-century Zulu history reveals that the period of most intense sexual repression coincided with the most draconian period of terror (Walter, 1969: 147–149, 198). Evidence from other collectivity types is less abundant but supportive. The use of physical punishment in families, for example, is positively correlated with stricter sexual control (Goode, 1971: 629).

The contention that punishment practices will vary inversely with the intensity of self-directed aggression within a collectivity remains largely untested. A cross-sectional study of stateless societies revealed that the intensity of punishment, homicide, and suicide all vary together, suggesting that penal severity may reflect aggressive inclinations in general. On the other hand, the American medical profession, with a significantly low rate of sanctioning, has a relatively high rate of suicide. The extent to which this explanation can be extended to other nongovernmental collectivities must await further research.

THE FORM OF PUNISHMENT:
STRUCTURAL DETERMINANTS

The most basic change in the form of punishment lies in the transition from informal sanctioning to the formal administration of penalties. The form of punishment appears to be a function of both the size of a collectivity and its relationship to its host society. Such methods as ostracism and public or private rebuke tend to characterize small, intimate settings. Often membership in the collectivity is of great salience to the conception of self, and there are few sources of economic or social support outside of the group. This explanation accounts for the salience of informal sanctions in Eskimo societies, where social isolation places the individual alone against the Arctic wastes, or in Japanese society, where one's psychic well-being is so inextricably bound up with one's membership in a collectivity.

As a social unit increases in size, however, and the relational distance between members tends to increase, informal sanctions are employed with decreasing frequency (see Black, 1976: 45–46). The emergence of incarcerative institutions in American society provides an illustrative example (Rothman, 1971). As the scale of society and the geographic mobility of its members increased, family and community were replaced as agents of social control by prisons and asylums. This pattern of penal evolution fits quite well with anthropological evidence on the overwhelming informality of sanctions that characterizes small-scale societies.

THE FORM OF PUNISHMENT:
ECONOMIC IMPERATIVES

There is some evidence from nongovernmental collectivities to support the general thesis that changes in the form of punishment serve the interests of the sanctioning agents. During the nineteenth century when labor was in relatively short supply, for instance, it was not uncommon to deduct a certain amount from a transgressor's pay for a breach of factory discipline. Today, in societies plagued with chronic unemployment, suspension without pay or outright termination of employment is the dominant response (Gersuny, 1976). During the era of slavery in the United States, the value of a slave's labor time militated in favor of corporal punishment in lieu of incarcerative sanctions (Fogel and Engerman, 1974: 147).

Conclusion

Durkheim, Sorokin, and several more recent scholars, such as the neo-Marxians, have contributed to the foundation of a general theory of punishment. Findings from a wide variety of settings reviewed in the preceding pages suggest that two basic properties of collectivities are of greatest utility in explaining variations in the form and intensity of penal sanctions: All else equal, social groups become more punitive and administer sanctions with greater formality as the relational distance between members widens and as the group undergoes stressful change.

Moreover, large, heterogeneous, stratified collectivities in which authority is centralized will be more punitive as well. It is hardly surprising, therefore, that the Republic of South Africa is more punitive than is Sweden, that the Tasaday should be renowned for their gentleness and the Zulu for their ferocity, and that the International Association of Chiefs of Police lacks a reputation for harsh treatment of its members.

These general patterns merit further scrutiny in a wider variety of settings in time and space, as does the nature of interaction between stressful change and aggregate relational distance. It seems quite likely that further inquiry will reveal new principles and explanatory phenomena that have been ignored or understated in these pages. Whatever the case, the path that lies ahead is inviting.

References

Alexander, F., and H. Staub
  1931   *The Criminal, the Judge, and the Public.* New York: Macmillan.
American Bar Association Center for Professional Discipline
  1978   "Statistical report: Public discipline of lawyers by state disciplinary agencies, 1974–1977." Unpublished paper. Chicago: American Bar Association.
American Behavioral Scientist
  1963   "The politics of science and Dr. Velikovsky." 7: 3–68.
American Medical Association Judicial Council
  1964   "Disciplinary action in the medical profession." *Journal of the American Medical Association* 83:1077–1078.
Archer, Dane, and Rosemary Gartner
  1976   "Violent acts and violent times: A comparative approach to postwar homicide rates." *American Sociological Review* 41: 937–963.
Associated Press
  1978   "Number of doctors disciplined reported up six times in six years." *New York Times* (December 3): 73.
Auerbach, Jerold S.
  1976   *Unequal Justice: Lawyers and Social Change in Modern America.* New York: Oxford University Press.
Barber, Benjamin
  1978   "Control and responsibility in the powerful professions." *Political Science Quarterly* 93: 599–615.
Baxi, Upendra
  1974   "Durkheim and legal evolution: Some problems of disproof." *Law and Society Review* 8: 645–651.
Bensman, Joseph, and Israel Gerver
  1963   "Crime and punishment in the factory: The function of deviancy in maintaining the social system." *American Sociological Review* 28: 588–598.
Ben Yehuda, Nachman
  1980   "The European witch craze of the 14th to 17th centuries: A sociologist's perspective." *American Journal of Sociology* 86: 1–31.

Berg, Charles
    1945   "The psychology of punishment." *British Journal of Medical Psychology* 20:
           295–313.
Bergesen, Albert J.
    1977   "Political witch-hunts: The sacred and the subversive in cross-national perspec-
           tive." *American Sociological Review* 42: 220–233.
Berkowitz, Leonard, and A. Frodi
    1979   "Reactions to a child's mistakes as affected by his/her looks and speech." *Social
           Psychology* 42: 420–425.
Biles, D., and Glenn Mulligan
    1973   "Mad or bad? The enduring dilemma." *British Journal of Criminology* 13:
           275–279.
Black, Donald
    1976   *The Behavior of Law*. New York: Academic Press.
Blumstein, Alfred, and Jacqueline Cohen
    1973   "A theory of the stability of punishment." *Journal of Criminal Law and Criminol-
           ogy* 64: 198–207.
Blumstein, Alfred, J. Cohen, and D. Nagin
    1976   "The dynamics of a homeostatic punishment process." *Journal of Criminal Law
           and Criminology* 67: 317–334.
Blumstein, Alfred, and J. Moitra
    1979   "An analysis of time series of the imprisonment rate in the states of the United
           States: A further test of the stability of punishment hypothesis." *Journal of
           Criminal Law and Criminology* 70: 376–390.
Bradley, Bill
    1977   *Life on the Run*. New York: Bantam Books.
Brenner, M. H.
    1976   "Effects of the economy on criminal behavior and the administration of crimi-
           nal justice in the United States, Canada, England and Wales and Scotland."
           Pages 25–65 in *Economic Crises and Crime*, issued by United Nations Social
           Defense Research Institute. Rome:UNSDRI.
Caffey, John
    1972   "The parent–infant traumatic stress syndrome." *American Journal of Roentgenol-
           ogy, Radium Therapy, and Nuclear Medicine* 114: 218–229.
Cain, Maureen, and Alan Hunt (editors)
    1979   *Marx and Engels on Law*. London: Academic Press.
Carlin, Jerome
    1962   *Lawyers' Ethics*. New York: Russell Sage Foundation.
Chambliss, William J.
    1964   "A sociological analysis of the law of vagrancy." *Social Problems* 12: 67–77.
Christie, Nils
    1968   "Changes in penal values." *Scandinavian Studies in Criminology* 2: 161–172.
    1975   "Utility and social value in court decisions on punishment." Pages 281–296 in
           Crime, Criminology and Public Policy, edited by Roger Hood. New York: Free
           Press.
Clarke, Michael
    1976   "Durkheim's sociology of law." *British Journal of Law and Society* 3: 246–255.
Cohen, Yehudi
    1969   "Ends and means in political control: State organization and the punishment of
           adultery, incest, and violation of celibacy." *American Anthropologist* 71: 658–687.

Cotterrell, R.B.M.
  1977 "Durkheim on legal development and social solidarity." *British Journal of Law and Society* 4: 241–252.
Durkheim, Emile
  1893 *The Division of Labor in Society.* New York: Free Press, 1964.
  1895 *The Rules of Sociological Method.* Chicago: University of Chicago Press, 1938.
  1900 "Two laws of penal evolution." *University of Cincinnati Law Review* 38(1969): 32–60.
Dye, Thomas R.
  1969 "Inequality and civil rights policy in the States." *Journal of Politics* 31: 1080–1097.
Ellis, Joseph, and Robert Moore
  1974 *School for Soldiers: West Point and the Profession of Arms.* London: Oxford University Press.
Engels, Friedrich
  1845 "The condition of the working classes in England." Pages 295–596 in *Collected Works* of Karl Marx and Friedrich Engels, vol. 4. London: Lawrence and Wishart, 1975.
Erikson, Kai T.
  1966 *Wayward Puritans: A Study in Sociology of Deviance.* New York: Wiley.
Etzioni, Amitai
  1968 "Social control: Organizational aspects." Pates 396–402 in *International Encyclopedia of the Social Sciences*, vol. 14. New York: Macmillan.
Fabbro, David
  1978 "Peaceful societies: An introduction." *Journal of Peace Research* 15: 67–83.
Fogel, Robert W., and Stanley L. Engerman
  1974 *Time on the Cross: The Economics of American Negro Slavery.* Boston: Little, Brown.
Foucault, Michel
  1977 *Discipline and Punish: The Birth of the Prison.* New York: Pantheon.
Fraser, C. Gerald
  1978 "Videotapes of South Bronx youth gangs by French film maker in Whitney Series." *New York Times* (June 4): 60.
Freidson, Eliot, and Buford Rhea
  1972 "Processes of control in a company of equals." Pages 185–199 in *Medical Men and Their Work*, edited by E. Freidson and J. Lorber. Chicago: Aldine-Atherton.
Gelles, Richard J., and Murray A. Strauss
  1979 "Determinants of violence in the family." Pages 549–581 in *Contemporary Theories about the Family*, vol. 1, edited by W. Burr, R. Hill, F. Nye, and I. Reiss. New York: Free Press.
Gersuny, C.
  1973 *Punishment and Redress in a Modern Factory.* Lexington, Mass.: D. C. Heath.
  1976 "Devil in petticoats and just cause: Patterns of punishment in two New England textile factories." *Business History Review* 50: 131–152.
Gil, David G.
  1971 "Violence against children." *Journal of Marriage and the Family* 33: 637–648.
Gillin, John
  1934 "Crime and punishment among the Barama River Carib of British Guiana." *American Anthropologist* 36: 331–344.
Goode, William J.
  1971 "Force and violence in the family." *Journal of Marriage and the Family* 33: 624–636.

Greenberg, David F.
    1977   "The dynamics of oscillatory punishment processes." *Journal of Criminal Law and Criminology* 68: 643–651.
Griffin, Patricia
    1976   *The Chinese Communist Treatment of Counter-Revolutionaries.* Princeton, N.J.: Princeton University Press.
Grotius, Hugo
    1853   *De Jure Belli et Pacis.* Cambridge: Cambridge University Press.
Gurr, Ted R.
    1976   *Rogues, Rebels, and Reformers.* Beverly Hills, Calif.: Sage Publications.
Hagstrom, Warren O.
    1965   *The Scientific Community.* Carbondale, Ill.: Southern Illinois University Press.
Hall, Jerome
    1935   *Theft, Law and Society.* Indianapolis, Ind.: Bobbs-Merrill.
Hart, R. J.
    1978   "Crime and punishment in the army." *Journal of Personality and Social Psychology* 36: 1456–1471.
Hilberg, Raul
    1961   *The Destruction of the European Jews.* New York: Quadrangle.
Hirst, Paul Q.
    1972   "Marx and Engels on law, crime, and morality." *Economy and Society* 1: 28–56.
Ignatieff, Michael
    1978   *A Just Measure of Pain.* New York: Pantheon.
Jankovic, Ivan
    1977   "Labor market and imprisonment." *Crime and Social Justice* 8: 17–31.
Jessop, Bob
    1980   "On recent Marxist theories of law, the state, and juridico-political ideology." *International Journal of the Sociology of Law* 8: 339–368.
Kann, Robert
    1941   "Criminal law and aggression." *Psychoanalytic Review* 28: 384–406.
Katz, Jack
    1977   "Cover-up and collective integrity: On the natural antagonisms of authority internal and external to organizations." *Social Problems* 25: 3–17.
Konold, Donald E.
    1962   *A History of American Medical Ethics: 1847–1912.* Madison, Wis.: State Historical Society of Wisconsin.
Kuhn, Thomas S.
    1962   *The Structure of Scientific Revolutions.* Chicago: University of Chicago Press.
Lieberman, Jethro K.
    1970   *The Tyranny of the Experts.* New York: Walker.
Lueschen, Guenter
    1976   "Cheating in sport." Pages 67–77 in *Social Problems in Athletics: Essays in the Sociology of Sport,* edited by Daniel M. Landers. Urbana, Ill.: University of Illinois Press.
Lukes, Steven
    1973   *Emile Durkheim: His Life and Work: A Historical and Critical Study.* New York: Harper & Row.
Maden, Mark F., and David F. Wrench
    1977   "Significant findings in child abuse research." *Victimology* 2: 196–224.
Malinowski, Bronislaw
    1926   *Crime and Custom in Savage Society.* Paterson, N.J.: Littlefield, Adams, 1976.

Marx, Karl
   1842   "The law on thefts of wood." Pages 20–22 in *Karl Marx: Selected Writings,* edited
          by D. McLellan. Oxford: Oxford University Press, 1977.
   1867   *Capital.* New York: International Publishers, 1967.
Melossi, Dario
   1976   "The penal question in *Capital.*" *Crime and Social Justice* 5: 26–33.
Milgram, Stanley
   1974   *Obedience to Authority: An Experimental View.* New York: Harper & Row.
Moore, Wilbert E.
   1970   *The Professions.* New York: Russell Sage Foundation.
O'Malley, P., and S. D. Webb
   1973   "Economics, ideology, and criminal policy: Sentencing and penal reforms in
          New Zealand, 1954–1970." *International Journal of Criminology and Penology* 1:
          363–374.
Penrose, L.
   1939   "Mental disease and crime: Outline of a comparative study of European statis-
          tics." *British Journal of Medical Psychology* 28: 1–15.
Phelps, Orme W.
   1959   *Discipline and Discharge in the Unionized Plant.* Berkeley, Calif.: University of
          California Press.
Poole, Eric D., and R. M. Regoli
   1980   "Race, institutional rule breaking, and disciplinary response." *Law and Society
          Review,* 14: 931–946.
Pospisil, Leopold
   1971   *Anthropology of Law: A Comparative Theory.* New York: Harper & Row.
Prescott, James W.
   1975   "Body pleasures and the origins of violence." *Bulletin of the Atomic Scientists* 31:
          10–20.
Ranulf, Svend
   1938   *Moral Indignation and Middle Class Psychology: A Sociological Study.* New York:
          Schocken Books, 1964.
Ravetz, Jerome R.
   1971   *Scientific Knowledge and its Social Problems.* New York: Oxford University Press.
Riches, D.
   1974   "The Netsilik Eskimo: A special case of selective female infanticide." *Ethnology*
          13: 351–361.
Riewald, Paul
   1950   *Society and Its Criminals.* New York: International Universities Press.
Robertson, Roland, and Laurie Taylor
   1973   *Deviance, Crime, and Socio-Legal Control.* London: Martin Robertson.
Robin, G. D.
   1967   "The corporate and judicial disposition of employee thieves." *Wisconsin Law
          Review* 1967: 685–702.
Rothman, David J.
   1971   *The Discovery of the Asylum: Social Order and Disorder in the New Republic.* Boston:
          Little, Brown.
Rusche, Georg, and Otto Kirchheimer
   1939   *Punishment and Social Structure.* New York: Columbia University Press.
Schwartz, Richard D.
   1974   "Legal evolution and the Durkheim hypothesis: A reply to Professor Baxi." *Law
          and Society Review* 8: 653–368.

Schwartz, Richard D., and Miller, James C.
    1964 "Legal evolution and societal complexity." *American Journal of Sociology* 70: 159–169.
Scott, Robert A.
    1976 "Deviance, sanctions, and social integration in small scale societies." *Social Forces* 54: 604–620.
Scudder, Kenyon T.
    1954 "The open institution." *The Annals of the American Academy of Political and Social Science* 293: 80–87.
Scull, Andrew T.
    1977 *Decarceration*. Englewood Cliffs, N.J.: Prentice-Hall.
Sellin, J. Thorsten
    1976 *Slavery and the Penal System*. New York: Elsevier.
Slichter, S. H., J. J. Healy, and E. R. Livernash
    1960 *The Impact of Collective Bargaining on Management*. Washington: The Brookings Institution.
Sorokin, Pitirim
    1937 *Socio-cultural Dynamics*. New York: American Book Company.
Sparks, Richard
    1980 "A critique of Marxist criminology." Pages 159–210 in *Crime and Justice: An Annual Review of Research*, vol. 2, edited by N. Morris and M. Tonry. Chicago: University of Chicago Press.
Spitzer, Steven
    1975a "Punishment and social organization: A study of Durkheim's theory of penal evolution." *Law and Society Review* 9: 613–638.
    1975b "Toward a Marxian theory of deviance." *Social Problems* 22: 638–651.
Steele, Erich H., and Raymond T. Nimmer
    1976 "Lawyers, clients and professional regulation." *American Bar Foundation Research Journal* 1976: 917–1019.
Straus, Murray A.
    1977a "Societal morphogenesis and intrafamily violence in cross-cultural perspective." *Annals of the New York Academy of Sciences* 285: 717–730.
    1977b "A sociological perspective on the prevention and treatment of wifebeating." Pages 194–238 in *Battered Women*, edited by Maria Roy. New York: Van Nostrand Reinhold.
Sutherland, Edwin H., and Donald R. Cressey
    1974 *Principles of Criminology*. 9th edition. Philadelphia: Lippincott. (1st edition, 1924).
Thompson, E. P.
    1975 *Whigs and Hunters: The Origin of the Black Act*. New York: Pantheon Books.
Turkel, G.
    1979 "Testing Durkheim: Some theoretical considerations." *Law and Society Review* 13: 721–738.
Udy, Stanley
    1965 "The comparative analysis of organizations." Pages 678–709 in *Handbook of Organizations*, edited by James G. March. Chicago: Rand McNally.
Waller, I., and J. Chan
    1974 "Prison use: A Canadian and international comparison." *Criminal Law Quarterly* 17:47–71.

Walter, E. V.
   1969   *Terror and Resistance.* New York: Oxford University Press.
Yeager, Matthew G.
   1979   "Unemployment and imprisonment." *Journal of Criminal Law and Criminology*
          70: 586–588.
Zald, M. N.
   1978   "On the social control of industries." *Social Forces* 57: 79–102.

7

Compensation in Cross-Cultural Perspective

VIVIAN J. ROHRL

Compensation as a style of social control has been found in many if not all cultures. Characteristically the compensatory style is initiated by a victim, and the problem is seen as a debt that resulted from the failure of someone to fulfill an obligation. The solution consists of a payment by the debtor. As Donald Black (1976: 6–8) states, it is possible to explain this and other styles of social control in relation to the social settings in which conflicts arise. The following pages contain an overview of several aspects of the compensatory style. A common denominator found in all systems of compensation will be explored, followed by a review of theories of the history of law, with special attention given to societies in which compensation is most clearly developed. A central question to be addressed in developing a theory of compensation is, What are the main types of compensation, and under what conditions are each of these different types emphasized? This question will be explored through a survey of related theoretical and descriptive literature. A model will be presented in which subtypes within the compensatory style will be related to other aspects of social life. Compensation will be considered in the context of several broader modes of social control: reciprocity oriented, negotiative, mediative–arbitrative, and adjudicative. Each of these modes can be seen in relation to a characteristic sociocultural system, and examples of such systems will be given.

191

TOWARD A GENERAL THEORY OF SOCIAL CONTROL
Volume 1: Fundamentals

Compensation encompasses a wide variety of behavior, including the "making up" for an injury, a misdeed, or a crime. Within this variety of possibilities, compensation as social control includes the right of a publicly sanctioned person, or group of officials, to demand the payment—create a debt—of something in order to set to rights an infraction on the part of the debtor.

A common denominator of all modes within the compensatory style is the standard of obligation. *Obligation,* traced back to its Latin root, derives from two words: *ob,* meaning 'to' or 'toward,' and *ligatio,* meaning 'to tie' or 'bind'. And, indeed, it often seems that an underlying principle of compensation is the binding or tying together of people. The dictionary definition states that an obligation is "something (as a formal contract, a promise, or the demands of conscience or custom) that obligates one to a course of action [Merriam-Webster, 1977: 792]." It happens that compensation has meant each of these in different times and places.

Compensation long ago received attention in the Old Testament and in the code of Hammurabi as the law of talion. The Old Testament contains many refinements of the compensatory principle. For example, the often-quoted *lex talionis*—"life for life, eye for eye, tooth for tooth, hand for hand, foot for foot"—is set forth with rules as to its application:

> If the witness be a false witness, and hath testified falsely against his brother; then shall ye do unto him, as he has purported to do unto his brother; so shalt thou put away the evil from the midst of thee. And those that remain shall hear, and fear, and shall henceforth commit no more any such evil in the midst of thee. And thine eye shall not pity: life for life [Deuteronomy 19: 18–21].

The talion principle did not apply strictly or mechanically, and under other circumstances, people's lives were spared. Much attention is given to the details of circumstances, relationships, and intentions. For example,

> And this is the case of the manslayer, that shall flee hither and live: whoso killeth his neighbour unawares, and hated him not in time past; as when a man goeth into the forest with his neighbour to hew wood, and his hand fetcheth a stroke with the axe to cut down the tree, and the head slippeth from the helve, and lighteth upon his neighbour, that he die; he shall flee unto one of these [sanctuary] cities and live; lest the avenger of blood pursue the manslayer, while his heart is hot, and overtake him, . . . and smite him mortally; whereas he was not deserving of death, inasmuch as he hated him not in time past. . . . But if any man hate his neighbour, and lie in wait for him, and rise up against him, and smite him mortally that he die; and he flee into one of these cities; then the elders of his city shall send and fetch him thence, and deliver him into the hand of the avenger of blood, that he may die [Deuteronomy 19: 4–12].

It is notable that the issue of responsibility is not dealt with in the preceding passage—only liability as related to intention. This separation of responsibility from liability will be discussed further later in the chapter. But first we shall examine the continuum of compensation, from lawless to lawful and from the feud to adjudication.

The Context of Compensation

Feud can be defined as "a state of conflict between two kinship groups within a society, manifest by a series of unprivileged killings and counter-killings between the kinship groups within a society, usually initiated in response to an original homicide or other grievous injury [Hoebel, 1973: 8]." In a study of the function of feud, Hoebel concludes that it occurred far less frequently than anthropologists heretofore thought. For example, there was not one case of feud reported among the Trobrianders of Melanesia. Although a talion-like idea was present, it was rarely regarded as obligatory except "in cases of a male adult of rank or importance. . . . In other cases, . . . it is still evaded by the substitution of blood-money (*lula*) that would relieve the survivors from the duty of talion [Malinowski, 1926: 118–119]." Hoebel concludes that "actual feud is not nearly as common as we have allowed ourselves to believe [1973: 10]." It is the image of feud that is prevalent. Feud, as unchecked killing and counterkilling, represents the breakdown of society. A fear of the idea of feud and of what it represents is, in a sense, however, the sustenance of law and leads to compensatory and other lawful behavior. "Law consists of procedures designated to obviate feud [Hoebel, 1973: 13]." Restated, compensation is tied to obligation, the centripetal principle that links members of a society together. Feud, or "blood revenge," is tied to centrifugal or anarchic influences. The two phenomena can be seen as opposite sides of the same coin.

This close relationship between feud and compensation can be seen among the Nuer of the Sudan, among whom feuds could occur. Before such a feud devastated the society, a "leopard-skin chief" was called on to intervene and to assist in negotiating a compensatory settlement between the lineage of the killer and the victim's lineage (Evans-Pritchard: 1940; 1941). The Nuer had customary preset compensation in specified numbers of cattle for murders as well as for other injuries to a person.[1]

[1]For examples of exact schedules of compensation for injuries, see Howell (1954: 70) and Diamond (1971: 58–59, 65–66, 269–279). Among the Northern Somali of East Africa, as among many pastoral nomads, tension and rivalry can occur between different lineage groups, and such conflicts can result in feuds and in positively sanctioned self-help. Such

Again, without considering responsibility, the liability was set and understood among the entire community.

Among the Trukese of Micronesia, a feud could occasionally wipe out an entire lineage segment. But at some point, an acknowledged end to hostilities was made (Goodenough, 1966: 148–153).

Self-help or *vengeance* can, but does not always, lead to feud. If a community disapproves of such retaliatory killing, as in the hypothetical example in Deuteronomy given earlier, then further killing and counterkilling can continue. As is also seen in that example, however, if a murder is viewed by the community as the righting of a wrong caused by an earlier murder, then the matter can be closed. Similarly, in the Albanian mountain culture, feud shades into positively sanctioned self-help or vengeance. Compensation may or may not be permitted in lieu of such a killing, depending on the circumstances, the relationships of the people involved, and the individual village's unwritten laws (Hasluck, 1954). In certain villages, people could avenge a murder only with a counterkilling. In other villages, the murderer might have a number of alternative courses. He might be subject to a counterkilling, which resulted in a feud. Or he could expiate himself, in the form of "blood money," in those villages where such compensation was permitted. In the villages where it was not, "peace was seldom made until the same number had been killed on both sides [Hasluck, 1954: 256]." But then, peace ultimately was made; this demonstrates the lawlessness of feud, as universally defined. Whether a counterkilling led to a feud depended on whether such a murder was negatively or positively sanctioned by the community. In certain villages, "when a life had been paid for a life, peace was made. But when an inferior killed his superior, the latter's relative would not make peace till he had killed two of the other's men. At the peace-making the first was paired with the original victim and for the second the superior's relative paid blood money [Hasluck, 1954: 129]." In this setting, then, feud shades into negatively or positively sanctioned self-help or vengeance, with the ultimate possibility, at times, of compensation.

To restate the analysis so far: Where feud occurs, it is an expression of

---

feuding appears to be correlated with kinship-oriented conflict. Several principles are involved in the way in which such matters will be settled: "Whether or not the aggressors are . . . prepared to pay compensation depends on the structural distance between the adversaries, on their relative strengths, and on the force of administrative invervention. The nature of the wrong also influences the course of events. A minor issue such as stock-theft is less likely to create serious tension than a graver injury such as homicide [Lewis, 1961: 244]." In this segmented society, feud and self-help alternate with (mediated) compensation.

negatively sanctioned self-help or vengeance. For whatever reason it may occur, it is the result of a deed against a person that is not mutually agreed on as "right" by the doer and by the victim.[2] The victim's family retaliates, and this can lead to feud. Thus, feud is negatively sanctioned killing and counterkilling. In this sense, it is negative reciprocity, "a life for a life" (compare the concept of negative reciprocity in Sahlins, 1965: 168–169).[3]

Contract is said to characterize the modern urbanized society (see Maine, 1861: 165; compare Hoebel, 1954: 327–328). Nevertheless, the contract has its counterparts in primitive society, for example, among the Cheyenne of the American Plains, where unwritten "contracts" occur. The primary difference between the Cheyenne contract and that of a modern legal system is that the former is usually in the nature of a negotiated promise: The expectation of fulfillment is more a matter of mutual agreement and societal expectation than court-enforceable order, although for the Cheyenne *repeated* violation of such promises could lead to punitive action on the part of the community. Even though they were unwritten, rules for such behavior were contained in the oral tradition, and what constituted a breach was clear. The compensatory settlements for breaches of such contractual promises were determined among the parties involved, with the approval and consensus of members of the community. Exact amounts of compensation, or "damages," were not set beforehand.

Llewellyn and Hoebel (1941: 127–128) describe such a "trouble-case," involving the nonreturn of a borrowed horse after a year and the resultant spontaneous contractual settlement. In that case, the original owner (Wolf Lies Down) invited the chiefs of his military society (Elk Soldiers) to search for the borrower and to inquire as to his intentions. The borrower subsequently explained his circumstances and offered the return of the horse and an additional one of his own. Wolf Lies Down chose to accept one of the borrower's horses as complete compensation. The Elk Soldier chiefs declared the matter closed. It should also be noted that such a settlement in a society without formal written law, like the

[2]In this context, reference to the offender and the victim in such a community refers also to each party's kin and the community at large. See also Barton (1919: 77). For a discussion of self-help in the context of American society, see Black and Baumgartner (1980).

[3]Additional examples of feud that could move toward sanctioned vengeance (punishment) or compensation are found in such diverse cultures as the hunting-fishing-gathering Yurok Indians of northern California (Spott and Kroeber, 1943: 182–299) and the pastoral Somali (see Lewis, 1961: 64). Examples of the significance of timing—whether a counterkilling is done at once or later in "cold blood"—are found in some Albanian villages (Hasluck, 1954: 224).

| Feud | Negatively sanctioned self-help | Positively sanctioned self-help | Contract | Ordered compensation |

Lawless ————————————————————————————— Lawful

FIGURE 7.1. The evolution of compensation.

Cheyenne, can result, as it did in that instance, in the initiation of a relationship of continuous reciprocity-oriented exchanges, to be described later in the chapter. For example, a result of the preceding Cheyenne trouble-case was that "the chiefs declared, 'Now we have settled this thing. . . . Our society and his shall be comrades. Whenever one of us has a present to give, we shall give it to a member of his soldier society' [Llewellyn and Hoebel, 1941: 128]."

Cases such as the preceding demonstrate the nature of the quasi-contractual agreement among preindustrialized societies. Such promissory contracts have something in common with modern, court-ordered compensation, namely, that violation of the terms of such an agreement can lead to community-initiated punitive or compensatory action.

In the modern court system, with *ordered compensation*, the shift to "contract law" is complete. Rules are based on the individual-oriented rather than on the kin-oriented or locality-based community. Rules and procedures are clearly spelled out, and determinations are based on such laws in connection with written precedent. Adjudication results in enforceable orders.

Figure 7.1 is thus a typology of stages in the evolution of compensation. But can we be more specific about when compensation appears as a sanction and when the law is punitive? The first theory to deal extensively with such a question in evolutionary perspective is found in the work of Emile Durkheim (1893).

The Social Organization of Compensation

Durkheim posits a development over time of repressive to restitutive social sanctions. Such sanctions, in turn, are related to the structure of society. Thus, in simpler societies, social cohesion is based primarily on likenesses across people rather than on the differences inherent in a division of labor. In such a preindustrialized society, the collective whole is placed above any one individual in its importance, and a breach of custom is thus connected with a breach of supernatural forces that stand for the society in its entirety. Punishment, he argues, will tend to be harsh or repressive: "Punishment consists, then, essentially, in a passionate reaction . . . that society exercises through the medium of a body acting upon those of its members who have violated certain rules of conduct [Durkheim, 1893: 96]." He called the system of social integration under these conditions *mechanical solidarity*. In contrast, modern, industrialized social organization is based on organic solidarity; here, human society has developed into a complex, inderdependent entity. Rather than the fusion of many similar parts, the society of persons is seen as complementary: Each individual has a different status and a different role to perform in production, and, as a consequence, the individual becomes increasingly important. The individual contract is given more importance, and one result is that when a breach is committed, the offender is required to restore what was damaged to its former state, that is, to provide compensation (Durkheim, 1893: 226–229).

Several scholars have questioned Durkheim's formulation. A. S. Diamond, for example, in a detailed study of the development of law, seems to say the opposite, namely, that laws involving physical punishment did not develop until after compensation in the history of humankind. For example, he states that "the principle of the *talio* . . . is a late development which appears at a stage shortly before that represented in the Code of Hammurabi where it is at its height. The Eshnunna laws [dating to 200 years before the code of Hammurabi] contain no trace of such a rule; the sanctions for wounds are all 'pecuniary' [1951: 6]." Diamond indicates that the social control of hunters and gatherers—the earliest in time—is the *least* repressive and that such societies have a less developed sense of individual property. Among the "cattle people," material compensation is more common because they have more property (Diamond, 1951: 22). State-ordered punishment such as the *lex talionis* developed still later (Diamond, 1951: 86–103).

In a study that utilized cross-cultural data in the Human Relations Area Files, Schwartz and Miller demonstrate that legal organization is tied in with regularities in societal development: "It may be necessary . . . for a society to accept the principles of mediation and compensation *before* formalized agencies of adjudication and control can be evolved [Schwartz and Miller, 1964: 381]." The findings of this study appear "directly contradictory to Durkheim's major thesis . . . that penal law—the effort of organized society to punish offenses against itself—occurs in societies with the simplest division of labor," and it is further suggested that "the restitutive principle is not contingent on social heterogeneity [Schwartz and Miller, 1964: 388–389; see also Black and Mileski, 1973: 11–12]."

Spitzer has also examined with cross-cultural materials the Durkheimian theory, and also the later elaboration found in Durkheim's "Two Laws of Penal Evolution" (1899–1900), and concludes that the hypotheses are erroneous (1975: 614). Spitzer substitutes a curvilinear development for Durkheim's linear one and brings in two important political and economic variables, which themselves are interrelated. Thus, in comparing "simple egalitarian [reciprocal] societies" with "non-market [redistributive] complex societies" and "established market societies," he finds that the redistributive type contains the most severe sanctions, whereas the reciprocal type as well as the established market societies are more lenient and compensatory. He attributes the decline of material sanctions (as in compensation) and the rise of punitive ones in the Middle Ages to the development of class differentiation and the "inability of lower-class evildoers to pay fines of money." Thus, another important variable related to material sanctions rather than punitive ones may be the absence of "vast disparities in wealth [Spitzer, 1975: 633]."

Posner (1980) also examines economic life in order to explain legal institutions. Like Spitzer, he works with the threefold division of societies into those having "reciprocal exchange," "centralized redistribution," and "market exchange," following the evolutionary sequence of the economist Karl Polanyi (1944). Like Schwartz and Miller and Spitzer, but unlike Durkheim, he sees punitive law as more characteristic of the not-yet-industrialized complex society that began with the "centralized redistribution" phase, in which a central authority collects dues from food producers and redistributes it to the population. For primitive society, Posner posits an earlier phase of "retaliation" or vengeance—which could lead to feud—that "yields in time to a system of compensation (bloodwealth, 'composition,' 'wergelds') paid to the victim or his kin by the injurer or his kin [1980: 43]." He attributes this shift to a compensatory style from the retaliatory one "not to . . . diminishing bloodthirstiness . . . but simply to growing wealth. A system of compensation will not work unless injurers and their kin have a sufficient stock of goods in excess of their subsistence needs to be able to pay compensation for the injuries they inflict on others [Posner, 1980: 43]." Posner gives particular emphasis to *strict liability* in primitive law, that is, the obligation to pay for an injury *regardless of the offender's intentions and guilt or responsibility*. This obligation, as was said earlier, is particularly prominent in cattle-raising tribes, and an additional relevant variable that may explain it is presented in Posner's study: Strict liability is most likely in situations where "the determination of fault is more costly . . . than the determination simply whether the defendant injured the plaintiff [Posner, 1980: 49]."

It now becomes possible to suggest several propositions that may help to explain the development of the compensatory style across societies, in particular, the pure form associated with strict liability:

Proposition I   *The compensatory style is likely to develop only in situations where there is a sufficient accumulation of wealth.*

Proposition II   *The compensatory style is likely to remain dominant only as long as extreme inequalities of wealth do not develop.*

Proposition III   *The compensatory style is likely to be preferred in situations in which the informational cost of determining guilt is substantially higher than the cost of determining that an injury occurred under particular social conditions.*

Proposition IV   *The compensatory style is more likely to be adopted in societies where all parties know the exact liability and where it is established that all liability is ended after the compensation has been given* (see Macaulay and Walster, 1977: 275).

It might be noted that the well-known adage of Henry Sumner Maine that law shifts from "status to contract" has been modified by Hoebel, who observes that primitive man had a form of contract (1954: 127–128, 327–328; see also pages 195–196 earlier in this chapter). It should also be added that "status law" has not disappeared in the industrialized society: Dispute processing can be related to *who* a person is in relation to the rest of the community. Thus, a set of variables that correlate modes of compensation with other aspects of society and culture can supplement or possibly even supplant aspects of the above-described evolutionary sequences.

Modes of Compensation

Table 7.1 posits four modes or subtypes of compensation, presented in a continuum from the most simple social organization to the most complex. Each of these four modes will be described, and then eight variables, which may be related to the predominance of one over another mode in the societies given as examples, will be examined in more detail.

TABLE 7.1.
Modes of Compensation

Mode	1 Prevailing subsistence	2 Economy type	3 Nature of group relationships	4 Prevailing value orientation(s)	5 Group type	6 Main sanctioner and type of sanction	7 Time of compensation	8 Example of mode	9 Example of society
A. Reciprocity oriented	Hunting and gathering; some gardening	Generalized reciprocity	Multiplex	Collateral	Cohesive, with relevant public; Linton's primary group; small face-to-face community	Offender; informal sanction	After settlement; following restitution	Gift exchange and donation	Chippewa, Andamanese, Kalahari, Bushmen
B. Negotiative	Farming and/or herding or industrialized	Balanced reciprocity or market–monetary; unitary value in kind	Simplex or multiplex	Collateral or individualistic	Variable	Both parties; formal or informal sanction	Before settlement	Bargaining; "out-of-court" negotiative settlement	Urban United States, Ndendeuli
C. Mediative–Arbitrative	Farming and/or herding	Unitary value in kind; balanced reciprocity	Simplex and multiplex	Lineal or collateral	Cohesive, but with subgroups	Arbitrator and/or mediating group	At settlement	Strong suggestion or order	Kpelle, Reu'la, Zapotec
D. Adjudicative	Farming or industrialized	Market–monetary or balanced reciprocity	Simplex or multiplex	Lineal or individualistic	Least cohesive	Judge; formal sanction	At settlement	Order; decree	Urban United States

RECIPROCITY-ORIENTED COMPENSATION

Considered in the context of social control, reciprocity is the most marginal mode of compensation, strictly speaking, because it involves continuous, more or less voluntary contributions by each to all, at least by those able to do so, whereas only occasionally does it involve the payment of goods in compensation for a wrong. As Posner (1980) indicates, such an economy was a form of insurance in a hunting-and-gathering society where food storage and redistribution were not possible on a large scale. Where breaches occurred, they could be mended with such informal sanctions as ridicule or avoidance of the offender, and such sanctions were usually sufficient. In the case of more serious breaches, the two parties could eventually meet, and, frequently, the offender would *volunteer* compensation, as in the case of the Cheyenne horse borrower described earlier (for a similar situation among contemporary Chippewa of the North American Great Lakes, see Rohrl, 1981).

NEGOTIATIVE COMPENSATION

The negotiative mode of compensation is rare as a dominant form. Here, two parties negotiate a settlement without bringing in a third, mediative or arbitrative, party. Among the Ndendeuli of Tanzania, two litigants could negotiate a compensatory settlement; in most cases, each would be supported or represented by kinsmen. At times, members of the community served as an audience, or a *moot,* without necessarily having a voice in the decision, which was arrived at by mutual agreement (Gulliver, 1971: chap. 5).

Gulliver has set forth conditions under which successful negotiations take place; in a detailed comparison, he describes common denominators between dyadic, or two-party, dispute processing, which characterizes the negotiative mode among the Arusha of Tanzania, and American labor–management relations (1979: 233–264). In one case involving the Arusha, for instance, the dispute began between two men over their mutual claim to land that rested between their two properties. When neither gave in, negotiation developed, with kinsmen backing up each party. Several secondary issues came in, with claims and counterclaims, ranging from demands of compensation for animals of one party wandering over the property of the other to demands for compensation for an implied supernatural curse. All issues were defined and aired, and in the end each party made compensatory concessions; in addition, the original land that had been under dispute was divided, also with mutual agreement.

An illustrative labor–management dispute has much in common with the preceding example. An agreement on wages was reached primarily through management's use of comparative data of other companies, and management also agreed to a contract stipulation regarding seniority in order to conclude the dispute. In the individualistic American culture, a feeling of hostility prevailed even after the agreement, in contrast with the Arusha, who had a stronger need to maintain harmonious relationships among persons in a common community who knew one another well, who were members of the same age group, and who were also neighbors. "In each case, both parties in their negotiations acknowledged the importance of reaching agreement in their dispute, however pronounced their antagonism [Gulliver, 1979: 262]." That statement summarizes a prerequisite for negotiation, which apparently can take place in many types of culture; however, it usually exists side by side with other modes of compensation, such as the mediative–arbitrative or adjudicative, in case it fails.

MEDIATIVE–ARBITRATIVE COMPENSATION

As Gulliver (1971) indicates, even among such pastoral tribes as the Arusha and the Ndendeuli, where the negotiative mode is highly developed, it does not occur universally. At some point, where resolution does not seem possible, mediators may be called in to participate. But when a third party is called on, it is more as reconciler, a *mediator*, and not as an *arbitrator* with any binding or decisive voice. In any event, the common denominator of the mediative–arbitrative mode is the presence of a third party. Among the Nuer of the Sudan, compensation is normally made among persons of the same community. Among distant peoples, retaliation and feud can arise, but even in such instances compensation—with the help of a third party—may resolve the situation:

> When a man has killed another, he must at once go to a chief. . . . Within the next few months the chief elicits from the slayer's kin that they are prepared to pay compensation to avoid a feud and he persuades the dead man's kin that they ought to accept compensation. The chief then collects the cattle—till recently some forty to fifty beasts—and takes them to the dead man's home, where he performs various sacrifices of cleansing and atonement. Such is the procedure of settling a feud [Evans-Pritchard, 1940: 291].[4]

---

[4]A complete discussion of psychological variables in relation to compensation will not be presented here. However, it has been noted that such tribes as the Nuer are "predominantly pastoral in sentiment [Evans-Pritchard, 1940: 272]." The relation of a Nuer man to his herds of cattle is such that, in many instances, and for many ritual purposes, a certain number of cows are presented from one kin group to another. For example, the "giving" of a spouse from one kin group to another is acknowledged with "bridewealth," a set

The authority of the "leopard-skin chief," who was called on to end a Nuer feud, was more mediative than arbitrative—his ritual authority was used to symbolize approval and acceptance, on both sides, of the offered compensation.

Mediation can at times shade into arbitration, as is found among the Mexican Zapotec. Here, villagers elect a man to mediate disputes, the *presidente*, and while he presides, eliciting the views and feelings of both sides, he assists in a compromise solution. He can also arbitrate and state a required compensation, however, and each side is then expected to accept his decision (Nader, 1972b).

In Lebanese villages, "mayors frequently function as mediators and intermediators speaking on behalf of other parties, exerting social pressure, or tempering violence. . . . The outcome [compensation] is a higher priority than the 'truth' about a particular incident; this is particularly true when personal injury is not an issue for compensation [Witty, 1980: 53]." Thus, in the village of Shehaam, Abraham, a Maronite, discovered one of his sheep was missing. Subhi, a Moslem, reported that a 17-year-old boy who appeared rather impulsive and irresponsible was seen early in the morning with blood on his clothes and carrying a knife. Abraham and Subhi spoke to the boy's father, Aziz, who later questioned the boy, Abdul, while the suspicious visitors were present. No conclusions about guilt were reached; 2 weeks later, however, the Moslem mayor was summoned, and it was agreed that the father would compensate the family of Abraham for the price of the missing sheep. All agreed, and Abraham and Aziz came to an agreement as to the exact sum. "The money was [immediately] produced, between Aziz and his uncle, and handed to Abraham. He thanked them. . . . Coffee was brought out and they all drank, the guests served first. Shortly after, they departed [Witty, 1980: 49–52]."

ADJUDICATIVE COMPENSATION

Adjudication—formal legal procedures involving full-time specialists—characterizes modern, urbanized, industrialized cultures. As indi-

---

number of cattle that passes to the kin group of the bride to acknowledge the transfer of rights over her labor and children to the groom's kin group. Although such exchanges are not in themselves social control, they indicate an aspect of the sociocultural background for the "blood wealth" or "wergeld" tables of exact compensation that are well known among pastoral tribes of Africa and of the Old Testament as well as in early European laws. As a market–monetary system developed, silver and other precious metals were substituted for cattle as payment.

cated in Table 7.1, numerous examples are found in modern America, where compensation is ordered or decreed in courts of law, and this order marks the settlement. The main sanctioner is the judge. In this mode, the society is the least cohesive of the four types. The value orientation is generally individualistic. Particularly in the modern urban setting, the relationships are simplex, that is, with few connecting links among the members. The prevailing subsistence pattern is primarily one of industrialization, and the economy type is market–monetary, although at times it can be a system of balanced reciprocity in which there is a concept of equal values.

It appears, on the basis of the preceding subsections, that a number of independent variables contribute to the prevalence of each mode of compensation. For example, in Columns 1 and 2 of Table 7.1 each subsistence pattern is linked with a characteristic economy type, following the categories of Polanyi (1944), as defined earlier. To those categories a fourth has been added here, namely, the herding or pastoral type. Compensatory social control is the most dominant style in societies that characteristically are large enough so that there is some distance among subgroups yet small enough so there is less cultural distance than in societies where penal law predominates (see Black, 1976: 78–79), and these include many pastoral–herding societies. The four propositions presented earlier fit the conditions in these societies, and it might also be noted that head of livestock lend themselves especially well to clear, unitary values in kind such as compensation typically involves. Most societies contain more than one mode of compensation, however. Table 7.1 therefore deals with ideal types, on the assumption that, in conjunction with a cluster of the variables listed in Columns 1–8, one or another mode shown in the left-hand column will assume more importance.

Column 3 classifies group relationships, following Gluckman (1955: 1–21). Although that classification cannot in itself predict whether a mode will be negotiative, mediative–arbitrative, or adjudicative, it can be seen as one of the eight variables that, taken together, can contribute to predicting a mode of compensation. In other words, if five or six columns follow a pattern that is consistent with a row shown across Column A, B, C, or D, it would indicate a likelihood of predominance for the mode indicated. One variable alone is not necessarily diagnostic; however, consistency in a cluster of variables could be indicative. Furthermore, the eight variables are by no means exhaustive. They are merely an indication of one way in which to proceed with a theory of compensation.

Column 4, prevailing value orientations, reflects Variables 1, 2, and 3 (see Kluckhohn and Strodtbeck 1961; Rohrl, 1981). The value orientations shown suggest how people in a given society characteristically relate to other persons. The individualistic orientation characterizes members of a modern industrialized society such as the United States, in which each individual, at least theoretically, has an equal and independent voice and does not necessarily seek consensus. The collateral orientation characterizes many American Indian societies and involves a need for consensus, in which nearly every member voices agreement. The lineal orientation involves respect for elders and for authority figures in government and gives such figures much power in social control. Columns 5–9 are self-explanatory.

ADDITIONAL REMARKS

It should be restated here that Table 7.1 represents a continuum with clusters of indexes that would incline a group toward one or another mode of compensatory settlement. Within one culture—in particular, the large, urban, industrialized society—all modes exist, depending on region, situation, context, relationship of litigants, type of case, and other variables that deserve further study. Two matters not included in Table 7.1 are psychological variables and the question of responsibility versus liability. Gibbs's (1972) pioneering study of the Kpelle of Liberia indicates that certain patterns of compensation and of liability are related to sociopsychological aspects of the culture. For example, in Kpelle divorces, the plaintiff (usually a woman) is considered liable, in the sense that she is required to return the bridewealth paid to her family at marriage. Indeed, the commencement of such suits is phrased in a traditional way that includes her offer to return the bridewealth. Gibbs suggests that our judicial ideas of guilt or innocence are not adequate to explain Kpelle law. The Kpelle method of handling disputes reveals an androcentric bias, a psychological factor that emphasizes male domination, present not only as a structural fact in the culture but also as a psychological factor among Kpelle individuals. As Gibbs indicates, such psychological variables still require further study in order better to understand legal processes.

In order to clarify such determinations of innocence or guilt, Koch reminds us that in our culture responsibility, as "guilt," or "subjective moral fault," is usually equated with liability, or jural obligation, even though the two notions are not actually the same:

> A logical distinction exists between *responsibility*, or subjective moral fault or mental disposition, and *liability*, as a jural obligation to suffer the consequences of an injurious action or a breach of duty. Consequently, some rules must define a party's

guilt for damaging another party's reputation, health, or property, and other rules must translate a party's responsibility into its own or other's liability to compensate the injured party and/or to suffer punishment [Koch, 1977: 314].

Koch thus reminds us that the two concepts are separable; whether and how they coincide varies from society to society and is a "core issue in any debate about the purpose and reason of law enforcement [Koch, 1977: 314]." It should also be recognized as a core issue in a theory of compensation.

A Note on International Compensation

International law, a recent concept in the history of cultures, raises questions of direction and development in compensatory social control. The United Nations, although a representative association, has no binding force over modern nations. Thus, policies are developed in many cases in a manner resembling tribal conflict management. For example, for a long time the neighbors in the Middle East, Israel and Egypt, were dealing with a Nuer-type "leopard-skin chief" in the person of United States Secretary of State Henry Kissinger, who acted as a mediator. At the time of this writing, however, Ndendeuli-style negotiation continues between the two nations. Moreover, a compensatory issue is involved, namely, return of certain territory captured during wars.

Anthony D'Amato examined some aspects of the June 1981 Israeli attack on Iraqi nuclear facilities. Questions of responsibility and liability were raised. He suggested that regardless of which party was more or less guilty, some compensation could be arranged. Israel could compensate Iraq for the nuclear reactor without any admission of guilt. "An analogy is found in the American law of eminent domain as well as the international law of expropriation; the government may take away private property for a public purpose but it nevertheless must award compensation to the person whose property was taken. The primary act is not illegal even though compensation must be paid [1981]." At the same time, even if Israel were deemed not guilty, or less guilty, it would not set a precedent, let alone a rule, that "any nation can pre-empt the nuclear capacity of its neighbor." Thus, "international law must be rethought not as a collection of dos and don'ts, but as a purposive system designed to ensure peace and fundamental human values [D'Amato, 1981]."

Shortly after this opinion was printed, the United Nations General Assembly voted to reprimand Israel's action without requiring compensation. Even though the compensatory solution suggested by Professor D'Amato did not take place, it is significant that he raised the question of compensation in lieu of assigning guilt.. That this suggestion was raised and printed may indicate that the potential for such a compensatory mode is present within the international culture and its value systems (see Hsu, 1963). It is possible that policies and modes of compensation should, indeed, precede steps toward defining policy and adjudicatory structures and procedures among nations: Compensation preceded modern law in the history of cultures, and negotiation, in the broad spectrum or continuum described by Gulliver (1977), is effective in situations where the two parties concur that any other "solution" would be at too great a cost. Although the trend of international law, as well as of national laws, remains to be seen, it seems clear that theoretical knowledge of the sociocultural variables that accompany each type of social control mechanism could assist in effectuating settlement in certain cases (see Schwartz and Miller, 1964: 381; Witty, 1980).

In summary, the concept of compensation has a number of dominant ways of finding expression within systems of social control. Such ways or modes have correlates in the sociocultural system. It remains for future research to determine more precisely the significant conditions or independent variables that are related to one or another mode of compensation.

ACKNOWLEDGMENTS

I would like to express appreciation to Donald Black for the initial inspiration in his work as well as his comments on earlier drafts and to E. Adamson Hoebel, David E. Aaronson, James L. Wood, Jr., Daniel D. Whitney, Mohammed El-Asal, Rabbi T. Kaplan, George Kirkpatrick, Amyra Grossbard-Schechtman and Mark Cooney for discussions and comments at various phases of the manuscript. Of course, I claim responsibility for the final form. Assigned time for research within the College of Arts and Letters and the Department of Anthropology, San Diego State University, freed me for writing.

References

Aaronson, David E., Bert H. Hoff, Peter Jaszi, Nicholas N. Kittrie, and David Saari
    1977   The New Justice: Alternatives to Conventional Criminal Adjudication. Washington, D.C.: U.S. Government Printing Office.
Barton, Roy
    1919   Ifugao Law. Berkeley, Calif.: University of California Press, 1969.
Black, Donald
    1976   The Behavior of Law. New York: Academic Press.

Black, Donald, and M. P. Baumgartner
  1980   "On self-help in modern society." Pages 193–208 in *The Manners and Customs of the Police*, by Donald Black. New York: Academic Press.
Black, Donald, and Maureen Mileski
  1973   "Introduction." Pages 1–14 in *The Social Organization of Law*, edited by Donald Black and Maureen Mileski. New York: Seminar Press.
Clark, Walter van Tilburg
  1970   *The Ox-Bow Incident*. New York: The Press of the Readers Club.
D'Amato, Anthony
  1981   "Imagining a judgment in the case of Iraq vs. Israel." *Washington Star* (June 15): editorial page.
Diamond, Arthur S.
  1951   *The Evolution of Law and Order*. London: Watts Publishing Company.
  1971   *Primitive Law, Past and Present*. London: Methuen.
Durkheim, Emile
  1893   *The Division of Labor in Society*. Glencoe, Ill.: Free Press, 1933.
  1899– "Two laws of penal evolution." *University of Cincinnati Law Review* 38 (1969):
  1900   32–60
Epstein, A. L.
  1968   "Sanction." Pages 1–5 in *International Encyclopedia of the Social Sciences*, vol. 14. New York: Macmillan.
Evans-Pritchard, E. E.
  1940   "The Nuer of the southern Sudan." Pages 272–296 in *African Political Systems*, edited by M. Fortes and E. E. Evans-Pritchard. London: Oxford University Press.
  1941   *The Nuer*. London: Clarendon Press.
  1952   "Introduction." Pages v–x in *The Gift: Forms and Functions of Exchange in Archaic Societies*, by Marcel Mauss. New York: W. W. Norton, 1967.
Gibbs, James L.
  1972   "Law and personality: Signposts for a new direction." Pages 178–207 in *Law in Culture and Society*, edited by Laura Nader. Chicago: Aldine Press.
Gluckman, Max
  1955   *The Judicial Process among the Barotse of Northern Rhodesia*. Manchester: Manchester University Press.
Goodenough, Ward H.
  1966   *Property, Kin, and Community on Truk*. Hamden: Archon Books.
Gravel, Pierre Bettez
  1967   "The transfer of cows in Gisaka (Rwanda): A mechanism for recording social relationships." *American Anthropologist* 69: 322–331.
Gulliver, Phillip H.
  1971   *Neighbours and Networks: The Idiom of Kinship in Social Action among the Ndendeuli of Tanzania*. Berkeley, Calif.: University of California Press.
  1977   "On mediators." Pages 15–52 in *Social Anthropology and Law*, A.S.A. Monograph 14, edited by Ian Hamnett. London: Academic Press.
  1979   *Disputes and Negotiations*. New York: Academic Press.
Hasluck, Margaret
  1954   *The Unwritten Law in Albania*. Cambridge: Cambridge University Press.
Hoebel, E. Adamson
  1954   *The Law of Primitive Man: A Study in Comparative Legal Dynamics*. Cambridge, Mass.: Harvard University Press.

1972   *Anthropology: The Study of Man.* New York: McGraw-Hill.
1973   "Feud: Concept, reality and method in the study of primitive law." Pages 1–15 in *Essays on Modernization of Underdeveloped Societies,* vol. 1, edited by A. R. Desai. Bombay: Thacker.
Howell, P. P.
1954   *A Manual of Nuer Law.* London: Oxford University Press.
Hsu, Francis L. K.
1963   *Clan, Caste, and Club.* Princeton, N.J.: D. Van Nostrand.
Kluckhohn, Florence, and Fred Strodtbeck
1961   *Variations in Value Orientations.* Evanston, Ill.: Row Peterson.
Koch, Klaus-Friedrich
1977   "The anthropology of law and order." Pages 300–318 in *Horizons on Anthropology: Second Edition,* edited by Sol Tax and Leslie G. Freeman. Chicago: Aldine Press.
Lewis, I. M.
1961   *A Pastoral Democracy: A Study of Pastoralism and Politics among the Northern Somali of the Horn of Africa.* London: Oxford University Press.
Llewellyn, Karl N., and E. Adamson Hoebel
1941   *The Cheyenne Way: Conflict and Case Law in Primitive Jurisprudence.* Norman, Okla.: University of Oklahoma Press, 1973.
Lowie, Robert H.
1947   *Primitive Society.* New York: Liveright.
Macaulay, Stewart, and Elaine Walster
1977   "Legal structures and restoring equity." Pages 269–276 in *Law, Justice, and the Individual in Society,* edited by June Louin Tapp and Felice J. Levine. New York: Holt, Rinehart and Winston.
Maine, Henry Sumner
1861   *Ancient Law.* London: J. Murray, 1906.
Malinowski, Bronislaw
1926   *Crime and Custom in Savage Society.* London: G. Routledge and Sons, 1932.
Mauss, Marcel
1952   *The Gift: Forms and Functions of Exchange in Archaic Societies.* New York: W. W. Norton, 1967.
Merriam-Webster
1977   *Webster's New Collegiate Dictionary.* Springfield, Mass.: Merriam.
Nader, Laura
1972a   "Introduction." Pages 1–10 in *Law in Culture and Society,* edited by Laura Nader. Chicago: Aldine Press.
1972b   "Styles of court procedure: To make the balance," Pages 69–91 in *Law in Culture and Society,* edited by Laura Nader. Chicago: Aldine Press.
O'Connell, John F.
1977   *Remedies.* St. Paul, Minn.: West Publishing Company.
Polanyi, Karl
1944   *The Great Transformation.* New York: Farrar and Rinehart.
Posner, Richard A.
1980   "A theory of primitive society with special reference to law." *The Journal of Law and Economics* 23: 1–53.
Redfield, Robert
1955   *The Little Community.* Chicago: University of Chicago Press.

Rohrl, Vivian J.
    1981   "A Chippewa trouble-case: Toward an expanded model of conflict resolution."
            Pages 57–66 in *The Anthropology of Law: New Developments in Teaching and Ap-*
            plication, edited by Vivian J. Rohrl. Special issue of *American Behavioral Scientist*
            25(1).
Sahlins, Marshall D.
    1965   "On the sociology of primitive exchange." Pages 139–236 in *The Relevance of*
            Models for Social Anthropology. London: Tavistock.
Schwartz, Richard D., and James C. Miller
    1964   "Legal evolution and societal complexity." *American Journal of Sociology* 70:
            159–169.
Spitzer, Steven
    1975   "Punishment and social organization: A study of Durkheim's theory of penal
            evolution." *Law and Society Review* 9: 613–635.
Spott, Robert, and Alfred L. Kroeber
    1943   *Yurok Narratives.* Berkeley, Calif.: University of California Press.
Tönnies, Ferdinand
    1887   *Fundamental Concepts of Sociology (Gemeinschaft und Gesellschaft).* New York:
            American Book Company, 1940.
Weber, Max
    1904   *The Protestant Ethic and the Spirit of Capitalism.* New York: Charles Scribner's
            Sons, 1958.
Witty, Cathie J.
    1980   *Mediation and Society: Conflict Management in Lebanon.* New York: Academic
            Press.

8

Therapy and Social Solidarity[*]

ALLAN V. HORWITZ

In *The Division of Labor in Society,* Emile Durkheim (1893) developed the thesis that types of social control systems reproduce the principal forms of social solidarity. Durkheim predicted that societies based on mechanical solidarity, in which each member is similar to the others, develop repressive forms of social control. In repressive control, suffering is imposed on wrongdoers to deprive them of something of value such as money, liberty, honor, or life. On the other hand, societies held together by organic solidarity, marked by a differentiation of individuals, develop restitutive forms of social control. In restitutive control, wrongdoers are forced to compensate their victims for the harm that they have done. Although Durkheim's association of repressive control with simple societies and restitutive control with complex ones has proven to be incorrect (Schwartz and Miller, 1964; Chambliss and Seidman, 1971: chap. 3; Spitzer, 1975; Black, 1976: chap. 3), his central contribution was to ground the study of social control in the nature of social relationships.

Durkheim sharply differentiated repressive and restitutive styles of social control, but in a broader sense both are coercive forms of social

---

[*]An expansion of the approach in the present chapter appears in my recent book, *The Social Control of Mental Illness* (1982).

TOWARD A GENERAL THEORY OF SOCIAL CONTROL
Volume 1: Fundamentals

control that are imposed on offenders. In both styles, parties to a dispute via against each other, there is a winner and a loser, and a decision is imposed on the parties regardless of their wishes (Black, 1976: 4). In addition, both styles are associated with the law of the state, with the criminal law illustrating the repressive style and parts of the civil law such as contracts and torts representing the restitutive style. Most sociological studies in the area of social control focus on these coercive styles of social control.

In contrast, most anthropologists who have studied social control have emphasized conciliatory styles of social control (Gluckman, 1967; Nader, 1969; Black and Mileski, 1973). Conciliatory social control uses mechanisms of dispute processing such as mediation and negotiation that do not impose decisions on disputants but rely on solutions cooperatively agreed on by all parties (Black, 1976: 5). Unlike coercive forms of social control, there are no winners or losers, but each party to the dispute "gives a little and gets a little" in the interest of compromise and consensus (Nader, 1969). The goal in conciliatory control is not the punishment of offenders but the attainment of social harmony. Coercive styles of social control are usually embedded in legal systems and are found when disputes arise among strangers, whereas conciliatory styles of social control are commonly found in informal settings when disputes arise among intimates (Black, 1976: 47).

Despite their differences, one factor shared by coercive and conciliatory styles of social control is that they are directed at the control of *conduct*. Both are used only after some behavioral deviation has occurred, and both are satisfied when conformity in the outwardly visible conduct of the offenders has been achieved. Indeed, the notion of social control itself is usually defined as control over nonconforming behavior rather than control over nonobservable states of individual personality (e.g., Clark and Gibbs, 1965; Toby, 1973; Gibbs, 1977). For example, in his influential work *A Theory of Social Control* (1954), Richard LaPiere states that "the proper concern of social control is with how persons act overtly rather than with their private selves [p. 56]." In this view, whatever is open to public scrutiny is subject to social control, whereas whatever is within the "inner self" is solely of private concern and not subject to social control.

The unfortunate consequence of identifying the study of social control with the control of overt conduct has been the neglect of the study of the social control of personality systems. With a few exceptions (e.g., Parsons, 1951: chap. 6), sociologists have been unconcerned with the social control of personality systems and, by default, have left the field to psychiatrists and psychologists, who are unconcerned with sociological questions regarding this topic. Yet, although a general sociological theory of therapeutic social control does not exist, there is no reason why the control of personalities is any less important a topic for sociological exploration than the control of conduct.

Following Donald Black (1976), I assume that the central task of a general theory of psychotherapy is to use characteristics of the social system to predict variations in therapeutic control systems across social space and time. The first requirement of such a theory is that it be grounded in an adequate concept of therapeutic social control. Like all concepts, a concept of therapeutic control is not true or false but only more or less useful for the purpose at hand (Brodbeck, 1968). For the purpose of developing a general theory of therapeutic control, the concept of psychotherapy must not be limited to the particular techniques called psychotherapy in contemporary Western culture but must encompass all generically similar techniques in a broad cross-cultural perspective. Second, I limit the term *psychotherapy* to techniques that attempt to change *personalities*, not bodies, and will not consider any types of physical therapies. In addition, in order to keep the subject matter manageable, the concept must be limited to *intentional* efforts at social control. I shall not, therefore, be concerned with broader social and cultural arrangements that may be "therapeutic" in their effects (see, e.g., Parsons, 1951; Rieff, 1966). Finally, to keep therapeutic control from encompassing the field of socialization in general, I shall be concerned only with intentional efforts to control *deviant* or undesirable states of mind.

The purpose of the typology in Figure 8.1 is not to construct an exhaustive grouping of social control systems but to illustrate the distinctive aspects of psychotherapeutic social control. I define *therapeutic social control* as the *persuasive social control of the personality.* As Figure 8.1 indicates, this definition stems from dividing styles of social control along two dimensions: whether the control is coercive or persuasive and

Focus of control effort	Relationship between parties: Coercive	Relationship between parties: Persuasive
Conduct	Adjudicatory	Conciliatory
Personality	Indoctrinatory	Therapeutic

FIGURE 8.1. Styles of social control systems.

whether it is directed at changing conduct or the personality. The first dimension involves the voluntariness of the control: Is it imposed on parties regardless of their wishes, or is a solution reached through persuasive means? Whenever coercive efforts to change conduct are imposed by third parties and are ultimately backed by coercive force, the style of social control is *adjudicatory* (Weber, 1925; Felstiner, 1975). Adjudicatory control encompasses both the repressive and restitutive styles of social control. When persuasive means are used to secure conformity in conduct, as in mediation or negotiation, a *conciliatory* style of social control is present (Black, 1976). There are analogies to both adjudicatory and conciliatory styles of social control in the response to mental illness. Sometimes coercive techniques, such as electric shock, the forced administration of drugs, operations such as lobotomies, or physical restraint are used as means of control. None requires the cooperation of patients, and all can be imposed on them against their will. On the other hand, some techniques that operate directly on the body are administered to willing patients, such as the voluntary taking of medication. In both styles, the control effort acts directly on the physical organism and does not use symbolic means to change the personality. Hence, they are not considered to be instances of *psychotherapy*, as the term is used in this chapter, and I shall not discuss these styles here.

The second dimension that distinguishes styles of social control is their focus: Is the control effort directed at changing the outward conduct of individuals, or at their personalities? Both adjudicatory and conciliatory social control accomplish their purposes through efforts to change overt conduct. Social control can also attempt to change motives, ideas, values, emotions, meaning systems, and the like. I use the term *personality* in its broadest sense to refer to all of these states that are defined as existing "inside" of the individual. For my purposes, the terms *mind, self, identity,* or *soul,* are interchangeable with the term *personality,* and I shall sometimes use them as such.

There is no sharp distinction between the social control of conduct and of personality. When the control effort is directed at the personality, the ultimate goal may be to change the conduct of the deviant. This goal is always achieved through changing the personality, however. Similarly, adjudicatory and conciliatory control may alter the personality, but they do this through the mechanism of changing conduct. In the response to mental illness, there is a central difference between the manipulation of the body and of the mind. When techniques are directed at changing the body, the patient need not participate actively in the change effort or even be conscious of the effort at all. In contrast, when the focus is on the personality, the patient must participate actively if the personality can be altered. Although the distinction between the social control of conduct and of personality should not be overemphasized, it is nevertheless a useful one.

When the distinction between coercive and persuasive styles of social control is applied to the control of personalities, two additional styles of control emerge, the *indoctrinatory* and the *therapeutic*. Indoctrinatory social control refers to the coercive control of the personality. It occurs whenever controllers attempt to change the attitudes, beliefs, motivations, and so on, of unwilling deviants. Religious inquisitions (Ladurie, 1978), brainwashing (Frank, 1973: chap. 4), and political indoctrination (Parsons, 1942) are instances of indoctrinatory social control. In addition, all contemporary "rehabilitation" programs that attempt to change the personalities of unwilling deviants such as delinquents, criminals, drug addicts, and alcoholics are forms of indoctrinatory, rather than of therapeutic, control. Although these programs are commonly associated with the rise of the "therapeutic" state (Kittrie, 1971), my definition views any involuntary therapy as a contradiction in terms.

There are a number of inherent differences between coercive and persuasive styles of personality change that should keep these two styles from being assimilated into the same category of social control. As I indicate later, different variables predict these two styles, so it is not possible to develop a single theory of them. In addition, the dynamics of indoctrinatory control are very different from those of therapeutic control. Changes in conduct can be imposed on individuals regardless of their wishes, but coercive changes in personality are more difficult to accomplish. The personality is, by definition, not observable to control agents, so it is always possible for deviants inwardly to resist control efforts while outwardly conforming to them. In addition, if deviants resist the attempts of controllers to change their personalities, there is little controllers can do except to resort to coercive control over conduct. With some exceptions, such as certain forms of drug treatment, changes in personality cannot be coerced but require cooperation between controllers and deviants. Because controllers find it extremely difficult to produce changes in the personalities of unwilling deviants, there is a tendency for coercive attempts to change personalities to become coercive attempts to change behavior, so pure cases of indoctrinatory social control are rare. Therefore, I reserve the label *therapeutic* for persuasive attempts to change the personality. This use maintains both the spirit of the word and the scientific necessity to create homogeneous categories. Although indoctrinatory social control is almost as neglected an area of study as is therapeutic social control, its unique dynamics require separate consideration, and I shall not deal with it in this chapter.

Several elements distinguish psychotherapy from other forms of social control. First, because it is directed at changing personality systems,
therapeutic social control can occur only through the manipulation of
symbols. Therapeutic control attempts to change attitudes and beliefs so
that patients are persuaded to think and feel differently than they did in
the past. Changes in the self can come about only when the therapeutic
techniques are *meaningful* to the individual undergoing the change attempt. This means that social control must rely mainly on the power of
language to achieve conformity. Words, rather than force, are the major
mechanism of social control (Entralgo, 1970). Although the social control
of behavior need not be understood by deviants, changes in their personalities can be accomplished only through the use of cultural symbols.

A second aspect of therapeutic social control is that the seeker of
therapy must believe in the efficacy of the therapeutic technique (Frank,
1973). Because the symbolic reorganization of the personality is impossible without belief, all schools of therapy find it impossible to cure someone who is skeptical about the efficacy of the particular therapeutic
orientation. Hence, the practitioners of therapy must be people who are
able to mobilize the belief necessary for effective therapy. The association of formal therapeutic agents with medical and religious roles in a
wide variety of social settings is understandable in light of this fact, for
in all groups medical and religious healers occupy roles that mobilize
symbolic commitments (Parsons, 1942).

A third element of therapeutic social control is that a relationship of
trust must be established between patients and therapists (Parsons,
1942; Frank, 1973). Because therapeutic control is not backed by coercive
sanctions, patients will accept therapists' authority only if they trust
their therapists. Without the condition of trust, patients would not provide therapists access to the inner thoughts, feelings, and emotions that
are the object of the control effort. If patients do not trust their therapists
and fear sanctions for revealing their personalities, they can simply refuse to engage in the therapeutic effort, rendering therapeutic control
inoperative. Because of its use of language and need for belief and trust,
therapeutic control can occur only when seekers and providers of therapy share a common symbolic universe. It also sets therapeutic control
apart from other forms of social control that can, and usually do, occur
across wide social distances (Black, 1976: chap. 2). Another implication
of the reliance of therapeutic control on symbolic systems is the inability
of this style of control to deal with severe psychotics who, by definition,
do not share the symbolic system of the other members of the society.
Hence, therapeutic control should not be identified with the social control of severe mental illness, because this form of control is incapable of

bridging wide differences in symbolic meaning systems (compare Laing, 1967). Unlike other forms of social control, therapeutic control is intrinsically connected to cultural systems of meaning.

In this chapter I begin to develop a general theory of therapeutic social control. This theory uses variations in social and cultural systems to predict variations in the nature of therapeutic control. Systems of psychotherapy reflect the nature of social relationships. In addition, a general theory of therapeutic control should predict the style of psychotherapy within a broad range of cross-cultural and historical settings. To outline such a theory in the space of a chapter requires considerable oversimplification. Nevertheless, I hope the general nature of this chapter can serve as a useful corrective to the narrow empirical base of most previous work on the subject.

Toward a Theory of Therapeutic Social Control

Most previous work about psychotherapy does not provide a strong base for the development of a general sociological theory of therapeutic social control. For example, traditional histories of psychiatry usually adopt an evolutionary view of the subject (e.g., Zilboorg, 1941; Ackerknecht, 1959; Alexander and Selesnick, 1966). Psychotherapy is viewed as a branch of medicine, and the therapeutic techniques developed prior to the twentieth century are seen as inferior to the scientific psychiatry that has developed in this century. Modern styles of therapy are contrasted to the "demonological" explanations of mental illness that prevailed until recent times, and Freud is credited as the first major figure who "introduced a sound and scientific kind of psychological reasoning that did not appear to threaten medicine with relapse into its magical and animistic origins [Alexander and Selesnick, 1966: 23]." In this view, modern techniques that find the cause of personality problems within individual experience represent scientific advances over previous styles of therapy that relied on religious, magical, or demonological explanations.

Most sociologists have accepted the distinction between modern scientific therapies and alternative therapeutic styles. The bulk of sociological work has focused on the attitudes of the different social classes toward therapy (e.g., Hollingshead and Redlich, 1958; Suchman, 1965; Gove and Howell, 1974). Lower- and working-class individuals are viewed as relying on superstitious or physical explanations of personality problems while they reject insight-oriented therapies. Because of the allegedly inferior knowledge of these social classes regarding the causes of personality problems, "the obvious, but difficult answer to this problem lies in the development of a greater congruence between modern scientific medical and public health practice and the needs of a still largely popular or folk-oriented public [Suchman, 1965: 14]." In contrast, the upper and middle classes have more scientific and sophisticated views of mental illness and are better able "correctly [to] identify" the causes and nature of personality problems because of their greater knowledge and sociocultural value systems (Hollingshead and Redlich, 1958: 177).

With few differences, sociologists' portrayals of the values of the working and lower classes reflect the views of medical historians regarding pre-twentieth-century therapies, whereas the attributed values of the middle and upper classes correspond to modern scientific therapies. Both bodies of literature accept modern analytic techniques of modern psychiatry as more scientific and "better" than alternative folk belief systems. Moreover, neither considers that both modern and folk styles of therapy may represent alternative forms of therapeutic styles that reflect different underlying forms of social experience.

Two major attempts to view therapeutic control as a symbolic system rather than as an objective science are found in the works of Jerome Frank (1973) and Talcott Parsons (1942; 1951: chap. 6). Frank's broad comparative survey of therapeutic techniques locates the central aspect of therapeutic healing in the ability of therapists to tie sufferers' experiences to the communal symbols of the group. Various therapies are more or less effective not through being scientific or unscientific but through the efficacy with which they can arouse expectations of help. For Parsons (1942), the essence of therapy lies in the degree of group support, the permissiveness to reveal true feelings, and the denial of reciprocity and manipulation of rewards by the therapist. Because therapeutic control is not backed by coercive sanctions, the therapist must assume a cultural role that maximizes the trust placed in its occupant. Neither Frank nor Parsons, however, provides a *theory* of therapeutic control that allows the prediction of variations in the nature of therapy from the nature of the social group. Rather, Frank is concerned with the conditions leading to the effectiveness of therapeutic techniques, and Parsons, with defining what therapy is and not the conditions under which it occurs.

A more adequate attempt to link variations in the style of therapy to variations in cultural systems is found in Philip Rieff's work, *The Triumph of the Therapeutic* (1966). Rieff distinguishes two major styles of therapeutic control: commitment and analytic therapies. Whenever the common culture is strong, commitment therapies develop. These therapies, through the presence of healers who represent the group, serve to tie sufferers to the common symbolic system of the community. According to Rieff, until the nineteenth century all therapies were commitment therapies because cultural systems were strong. The rise of analytic therapies in Freud and his followers was a response to the decline of a common symbolic culture in the West. Analytic therapies aim to increase the range of individual choice and to expand self-awareness rather than to integrate the individual into the community. No longer finding meaning in communal belief systems, Western men and women find symbolic meaning within their personal experiences.

Rieff's work goes beyond other studies of therapeutic control in its use of cultural systems as predictive of different styles of psychotherapy. Even so, it is too limited to serve as a general theory of therapeutic social control. Rieff examines only the nature of cultural systems and ignores the structural factors that are associated with symbolic systems. In addition, his work examines only the last century of Western culture, and he provides no examples of therapies in other historical and cultural contexts. Even within modern society, Rieff is concerned only with types of therapy that appeal to the intellectual elite rather than with a broader range of therapeutic styles. Nevertheless, his work provides invaluable insights into the cultural experiences that have led to the emergence of the analytic style of therapy.

Rieff's distinction between commitment and analytic therapies provides a basis for distinguishing two major styles of therapeutic control. Because his commitment style is tied to belief in religious systems of meaning and his analytic style to psychoanalytic theory, however, these labels are too narrow for a more general theory of therapeutic social control. Instead, I shall use the term *communal* to refer to therapies that bind the individual to the group and the term *individualistic* to refer to therapies that promote the independence of the person. My central thesis is that *the style of therapeutic social control found in a group reflects its major form of social solidarity.* Communal therapies emerge in groups that grip each member in a tight network of social relationships and bind them to communal purposes. In contrast, individualistic therapies arise when people are freed from group ties and the autonomy of the individual becomes the highest value of the group. When the group is communal, therapeutic control deemphasizes the relevance of individual motivation and promotes strong common symbols, the likeness of the self to others, and ties between the individual and the group. On the other hand, in the individualistic group, therapeutic control focuses on the inner experience of the person, stresses the uniqueness of the self, and enhances self-awareness and adaptability. In each case, the social control of the personality corresponds to the nature of social relationships in the group.

In general, the distinction between communal and individualistic forms of social solidarity corresponds to many of the most common typologies in social science including mechanical and organic solidarity (Durkheim, 1893), *Gemeinschaft* and *Gesellschaft* (Tönnies, 1887), folk and urban (Redfield, 1947), and status and contract relationships (Maine, 1861). In contrast to these distinctions, however, I do not view communal and individualistic groups from an evolutionary perspective. Although individualistic societies are almost exclusively limited to the modern West, all modern societies have some pockets of cohesiveness such as some urban ethnic communities and some small towns. In addition, some contemporary societies, such as the People's Republic of China, are purposely organized around communal principles. The potential power of a theory of therapeutic control based on forms of social solidarity is that it predicts that similar styles of psychotherapy will arise whenever similar styles of social solidarity exist, despite divergences in the historical context.

There is both a structural and a cultural aspect to the distinction between communal and individualistic forms of social solidarity. *Culture* refers to the system of meaning and symbols that interpret experience and guide social action, whereas *structure* refers to the patterned network of social relationships between people (Geertz, 1973: 144–145).

In the social structure of the communal group, every member of the group knows the others, so that interaction occurs within the same interlocking network of relationships (Bott, 1957). Relationships tend to be multiplex, with persons bound together in a number of different ways, rather than only for a single purpose (Gluckman, 1967: 19–20). Geographic and social mobility is low, and individuals are likely to spend their entire lives among the same interlocking groups of kin, friends, and neighbors. The cultural system of communal groups emphasizes standardized and formal modes of expression that are used by all members of the group with little variation in individual meaning (Douglas, 1973). Group cohesion is high, and the subordination of the individual to the demands of the group is stressed. Communal groups have been by far the most common form of social experience, with the only major exception being modern Western societies and their immediate precursors.

The individualistic group features fewer ties between its members than does the communal group. Each individual interacts with many different people, most of whom do not know the others. Relationships are typically uniplex, serving one particular interest, and individuals have few encompassing relationships with other people (Gluckman,

1967: 19–20). Geographic and social mobility is high, serving to break established group ties and to make most relationships transitory rather than permanent. Individuals and nuclear families become detached from broader structural ties and become relatively separate and autonomous (Bott, 1957). Society is viewed as an aggregate of separate individuals, each of whom pursues his or her particular interests. The individual stands at the center of group life with individualism as the reigning cultural principle. Symbolic systems emphasize the expression of individual meaning and denigrate the use of standardized expressions (Douglas, 1973). The structure and culture of the group reflect a form of social experience stemming from the association of separate individuals.

Communal and individualistic groups produce different general styles of social control (see generally Black, 1976: chap. 3). Social control is communal groups emphasizes the promotion of group cohesion and serves to reinforce the ties between group members (Gluckman, 1967). The emergence of individuality represents a threat to such groups, and many control mechanisms such as gossip and mockery exist to subordinate the individual to the group (Fernandez, 1978). Tightly knit social networks in modern urban societies also illustrate these principles (Bott, 1957; Laumann, 1973). When members of the network are in constant and close contact with one another, normative consensus arises and strong pressure can be exerted on each member to conform to group norms. In addition, because members interact with one another in a number of different contexts, it is more difficult for an individual in a communal structure to withdraw from participation in group activities. Therefore, when deviance arises, the group can react strongly to incorporate the deviant back into it. Research on small groups also shows that communal groups exert more pressure on their members to conform than do individualistic groups (Laumann, 1973: 115). In general, the greater the extent to which individuals are encapsulated by the group, the greater is the pressure to conform to group norms.

In contrast, when the group is individualistic, most of the persons an individual knows do not interact with one another. Social control in such a situation becomes more fragmented and less consistent (Bott, 1957). Diverse norms emerge, and more variation in individual behavior becomes possible. Each individual becomes unique as he or she is involved in a different web of interpersonal relationships (Simmel, 1908). Individuals who are able to adapt to diverse situations and transitory relationships are functional in this situation (Lofland, 1969). A heightened emphasis on individual uniqueness accompanies the weakening of pressures to conform to group norms.

The form of social solidarity should also predict the social control of the personality. My central thesis is that when the social group grips its members in tight communal bonds, therapeutic social control submerges the personality into the group. In contrast, when the grip of the social group is relaxed, therapeutic social control enhances the autonomy of the personality. Durkheim (1893: 130) anticipated this thesis in his discussion of personalities in societies marked by mechanical and organic solidarities:

> Solidarity which comes from likenesses is at its maximum when the collective conscience completely envelops our whole conscience and coincides in all points with it. But, at that moment, our individuality is nil. It can be born only if the community takes smaller toll of us. . . . We cannot, at one and the same time, develop ourselves in two opposite senses. If we have a lively desire to think and act for ourselves, we cannot be strongly inclined to think and act as others do. If our ideal is to present a singular and personal appearance, we do not want to resemble everybody else. Moreover, at the moment when this solidarity exercises its force, our personality vanishes . . . for we are no longer ourselves, but the collective life.

Therapeutic social control in communal groups absorbs the individual personality into the collective life, whereas in individualistic groups it enhances the individual personality. In the communal group, personality problems should be viewed within standardized categories rather than as reflective of the uniqueness of the individual. In this setting, therapy turns the individual away from the self and toward the group. The stress is on the similarities, rather than the differences, between the individual and others in the group. The goal is to integrate the personality into the collective life of the group.

When the form of social solidarity is individualistic, the style of therapeutic control reflects different patterns of social relationships. Problems are viewed within the framework of the unique experience of the individual rather than through common social categories. The goal of therapy is to enhance personal autonomy and self-awareness. The symbolic interpretation of personality problems focuses on either the private history or the current experiences of each individual. As individuals become the principal focus of social life, their unique personal qualities become the focus of therapeutic control. The individualistic explanations and control of personality problems found in modern psychiatry are thus predicted by the nature of social solidarity in contemporary Western societies.

To test the thesis that communal forms of solidarity lead to communal psychotherapies whereas individualistic forms lead to individualistic therapies requires examining forms of social solidarity in a wide variety of historical and cultural contexts. I begin by examining therapeutic control in tribal societies and then generalize the style of therapy found in these contexts to communal settings as diverse as modern China, communes, religious cults, and tightly knit social networks in modern societies. Because individualistic forms of solidarity are a peculiarly modern phenomenon, it is impossible to utilize the same range of data to test my thesis. Instead, I show how those individuals who are least encapsulated by strong social groups are the ones who are most likely to utilize individualistic styles of therapy. Although much of my argument will be speculative, the available evidence suggests that the major styles of therapeutic social control are associated with the major forms of social solidarity.

Therapeutic Social Control in Tribal Societies

In many ways, tribal societies provide the prototype of communal social life. Although there are many differences between different tribal groups, in contrast to modern individualistic societies, the similarities among them are far greater. Individuals are typically bound to a small number of kinsmen and tribesmen with whom they spend their entire lives. Relationships endure throughout the life of the individual, and the supreme values are the kinship and tribal groups. When problems arise in such settings, they not only are problems of the individual but also radiate throughout the interlocking network of relationships. In such settings, the social control of the personality serves to turn individuals away from their private preoccupations toward the communal life of the group.

Despite differences in particulars, there are a number of similarities in the style of therapeutic social control found in tribal groups. First, problems are interpreted through a small number of ritualized categories. The public nature of these categories allows the individual, family, and community to connect the problematic experiences to the communal symbolism of the group. Second, therapy emphasizes the likeness of the individual to others in the group and stresses the need for conformity to group norms. The therapeutic process reaffirms the normative order of the group for both the sufferer and other group members. Third, the structure of the healing process integrates the patient into the group by affirming the values of the collectivity and devaluing the unique aspects of the self. In these ways, the process of therapeutic control is an encapsulating one, combating individuality and stressing commonality.

Tribal groups use a small number of ritualized categories of explanations to interpret the personality problems of their members. In a world-wide survey of the ethnographic literature, Clements (1932) found that tribal groups have only a few basic categories of disease causation. The most common explanations involve the departure of the soul from the body, the breach of a taboo, witchcraft, and the intrusion of some foreign object or spirit into the body. The importance of such explanations is that they provide culturally conventional and ritualized expression for idiosyncratic experiences (Devereux, 1958). People who have violated taboos, are possessed by demons, have lost their souls, or have been bewitched have not unique problems but problems that are articulated with the common symbolic system of the group. For example, when people believe they are bewitched, they do not have to explore any personal factors in their experience, because their symptoms are readily comprehensible within an idiom that is part of the common culture (Opler, 1936). Similarly, when a Taiwanese is told "your soul has been away from the body and has not returned yet" to explain an illness (Tseng, 1976: 166), the experience is anchored in the communal symbolism of the group rather than in the idiosyncratic experience of personal life. Or, if mental illness is explained as stemming from the intrusion of a spirit, this spirit may be driven out through a healing ritual common to all members of the group who are so inflicted, without exploring the individual psyche (Gelfand, 1964; see also Obeysekere, 1970).

There is a twofold importance to the use of ritualized, external explanations in tribal contexts. First, in contrast with the practice in many Western psychotherapies, in tribal groups psychotherapies ignore the inner motivations and unique aspects of experience (Kaplan and Johnson, 1964: 227; Murphy, 1964: 79; Prince, 1964: 115). Unlike the language of modern psychological symbolism such as "repression," "low self-esteem," "self-awareness," or "conflicting emotions," which refer to elements within the personality of the individual, tribal explanations relate the experience of symptoms to the broader cultural system of the group (Obeysekere, 1970: 104). Mental symptoms are divorced from the character and uniqueness of the individual and are transformed into elements of a social category rather than of a personal state. Whatever idiosyncratic aspects of the illness are present are forced into the standardized categories of group expression. Second, from the point of view of the group, the experience of the individual becomes accessible to the community. The family and the group, as well as the patient, are able to grasp the experience within a mutually comprehensible idiom (Obeysekere, 1970). Feelings are no longer private but become part of the culturally patterned mode of expression.

An additional element of therapeutic social control in tribal groups is its promotion of conformity to group norms. Regardless of the particular interpretation of the problem, cure is obtained through redirecting the patient to social conformity (Cawte, 1974). One commonly used method to attain conformity in tribal groups is confession. Confession in these settings, however, does not involve a detailed inquiry into the patient's background and early experience, as in some styles of individualist therapies, but is a ritualized mechanism used to promote conformity (Opler, 1936; Berndt, 1964; Fernandez, 1978). For example, the Saint Lawrence Eskimo believe that disease emerges after someone violates group norms. Therefore, it can affect the well-being of the entire group as well as the individual. Cure occurs after an elaborate ritual of public confession and acts of expiation (Murphy, 1964). Among the Temne of Sierre Leone, women often become violent and hysterical after their children die (Dawson, 1964). The native healers then accuse them of witchcraft and tell the women they must confess their deviant activities. In a stereotyped confession, common to all women so inflicted, the individual admits her involvement in witchcraft, after which the healer performs rites that reintegrate the women into society. The Aurohuaca Indians of Colombia believe that all sickness is inflicted as a punishment for sin (LaBarre, 1964). The healer will refuse to treat patients until they have confessed their sins. After confession, the sins can be transferred onto objects such as shells or stones, exposed to the sun, and expiated. Through confession, the sick individual, as well as other members of the group, learn that psychic well-being is found only through conformity with group norms.

Just as the cause of illness is commonly found in deviation from group norms, so is conformity to these norms often prescribed as the appropriate cure. Among the aboriginal tribes in Australia, hysteria is a common form of mental disturbance that typically develops after a woman leaves her own clan and finds herself among strangers in the clan of her husband. To cure the illness, there is an elaborate ritual dance, during which the woman is told she must obey her husband, be respectful and obedient to the other clan members, and conform to food, dress, and behavioral taboos (Berndt, 1964). Taiwanese folk healers often prescribe observance of the duties and obligations of kinship as the remedy for illness (Li, 1976). Similarly, the Luo of Kenya accompany ritual cures with the warning that mental health depends on the mainte-nance of harmonious relations with members of the home and that the violation of any taboos will lead to another attack of illness (Whisson, 1964). Lambo reports that Africans usually believe that the best protec-tion from disease is found through "peaceful living with neighbors, abstention from adultery, and keeping the laws of gods and men [1964: 446]." In general, healing in tribal groups involves the promotion of conformity to group norms. In this way, the cure of individual problems provides an occasion for reaffirming group norms and stressing the solidarity of all group members.

Not only the symbolism but also the structure of therapy in tribal groups reinforces the merging of individual experience into the shared beliefs of the group. Therapy in tribal groups typically occurs in the presence of family and community members. For example, ritual confession of sins is a universal trait among American Indians (LaBarre, 1964: 37). This confession usually occurs at periods of especially intense collective activity, such as hunts, festivals, and before warfare, heightening the merging of individual experience with the collective representations of the group. Cures commonly take place in settings involving the collective activities of the group, such as feasts and dancing, during which the individual is placed at the center of group attention, (Kaplan and Johnson, 1964: 228; Lambo, 1964: 448; Murphy, 1964: 80; Prince, 1964: 107; Turner, 1964: 258–259; Whisson, 1964: 303; Frank, 1973: 58–66; Geertz, 1974: 104–105). In Ethiopia, women who become psychologically disturbed are commonly diagnosed as being possessed with a *zar* spirit (Messing, 1959; see also Kennedy, 1967). This spirit is feasted in a collective ceremony, and the patient is inducted into membership into the *zar* cult group. Similarly, in Sierra Leone, members of the Mende who become ill are inducted into healing societies where they are treated by others of their group who have undergone the same type of experience (Dawson, 1964: 334). Distressed Pueblo Indians of North America are sometimes cured through providing them membership in a new clan group (Fox, 1964). Among the Plains Indians of North America, a disturbed individual may take peyote within a collective setting, confess his or her sins, and then become reintegrated into the group through collective discussion (Kiev, 1972: 112). Group participation in healing ceremonies among the Navaho is involved to the extent that "when hot pokers were applied to the patient's body, the others would receive the same treatment [Kiev, 1964: 25–26]." The healing process in tribal groups is one in which kin and tribe are intensely involved. The involvement of a broad social network in therapy further serves to draw individuals away from unique experiences toward a commitment to the values of the group.

Both the symbolic and the structural aspects of therapy in tribal groups promote the reintegration of the individual into the group and reinforce the solidarity of the communal body. The interpretation of problems through standardized ritual categories ties the experiences of the individual to the common categories of the group. The healing ritual itself occurs within a highly charged emotional context, with the patient placed at the center of group attention. Explanations are drawn from the stock of collective representations rather than from the inner experiences of the individual. The privatization of the self cannot be tolerated, and withdrawal into the self represents a threat to the well-being of the group. Therapeutic social control meets this threat by affirming the bonds between the individual and the group and the value of group solidarity. All aspects of the therapeutic process stress the similarity of the individual to the group, the promotion of conformity to group norms, and the values of the collectivity. Both the individual and the community learn that cure for ills of the personality comes about only through obedience to the demands of the group.

Modern psychiatrists who have studied tribal healing practices are often critical of these techniques. For example, the authors of a study of Malayan folk healers conclude with this statement:

> Certain problems with the approach of the native healer must be mentioned. It is rare for any of them to engage the patient in private consultation outside the group and to encourage the patient to state personally how he sees his problems. In this sense it has strengthened denial, repression, and rationalization. Our own experience with many patients in the same cultures indicate that many feel extremely relieved to be able to discuss personally and privately their own problems. In many of the native therapies, the diagnosis is entirely a work of magical, religious speculation and has nothing to do with the patient's own interpretations of the difficulty. It is extremely rare to go into the depths of the personality of the patient, and the interpersonal and intrapsychic stresses that he may be feeling [Kinzie, Teoh, and Tan, 1976: 143–144].

These researchers accurately characterize the nature of therapy in tribal groups, but they do not associate the nature of this healing with the dynamics of tribal social systems. According to the view presented in the present chapter, by contrast, what these authors call "magical, religious speculation" is one style of symbolic interpretation that emerges when persons are tightly bound together in communal groups. On the other hand, symbolic interpretations such as "denial, repression, and rationalization," emerge only within societies in which individuals have been freed from encompassing group ties. Just as the exploration of the inner feelings of individuals emerges within a particular type of social system based on the principles of individualism, the "denial" of these feelings through symbols that merge the self with the collectivity is also the product of a particular type of social life. Not superstition or ignorance, but the demands of group solidarity, shape the nature of therapeutic social control in these groups.

If my thesis is correct, there is nothing "primitive" about therapy in tribal societies. Rather, certain similarities in the style of therapy should be expected to emerge whenever a communal form of social solidarity exists. In communal groups, the symbolic and structural aspects of therapeutic social control will devalue the unique aspects of the individual and promote conformity to group norms. A test of this thesis requires an examination of therapy in communal settings in widely varied cultural and historical contexts.

Therapeutic Social Control in Other Communal Groups

My thesis specifies how the nature of therapeutic control reflects the nature of social solidarity. Accordingly, groups that feature strong social ties between members and a strong collective value system should be expected to develop similar styles of responding to the mentally ill. The nature of therapy in communal groups subjects the individual to collective interests. This is done in several ways. First, the interpretation of the problem takes a *ritualistic* form, focusing on concrete and formal sources with little variation across individuals. Intrapsychic factors and individual motivation are irrelevant in the interpretation of the problem. Second, therapy has a strongly *normative* component, so that personality problems are seen as stemming from deviations from group norms. Cures arise when conformity to norms is achieved. Third, treatment should take a *collective* form, usually involving the patient's significant others and community members. The therapeutic process heightens the integration of the patient into the group and reaffirms the normative order. In each of these ways, therapy both reflects the communal nature of social relationships and reinforces these tightly knit bonds between people. If this is true, there should be similar elements in therapeutic social control in communal groups in widely divergent cultural and historical settings.

One setting reflecting a communal form of social solidarity is the People's Republic of China under the leadership of Mao Zedong. In the 1950s, there was a deliberate attempt to implement a communal value system based on the ideology of Mao Zedong. One way the Chinese accomplished it was to create encapsulating groups of 8–15 members called *hsiao-tsu* (Whyte, 1974). These groups carried out activities such as work, military training, and academic study and met on a regular basis to engage in political study. Their major function was "the encapsulation of individuals in all walks of life into *hsiao-tsu*, and then the manipulation of interactions and emotions within these groups through political study and mutual criticism [Whyte, 1974: 230]." The primary goal of these groups was to promote group solidarity and conformity to the dominant ideology.

The social control of mental illness in China during this period reflected the collective organization of the group. The same ideology of Mao Zedong that these groups were organized to transmit was also used to interpret the private problems of individuals. The aim of therapy was to subject the individual to the authority of the group through a ritualistic interpretation of the problem common to all persons so inflicted. In one case, the person reported:

> My trouble was that I had subjective thinking which was not objectively correct. My wife had not written letters wanting to divorce me; my wife actually loves me. My subjective thinking was divorced from the practical condition and my disease was caused by my method of thinking. I was concerned with the individual person; I was self-interested. I haven't put revolutionary interests in the first place but if I can put the public interest first and my own interest second I can solve the contradictions and my mind will be in the correct way. From now on I will study Chairman Mao and apply his writings [Sidel, 1975: 128].

In this case, the problem of the individual, who had been diagnosed as a paranoid schizophrenic, is viewed as an excessive degree of self-absorption. The cure is found through tying his problem to the symbolic system of the group. The self is to be submerged into the ritualized symbolism of the collectivity. As another patient states: "Now whenever I have hallucinations, I study the works of Chairman Mao and attract my mind and my heart so I will get rid of my trouble [Sidel, 1975: 128]."

The symbolic interpretations of mental problems in Chinese psychiatry are far removed from explanations involving witchcraft, soul loss, or spirit possession. Yet although grounded in a thoroughly secular political ideology, their ritualized nature is similar and all problems are interpreted in like manner. Their function is the same as in tribal groups: to direct attention away from self-exploration and to subordinate individual interests to the common goals of the culture. One student of Chinese psychiatry notes: "Instead of supporting the patient's efforts to achieve private ambition and promote personal growth as American therapists might do, Chinese doctors discourage private ambition and desire for personal gain, while urging identification with the collectivity and its common goals [Lu, 1978: 107]." The structure of Chinese psychiatry also takes a collective emphasis. Within the hospital, therapy focuses on the intensive study of Mao Zedong's writings in group sessions (Sidel, 1975). Heavy reliance is also placed on mobilizing the patient's significant others to deal with all areas of the problem (Lu, 1978: 10). Both the symbolic and the structural nature of Maoist psychiatry serve to denigrate individuality and reinforce ties to the communal group.

Students of Chinese psychiatry have explained this style of therapy as emergent from the distinctive value system of this society. Lu, for example, speaks of "the Chinese experiment in the collective approach to the treatment of mental illness [1978: 12]." Yet the stress on a formal, ritualistic interpretation of the problem, the cure through identification with the group and through conformity to group norms, and the mobilization of the group to deal with personality problems all mirror the formal elements of therapy in tribal groups. In the Chinese case, the society is deliberately organized to implement a secular ideology rather than to transmit religious or "superstitious" customs that have persisted for centuries. Nevertheless, both settings involve a communal type of social solidarity that emphasizes the collectivity and devalues the individual personality in the interest of group solidarity. The style of Chinese psychiatry is predictable from the general proposition that communal therapies emerge whenever group ties are strong.

The Soviet Union is another modern, secular society with a collectivist orientation. Although Soviet social structure is not as tightly knit as the Chinese structure, the value system is one in which individual interests are subordinated to those of the group. Soviet psychiatry, like Chinese psychiatry, reflects the communal nature of the society. In the Soviet Union, psychiatry is marked by a "violent rejection" of Freud because of his stress on the exploration of the inner self of individuals (Field, 1960: 290). Instead, problems are interpreted within a purely mechanistic framework that suppresses any unique aspects of the individual and provides similar explanations of the problems of all individuals regardless of their particular situations. Treatment, in addition to physiological therapies, focuses on reeducating patients to conform to the dominant ideology, not on the exploration of personal factors underlying problems. As in other communal settings:

> Personal mental adjustment is to be found in the submerging of one's wishes and desires to the needs of the group or society, in the assumption that society has rights against the individual and not vice-versa. It is stressed to the patient that he must give to others and not be concerned with himself, that he must not isolate himself from others. Even if his family rejects him, his fellow citizens are ready to welcome him with open arms [Field, 1960: 294].

To implement these goals, most treatment occurs within the community and often involves the participation of family members as well as patients (Field, 1960). In providing standardized interpretations of problems, denying the relevance of individual factors, and treating mental illness through promoting conformity to social norms, Soviet psychiatry reflects the nature of collectivist societies.

Both China and the Soviet Union are modern societies organized to implement a secular, communist ideology. It is not this ideology, however, that is responsible for the style of therapy but the significantly communal nature of these societies. For example, modern Japan emphasizes a value system totally different from either China's or the Soviet Union's. Japanese culture is a traditional one where individual deference to the kin and communal group is extremely strong. It is not surprising that, as Doi explains, "psychoanalytic therapy has never caught the fancy of Japanese people [1976: 276]," because their orientation to communal living makes them uncomfortable about searching within the individual to find the source of personality problems. Instead, "the emphasis in Japanese psychotherapies is not so much upon seeking a hidden secret as upon rescuing the person entrapped in his hiding place and bringing him back to communal living [Doi, 1976: 275]." As in other communal groups, therapy turns patients away from themselves toward participation in group life and culture.

The denigration of the personality in the service of the group is also found in contemporary religious sects that are marked by tight bonds between their members. In some religious communes in nineteenth-century America, "excessive introspection was considered a sin" and confession of sins was commonly used to obtain conformity (Kanter, 1972: 16; see also Zablocki, 1971). Hasidic Jewish groups also forbid excessive introspection and believe that therapeutic cures arise "not through insight but through 'exsight,' not by being preoccupied with one's own problems but by being involved with the others to whom one is responsible [Rotenberg, 1978: 154]." In such groups, the treatment of the mentally ill often involves the participation of the collectivity, as in the "powwowing" ceremonies among the Pennsylvania German religious sects in which the entire group lays its hands on the patient while repeating prayers and incantations (Guthrie and Noll, 1966). In these kinds of groups, the cure for mental illness is found not within self-exploration but through reliance on the collective ideology and on other members of the group.

If my thesis that the style of therapeutic social control reflects the form of social solidarity is correct, then those individuals in contemporary American society who are bound within communal groups should be expected to deal with mental illness through communal rather than individualistic therapies. When people are tied to tightly knit social groups, they should deemphasize the importance of inner life and seek cure through formal and ritualized means. If this is so, the rejection of

insight-oriented therapies by members of groups distant from the culture of psychiatrists (such as those who lack education or are members
of the working class) may reflect, in part, the nature of social relationships among these people. Conversely, the "greater knowledge" presumably possessed by more educated members of society may reflect
the more individualistic nature of the social life in which they participate. In fact, there is some evidence from studies of communal groups in
modern societies that the values and attitudes toward psychotherapy of
various "folk" and working-class groups does reflect a particular form of
social solidarity.

A study of therapy among the Hutterites, an Anabaptist group who
live in self-contained tightly knit communities in the upper Midwest and
southern Canada supports the central thesis: "Hutterite 'psychiatry'
emphasizes the importance of the patient's social and value milieu in
treatment, with little consideration of the individual. It contrasts sharply
with much of modern psychiatry, which is much more psychologically
oriented and is focused on the patient [Eaton and Weil, 1955: 176]."
Treatment among the Hutterites does not encourage thought about past
events or introspection; healing is thought to arise from faith in the
religious beliefs of the group. Although Eaton and Weil believe that
"much more could be done for Hutterite patients if their problems were
viewed in more intrapersonal or psychological terms [1955: 177]," the
system of therapeutic healing they describe is one that perfectly reflects
the communal character of Hutterite life. The denigration of individual
motivation, emphasis on conformity to group norms, and public involvement in treatment reflect the healing processes of mental illness
within tightly knit communities in general.

A very different form of communal solidarity is found among some
urban ethnic communities in the United States. For example, in an Italian neighborhood in Boston marked by tightly interlocking kinship and
friendship groups, psychosomatic and mental symptoms were viewed
as deviations from group norms and interpreted as moral rather than as
pathological problems (Gans, 1962: 138–139). Treatment consisted of
attempts to integrate the individual into the group and, integration failing, through punishment of the deviant. Personality problems were
regarded not only as problems of the individual but also as problems
that threatened to disrupt the solidarity of the group (Gans, 1962: 266).
Although Gans attributes the style of interpretations and the response to
mental illness to "working-class culture," the similarity of "therapy"
within this Italian community to that of other communal groups with
widely differing cultures indicates that their response to mental illness
may reflect not working-class culture but rather the nature of the group
life within this community.

Another ethnic group in the United States that is oriented to close and interdependent familial relationships is the Mexican-Americans. The explanation for the development of mental illness among Mexican-Americans commonly is found in the violation of their moral and ethical codes; the illness is viewed as a punishment for sins (Madsen, 1964). They believe cure often is achieved after the confession of sins. As in many communal groups, the healing ceremony takes place within a collective setting:

> The family of the patient is present throughout the curing session and becomes intimately involved. They may be specifically told how to help the patient, or to make votive offerings. This enables the *curandero* to make extensive use of family and social manipulation if he wishes. Thus, treatment is not merely the result of the doctor–patient relationship but is instead a form of social reintegration through socially reorganized methods [Torrey, 1972: 121].

In their interpretation and treatment of emotional problems, Mexican-Americans are similar to other groups with communal forms of social solidarity. Individual symptoms are interpreted and treated not as intrapsychic problems but as deviations from interpersonal and community norms.

The development of "therapeutic communities" and other forms of group therapies in modern societies is sometimes seen as similar to tribal-like therapies (Jones, 1968). The therapy that occurs in therapeutic communities, milieu therapies, encounter groups, sensitivity sessions, and various forms of self-help groups, however, is usually "communal" in only the most superficial sense. The "group" is usually no more than a collection of strangers with whom each member shares only the tie of membership in the therapy group, and there are no communal symbols to which members can tie their experiences (Fernandez, 1978). Not surprisingly, the values of these groups involve the promotion of individual growth and self-awareness rather than integration into the community (Marx and Seldin, 1973). Most forms of modern group therapies mirror an individuated form of solidarity in which individuals explore the nature of their selves in the company of a fleeting group of strangers.

Some forms of modern group therapy, however, do bear some resemblances to communal therapies. One of the best known examples is Alcoholics Anonymous (AA). Therapy in the AA program occurs within group sessions, all members at some time having been alcoholic. Each member, without exception, proceeds through the same "12-step" formula of treatment. The problem of the alcoholic is interpreted through a purely standardized explanation, and the AA member learns to tie his or her drinking problem to a "Power greater than the self and to transfer his worries and the direction of his will to that Power [Bales, 1962: 573]."

Alcoholism is viewed as an "allergy," and participants learn that they are not different from any other alcoholic.

For my purposes, what is important about the Alcoholics Anonymous program is that the ritualized style of explanation of problems it provides is accompanied by the creation of a communal-like social structure. The AA program involves an enveloping round of group activities (see Lofland, 1969: chap. 11). Group meetings take place every night of the week, special activities are held on weekends and holidays, and members are encouraged to have only other AA members as friends. Spouses and children of AA members also often become involved in the therapy process through adjunct programs such as Al-Anon and Al-Ateen. Although hardly comparable to a tribal setting, membership in AA becomes as encompassing as is possible for a middle-class person in American society. Without the creation of a communal-like social setting, it is doubtful that AA could effectively utilize a communal style of therapy.

In the Alcoholics Anonymous program, the form of social solidarity reproduces the form of therapeutic social control, rather than vice versa. This program was constructed on the basis of a therapeutic ideology. Yet it illustrates the principle that if individuals can tie their personalities to communal types of symbolic systems, the symbolism must be grounded in an interlocking network of social relationships. Communal styles of therapy can be maintained only within tightly binding social structures. Similarly contemporary religious sects such as the Hare Krishnas or Children of God couple a ritualistic set of beliefs with an encapsulating communal group structure. Given the conditions of modern social existence, if any group wishes to promote a ritualistic form of expression, it must also create the type of group solidarity that can maintain this symbolic style.

What programs such as Alcoholics Anonymous have in common with tribal societies, the People's Republic of China, or religious sects is that in them the unique qualities of individuals and their unique motivations become irrelevant to the interpretations and treatments of personality problems. The view of alcoholism as an "allergy," for example, is similar in form to the view of personality problems as instances of "sin," "demonic possession," or "ideological deviation." In each interpretation, the experience of the individual is grounded in the collective representations of the group. Through the use of standardized interpretations, the individual is turned away from the self and outward toward the group. Such interpretations, however, can be sustained only when they are situated in a form of social solidarity that envelops individuals and commits them to the common life of the group. When individuals can align their experiences to strong and binding groups and symbolic systems, the explanation and treatment of personality problems is not likely to be found within individual selves. Individualistic interpretations and treatments of personality problems emerge only when people cannot turn to their own social groups or cultural values for solace and healing.

Therapeutic Social Control in Individualistic Groups

The form of social solidarity in communal groups promotes the welfare of the group over that of the individual and submerges individual identity into the collectivity. Therefore, communal groups produce therapeutic styles that are oriented to ritualistic expression, social conformity, and collective participation. When the form of social solidarity becomes individualistic, the style of therapy should be expected to change as well. Individualistic groups do not have the same requirements for group orientation and social conformity as communal groups. With the development of individualism, therapeutic social control comes to emphasize the individual elaboration of meaning, the promotion of autonomy, and a privatized therapeutic relationship.

Groups that feature an individualistic form of social solidarity are rare. Louis Dumont has stated: "Among the great civilizations the world has known, the holistic type of society has been overwhelmingly predominant: indeed, it looks as if it has been the rule, the only exception being our modern civilization and its individualistic type of society [1976: 4]." Because of this, it is not possible to make broad cross-cultural and historical comparisons among individualistic groups. Individualistic styles of therapy are virtually unique to modern Western societies.

Beginning at about the end of the eighteenth century and continuing throughout the nineteenth and twentieth centuries, Western societies have been marked by increasing individualization. Industrialization and the accompanying division of labor broke down the tightly knit communal groups that had predominated in previous eras. Large-scale movements from rural to urban areas created a great amount of geographic and social mobility, further breaking down ties to kin and community groups. Political and cultural values became oriented to the sovereignty of the autonomous individual, and the individual, rather than the group, became the bearer of rights and duties (Unger, 1975). Because of these structural and cultural changes, individuals in modern Western societies are far more autonomous than ever before. Freed of binding group ties, the individual has become the center of group life and culture.

Only in the last 200 years or so, and only in the West, has individualism become the predominant structural and ideological order of entire societies. Consequently, in the modern world, the notion that mental illness is a problem rooted in the personality of individuals is a fairly recent conception. Foucault locates this shift as occurring in the latter part of the eighteenth century in Europe when madness became: "inscribed within the dimension of interiority; and by that fact, for the first time in the modern world, madness was to receive psychological status, structure, and signification [1976: 72]." The notion of therapeutic social control as involving the comprehension of the private states of individuals, now taken for granted in psychotherapy, is a new development. Modern individualistic styles of therapy have emerged within the context of social and cultural changes that are a unique feature of modern Western societies.

Sigmund Freud's system of psychoanalysis, developed at the end of the nineteenth and beginning of the twentieth centuries, represents a dramatic shift in the nature of therapeutic social control. Therapy no longer serves to tie individuals into the community but, instead, is designed to free them from group ties. The goal of psychoanalytic treatment is to allow patients to become autonomous and regulate their lives by norms of their own choosing. To achieve this goal, the individual personality becomes the center of therapeutic concern, and therapeutic techniques turn individuals inward to gain insight into how their past experiences have led to their current problems. The primary technique of analysis is introspection, and "psychoanalysis is learnt first of all on oneself through the study of one's own personality [Freud, 1924: 23]." Just as the interpretation of problems comes to be found in private experience, so does the structure of therapy become privatized. Therapy becomes limited to a dialogue between the patient and the therapist, with no participation by outside family or community members. Within this isolated setting, patients communicate their private feelings that they keep hidden from the social world.

Psychoanalysis inverts each element of communal therapy (Lévi-Strauss, 1964: 193). Symbols drawn from self-experience, not ritualized and communal symbols that do not correspond to a personal state of mind, are used to interpret personality problems. Cure occurs through self-exploration and consequent self-awareness, not through conformity to the normative order of the group. The individual personality is not denigrated in the therapeutic process but comes to be of paramount concern in therapy. Finally, the therapeutic process itself becomes a private oasis from the social world, rather than a communal affair mobilizing the energies of the community. In each of these aspects, psychoanalytic therapy reflects the development of an individualistic society and the liberation of the individual from the ties of the communal group.

Psychotherapy after Psychoanalysis

Although psychoanalysis was the first widely institutionalized form of individualistic therapy in the modern West and still stands as its paradigmatic case, in recent decades it has declined in popularity. On the one hand, among many psychiatric professionals drug-oriented therapies and behavior modification have enjoyed growing popularity (Murray, 1979). These therapies are primarily directed toward changing the physical organism or outward behavior and are little concerned with the symbolic aspects of the personality. Hence, they do not fit my definition of psychotherapy and I shall not consider them here. On the other hand, especially during the late 1960s and early 1970s, a tremendous number and variety of alternative psychotherapeutic approaches arose. Largely appearing outside of the psychiatric profession, existential therapy, Gestalt therapy, self-actualization, client-centered therapy, and many other therapies became popular.

The proponents of most of these newer styles of therapy view them as a reaction against Freudian theory and techniques (e.g., Rogers, 1951; Laing, 1967; Bart, 1974). From a broader sociological point of view, however, they reflect an *intensification* of the individualistic nature of therapy as compared with psychoanalysis. The emphasis on the individual self and the denigration of social convention found in the newer psychotherapies is unprecented in the history of psychotherapy.

What unites the practitioners of the multitude of contemporary individualistic therapies in their rejection of psychoanalysis is their belief that psychoanalysis, because of its mechanistic nature, does not do enough justice to the uniqueness of the individual personality. Instead, the advocates believe that more attention should be paid to individuals' internal subjective experiences. For example, Carl Rogers (1951) claims that psychoanalysis constructs barriers to seeing the uniqueness of patients, overestimates the importance of past experiences and consequently underestimates the importance of the immediate moment, and prevents clients from total "self-actualization." Similarly, the Gestalt therapy developed by Fritz Perls (1964) rejects any study of personal history, or even any intellectualization of problems, because this impedes a focus on the unique present. The encounter-group movement also strove to liberate people from their past, utilizing immediate contacts with others in the present moment for therapeutic effect (Back, 1973).

In contrast with communal therapies, which rely on strict rituals, and even with psychoanalysis, which utilizes specific therapeutic techniques, there is no formal agenda in the variety of contemporary psychotherapies. Instead, treatment occurs through a constant analysis of the feelings and dynamics that occur within relationships formed in the present situation (see Back, 1973). Self-expression rather than social norms, nonverbal exploration of feelings and senses instead of language, and immediacy and not habit are the central dynamics in these therapies. The cure for problems lies in a celebration of the unique aspects of the self and in the exploration of one's self free from all preconceived social categories. Unlike psychoanalysis, contemporary psychotherapies reject the examination of personal history, enduring social structures, or even the symbolization of experience. Instead, they discard the "language of symbols in favor of direct experience and action [Back, 1973: 79]."

Just as the development and diffusion of psychoanalysis reflected the changes that occurred in Western societies in the late nineteenth and early twentieth centuries, the development of the new individualistic therapies reflect new forms of social existence. These therapies have had great appeal only in the United States, and there only among a particular segment of the American population. Their participants are typically mobile, affluent, and white members of the upper middle class (Back, 1973). Moving from one relationship to another, these individuals in their own lives are differentiated from binding group ties. In addition, they feel no commitment to any strong belief system. Freud and his followers were still burdened by a cultural heritage they sought to overcome, whereas the clients of the modern therapies, who often have grown up in suburbia, have never suffered from oppressive social and cultural restraints.

The Users of Individualistic Therapies

My thesis predicts that the development of individualistic styles of therapy and the decline of communal therapies is produced by changing forms of social solidarity. This thesis predicts not only the content of therapeutic styles but also the characteristics of individuals who use individualistic therapies. In particular, individuals who are least committed to communal symbolic systems and least tied to strong social groups are expected to be the ones who are most likely to utilize individualistic styles of psychotherapy.

All forms of contemporary individualistic psychotherapies in the

United States have a greater appeal to people of higher social status than to those of lower status. It is also in this segment of society that the development of autonomous selves is highest and that individuals are oriented to unique motivations and feelings rather than to systems of rules (Bernstein, 1971). Socialization centers around the development of individuated selves and internalized controls and not, as in the lower and working classes, to conformity to an external system of authority (Miller and Swanson, 1958; Kohn, 1959; Bronfenbrenner, 1961). In addition, highly educated professionals are the most geographically mobile group in the population (Ladinsky, 1967). This mobility tends to weaken long-standing social ties and to enhance the autonomy of individuals who have been detached from stable social groups.

In light of the preceding facts, it is not surprising that ascending social class is strongly related to the use of individualistic styles of psychotherapy. Back associates the recent rise in popularity of sensitivity training and encounter groups with the geographic mobility of the professional middle classes and calls these therapy groups: "Lonely hearts clubs for newcomers or those without roots in a community [1973: 33]." More traditional forms of analytic therapy are also associated with high social class status. Higher-status people are more likely than lower-status ones to define problems as stemming from psychological factors (Hollingshead and Redlich, 1958); to see problems as indicative of mental illness (Dohrenwend and Chin-Shong, 1967); to define themselves as in need of psychiatric treatment (Gurin, Veroff, and Feld, 1960; Kulka, Veroff, and Douvan, 1979); and to seek this treatment voluntarily and in shorter periods of time (Hollingshead and Redlich, 1958; Myers and Roberts, 1959; Gove and Howell, 1974).

The amenability of the higher social classes to individualistic therapies is not due to a higher rate of psychiatric impairment. For example, in midtown Manhattan, upper-class persons were less likely than others to display psychiatric impairment but were 4 times as likely as middle-class persons and 19 times as likely as lower-class persons to enter psychiatric treatment (Srole, Langner, Michael, Opler, and Rennie, 1962). Nor are the higher utilization rates of psychiatric facilities by persons of higher class status solely a function of their ability to pay for this treatment. A nationwide study of 2264 adults conducted in 1976 shows that education is more predictive than income of the utilization of psychiatrists (Kulka et al., 1979: 10). Whereas 11% of college graduates had visited a psychiatrist or psychologist, 7% of high school graduates, and only 3% of persons with a grade-school education had done so. This study also finds that, controlling for the level of psychiatric distress, more highly educated people are considerably more likely than the less educated to define their problems in psychiatric terms (Kulka *et al.*, 1979). In addition, once treatment is sought, higher-status persons are more likely to remain in therapy for longer periods of time than are lower-status persons (Hollingshead and Redlich, 1958: 235; Miller and Mishler, 1964: 30), although this relationship appears to be declining in the 1970s (Stern, 1977). It is only speculation to explain the association between social class status and the utilization of individualistic forms of therapy through the more individualistic culture and social structure of the higher social classes. At least, however, the evidence regarding social class and psychotherapy is consistent with the general proposition that the style of therapeutic social control reflects the form of social solidarity.

In addition to social class, the degree to which individuals participates in cosmopolitan cultures also predicts their amenability to individualistic styles of therapy. Although there is no agreed-upon meaning for the term *cosmopolitan*, it generally refers to a broad awareness of different cultural trends and a humanistic and liberal outlook on the world. In contrast to participation in communal groups, which is associated with total commitment to the symbolic system of the group, participation in cosmopolitan cultures is usually associated with an acquaintance with many symbolic systems but no binding commitment to any particular system.

Individualistic therapies flourish in centers of cosmopolitan cultures. Psychoanalysis itself developed in a major cosmopolitan center, late nineteenth- and early twentieth-century Vienna, and its founder and most of his followers were members of a cosmopolitan Jewish ethnic group (Ellenberger, 1970). Jews are still considerably more likely than other ethnic groups to enter individualistic forms of therapy. In midtown Manhattan, Jews report no more psychiatric symptoms than Protestants and Catholics but are four times as likely to enter psychotherapy (Srole *et al.*, 1962). Jewish students are more likely to seek therapy than are members of other religious groups (Scheff, 1966; Linn, 1967; Greenley and Mechanic, 1976) and to define problems as indicative of mental illness (Dohrenwend and Chin-Shong, 1967). Within universities, students of the humanities and the social sciences are more likely to seek psychotherapy than are those in the natural sciences, and students who seek therapy are more likely than those who do not participate in cosmopolitan cultures marked by the viewing of foreign films, an interest in psychology, and an emphasis on introspection (Scheff, 1966; Linn, 1967; Greenley and Mechanic, 1976). In addition, urban areas, everywhere the centers of cosmopolitan culture, have higher rates of psychiatric therapy than do rural areas, controlled for the size of the population (Gurin *et al.*, 1960).

In the centers of cosmopolitanism, large metropolitan areas, individualistic therapy can sometimes become part of the culture itself. A social circle that Kadushin (1969) calls "the friends of psychotherapy" develops in urban areas among persons who work in occupational milieus such as teaching, the arts, communication, and the health professions that emphasize artistic and psychological phenomena. The members of this culture openly discuss their personal problems and therapeutic experiences with others, and participation in psychotherapy itself is a central aspect of their lives.

In addition to social class and cosmopolitan culture, the lack of integration into social networks predicts the utilization of individualistic therapy. In the contemporary United States, the admission rate to outpatient psychiatric treatment is over five times higher for separated and divorced people than for married people (NIMH, 1970). People who have never married are twice as likely and the widowed three times as likely as the married to seek psychiatric treatment (NIMH, 1970). Among married persons, individuals with weak kinship and friendship ties seek therapy in shorter periods of time than those with more ties (Lowenthal, 1964; Horwitz, 1977a). People who are geographically mobile have higher utilization of psychiatric guidance facilities than do long-term residents of the same communities (Raphael, 1964). And, controlled for the level of psychiatric distress, students who are least likely to participate in religious, extracurricular, and organizational activities are the most likely to seek psychiatric treatment (Scheff, 1966; Linn, 1967; Greenley and Mechanic, 1976). All of these findings are predictable from the general proposition that structural individuation is associated with the utilization of individualistic styles of therapy.

The common factor that seems to unite the major users of individualistic styles of psychotherapy—those with high social class status, cosmopolitan culture, and lack of integration into strong social networks—is the lack of commitment to particular belief systems and/or to social groups. More research that specifically tests this thesis must be conducted before such an explanation can be regarded as definitive. The individualistic emphasis and control of personality problems found in modern styles of therapy, however, appears to reflect the individualistic form of social experience of the people who are likely to utilize these therapies. If so, the notion that higher-status people are more knowledgeable and better able correctly to identify the nature of personality problems than are lower-class people would be a misunderstanding of the nature of these issues. Only within a particular type of social order are problems of the self tied to individual experience rather than to ritualized expressions of collective identity. Each style of therapy corresponds to the nature of the social ties that bind individuals to one another.

Conclusion

In this chapter I have tried to show how therapeutic social control is predictable from the nature of group life. Like all styles of social control, therapy responds to deviations from normative standards, in this case standards of "healthy" and "unhealthy" personalities. The standards of mental health that contemporary psychiatric professionals and highly educated members of modern society take for granted, such as self-fulfillment, spontaneity, freedom, autonomy, and so on, are premised on the notion of an individuated personality that is unique in history. In contrast, mental health traditionally has been found through conforming to the demands of the group and by suppressing individuality in the service of the collectivity. The obsession with the self of contemporary, educated people is as predictable from their form of social experience as the use of ritual is among tribal peoples.

I have focused on the association of one broad aspect of social experience, the form of social solidarity, with the nature of therapeutic social control. From the myriad diversity of social life, I have isolated two ideal types of social solidarity: the communal and the individualistic. In the communal group, the individual is bound to other members of society through interlocking social ties and through a value commitment to the collectivity. In contrast, the individualistic group is marked by an absence of enduring social bonds and communal symbolic systems. Although useful as a heuristic device, these two styles only sketch the basic forms of social solidarity in the broadest strokes. One of the major tasks of a more comprehensive theory of therapeutic social control is to examine in greater detail the variations of these two general types of social experience, as well as to isolate the various elements that comprise the general notion of social solidarity. In addition, more work should focus on the relationship between stratification, social solidarity, and therapeutic social control.

Until the present, individualistic styles of social solidarity and psychotherapy have been limited to a narrow segment of the population in modern Western societies. Many indicators, however, point to a continual expansion and flourishing of individualistic styles of psychotherapy. For example, Donald Black describes the movement of modern social structures as follows:

> Traditional ties have been loosening, even falling apart altogether. The community is weaker than ever before, and so is the neighborhood and family. The life span of relationships grows shorter and shorter. Increasingly, marriage does not last, for instance, and friends fluctuate from month to month, if not from week to week or day to day. Encounters replace the social structures of the past, and people increasingly have closeness without permanence, depth without commitment [1976: 135].

Black sees these trends leading to a decline of law and to an emergence of an anarchic style of social control. If these trends continue, they will also be consistent with an expansion of individualistic styles of therapeutic social control. Individuals cut adrift from encompassing belief systems and social groups will turn increasingly to individualistic therapy as a way of finding some meaning in their lives.

One possible outcome of these trends is that the therapeutic experience may replace the loss of stable commitments and permanent relationships. This is the belief of Carl Rogers, one of the leading proponents of "humanistic" forms of individualistic therapy. Rogers feels that in therapeutic groups, "there will be possibilities for the rapid development of closeness between and among persons, a closeness which is not artificial, but is real and deep, and which will be well suited to our increasing mobility of living. Temporary relationships will be able to achieve the richness and meaning which heretofore have been associated only with lifelong attachments [1968: 268–269]." If so, the newer forms of individualistic therapy will be ideal treatments for the personality problems of individuals who have been freed from long-standing commitments.

On the other hand, if a central thesis of Durkheim's work (e.g., 1893; 1897) is correct, that the meaning of life is found in strong group attachments, the continuing individuation of society will make meaningful social existence less possible. People who are freed of group ties and symbolic commitments may eagerly seek individualistic therapies to resolve their problems, and yet the emphasis in these therapies on unique experience, self-awareness, and autonomy may only reinforce the conditions that led them to seek help in the first place. The aphorism of the Viennese satirist Karl Kraus, "Psychoanalysis is the disease of which it pretends to be the cure [1977:227]," may aptly apply to all styles of individualistic therapy. But then structural individuation and the breakdown of communal belief systems have undermined the possibilities for therapies of the earlier kind. Perhaps only the emergence of new forms of social existence can turn modern individuals away from the focus on the self that they now experience in psychotherapy toward some new, as yet unknown, style of therapeutic social control.

References

Ackerknecht, Erwin H.
    1959   *A Short History of Psychiatry*. New York: Hafner.
Alexander, Franz, and Sheldon Selesnick
    1966   *The History of Psychiatry*. New York: Harper & Row.
Back, Kurt W.
    1973   *Beyond Words: The Story of Sensitivity Training and the Encounter Movement*. Baltimore: Penguin.
Bales, Robert F.
    1962   "The therapeutic role of Alcoholics Anonymous as seen by a sociologist." Pages 572–576 in *Society, Culture, and Drinking Patterns*, edited by David J. Pittman and Charles R. Snyder. Carbondale, Ill.: Southern Illinois University Press.
Bart, Pauline B.
    1974   "Ideologies and utopias of psychotherapy." Pages 9–57 in *The Sociology of Psychotherapy*, edited by Paul M. Roman and Harrison M. Trice. New York: Jason Aronson.
Berndt, Catherine H.
    1964   "The role of native doctors in Aboriginal Australia." Pages 264–282 in *Magic, Faith, and Healing*, edited by Ari Kiev. New York: Free Press.
Bernstein, Basil
    1971   *Class, Codes and Control: Theoretical Studies towards a Sociology of Language*. Boston: Routledge & Kegan Paul.
Black, Donald
    1976   *The Behavior of Law*. New York: Academic Press.
Black, Donald, and Maureen Mileski (editors)
    1973   *The Social Organization of Law*. New York: Seminar Press.
Bott, Elizabeth
    1957   *Family and Social Network*. London: Tavistock.
Brodbeck, May
    1968   "General introduction." Pages 1–11 in *Readings in the Philosophy of the Social Sciences*, edited by May Brodbeck. New York: Macmillan.
Bronfenbrenner, Uri
    1961   "The changing American child—a speculative analysis." *Journal of Social Issues* 17: 6–18.
Cawte, David
    1974   *Medicine Is the Law: Studies in Psychiatric Anthropology of Australian Tribal Societies*. Honolulu: University Press of Hawaii.
Chambliss, William, and Robert Seidman
    1971   *Law, Order, and Power*. Reading, Mass.: Addison-Wesley.
Clark, Alexander, and Jack P. Gibbs
    1965   "Social control: A reformulation." *Social Problems* 12: 398–415.

Clements, Forrest E.
   1932   "Primitive Concepts of Disease." *University of California Publications in American Archaeology and Ethnology* 32: 185–252.
Dawson, John
   1964   "Urbanization and mental health in a West African community." Pages 305–342 in *Magic, Faith, and Healing*, edited by Ari Kiev. New York: Free Press.
Devereux, George
   1958   "Cultural thought models in primitive and modern psychiatric theories." *Psychiatry* 21: 359–374.
Dohrenwend, Bruce, and Edwin Chin-Shong
   1967   "Social status and attitudes toward psychological disorder." *American Sociological Review* 32: 417–433.
Doi, L. Takeo
   1976   "Psychotherapy as 'hide and seek.'" Pages 273–277 in *Culture-Bound Syndromes, Ethnopsychiatry, and Alternative Therapies*, edited by William Lebra. Honolulu: University press of Hawaii.
Douglas, Mary
   1973   *Natural Symbols: Explorations in Cosmology.* New York: Vintage.
Dumont, Louis
   1976   *From Mandeville to Marx.* Chicago: University of Chicago Press.
Durkheim, Emile
   1893   *The Division of Labor in Society.* New York: Free Press, 1964.
   1897   *Suicide: A Study in Sociology.* New York: Free Press, 1951.
Eaton, Joseph W., and Robert J. Weil
   1955   *Culture and Mental Disorders.* Glencoe, Ill.: Free Press.
Ellenberger, Henri F.
   1970   *The Discovery of the Unconscious: The History and Evolution of Dynamic Psychiatry.* New York: Basic Books.
Entralgo, Pedro Lain
   1970   *The Therapy of the Word in Classical Antiquity.* New Haven, Conn.: Yale University Press.
Felstiner, William L. F.
   1975   "Influences of social organization on dispute processing." *Law and Society Review* 9: 63–94.
Fernandez, James W.
   1978   "Passage to community: Encounter in evolutionary perspective." Pages 7–32 in *In Search for Community: Encounter Groups and Social Change*, edited by Kurt Back. Boulder, Colo.: Westview Press.
Field, Marc G.
   1960   "Approaches to mental illness in Soviet society." *Social Problems* 7: 277–297.
Foucault, Michel
   1976   *Mental Illness and Psychology.* New York: Harper & Row.
Fox, J. Robin
   1964   Witchcraft and clanship in Cochiti therapy. Pages 174–202 in *Magic, Faith, and Healing*, edited by Ari Kiev. New York: Free Press.
Frank, Jerome
   1973   *Persuasion and Healing.* 2d edition. Baltimore: Johns Hopkins University Press (1st edition, 1961).
Freidson, Eliot
   1970   *Profession of Medicine.* New York: Harper & Row.

Freud, Sigmund
    1924   *A General Introduction to Psychoanalysis.* New York: Washington Square Press,
            1960.
Gans, Herbert
    1962   *Urban Villagers.* New York: Free Press.
Geertz, Clifford
    1973   *The Interpretation of Cultures.* New York: Basic Books.
Gelfand, Michael
    1964   Psychiatric disorders as recognized by the Shona. Pages 156–173 in *Magic,
            Faith, and Healing,* edited by Ari Kiev. New York: Free Press.
Gibbs, Jack
    1977   "Social control, deterrence, and perspectives on social order." *Social Forces* 56:
            408–423.
Gluckman, Max
    1967   *The Judicial Process among the Barotse of Northern Rhodesia.* 2d edition. Manches-
            ter: Manchester University Press (1st edition, 1955).
Gove, Walter, and Patrick Howell
    1974   "Individual resources and mental hospitalization." *American Sociological Review*
            39: 86–100.
Greenley, James R., and David Mechanic
    1976   "Social selection in seeking help for psychological problems." *Journal of Health
            and Social Behavior* 17: 249–262.
Gurin, Gerald, Joseph Veroff, and Sheila Feld
    1960   *Americans View Their Mental Health.* New York: Basic Books.
Guthrie, George, and G. Noll
    1966   "Powwow in Pennsylvania." *Pennsylvania Medicine* 69: 37–40.
Hollingshead, August, and Frederick Redlich
    1958   *Social Class and Mental Illness.* New York: Wiley.
Horwitz, Allan V.
    1977a   "Social networks and pathways into psychiatric treatment." *Social Forces* 56:
            86–101.
    1977b   "The pathways into psychiatric treatment: Some differences between men and
            women." *Journal of Health and Social Behavior* 18: 169–178.
    1982   *The Social Control of Mental Illness.* New York: Academic Press.
Jones, Maxwell
    1968   *Social Psychiatry in Practice: The Idea of the Therapeutic Community.* London:
            Penguin.
Kadushin, Charles
    1962   "Social distance between client and professional." *American Journal of Sociology*
            68: 517–531.
    1969   *Why People Go to Psychiatrists.* New York: Atherton.
Kanter, Rosabeth Moss
    1972   *Commitment and Community.* Cambridge, Mass.: Harvard University Press.
Kaplan, Bert, and Dale Johnson
    1964   "The social meaning of Navaho psychopathology and psychotherapy." Pages
            203–230 in *Magic, Faith, and Healing,* edited by Ari Kiev. New York: Free Press.
Kennedy, J. G.
    1967   "Nubian *zar* ceremonies as psychotherapy." *Human Organization* 26: 185–194.

Kiev, Ari
1964 "The study of folk psychiatry." Pages 3–35 in *Magic., Faith, and Healing,* edited by Ari Kiev. New York: Free Press.
1972 *Transcultural Psychiatry.* New York: Free Press.
Kinzie, David, Jin-Inn Teoh, and Eng-Seong Tan
1976 Native healers in Malaysia. Pages 130–146 in *Culture-Bound Syndromes, Ethnopsychiatry, and Alternative Therapies,* edited by William Lebra. Honolulu: University Press of Hawaii.
Kittrie, Nicholas
1971 *The Right to Be Different.* Baltimore: Johns Hopkins University Press.
Kohn, Melvin
1959 "Social class and parental values." *American Journal of Sociology* 64: 337–351.
Komarovsky, Mirra
1964 *Blue Collar Marriage.* New York: Random House.
Kraus, Karl
1977 *No Compromise: Selected Writings of Karl Kraus,* edited by Frederick Ungar. New York: Frederick Ungar.
Kulka, Richard A., Joseph Veroff, and Elizabeth Douvan
1979 "Social class and the use of professional help for personal problems: 1957 and 1976." *Journal of Health and Social Behavior* 20: 2–17.
LaBarre, Weston
1964 "Confession as cathartic therapy in American Indian tribes." Pages 36–49 in *Magic, Faith, and Healing,* edited by Ari Kiev. New York: Free Press.
Ladinsky, Jack
1967 "Occupational determinants of geographic mobility among professional workers." *American Sociological Review* 32: 258–264.
Ladurie, LeRoy
1978 *Montaillou.* New York: Braziller.
Laing, R. D.
1967 *The Politics of Experience.* New York: Pantheon.
Lambo, T. Adeoye
1964 "Patterns of psychiatric care in developing African countries." Pages 443–453 in *Magic, Faith, and Healing,* edited by Ari Kiev. New York: Free Press.
LaPiere, Richard T.
1954 *A Theory of Social Control.* New York: McGraw-Hill.
Laumann, Edward O.
1973 *Bonds of Pluralism.* New York: Wiley.
Lee, Nancy Howell
1969 *The Search for an Abortionist.* Chicago: University of Chicago Press.
Lévi-Strauss, Claude
1964 "The effectiveness of symbols." Pages 181–201 in *Structural Anthropology.* Garden City, N.Y.: Anchor.
Li, Yih-Yuan
1976 "Shamanism in Taiwan: An anthropological inquiry." Pages 179–188 in *Culture-Bound Syndromes, Ethnopsychiatry, and Alternate Therapies,* edited by William Lebra. Honolulu: University Press of Hawaii.
Linn, Lawrence S.
1967 "Social characteristics and social interaction in the utilization of a psychiatric outpatient clinic." *Journal of Health and Social Behavior* 8: 3–14.

Lofland, John (with the assistance of Lyn H. Lofland)
    1969   *Deviance and Identity*. Englewood Cliffs, N.J.: Prentice-Hall.
Lowenthal, Marjorie Fiske
    1964   *Lives in Distress: The Paths of the Elderly to the Psychiatric Ward*. New York: Basic
           Books.
Lu, Yi-Chuang
    1978   "The collective approach to psychiatric practice in the People's Republic of
           China." *Social Problems* 26: 2–15.
Madsen, William
    1964   "Value conflicts and folk psychotherapy in South Texas." Pages 420–440 in
           Magic, Faith, and Healing, edited by Ari Kiev. New York: Free Press.
Maine, Henry
    1861   *Ancient Law: Its Connection with the Early History of Society and Its Relation to
           Modern Ideas*. Boston: Beacon Press, 1963.
Marx, John H., and Joseph E. Seldin
    1973   "Crossroads of crisis: 1. Therapeutic sources and quasi-therapeutic functions of
           post-industrial communes." *Journal of Health and Social Behavior* 14: 39–50.
Messing, Simon D.
    1959   "Group therapy and social status in the *zar* cult of Ethiopia." Pages 319–332 in
           Culture and Mental Health, edited by Marvin Opler. New York: Macmillan.
Miller, Daniel R., and Guy E. Swanson
    1958   *The Changing American Parent*. New York: Wiley.
Miller, S. M., and Elliot G. Mishler
    1964   "Social class, mental illness and American psychiatry: An expository review."
           Pages 16–36 in *Mental Health of the Poor*, edited by F. Riessman, J. Cohen, and
           A. Pearl. New York: Free Press.
Murphy, Jane M.
    1964   "Psychotherapeutic aspects of shamanism on St. Lawrence Island, Alaska."
           Pages 53–83 in *Magic, Faith, and Healing*, edited by Ari Kiev. New York: Free
           Press.
Murray, Robin M.
    1979   "A reappraisal of American psychiatry." *Lancet* 8110 (February 3): 255–258.
Myers, Jerome K., and Bertram H. Roberts
    1959   *Family and Class Dynamics in Schizophrenia*. New York: Wiley.
Myers, Jerome K., and Lawrence Schaffer
    1954   "Social stratification and psychiatric practice: A study of an outpatient clinic."
           American Sociological Review 19: 307–310.
Nader, Laura
    1969   "Styles of court procedure: To make the balance." Pages 69–91 in *Law in Culture
           and Society*, edited by Laura Nader. Chicago: Aldine Press.
National Institute of Mental Health
    1970   *Statistical Note 35*. Washington, D.C.: U.S. Government Printing Office.
Obeysekere, Gananath
    1970   "The idiom of demonic possession: A case study." *Social Science and Medicine* 4:
           97–111.
Opler, Marvin
    1936   "The influence of aboriginal pattern and white contact on a recently introduced
           ceremony: The Mescalero peyote rite." *Journal of American Folk-Lore* 49: 143–166.
Parsons, Talcott
    1942   "Propaganda and social control." *Psychiatry* 25: 591–572.
    1951   *The Social System*. New York: Free Press.

Perls, Fritz
 1964 *Ego Hunger and Aggression.* New York: Random House.
Prince, Raymond
 1964 "Indigenous Yoruba psychiatry." Pages 84–120 in *Magic, Faith, and Healing,* edited by Ari Kiev. New York: Free Press.
Raphael, Edna E.
 1964 "Community structure and acceptance of psychiatric aid." *American Journal of Sociology* 69: 340–358.
Redfield, Robert
 1947 "The folk society." *American Journal of Sociology* 52: 293–308.
Rieff, Philip
 1961 *Freud: The Mind of the Moralist.* Garden City, N.Y.: Anchor.
 1966 *The Triumph of the Therapeutic.* New York: Harper & Row.
Rogers, Carl
 1951 *Client Centered Therapy in Current Practice: Implications and Theory.* Boston: Houghton Mifflin.
 1968 "Interpersonal relationships: U.S.A., 2000." *Journal of Applied Behavioral Science* 4: 208–269.
Rotenberg, Mordechai
 1978 *Damnation and Deviance: The Protestant Ethic and the Spirit of Failure.* New York: Free Press.
Scheff, Thomas
 1966 "Users and non-users of a student psychiatric clinic." *Journal of Health and Human Behavior* 7: 114–121.
Schwartz, Richard D., and James C. Miller
 1964 "Legal evolution and societal complexity." *American Journal of Sociology* 70: 158–169.
Sidel, Ruth
 1975 "Mental diseases in China and Their treatment." Pages 119–134 in *Labeling Madness,* edited by Thomas Scheff. Englewood Cliffs, N.J.: Prentice-Hall.
Simmel, Georg
 1908 *The Sociology of Georg Simmel,* edited by Kurt H. Wolff. New York: Free Press, 1950.
Slobin, Dan, Stephen Miller, and Lyman Porter
 1968 "Forms of address and social relations in a business organization." *Journal of Personality and Social Psychology* 8: 289–293.
Spitzer, Stephen
 1975 "Punishment and social organization: A study of Durkheim's theory of penal evolution." *Law and Society Review* 9: 613–635.
Srole, Leo, Thomas Langner, Stanley Michael, Marvin Opler, and Thomas Rennie
 1962 *Mental Health in the Metropolis: The Midtown Manhattan Study.* New York: McGraw-Hill.
Stern, Maxine Springer
 1977 "Social class and psychiatric treatment of adults in the mental health center." *Journal of Health and Social Behavior* 18: 317–325.
Suchman, Edward A.
 1965 "Social patterns of illness and medical care." *Journal of Health and Human Behavior* 6: 2–16.
Toby, Jackson
 1973 "The socialization and control of deviant motivation." Pages 85–100 in *Handbook of Criminology,* edited by Daniel Glaser. Chicago: Rand McNally.

Tönnies, Ferdinand
    1887   *Community and Society.* New York: Harper & Row, 1963.
Torrey, E. Fuller
    1972   *The Mind Game: Witchdoctors and Psychiatrists.* New York: Emerson-Hall.
Tseng, Wen-Shing
    1976   Folk psychotherapy in Taiwan." Pages 164–178 in *Culture-Bound Syndromes, Ethno-psychiatry, and Alternate Therapies,* edited by William Lebra. Honolulu: University Press of Hawaii.
Turner, Victor W.
    1964   "An Ndembu doctor in practice." Pages 230–264 in *Magic, Faith, and Healing,* edited by Ari Kiev. New York: Free Press.
Unger, Roberto Mangabeira
    1975   *Law in Modern Society: Toward a Criticism of Social Theory.* New York: Free Press.
Weber, Max
    1925   *Max Weber on Law in Economy and Society,* edited by M. Rheinstein. Cambridge, Mass.: Harvard University Press, 1954.
Whisson, Michael G.
    1964   "Some aspects of functional disorders among the Kenya Luo." Pages 283–304 in *Magic, Faith, and Healing,* edited by Ari Kiev. New York: Free Press.
Whyte, Martin King
    1974   *Small Groups and Political Rituals in China.* Berkeley, Calif.: University of California Press.
Zablocki, Benjamin
    1971   *The Joyful Community.* Baltimore: Penguin.
Zilboorg, Gregory
    1941   *A History of Medical Psychology.* New York: Norton.

9

The Logic of Mediation

WILLIAM L. F. FELSTINER

Activities directed toward dispute resolution can be divided into three forms: The parties act without the intervention of others, they agree or accept that an outcome will be imposed by another, or in negotiations they involve a third party who does not have the power to dictate an outcome. The conventional label for the third form is mediation. It includes a broad range of behavior and a wide variety of settings, from errand boy to powerful intervenor (Cohen, 1967: 54) as well as from international negotiations to parental involvement in the squabbles of children.

Because mediation implicates an immense slice of human activity and because many factors affect its content in specific cases, this chapter does not present a general theory of mediation, a limited theory of mediation, a general theory of some kinds of mediation, or even a limited theory of limited mediation. Rather, the boundaries are, first, that the chapter discusses one kind of dispute only—that between individuals—ignoring mediation in labor relations, commerce, politics, and international affairs. And second, that it is not theoretical if by *theory* one means an integrated view of behavior from which specific actions relevant to mediation are deduced. What the chapter does do is present a number of propositions about the factors that influence the success of interpersonal mediation. Some of these propositions may be related to

251

others by a common view of the determinants of behavior—for instance, that people have goals and seek to fulfill them efficiently or that people are influenced by culture (collective experience) and habit (individual experience). But these views are not necessarily related to one another, and several of the propositions speak directly to the structure of mediation and only indirectly to disputant behavior. Finally, a strong indication that these propositions are not generated from a unified theory is that they sometimes contradict one another.

Mediation is frequently described and rarely analyzed. Gulliver, who has observed more and written more about mediation than any anthropologist, notes that it "remains an inadequately understood process [1977: 44]." As with other forms of third-party intervention, "there is an abundance of specific detail, but no general knowledge [Rosenau, 1968: 150]." The propositions in this chapter are derived in part from the thin literature on mediation and a little on several of my earlier papers (1974, 1975; Felstiner and Drew, 1978; Felstiner and Williams, 1978), but for the most part they are ideas that either came or were suggested to me or colleagues during fieldwork in 1977 on mediation at the Dorchester Urban Court in Boston (see Felstiner and Williams, 1980).[1] They may, as a consequence, have more power in interpersonal disputes in so-called neighborhood justice centers in the United States than for activities such as marriage counseling and consumer mediation in the same society, but they are intended to apply to all interpersonal mediation involving disputants whose culture is that of a Western industrialized society.

There is one more preliminary matter. All of the propositions seek to explain the "success" of mediation—success is the dependent variable. But what do I mean by success? First, it is determined from the perspective of the disputants—the consequences of mediation for others are ignored. Second, it may have several operational forms:

1. Success may be an open judgment by the disputants. "On a scale of one to five, how successful was the mediation in which you were involved?" With this measure, success is subjective and interdisputant consistency is unknown.
2. Success may be a specified judgment by the disputants. "On a scale of one to five, how successful was mediation in solving the problems raised in the hearing?" This definition provides better assurance that success means the same thing to different disputants, but it narrows the criteria to the resolution of issues ex-

---

[1]Although the literature was thin when this paper was written, a special issue of the *Journal of Social Issues* devoted to mediation to be published in 1984 suggests that considerable research on mediation has been conducted recently.

plicitly raised at a hearing. Those disputants who believe that their relationship with another disputant has been substantially improved even though the issues at a hearing were not resolved would be forced to classify mediation as a failure, when in fact they considered it to be a success.

3. Success may be equivalent to reaching an agreement at a mediation hearing. This definition is easy to apply, but difficult to evaluate. Many agreements are empty gestures concluded to please mediators or terminate uncomfortable hearings. Others are unrealistic or simply fail to improve relations between the disputants. On the other hand, hearings that do not produce an agreement may nonetheless be helpful.

4. Success may be defined by an outsider's comparison of complaints voiced at a hearing with long-term outcome.

A choice among these measures or a composite of them is a difficult task for any researcher who sets out to test the propositions. But in understanding the propositions it is only necessary to assume that success means an improvement in the relationship between the disputants, whether the improvement comes from an agreement or from change in behavior or in attitude, and whether the disputants agree about the form of improvement. The only circumstance in which disputant satisfaction and success are unrelated is when a disputant wants mediation to harm a relationship with another disputant. (From the point of view of such a disputant, all the propositions may be reversed.) Success may also be a relative measure. Therefore, a proposition that asserts that success is related to X may mean either that if X, then success, or the more X, the more success.

The Propositions

There are 23 propositions. Nine relate success to aspects of the mediation process, 5 to the characteristics of mediators, 8 to those of disputes, and 1 to characteristics of disputants. Table 9.1 lists hypotheses by short title and independent variable.

Proposition 1   *Success in mediation is related to the cognitive orientation of disputants.*

Those disputants who exhibit a high degree of rights consciousness or whose attitude toward dispute processing is dominated by a court model will discount mediators as impotent judges and will feel that the

TABLE 9.1.
Table of Propositions

Number	Short title	Independent variable
1	Cognitive orientation	Disputants
2	Complexity	Dispute
3	Interests versus values	Dispute
4	Contra money, property	Dispute
5	Single incidents	Dispute
6	Money, property	Dispute
7	Continuing relationship	Dispute
8	Underlying cause	Dispute
9	Practical problems	Dispute
10	Outcome function	Mediators
11	Process function	Mediators
12	Psychotherapy—Yes	Process of mediation
13	Psychotherapy—No	Mediators
14	Affinity	Mediators
15	Sex, race	Mediators
16	Defining issues	Process of mediation
17	Confidentiality and moral neutrality	Process of mediation
18	Coercion	Process of mediation
19	Attitude versus behavior	Process of mediation
20	Form and function	Process of mediation
21	Manipulation	Process of mediation
22	Equality	Process of mediation
23	Sequencing	Process of mediation

anormative stance of mediation debases legitimate expectations (see Kurczewski and Frieske, 1978: 315). This proposition was first reported by researchers working in rural Poland but may be even more salient in the United States, where firsthand and vicarious experience with adjudication overshadows any experience with formal mediation.

On the other hand, the effect of a courtroom orientation may be reduced by a large volume of everyday experience. Presumably, success in problem solving in one context produces attempts to duplicate those techniques in others. Many people who have had no exposure to formal mediation will, nevertheless, have become comfortable with negotiations and compromise as a style of responding to conflict. Formal mediation will not appear to them to be either impotent or illegitimate, for it will parallel, and be reinforced by, their previous experience.[2]

---

[2]Many complainants may in fact prefer a mixed mode of dispute processing—mediation with its high degree of disputant participation in reaching an agreement coupled to some coercive power to enforce the consensual agreement.

Proposition 2 *Success in mediation is more likely in disputes involving several problems rather than a single issue.*

The core of mediation is compromise. Compromises may be of two sorts: Values may be traded on a single issue, or issues may be traded in multiproblem disputes. In simple cases, only single-issue adjustments may be made. A landlord will accept fewer dollars than he or she believes correct, and an ex-tenant will pay more than he or she believes is justified. But if the value at issue is individible, no compromise may be possible. Neither party in a traditional custody battle, for instance, may be satisfied with visitation rights.

In multiissue disputes, because both types of compromise are possible, an agreement is more likely. If a couple disputing over custody of a child is also contesting support levels and property divisions, significant gains on the material issues may persuade either disputant to relinquish his or her claim to custody (see Ross, 1970: 143).

Proposition 3 *Success in mediation is related to the nature of the dispute—whether it concerns interests or values.*

This notion was first suggested by Aubert (1963) and has been repeated so often that it may be considered The Proposition in the field of mediation. Interests are objects similarly prized by the disputants, for example, money, other property, or power. Values are religious, moral, political, or scientific convictions and include beliefs about factual truth. The Proposition asserts that compromise, and therefore mediation, of values is difficult because "a scent of the illicit often pervades such dealings: 'one cannot trade in values,' 'ideas are not for sale,' 'no bargain with the truth,' etc. This illicit nature of compromise on the level of value and of empirical truth makes it hard to discuss matters quite candidly, thereby decreasing the chances of reaching a solution [Aubert, 1963: 29]."

The Proposition thus claims that conflicts of values will be less likely than conflicts over interests to produce mediated agreements, for two reasons: (*a*) because of the principles involved in value conflicts, compromise may be rejected on principle; and (*b*) because of the principles involved in value conflicts, frank discussions between the disputants will be difficult and compromise will be jeopardized by the failure in communication.

I have amended The Proposition because my view of conflict over empirical truth may be different from Aubert's. Aubert appears to endorse the conventional understanding of facts as objective events that have happened in the past. Facts may be difficult to get straight, and participants will have different views about them, but they are stable data. I believe, on the other hand, in a transformation perspective (see Hosticka, 1979: 599; Felstiner, Abel, and Sarat, 1981) in which facts are subjective phenomena. They are subjective because they can frequently be "known" only as the experience of them is recalled. The process of recall is influenced by the attribution of motives: They frequently determine our understanding of behavior. If we are presented with new information that changes our attributions, our view of what happened in the past will also change—the facts have changed. Because of this process, compromise over facts is not necessarily illicit and may be unnecessary. As the compromise itself unfolds, the facts necessary to make that compromise tenable will emerge. The past will be formulated retroactively to rationalize the present.

The transformation perspective leads me to confine The Proposition to conflicts over values where values are defined to include only religious, moral, political, or scientific conviction and to exclude beliefs about factual truth.

Proposition 4 *Disputes concerning money or other property are less likely to be successfully mediated than are nonproperty disputes* (compare Witty, 1980: 18).

The objectives of mediation may be to correct the past or structure the future. When the objective is to correct the past, the means to do so are frequently of a zero-sum character: Every benefit secured by the compensated party is a loss to the party doing the compensating. Compromise is possible—the recipient may take less, and the payer pay more, than each would wish or believe fair. But whatever the concessions, in the residual one gains only at the other's expense. On the other hand, when a mediation agreement is concerned only with a relationship in the future, one disputant does not necessarily gain at the expense of the other. Each may agree to alter his or her behavior in ways that please the other but do not necessarily displease himself or herself or are less displeasing than they are pleasing to the other (see Walton and McKersie, 1965).

The second stage of this proposition is that zero-sum agreements are more difficult to produce than are positive-sum agreements simply because the costs of compromise are less in positive-sum cases. And the final stage is the empirical generalization that property disputes are more likely to be concerned with correcting the past and less likely to be concerned with structuring the future than are nonproperty disputes over matters such as fidelity, custody, physical abuse, nuisance, and power.

Proposition 5 *Mediation agreements are less likely to be reached in disputes growing out of single incidents than in those arising from sporadic misunderstandings or continual conflict.*

This notion is a derivative of Proposition 4. It depents on an assumption that single-incident disputes are more likely to demand corrections of the past and are, therefore, more likely to involve difficult, zero-sum adjustments.

Proposition 6 *This proposition is formally the opposite of 4; it asserts that disputes concerning money or other property are more likely to be successfully mediated than are nonproperty disputes.*

It is proposed without elaboration by Merry (1982), relying on research conducted on Florida citizen dispute-resolution programs. The thought, I presume, is that the more concrete the dispute, the more likely it is that a mediated agreement will be fulfilled (see Felstiner and Williams, 1980: 24).

It is possible that Propositions 4 and 6 are empirically consistent because they refer to judgments made at different points in dispute life cycles. Proposition 4 asserts that agreement is less likely in property disputes; Proposition 6 proposes that property agreements, if reached, are more likely to be kept.

Proposition 7 *Success in mediation is related to the existence of a relationship that the parties wish, or are forced, to maintain* (Witty, 1980: 15; Merry, 1982: 31).

Merry, for instance, believes that the tilt toward the future provides necessary coercion to compromise. Certainly, compromise is central to mediation. But a continuing relationship may be only an example of a more general proposition that asserts that success in mediation is related to the propensity of dispute types to accommodation: Any set of factors that make compromise feasible will better the chances of success. Thus, the wish to terminate a painful relationship may be as effective an incentive in mediation as the need to restructure continuing interaction, and mediation may prove a useful adjunct to so-called small-claims procedures (in the United States), although those cases infrequently involve continuing relationships (McEwen and Maiman, 1981: 251). For instance, the certainty of result and increased likelihood of payment in mediation may be adequate grounds for a creditor plaintiff to compromise even though he or she has no expectation of ever dealing with the debtor defendant again.

Proposition 8 *Mediation cannot ordinarily confront the underlying causes of disputes submitted to it.*

If underlying causes are social in origin or are rooted in patterns established by years of coping or reflect ingrained attitudes, mediation will not address them. Inadequate housing, unemployment, chronic violence, sexual inadequacy, and racial hostility, for instance, underlie many disputes referred to mediation, but mediators do not deal with the disputant's responses to such stresses (compare Wallerstein and Kelly, 1977: 8).

Proposition 9 *Mediation will be most effective in sorting out the practical problems of urban life.*

It can assist neighbors in controlling pets, children, and noise. It can help strike bargains over restitution for property damage and theft. It is likely to be effective where intimates want to separate. It then works to reduce the likelihood of abrasive encounters, to divide property, and to set acceptable terms of child visitation and support. Mediators may also intervene successfully at the shallow end of maladaptations. Assume that he hits her when she nags, she nags when he drinks, and he drinks to ease the pain of living. Although mediation cannot cope with his underlying dissatisfaction, it may show her that if she breaks the cycle by not nagging when he has been drinking, she may avoid the beatings that brought her to mediation in the first place. I do not mean to advocate as a solution to physical abuse that the victim must avoid behavior that seems to provoke it. It would be better for her if he stopped drinking and might be better if she abandoned the relationship. But if he will not stop and she does not wish to go, mediation is an effective technique for helping people identify second-best solutions.

This proposition parallels Walton's suggestion that conflicts centering on substantive issues require bargaining and problem solving, whereas disagreements about emotions need "restructuring of a persons' perceptions and the working through of feelings between the principals [1969: 75]." Mediation, if limited to one or two sessions, is adapted to problem solving but cannot generally meet the needs of emotional rearrangement.[3]

Proposition 10   *Success in mediation is related to the mediator's ability to identify aspects of solutions that are not apparent to the disputants.*

This proposition emphasizes the so-called production function of mediation (see Danzig and Lowy, 1975: 689–691; Felstiner, 1975: 703; Todd, 1978: 108). It asserts that mediators contribute to agreements through substantive suggestions as well as by structuring a process of discussion and bargaining.

Proposition 11   *Success in mediation is related to the mediator's ability to facilitate communication between the disputants.*

Mediators, and the format in which they operate, may "increase, clarify and focus the exchange of information [Gulliver, 1977: 31; see also Deutsch, 1973], including information about the disputants' feelings.

Proposition 12   *Mediation is effective in part because it is therapeutic.*

It involves Parson's four necessary elements of psychotherapy (see Gibbs, 1967: 284):

1. Support: Parties are encouraged to express their complaints and feelings because they sense group support.
2. Permissiveness: Ordinary restrictions on making antisocial statements are reduced.
3. Denial of reciprocity: Antisocial statements and descriptions of antisocial behavior do not lead to sanctions or controlling behavior.
4. Manipulation of rewards: Conciliation is coaxed through group approval.

Proposition 13   *When mediation is confronted with marital difficulties and other problems between intimates, it is attempting to intervene in interpersonal systems, a task to which it is not well suited.*

---

[3]Propositions 8 and 9 may inadequately deal with divorce mediation. If divorce mediation is conducted by people with training in counseling rather than in law and if it is not limited to a small number of sessions, it may function as a form of brief therapy and may grapple with some of the deeper issues glossed over by neighborhood mediation.

A characteristic of these systems is that the difficulties usually have some advantages to the system participants. A second characteristic is the probability that attempts by individuals in the system to resolve the problems have instead made them worse. Mediators are generally not trained to connect specific negative behavior to the system of which it is an ingredient, or to perceive how some problem-solving behavior may make problems more intractable. As a result, mediation will not lead to positive change in dysfunctional interaction between intimates (see Weakland, Fisch, Wetzlawick, and Bodin, 1974).

This proposition rests on three assumptions: that some part of the caseload of mediation is indistinguishable from the problems encountered in brief psychotherapy, that psychotherapy is basically counterintuitive and therefore must be taught to paraprofessionals, and that its principles are not taught to mediators.

Proposition 14 *Success in mediation is related to the experiential and linguistic affinity between disputants and mediators.*

The relationship is derived from the following subpropositions:

1. Success in mediation requires a relatively candid recital of feelings, complaints, and requests.
2. Candor from the disputants requires that they trust the mediators to maintain confidentiality, to respect and validate the disputants' feelings, and to be able to understand their experience and the language in which it is expressed.

Proposition 15 *Success in mediation is not related to a sex or race correspondence between disputants and mediators or to coresidence in any particular community.*

Disputants care whether mediators understand their experience and manner of relating that experience. Generally, their experience and language is not sex, race, or community limited but is more a product of economic level, education, work, stage in the life cycle, and family situation. Exceptions will be in the area of race and sex rather than community: That is, urban life at any economic level in any neighborhood in any Western city is likely to be equivalent to that in any other.

Proposition 16 *Mediator attention to defining issues will be more constructive in cases of low rather than high conflict* (see Erickson, Holmes, Frey, Walker, and Thibaut, 1974).

In low-conflict situations, issue identification provides information necessary to direct activity toward reaching acceptable agreements. In high-conflict cases, on the other hand, issue identification inhibits agreements because it underscores the degree to which the disputants' objectives are incompatible.

Proposition 17 *Privacy and moral neutrality may handicap as well as promote success in Westernized mediation.*

In tribal societies, community representatives and disputant action sets (see Gulliver, 1971) are present at mediation sessions. They, as well as the mediators who tend to represent community values, provide a form of normative testing. In Western mediation, use of witnesses and lawyers is commonly discouraged and mediators are trained not to be judgmental. It is thus unlikely that anybody neutral or allied to disputants will tell them that they have been behaving badly and likely that some positions will be advanced by disputants who do not realize how inappropriate others might view their behavior.

Mediators who are anxious to be morally neutral, moreover, may have difficulty in understanding disputant perceptions when those perceptions are heavily influenced by value judgments.

Proposition 18 *The propensity of mediation sessions to produce agreements and of disputants to carry them out is related to the level of third-party coercion to which disputants are subjected.*

Coercion is defined as a prediction of negative consequences that are under the control of a third party. For instance, a warning of reactivated prosecution of the respondent is coercion as it is not administered by or under the control of the complainant. On the other hand, notice by a wife that she would leave her husband if he continued to drink is not coercion as the eventuality is the product of the will of a disputant, not of a third party. Coercion is an important independent variable because it may be applied in varying strength by strangers to the dispute.

Coercion is thought to be relevant because disputants are assumed to behave in response to conscious, rational choices. A prediction of negative consequences should, then, influence those choices if it is credible. The more credible and the more negative the prediction, the greater is the influence (see E. Fisher, 1975; Merry, 1982).

In a discussion of disputant threats rather than third-party coercion, Harold Kelley (1965: 101) suggests that a request phrased as a threat implies that the requested behavior is outside of the rules normally applied to the disputants' relationship. Otherwise, why would it have been communicated as a threat? Coercion need not assume this anormative coloration and may constitute or be masked as a prediction rather than a threat. As a result, it should be less likely to produce the aggression, fear, indignation, or other emotional states that are found as responses to threats.

Proposition 19 *Mediation between intimates leads to more change in attitude than in behavior.*

When a mediation hearing is effective for a dispute between such parties, it improves the disputants' understanding of one anothers' complaints and what they would like done about them (R. Fisher, 1969). The hearing, then, produces two different effects: It (*a*) changes each disputant's view of the other, enabling each to empathize with the perspective of the other disputant; and (*b*) makes more concrete the behavior change that each could make to please the other. The proposition asserts that there will be more change in attitude than in behavior because attitude change in this context is self-executing—it happens at the hearing— whereas behavior change requires a shift in habitual conduct that, despite the insight gained in mediation, may be difficult to make.

If this proposition is at all accurate, it ought to alter the conventional view of mediation agreements and success in mediation for disputes between intimates. Mediation agreements generally speak to behavior change—he agrees to come home before 12 or not to hit her; she agrees not to go out with other men or to hit their child. Agreements rarely speak to attitude change—I agree to understand that you are depressed or harried or worried about your health. Yet the proposition suggests that the product of mediation is more likely to be an understanding of why he stays out late or why she is depressed than a direct change in that behavior. This difference means two things: First, because of the attitude change alone, mediation may have been worthwhile even though no agreement is reached or kept. Second, the attitude change may even mean that it is not so important from the viewpoint of the other disputant that any agreement be kept. People's reactions to others are made up of two elements: the other's behavior and their own understanding of that behavior. When understanding changes, the reaction may change as definitively as when the behavior changes. If a disputant no longer feels aggrieved about another's behavior even though the behavior has not changed, it may be presumptuous for an outsider to assert that the mediation hearing that produced that change in attitude was any less successful than if it had led to a change in the originally disputed behavior.

Proposition 20   *Success in mediation is dependent on the degree to which its structure is appropriate to its function.*

Labor mediation, for instance, is episodic, complete, impersonal, and delayed. It is episodic in the sense that the disputes it is mobilized to settle tend to stay settled during the period of the agreement. Terms are not renegotiated and generally are followed. Although the differences in attitudes that form the basis of labor conflicts remain between points of mediation, the behavioral elements of those conflicts are fixed for a period of time and are generally uncontested for that period of time, and thus there is little need to pay attention to the parties' ability, or lack of it, to negotiate about those issues in the interim.

Labor mediation is complete in the sense that arbitration is available if any major issues are left for interim disposition. Labor mediation is impersonal in the sense that though the disputants' feelings about one another may be important, they are not crucial. They are not crucial because there is not necessarily any interaction involving the parties' negotiating representatives between mediator interventions and because substitutions can frequently be made among negotiators if aggravated problems in interpersonal relations do occur. Labor mediation is a delayed process in that it occurs only when the parties have failed to agree on contract terms after prolonged discussion of those very terms. Because labor mediation has these characteristics, its function is to secure an agreement to specific issues rather than to improve the parties' ability to communicate with one another.

On the other hand, in the senses in which these terms are used, mediation of many interpersonal cases is not *episodic, complete, impersonal* or *delayed*. In mediation, the disputants do not attempt to freeze the preponderance of their interaction for a substantial period. They are not writing detailed interaction contracts, and they do not attempt to forecast and provide a response to the many turns that their relationship will take over time. Substitutions are not possible. Parties to an interpersonal dispute that comes to mediation may well have tried for a long time to make their relationship more positive, but they may not have confronted directly the issues that prove to be, or ought to be, the gist of the mediation (see Felstiner and Williams, 1978). The stark consequence of all these contrasts with labor relations is that the ability of the disputants in interpersonal mediation to set the framework for continuing and important negotiations may be the core of what the mediation is about.

An important dimension on which the structure of mediation varies is the extent to which it uses direct and indirect communication. In direct communication, the exploration of issues and outcomes takes place with all parties present. In indirect communication—so-called shuttle diplo-

macy—the bulk of the mediation involves meetings between the mediator and one party at a time. Because shuttle diplomacy is an effective
technique to finding compromise outcomes on specific issues, it is well
adapted to labor mediation. But for mediation of interpersonal disputes,
where postmediation communication is more important than the specific issues being mediated, direct communication should be a more effective technique.

Proposition 21   *Mediation may be manipulative, and this dimension may
undermine its success.*

Disputants may be maneuvered into an agreement by ambiguous
representations or commitments, by suppression of conflict in the later
stages of a hearing, by the expression of mediator judgments, and by the
coercion of the alternative, especially the criminal court. A disputant
who feels that his or her freedom of action has been compromised by
such manipulation will respond by subverting the agreement, retaliating
against the other disputant in areas outside of the agreement, or by
shifting his or her resentment inward or toward a third party.

Proposition 22   *Success in mediation depends on status equality between
the disputants.*

One notion is that disparities in power prevent the weaker party from
the candid presentation of complaints and requests that is the foundation of useful mediation—the weaker party cannot trust the stronger not
to retaliate outside of mediation and outside of the interaction that is
being mediated. Mediation between adolescent children and their parents is, on these grounds, avoided by some American mediation projects: "The project's experience in unequal power cases was that arguments were one-sided because the superordinate party rarely gave away
anything and the subordinate party would not articulate its real demands [Felstiner and Williams, 1980: 5]."

Status inequality is predicted by different researchers to have different kinds of consequences. Cathie Witty asserts that "differences in
wealth and status do not appear to affect the outcomes of mediated
settlements [1980: 8]." Instead, faced with large differences in power,
mediation withers and is replaced by adjudication (Witty, 1980: 23).
Merry, on the other hand, after an extensive review of the ethnographic
literature, concludes that "mediated settlements between unequals are
unequal [1982: 32]," suggesting that expectations of imbalance aside,
they may not be successful from at least one disputant's perspective.
This result may be more a consequence of coercive agreements than of

inhibitions on full participation. This view is also endorsed by critical theorists. Santos, for instance, alleges that mediation of landlord–tenant and consumer disputes "assumes a repressive nature because the setting has no coercive power to neutralize, even at the individual level, the power difference between the parties [1980: 390]." On the other hand, mediation of such small commercial disputes is frequently a step in an adjudicative system in which coercive state power may be mobilized by tenants and consumers (see McEwen and Maiman, 1981).

Proposition 23 *Successful mediation follows the phase movement of other problem-solving techniques.*

The purpose of interpersonal mediation is problem solving. Either attention is directed to a specific dispute or a contentious course of conduct or set of attitudes. Other problem-solving processes are alleged to exhibit "phase movement" or predictable sequences of interaction and, within phases, different frequencies of types of interaction (see Bales and Strodtbeck, 1951). Robert Bales and his colleagues believe that their stipulated phase movement captures the cognitive and emotional reactions of individuals to the process of successful problem solving. As a consequence, the empirical claim is that deviation from the predicted phases and frequencies reduces the probability of problem-solving success. Other researchers have suggested that this proposition applies to various forms of mediation (see, e.g., Landsberger, 1955; Shaw, Fischer, and Kelley, 1973), including interpersonal mediation (Williams, 1980).

Conclusion

Developing a set of propositions about mediation or any dispute-related phenomenon is not so difficult. Much the more difficult task is constructing an empirical context in which the propositions can be explored. There are, moreover, major shortcomings in any of the orthodox approaches to this problem. Consider, for instance, an observation study in which notes or transcripts are coded and the presence or absence of independent variables is correlated with success measures, however they are operationalized. The magnitude of this effort and the resources that it would require are staggering. My own fieldwork on mediation as an alternative to criminal prosecution consumed about 5 hours of observer and coder time for every hour of mediation observed. If a researcher is trying to test 15–20 propositions, many of which will not be relevant to any particular mediation session, the number of sessions that will have to be observed is in the hundreds. As each mediation session may consume 1–2 hours (see McGillis, 1981: 26), the effort to test these propositions adequately by an observation study approaches at least one full-time research year. Moreover, the inability of a researcher to isolate sets of independent variables means that hypothesis testing in the ordinary sense may not be feasible even with hundreds of cases. This extensive effort is further compounded by problems of securing access to the many programs necessary to provide a representative sample of cases (see Felstiner and Williams, 1980: 2). On the other hand, exploration of these and similar propositions in a laboratory rather than in a natural setting could be accomplished with a reasonable level of resources at the same time that it would increase both the capacity to isolate specific variables and the size of samples. But laboratory research, on the other hand, might well be unable to meet the demands of external validity that have plagued a generation of jury research (see, e.g., Bray and Kerr, 1979; Konečni and Ebbesen, 1981: 486–492):

> We would prefer to base our conjectures about how people make various types of decisions on observations of the actual people making the actual decisions. Moreover, even if a real-world judge's decision strategies do change when certain features of his or her real-world legal task change—for example, because of administrative or legal modifications—such changes merely reflect the reality of decision making in the actual courts. Quite another matter are changes in decision strategies that are brought about by scientists' often arbitrary decisions to change this or that feature of the laboratory task; such changes typically have no substantive, let alone practical, importance or relevance, and their effects on subjects' decision strategies are therefore of minimal interest [Konečni and Ebbesen, 1981: 491].

My personal preference in this quandary is a third course: ethnography. I have, for instance, learned more about the operation of so-called adversarial and inquisitorial systems from Sybille Bedford's *The Faces of Justice* (1961), a reporter's account of specific trials in five countries, than I have from the exhaustive laboratory experiments comparing those systems conducted by Thibaut and Walker and colleagues, and I have as much faith in the accuracy and representativeness of what she described as I do in the relationship between their experiments and real trials (see Hayden and Anderson, 1979). Of course, good ethnography must be disciplined and intelligent. It must be as arduous when focused on modern domestic life as it is when used in traditional tribal settings. But to my knowledge, there are no published reports of such research on any mediation program in any Western industrial society.

ACKNOWLEDGMENTS

Richard Abel, Stewart Macaulay, Craig McEwen, and Sally Engle Merry commented on an earlier version of this chapter. I am even more indebted to my colleagues in fieldwork on mediation, Pauline Peters and Lynne Williams.

References

Aubert, Vilhelm
    1963   "Competition and dissensus: Two types of conflict and conflict resolution."
            Journal of Conflict Resolution 7: 26–50.
Bales, Robert F., and Fred L. Strodtbeck
    1951   "Phases in group problem-solving." *Journal of Abnormal and Social Psychology* 46:
            485–495.
Bedford, Sybille
    1961   *The Faces of Justice.* New York: Simon and Schuster.
Bray, Robert M., and Norbert L. Kerr
    1979   "Use of the simulation method in the study of jury behavior: Some meth-
            odological considerations." *Law and Human Behavior* 3: 107–119.
Cohen, Jerome A.
    1967   "Chinese mediation on the eve of modernization." *Journal of Asian and African
            Studies* 2: 54–76.
Danzig, Richard, and Michael J. Lowy
    1975   "Everyday disputes and mediation in the United States: A reply to Professor
            Felstiner." *Law and Society Review* 9: 675–694.
Deutsch, Morton
    1973   *The Resolution of Conflict.* New Haven, Conn.: Yale University Press.
Erickson, Bonnie, John G. Holmes, Robert Frey, Laurens Walker, and John Thibaut
    1974   "The functions of conflict: The role of a judge in pretrial conferences." *Journal of
            Personality and Social Psychology* 30: 293–306.
Felstiner, William L. F.
    1974   "Influences of social organization on dispute processing." *Law and Society Re-
            view* 9: 63–94.
Felstiner, William L. F.
    1975   "Avoidance as dispute processing." *Law and Society Review* 9: 695–705.
Felstiner, William L. F., Richard Abel, and Austin Sarat
    1981   "The emergence and transformation of disputes: Naming, blaming, and claim-
            ing." *Law and Society Review* 15: 631–654.
Felstiner, William L. F., and Ann B. Drew
    1978   *European Alternatives to Criminal Trials and Their Applicability in the United States.*
            Washington, D.C.: U.S. Government Printing Office.
Felstiner, William L. F., and Lynne A. Williams
    1978   "Mediation as an alternative to criminal prosecution." *Law and Human Behavior*
            2: 223–244.
    1980   *Community Mediation in Dorchester, MA.* Washington, D.C.: U.S. Government
            Printing Office.
Fisher, Eric
    1975   "Community courts: An alternative to conventional criminal adjudication."
            American University Law Review 24: 1253–1291.
Fisher, Roger
    1969   *International Conflict for Beginners.* New York: Harper & Row.
Fuller, Lon
    1971   "Mediation: Its forms and functions." *Southern California Law Review* 44:
            305–338.
Gibbs, James L., Jr.
    1967   "The Kpelle moot." Pages 277–291 in *Law and Warfare,* edited by Paul Bohan-
            nan. Garden City, N.Y.: The Natural History Press.

Gulliver, Phillip H.
    1971   *Neighbours and Networks: The Idiom of Kinship in Social Action among the Ndendeuli of Tanzania*. Berkeley, Calif.: University of California Press.
Gulliver, Phillip H.
    1977   "On mediators." Pages 15–52 in *Social Anthropology and Law*, edited by Ian Hamnett. London: Academic Press.
Hayden, Robert M., and Jill K. Anderson
    1979   "On the evaluation of procedural systems in laboratory experiments." *Law and Human Behavior* 3: 21–38.
Hosticka, Carl J.
    1979   "We don't care about what happened, we only care about what is going to happen: Lawyer–client negotiations of reality." *Social Problems* 26: 599–610.
Kelley, Harold H.
    1965   "Experimental studies of threats in interpersonal negotiations." *Journal of Conflict Resolution* 9: 79–105.
Konečni, Vladimir J., and Ebbe B. Ebbesen
    1981   "Social psychological approaches to legal issues." Pages 481–498 in *The Trial Process*, edited by Bruce D. Sales. New York: Plenum Press.
Kurczewski, Jacek, and Kazimierz Frieske
    1978   "The Social Conciliatory Commission in Poland." Pages 153–427 in *Access to Justice*, edited by Mauro Cappelletti and John Weisner. Milan: Dott A. Giuffre, Editore.
Landsberger, Henry A.
    1955   "Interaction process analysis of the mediation of labor–management disputes." *Journal of Abnormal and Social Psychology* 51: 552–558.
McEwen, Craig A., and Richard J. Maiman
    1981   "Small claims mediation in Maine: An empirical assessment." *Maine Law Review* 33: 237–268.
McGillis, Daniel
    1981   *Neighborhood Justice*. Washington, D.C.: National Institute of Justice.
Merry, Sally Engle
    1982   "The social organization of mediation in nonindustrial societies: Implications for informal community justice in America." Pages 17–45 in *The Politics of Informal Justice* (Vol. 2), edited by Richard L. Abel. New York: Academic Press.
Rosenau, James N.
    1969   "Intervention as a scientific concept." *Journal of Conflict Resolution* 13: 150–171.
Ross, H. Lawrence
    1970   *Settled Out of Court*. Chicago: Aldine Press.
Santos, Boaventura de Sousa
    1980   "Law and community, the changing nature of state power in late capitalism." *International Journal of the Sociology of Law* 8: 379–397.
Shaw, Jerry I., Claude S. Fisher, and Harold H. Kelley
    1973   "Decision-making by third parties in settling disputes." *Journal of Applied Social Psychology* 3: 197–218.
Thibaut, John, and Laurens Walker
    1975   *Procedural Justice: A Psychological Analysis*. Hillsdale, N.J.: Lawrence Earlbaum Associates.
Todd, Harry F., Jr.
    1978   "Litigious marginals: Character and disputing in a Bavarian village." Pages 86–121 in *The Disputing Process—Laws in Ten Societies*, edited by Laura Nader and Harry F. Todd, Jr. New York: Columbia University Press.

Wallerstein, Judith S., and Joan B. Kelly
    1977 "Divorce counseling: A community service for families in the midst of divorce." *American Journal of Orthopsychiatry* 47: 4–22.
Walton, Richard E.
    1969 *Interpersonal Peacemaking: Confrontations and Third-Party Consultation.* Reading, Mass.: Addison-Wesley.
Walton, Richard E., and Robert B. McKersie
    1965 *A Behavioral Theory of Labor Negotiations.* New York: McGraw-Hill.
Weakland, John H., Richard Fisch, Paul Watzlawick, and Arthur M. Bodin
    1974 "Brief therapy: Focused problem resolution." *Family Process* 13: 141–168.
Williams, Lynne A.
    1980 *Mediation as a Mechanism for the Resolution of Interpersonal Disputes.* Ph.D dissertation, Department of Psychology, University of Southern California.
Witty, Cathie J.
    1980 *Mediation and Society.* New York: Academic Press.

10

Rethinking Gossip and Scandal[*]

SALLY ENGLE MERRY

Villagers in a small, isolated Andalusian town of 2000 inhabitants wedged between dry Spanish mountains live in a world of lively, articulate, and omnipresent gossip and scandal: "People live very close to one another under conditions which make privacy difficult. Every event is regarded as common property and is commented upon endlessly. . . . People's observation is sharp, and they are quick to satirize each other behind their backs [Pitt–Rivers, 1971: 31]." To these people, the power of public opinion is very great. "It is recognized that people are virtuous for fear of what will be said [1971: 31]." In contrast, in an ethnically diverse neighborhood of 1200 people inhabiting a small, densely packed housing project in a major American city, gossip is pervasive but is of far less concern (Merry, 1981). It flows only within smaller, ethnically homogeneous subgroups of the neighborhood and, unlike gossip in the Spanish town, rarely crosses these social boundaries or stimulates a collective response.

Why do gossip and scandal play such different roles in these two social settings? What gives gossip its power to control behavior, and how is this

*I am grateful to the Center for Studies of Metropolitan Problems of the National Institute of Mental Health for support under grant no. 1 F31 MH 05088–01 for the research described in this chapter.

271

power affected by the social structure within which it occurs? Anthropologists have long assumed that gossip and scandal serve as effective modes of informal social control (Radcliffe-Brown, 1933; Benedict,
1934; Herskovitz, 1937: 74ff.; Kluckhohn, 1944; Yang, 1945; Schwartz,
1954; Loudon, 1961; Gluckman, 1963; Abrahams, 1970: 296; Pitt-Rivers,
1971). Yet, we know very little about the process through which gossip
actually impinges on individuals' lives or why it seems to deter deviance.
We have accepted the folk view, widely shared by pastoral and peasant
peoples, that gossip is to be feared and avoided, but we have not systematically examined the consequences of gossip or how these differ for
individuals in various social positions. This chapter examines what gossip does and why it is sometimes ignored.

My survey of much of the ethnographic literature on gossip suggests
that talk, by itself, is far less important in deterring deviance than we
imagine. Gossip is often part of larger social processes, however, that
lead to the implementation of powerful social, economic, and political
sanctions. Individuals vulnerable to these pressures are vulnerable to
gossip, whereas those who are not ignore and defy malicious talk. Gossip
controls behavior when the people who gossip exercise other forms of
social control over its victims. Ethnographies about gossip in small-scale,
face-to-face societies are studded with examples of people who persist in
breaking deeply entrenched rules despite a storm of gossip about their
heads, as well as people who are somehow above and beyond the reach of
gossip (e.g., Frankenberg, 1957; Barth, 1961; Bailey, 1971; Pitt-Rivers,
1971; Selby, 1974; Yngvesson, 1976). These tend to be persons who are
insulated from the social, political, and economic consequences of gossip
either by their wealth and control over scarce resources such as land, or
by their accepted marginal social status and economic self-sufficiency. It
is those in the middle of the social spectrum, vying with one another for
slight precedence in social affairs, who are most concerned about gossip
and most vulnerable to its consequences.

The role of gossip in achieving social control in stable, bounded,
morally homogeneous, and close-knit societies where escape and avoidance are difficult differs markedly from its function in large, fluid, open,
and morally heterogeneous communities where escape and avoidance
are realistic possibilities. In modern society, gossip is pervasive, yet it
seems to have little deterrent effect and is generally of minor concern
(e.g., Hannerz, 1967; Peattie, 1968; Liebow, 1967; Bott, 1971; Merry,
1981). This conforms with our general expectation that informal social
controls weaken and formal controls grow in strength and scope with
modernization and the transition from small-scale, face-to-face societies
to complex urban ones (Black, 1976: 107–108). Yet, in some urban situa-

tions gossip does become a source of concern, whereas in certain village settings, residents ignore gossip. A comprehensive theory of the role of gossip and scandal in social control must identify the social conditions under which it has real consequences for its victims in both small-scale and complex societies.

Anthropological Perspectives on Gossip

Although gossip is omnipresent in the daily life of the communities anthropologists typically study, they have given it surprisingly little explicit analysis. In part, this neglect may reflect the difficulties of studying gossip. Because the content of gossip is finely tailored to the identities of its audience, it is affected by the presence of an observer in a way that a ceremonial or political gathering is not. Anthropologists do hear gossip when people report what has been said, by accident, or when the anthropologist represents a dominant colonial or ruling power and gossiping to him or her becomes a way of winning favor and defeating rivals (e.g., Colson, 1953; Balikci, 1968; Wilson, 1974). But they are largely excluded from intimate gossip sessions. In my research on an American urban neighborhood, I heard what was being passed around as gossip but observed natural gossiping only when I was temporarily ignored by a gossiping group or when the subject of the gossip was more socially distant from the speaker than I was. I was able to trace the flow of information circulating around the neighborhood, but I had little access to those intimate moments when close friends talk about a third friend. I expect this is true for much ethnography on gossip. Gossip may be a phenomenon that must rely heavily on reports of participants rather than those of observers.

A second obstacle to the ethnographic examination of gossip is the complexity and truncated nature of the information being communicated. As John Haviland argues, to understand gossip is to be competent in the underlying rules, values, and expectations of the culture and to have mastered a vast body of information on particular individuals and their kin networks, reputations, nicknames, and idiosyncracies (1977; see also Loudon, 1961: 147–148). He suggests that when one can understand gossip, one has mastered the culture. Probably as a result of this difficulty, many ethnographic studies of gossip concern social situations culturally and linguistically familiar to the observer.

One of the earliest efforts to analyze systematically the social functions of gossip was Gluckman's paper called "Gossip and Scandal" (1963). He argued that gossip is not simply "idle talk" but performs

significant functions in maintaining the morals, values, and unity of
social groups by restating their moral codes, providing a way of controlling competing cliques and aspiring members, making possible the selection of leaders without direct confrontation and embarrassment,
maintaining exclusive "we" groups by excluding newcomers who are
unable to participate in the group's gossip, and providing a means of
controlling members indirectly while preserving a pretense of group
amity.

This analysis is pervaded by the British structural-functionalists' assumptions of social equilibrium, harmony, stability, and the notion that
all institutions further these ends, as well as by Gluckman's own belief
that social conflict creates social cohesion and order. It exaggerates the
harmonious consequences of gossip while ignoring its disruptive, oppressive, divisive, and destructive implications. Further, it concentrates
on the functions gossip performs for social groups, but not those for
individuals, and analyzes gossip only within small, morally homogeneous, and bounded social groups. Nevertheless, Gluckman's analysis
poses important questions about the social role and significance of gossip in the functioning of small social groups.

In a major attack on Gluckman's analysis and on the entire structural-
functional mode of analysis in which it is framed, Robert Paine argues
that gossip is a form of communication and information management, a
device individuals use to put forward and protect their own interests
and to attack their opponents in situations where open confrontation is
too risky (1967: 278–279). Gossip is a means of competing by broadcast-
ing favorable information about one's self while transmitting critical
facts about one's rivals. Values are asserted in gossip, but they simply
provide the terms in which claims and counterclaims are couched and
justified. Gossip does not necessarily lead to group cohesion; it can
destroy the group. Paine argues that Gluckman has ignored the perspective of the actor and his or her motivations for gossiping. As he points
out, "It is the individual and not the community that gossips [1967:
280]."

Unfortunately, this debate (see also Gluckman, 1968; Paine, 1968) has
sidetracked further discussion of the social functions of gossip by em-
broiling the question in the conflict between system-centered and actor-
centered modes of explanation. In fact, Gluckman's and Paine's perspectives are not mutually exclusive but complementary. One looks at
the functions gossip performs for social groups, the other at the motivations for actors to engage in gossiping. Neither perspective alone is
adequate: Gluckman is too preoccupied with social needs and latent
functional analysis, whereas Paine leaves the questions Gluckman raises
about the social role of gossip unanswered. If anthropologists limit

themselves to the actor's perspective, they will be reduced to reporting faithfully the commonsense understandings of individual actors and neglecting the larger forces and institutions that impinge on these actors even though they are unaware of them. Both the notion of a pervasive social equilibrium and the idea that all individuals are motivated entirely by self-interest are caricatures of reality.

Paine's emphasis on gossip as a form of information transmission, however, has proved fruitful to further analyses of the processes, if not the functions, of gossip. Just as an individual manipulates his or her physical appearance to achieve "impression management" (Goffman, 1959), so the individual seeks to manage and control the information spread about him or her through gossip (Paine, 1970a; 1970b). Gossip is information shared by a communicating group. One can examine the processes of transmitting this information (Handelman, 1973), the conditions under which it is transformed into a community consensus about an individual's moral standing (Yngvesson, 1978), and the implications of the distribution and availability of information about the private lives and secret actions of one's fellows for individuals and for groups. As John Roberts suggests, gossip can be viewed as a means of storing and retrieving information, particularly in nonliterate societies (1964: 441). The information is stored in the minds of its members, and the process of gossip is actually a slow scanning of the total information resource of the group. For example, among the Hopi Indians, gossip retrieves legal precedents and previous disputes relevant to ongoing trials and conflicts (Cox 1970). Using this conceptual framework, I now turn to the problem of defining what gossip is and elaborate its structures, processes, and consequences.

Definitions and Characteristics

Gossip is informal, private communication between an individual and a small, selected audience concerning the conduct of absent persons or events. Gossip thrives when the facts are uncertain, neither publicly known nor easily discovered. Gossip generally contains some element of evaluation or interpretation of the event or person, but it may be implicit or unstated.

Scandal occurs when gossip is elevated into the public arena, when "everyone knows that everyone knows." It is often precipitated by a public confrontation or by the violation of such a basic norm or tabu that the information about the alleged incident can circulate without an accompanying evaluation, because all agree about the meaning of the behavior (Bailey, 1971: 288). Bronislaw Malinowski, for example, describes a case where an incestuous love affair was allowed to persist, despite widespread public knowledge spread through gossip, until the jealous lover publicly accused and insulted his rival (1926: 77–81). The announcement converted gossip into scandal and forced the culprit to acknowledge and respond to his rule breaking. To atone and to punish his accuser, he jumped off a tree and killed himself.

Although we commonly understand gossip to contain criticisms and judgments, it can usefully be divided into two distinct forms: information sharing and judgmental (Hannerz, 1967). Information-sharing gossip transmits private information about the actions of an absent third party but does not contain evaluations or judgments of that behavior. Mobile American blacks, for example, gossip to catch up on the activities of mutual friends when they meet with old friends (Hannerz, 1967). Judgmental gossip, on the other hand, contains information joined with criticisms and evaluations. It is this second form of gossip that is often vindictive, malicious, and hostile. These two types often occur together, and the same conversation can contain some communications that are critical and others that are purely informational.

The distinction between innocuous or information-sharing gossip and judgmental or "bad" gossip appears in the terms used to describe gossip in a variety of cultural settings. On Saint Vincent in the British West Indies, the people make a distinction between *commess*, or harmless gossip, and *melee*, or malicious gossip (Abrahams, 1970: 196). Heppenstall finds that residents of an Austrian mountain village distinguish between chatter (*plaudern*) and gossip (*tratschen*), that which has malicious undertones (1971: 154). Bailey argues that this distinction is typical of many European Alpine communities (1971: 288).

Moreover, it is the judgmental gossiper who is widely condemned. He or she is viewed as an evil and destructive person and gossip as an immoral and dangerous form of behavior in societies ranging from American urban blacks (Hannerz, 1967; Rainwater, 1970; Merry, 1981) to Greek pastoral nomads (Campbell, 1964: 291), Indian and Ladino Mexican villagers (Hotchkiss, 1967: 717; Selby, 1974: 69), Austrian mountain villagers (Heppenstall, 1971), Spanish villagers (Pitt-Rivers, 1971: 144), and Chinese peasants (Yang, 1945; Wolf, 1972: 37–41). Because I am interested in the role of gossip in social control, the remaining pages of my discussion deal primarily with judgmental gossip.

STRUCTURAL CHARACTERISTICS

Gossip is a form of private information that symbolizes intimacy. It is a social statement that the recipient of gossip is as socially close or closer to the speaker as is the subject of the gossip. To the audience, gossip is a confidence, a sign of trust and closeness. As gossip becomes more judgmental, it becomes a more powerful statement of social intimacy and trust. This aspect of gossip explains its ability to create and maintain boundaries around exclusive "we" groups (Gluckman, 1963). Because gossiping with a socially more distant person about a socially more intimate one risks accusations of disloyalty from the intimate, gossip is inevitably confined to a group and kept from outsiders. Gossip thus becomes a useful idiom for demonstrating relative intimacy and distance and can become a device for manipulating relationships, for forging new intimate ones and discarding old, less attractive ones.[1]

Gossip flows most readily in highly connected, morally homogeneous social networks, and it is here that its impact is greatest. For gossip to occur, the two participants must know a third party in common. The more mutual friends they have, the more people they can discuss. Every individual is at the center of a network of people he or she knows. The extent to which the members of this network know one another, independent of their relationship to ego, can be described as their "degree of connectedness" (Bott, 1971). Gossip flourishes in close-knit, highly connected social networks but atrophies in loose-knit, unconnected ones.

Moreover, only when the gossipers share moral views is the soil fertile for gossip. The person sharing a juicy tidbit expects the listener to join in condemning that behavior, not to approve it. If only minor differences in norms exist, gossip can forge consensus, but where fundamental ideas of proper behavior differ, gossip will be stunted.

THE SUBSTANCE OF GOSSIP

Gossip is about reputation, particularly lapses between claims to reputation and reports of actual behavior (Wilson, 1974: 100). One does not gossip about a prostitute who turns "tricks," but one does gossip about the respectable matron who is observed with men sneaking into her house day and night. It is couched in moral terms, with reference to how people should act. When conflicting interpretations of an event are put

---

[1]The recent popularity of mass media "gossip" columns is an attempt to build on this social idiom of intimacy by implying that the general public is sufficiently close to the media personnel and public figures to be privy to information about the private lives of national leaders. It transfers the underlying social meaning of the term *gossip* to a new social context in the same way that the feminists' use of the term *sister* to refer to nonrelated women suggests the trust and closeness of siblings. In both cases, the transplanted symbol derives its potency from the meaning it carries in the original usage.

forward through gossip, each is usually justified in terms of a set of norms. For example, I heard two reports of the same fight between two young men in the urban neighborhood I studied. One report claimed that one of the young men had assaulted the other, knocked him to the ground, and left victorious while the other was bloodied and humiliated. The other report said that the assault had been cowardly, coming from behind as the victim sat in his car. When the victim rose in anger to defend himself, the attacker fled down the street. The facts are not contradictory, but the moral implications of the two stories are quite different. Both are based on the same standards of what constitutes a fair fight and a victory, however. June Starr describes a similar case in a small Turkish village in which gossip is used to evaluate a man's response to his wife's sexual adventures to determine if he is a cuckold or a pimp (1978: 175; see also Selby, 1974: 74).

Gossip circulates around ambiguous situations: those with multiple rules, conflicting versions of the facts or undetermined facts, and uncertainty about the application of moral rules. As Yngvesson argues, gossip is a process of applying abstract rules to the complex reality of daily life, of fitting morals to ambiguous situations with limited facts, to generate shared interpretations of the moral meaning of events (1978: 153–155; see also Bailey, 1971: 284–285; Haviland, 1977). It is a means of allocating responsibility and assessing liability (Gluckman, 1972). It often uses social types to evaluate behavior and reputation. The social type is a label for a style of behavior, a kind of person, and the associated evaluation of the moral worth of that behavior, such as "red-neck," "greenhorn," "turkey," and so on (Hannerz, 1980). Social types are part of a group's shared culture. The process of gossip classifies particular individuals into these categories or analogous ones such as "witch" or "troublemaker" (Selby, 1974).

Gossip focuses on areas of structural tension, where conflicting social obligations and expectations cause strains. In societies where men are expected to be virile and display their powers by predatory sexual conquests of women, whereas women are expected to be chaste and virginal, for example, gossip frequently concerns sexual liaisons (e.g., Campbell, 1964; Pitt-Rivers, 1971; Starr, 1978). Collier (Chapter 5, Volume 2 of this work) finds that bridewealth societies, in which young men are dependent on their seniors for bridewealth and must wait until they are older to marry, have more frequent gossip than brideservice societies, in which young men can acquire wives simply by performing regular services for a young woman's family. She attributes this difference to the greater need in bridewealth societies to monitor behavior in order to ensure that others fulfill their obligations. It may also reflect the increased tensions created by this social pattern, rooted in the exclusive control of vital resources by family elders.

Numerous examples suggest that gossip centers on areas where the cultural ideal is demanding and creates stress. Societies with food shortages gossip about food distribution and gift giving (Marshall, 1961); those with an ethic of equality but real differences in income and power gossip about those who are proud or ostentatious (Frankenberg, 1957; Bailey, 1971; Peters, 1972); and societies in which access to significant resources depends on legitimate descent although genealogies are uncertain and confusing gossip about ancestors (Colson, 1953). The reindeer-herding Lapps, for whom theft of livestock is easy and common, gossip about who has stolen which animal and where they are (Paine, 1970a). Societies that believe in witchcraft gossip constantly about who is a witch and, thus, who is responsible for the misfortunes people suffer (Kluckhohn, 1944; Bleek, 1976; Selby, 1974). A transient community of Euro-Canadians in the Arctic gossips intensely about social identities when newcomers flood in, speculating on the possible defects and failures that have driven each person to this isolated work situation (Koster, 1977).

PROCESSUAL CHARACTERISTICS

Gossip has three distinct phases. The first is the circulation of information about an event or action. The second is the formation of some consensus about the moral meaning of that event; how it is to be interpreted, and which rules are to be applied. Gossip does not always lead to such a consensus, however, and may simply produce two or more competing and conflicting interpretations. The third phase is the implementation of the consensus, the transformation of shared opinions into some form of action. This action can range from individual acts of snubbing to collective decisions to expel. It may be applied or simply threatened. The following section of this chapter discusses this implementation process in more detail, examining the range of consequences that follow from gossip.

The Role of Gossip in Small-Scale Societies

Gossip creates cognitive maps of social identities and reputations. It forms dossiers on each member of one's community: who is a good curer, who can be approached for loans, who is powerful, who is a witch, who is a good worker, and who is a thief (Hotchkiss, 1967; Bailey,

1971: 713; Pitt-Rivers, 1971; Haviland, 1977: 39). New pieces of information circulated through gossip add to the body of knowledge available within a community about its members. In some societies, an individual's black reputation can discredit his or her entire family. A young woman's sexual deviance, for example, destroys the honor of her whole kin group in many Mediterranean societies (Campbell, 1964; Pitt-Rivers, 1971; Denich, 1974; Mernissi, 1975; Starr, 1978). The following case study illustrates the formation of these dossiers and the ways they are implemented in one small-scale nomadic society.

THE SARAKATSAN NOMADS

Among the Sarakatsan shepherds of northwestern Greece, gossip and slander are haunting worries, as each family engages in a continuous competitive struggle for social prestige and honor against the claims and attacks of rival families (Campbell, 1964). When studied by J. Campbell in the mid-1950s, the Sarakatsani worked as transhumanant pastoralists with flocks of sheep and goats, moving between mountain summer pastures and rented winter pastures on the plains. Throughout the past decades, they had become increasingly incorporated into the Greek cash economy through sales of milk, sheep, and wool and the necessity of paying rent to sedentary villagers for rights to pasture lands. At the same time, their freedom of movement was considerably restricted by government efforts to control their migrations and by the increasing difficulties of obtaining winter pastures in the more settled coastal plains. Influential patrons in villages and local government became increasingly necessary in order to acquire these lands, enhancing the position of those wealthy shepherds with such contacts.

The basic social unit of the Sarakatsani is the bilateral kindred, a network of about 250 men, women, and children linked as siblings and cousins and dispersed throughout the grazing areas. As the smallest sheep management unit requires 4 adult males, most nuclear families join with kinsmen for purposes of herd management and negotiation for pasture rights (1964: 30–40).

Gossip is a pervasive aspect of Sarakatsani life. Campbell observed "interminable criticism of other people's failings [1964: 307]":

> The prestige of an individual, or a family, is constantly being evaluated in the community through gossip about personalities and events. To be gossiped about is in most cases to be criticized adversely, and since people enjoy this recreation, they laugh at and ridicule the object of their discussion. The knowledge, or the imagining, of this ridicule and laughter is an important element in a man's feelings of shame. For if the outside world judges him to be a failure he has also failed to live up to his own ideal image of himself which depends on success [1964: 312].

Gossip travels quickly, even in this dispersed community, and within 2 or 3 days an event becomes widely known (1964: 39, 313). The whole family suffers a loss of honor from the misbehavior of a single member, whether the sexual dalliance of one of its women or the lack of honor and manliness of one of its men. A man being ridiculed generally finds out first from a kinsman, who is anxious that the slur being circulated will not damage the prestige of the whole family (1964: 313).

Gossip not only attacks a person's honor and social prestige, however, but also leads to tangible political, economic, and social consequences. If a man loses his honor, he is denied full recognition and response from his community. He is rarely invited to major social events such as weddings, receives few visitors, and finds that his opinions in the coffee shop are ignored. When consensus concerning his moral standing emerges, he may find himself the subject of a satirical song, anonymously composed, which is remembered within the community and sung behind his back. It is a fate a man fears (1964: 313–314). The subject of gossip may be awarded a nickname ridiculing some aspect of his behavior. Campbell mentions public jokes and insults heaped on men of little honor, such as offering a man unable to hold his liquor water instead of ouzo at a large wedding party or inviting someone to sing when all know that his voice is execrable. If a man of higher prestige marries a woman of lesser honor, the community will deny him his more honorable patronym by labeling him with a nickname instead of his real name (1964: 300–301). In each of these forms of shaming, a man is not even able to counterattack to restore his honor, for the culprit is not an individual but the community as a whole.

Because gossip and scandal tarnish the name of an entire family, kinsmen are anxious to prevent family members from behaving in a dishonorable or immodest fashion. A person who refuses to behave appropriately risks losing the support of his family, a serious threat since life without kinsmen is virtually insupportable and kinsmen are irreplaceable (1964: 192). Without relatives, an individual has no one he can trust to provide information about the going prices for his precious milk and wool, to inform him about intrigues among other Sarakatsani, to assist him in times of hardship and economic disaster with loans and goods, to refrain from spreading gossip about him, to defend his name against gossip by others, to spring into a fight on his side, and, perhaps most important, to herd his animals with (1964: 95–96). Winter pastures must be rented by larger cooperating groups, and in this competitive and distrustful community, only kinsmen feel that they can rely on one another sufficiently for such cooperation.

A family's loss of reputation through damaging gossip affects the marriage prospects of all its members as well. All Sarakatsan families are anxious to arrange good marriages for their children, for only through marriage does a person achieve social adulthood (1964: 150). To remain unmarried is a humiliating and terrifying fate. Yet negotiations for marriage partners are delicate and fraught with hazards to honor, because only families equal in prestige can intermarry. An offer of marriage is thus a claim to social equality, and a rebuff a humiliating slap at the honor of the suitor's family. A broken betrothal demands vengeance to salvage the family's honor. Not surprisingly, considerable gossip surrounds matchmaking concerning the moral character, physical appearance, and strength of both parties as well as the relative prestige of their families and the size of the dowry.

The family of low prestige is also less able to defend its flocks and pastures. A family's reputation for manliness and courage discourages encroachment on its pasture land by other shepherds and in the past, before sheep stealing was outlawed by the state, deterred thieves. A flock owner who failed to retaliate against the theft of a few sheep advertised himself as a ready victim (1964: 206–207). Leaders of prestigious families have greater success negotiating for winter pastures in the plains and receive superior treatment from the village president, who controls summer pastures. Gossip also influences a family's political standing. Men of honor are more likely to find their comments respected and influential and to find kinsmen with powerful patrons willing to help them, and they are less likely to experience public mocking and social disengagement.

Thus, gossip and the reputations created by gossip impinge on a wide range of social and economic interests. Gossip controls individual Sarakatsani because they are economically dependent on one another. Because the community is small and bounded, they are also dependent on fellow Sarakatsani for all social ties including marriage partners. If exit from the community were made easy or if alternative marriage partners were available for those who lost honor, the grip of gossip might be loosened. The vulnerability of the average family to the economic control of others and their dependence on other families for vital and irreplaceable social relationships ensure that the reputations gossip creates will have serious consequences.

Yet, some Sarakatsani flagrantly defy the rules of their society despite the oppressive gossip. Campbell suggests that the very poor and the very rich both seem to be somewhat immune to assaults on their reputations (1964: 266–267). Members of wealthy, leading families lose prestige only with difficulty, whereas those who are very poor have none and seem unable to gain it even though they comport themselves as paragons of moral virtue. One-fifth of the families are either very rich or very poor. It is the other four-fifths of the Sarakatsan families, those roughly equivalent in prestige and wealth, who engage in the most intense competition for prestige, who experience the greatest doubt and insecurity about rank, and whose efforts to improve their own status by allusive gossip and criticism of others are most pervasive (1964: 272). Among these families, "the display of ostentatious pride, a touchy sense of honor, and a compulsive attempt to conform to accepted standards of conduct" is most intense (1964: 267).[2]

The wealthy are insulated from gossip by their economic power. The rich can always offer a generous dowry to offset a daughter's tarnished reputation, and affinal links to a powerful family appear advantageous to prospective suitors regardless of the woman's honor. Powerful families are beginning to send their children to school in the villages and into occupations outside the nomad society, thus decreasing their dependence on the economic cooperation of kinsmen. Leaders of powerful families who have influential patrons disproportionately control access to the vital winter pasture lands and therefore control many weaker Sarakatsan families. Only 5% of the Sarakatsani now marry out of the nomad community, but as this figure increases, the nomads' dependence on other Sarakatsan families for marriage partners will decline.

[2]Those who refuse to buckle under to the wagging tongues of gossip fall at either end of the social hierarchy. In one very poor family, the father failed to defend his son against the insult of being pelted with dung by another little boy, displaying to onlookers his inability to protect the honor of his family in more important ways (Campbell, 1964: 273). The same man looks dirty and uncouth despite gossip about his unkempt appearance, and his wife is criticized for laughing and joking, as it implies she may be guilty of sexual immodesty (Campbell, 1964: 110, 169). Although their daughter is apparently virtuous and chaste, she is tainted by her mother's immodesty, and no honorable man seeks her hand. Another poor man of low prestige apparently attacked and tried to seduce a woman in the pastures above the village, an act that was universally condemned by kinsmen and non-kinsmen alike and was immortalized in a mocking song (1964: 112–113). Campbell notes that this man was less severely affected than the average Sarakatsani would have been because his poverty had reduced him to herding the sheep of non-Sarakatsan villagers, a situation in which he did not depend on kinsmen for shared management of large flocks.

Members of wealthy, leading families also act in defiance of gossip. The leader of one prominent family married his daughter to her second cousin, a marriage the Sarakatsani consider illegitimate (Campbell, 1964: 267). After the initial shock within the community passed, his position of prestige and leadership was essentially unchanged. A young woman from a powerful and prestigious family was seduced in her youth by a young man from another wealthy and important family (1964: 303). Despite the explicit moral obligation of the father or brother to kill the girl and murder the seducer in order to avenge the family's honor, her family did nothing. She was even able to find a husband, although she had to wait until she was 39 and then could marry only a poor widower. Her family lost its reputation, but they did not conform to the norms of honorable behavior, in contrast with other families Campbell mentions who did kill their daughters under similar circumstances.

With the introduction of agricultural guards, the increasing intervention of the village president in the allocation of summer grazing lands, and state-enforced laws against sheep stealing, the need for reputations to protect flocks and pastures will probably diminish.

The very poor, on the other hand, ignore gossip because they cannot always afford to conform and because they have less to lose. Many poor families are being drawn into greater dependence on outsiders such as villagers. As they drop below the number of animals necessary to sustain a pastoral sheep-herding existence, they become wage laborers and subsistence farmers in the villages. Regardless of their moral character, they are unable to contract high-prestige marriages for their children and are treated as political nonentities because of their poverty.[3] It is Sarakatsan families in the middle who respond to gossip: those who are most vulnerable to the economic pressures of kinsmen, who are most in need of a good reputation to marry well, and who are least likely to leave the community.

CONSEQUENCES OF GOSSIP AND SCANDAL

Economic. In general, when individuals are dependent on one another for cooperative hunting, farming, herding, or for access to wage labor, gossip and the reputations it creates can have serious economic consequences. Hunters and herders form cooperative work groups and an individual with a poor reputation may find himself or herself unable to forge essential economic partnerships (e.g., Hoebel, 1954; Barth, 1961; Marshall, 1961; Pospisil, 1964; Paine, 1970a). Peasant villagers often depend on their neighbors for reciprocal field preparation and harvest work groups, whereas villages in which there is wage labor rely on reputations for trustworthiness, reliability, and industry in hiring workers (Herskovitz, 1937; Pitt-Rivers, 1971: 28).

Political. Gossip also serves as a device for political competition. Through the manipulation of information and interpretations of events, factions attempt to mobilize support and undermine the support of opposing factions (Paine, 1968: 282; Cox, 1970; Handelman, 1973: 233; Haviland, 1977: 45). Gossip is often an integral part of the factional fighting that leads to village fission (e.g., Turner, 1957). When access to leadership and power is ambiguous and undefined, gossip can strengthen or depose leaders because it influences followers in their choices of

[3]Frederik Barth notes that the process of sedentarization in the nomad population he examined in Iran affected primarily the wealthiest, who educated their children for the more lucrative urban occupations, and the very poor (1961). Both groups tended to marry out.

leaders (e.g., Barth, 1959; Sahlins, 1963). In small-scale societies in which open confrontations are highly disruptive, it serves as a mechanism for indirect attack and private, behind-the-scenes choice of leaders (Colson, 1953; Frankenberg, 1957). Weaker parties can use gossip to attack stronger parties whom they cannot challenge directly (Kluckhohn, 1944; Paine, 1967).

Although gossip is assumed to level social inequalities by providing channels of attack for less powerful parties (see Colson, 1953; Gluckman, 1963: 312), it often serves simply to reinforce existing power relationships. The spread of slander and gossip depends in part on the size and strength of each party's social network and its willingness to communicate his or her version of events. The more powerful person may achieve consensus behind his or her own perspective simply because of more extensive social connections through kinsmen, friends, patrons, and clients.

Gossip plays a central role in village disputing, particularly in societies that rely to a large extent on self-help. It serves to identify allies and indicate the extent of support before a public confrontation (e.g., Haviland 1977: 11). A disputant may forfeit his or her rights if that is the only way to avoid a public confrontation and he knows that his opponent possesses information about him acquired through gossip that could be humiliating if hurled as a public accusation (Starr, 1978: 174–175). The private knowledge available through gossip thus affects a disputant's political credit and ability to assert his or her rights and gather supporters in village disputes.

Social and Collective. Gossip leads to social consequences of both an individual and a collective nature. Individually, the victim of malicious gossip usually is ostracized, ignored, and ridiculed (Campbell, 1964; Pospisil, 1964; Briggs, 1970; Pitt-Rivers, 1971; Selby, 1974; Starr, 1978: 154, 160). Once a consensus forms, gossip leads to collective consequences such as derogatory nicknames (Pospisil, 1964: 423; Collier and Bricker, 1970: 290–291; Pitt-Rivers, 1971: 168–169; Haviland, 1977: 13), mocking songs by masked figures in village fiestas (Pitt-Rivers, 1971: 169–177; Haviland, 1977: 16), degrading songs sung by groups of young girls (Sansom, 1972: 218) or work crews (Herskovitz, 1937: 74), practical jokes by groups of young men (Peters, 1972), nightly attacks by an anonymous group singing mocking songs and shouting insults out of the darkness (Pitt-Rivers, 1971: 169–177), songs sung across the fires at night (Marshall, 1961), and the casting-out ritual of opinions shouted under the cover of darkness (Malinowski, 1926: 103). An accusation of witchcraft is a common device for converting the private but informal consensus achieved through gossip into a public statement of blame. In many societies every death or misfortune must be explained by witchcraft activity, so who is a witch is a common subject of gossip. Divination and witch doctors provide social mechanisms for converting this gossip into public accusations. These devices draw on information provided by gossip but legitimize their conclusions by reference to supernatural authority (see Evans-Pritchard, 1937; Kluckhohn, 1944: 120; Turner, 1957; Mair, 1969: 96–100; Peters, 1972: 151–153; Selby, 1974: 124).

When opinion crystallizes that a person is a troublemaker or a witch, he or she often faces expulsion or execution. The person regularly accused of lying, committing sorcery, killing, or breaking other rules may be exiled or executed among the Eskimo (Hoebel, 1954: 81–91), the Nandi of East Africa (Huntingford, 1953: 101–109), the Zapotec villagers of Mexico (Selby, 1974), the Navaho Indians (Kluckhohn, 1944: 98), and many African and European societies (Currie, 1968; Mair, 1969; Marwick, 1970).

The impact of expulsion varies with the ease of attaching oneself to another community and becoming a full member of it (Moore, 1972: 92–93). In societies where mobility is a normal part of social life, as among some pastoral nomads, no stigma attaches to mobility, and one can easily forge new ties in a new location. But among village farmers, exile generally poses severe difficulties in loss of rights to land, to the support of corporate kin groups, and to networks of patrons, clients, kinsmen, and friends. Intriguingly, witchcraft accusations seem to be relatively rare in some African pastoral societies which have witchcraft beliefs. The ease of movement forestalls interpersonal tensions and impedes the formation of a consensus about who is a witch (Baxter, 1972; Colson, 1974).

INDIFFERENCE TO GOSSIP

Despite these potent consequences to gossip, some individuals persist in defying gossip and continue to break basic social rules. As among the Sarakatsani, they tend to be the very rich and powerful and the socially marginal and weak. In general, people who ignore gossip are those who have significantly greater or lesser power and resources: those who are not subject to the economic and political control of those gossiping about them, those who are not entirely dependent on their local community for political support, economic assistance, or irreplaceable social relationships, and those who can leave the community easily. In the Spanish village, the "shameless" ones are gypsies, acknowledged village outsiders, and poor people who work as beggars, tinkers, hawkers, fortune-tellers, basket makers, or horse dealers (Pitt-Rivers, 1971: 184–185). The "shameless" ones do no agricultural work and will not be employed in any position that necessitates trust. The pueblo also includes a group of relatively rich and influential men who have social ties to elites in other villages and provincial and major towns (Pitt-Rivers, 1971: 209, 118–119). This mobility and social linkage outside the village allows them to escape the sanctions of the village and engage in illicit sex and other rule-breaking acts. Wealth and mobility shield them from local gossip.

Elites in small Alpine villages are similarly indifferent to local gossip (Bailey, 1971: 20). Despite continuous competition for reputation, those who are considered above or below oneself are not objects for rivalry. High-status leaders are beyond the reach of general personal criticism because, as Bailey argues:

> they cannot be cut down to size by depriving them of the help and civilities extended to equals: the point is they no longer need the help and can afford to demand deference in place of civilities. This does not, of course, put them beyond criticism: they are attacked for their performance "on the flat" so to speak, and they are vulnerable because the implementation of policy is seldom possible without some kind of cooperation from those who receive the orders [1971: 283].

Other studies of peasant villages report a similar immunity from gossip on the part of high-status individuals (Frankenberg, 1957: 156; Heppenstall, 1971: 56–59; Starr, 1978: 59). Among the Basseri nomads of Iran, a wealthy man who refused to be hospitable and lived a miserly life persisted in this behavior even though he was nicknamed D.D.T. Khan, implying that he was so miserly he ate his own lice (Barth, 1961: 102). In disputes over cash-crop land in a peasant Turkish village, rich men were willing to sacrifice traditional conceptions of honor in order to acquire control over valuable lands through the court (Starr, 1978; Abel, 1979). In the same village, a poor woman worked as a prostitute, despite widespread gossip, because she enjoyed her added wealth and as a poor person, had no other way to maintain her standards of consumption (Starr, 1978). Similarly, Yngvesson describes an individual who defies gossip in a Swedish fishing village who is closely linked to the important families of the village (1976).

This analysis of the social positions of individuals who defy gossip suggests a possible explanation for a question that has long puzzled anthropologists: How is responsibility for witchcraft allocated? (Mair, 1969; Gluckman, 1972). Black notes that it is primarily socially marginal people who are blamed and more integrated people who blame (1976:

56–59). In some societies, such as the Navaho, the rich and powerful are accused as well (Kluckhohn, 1944: 104; Gluckman, 1955; Macfarlane, 1970). Perhaps the very rich and the very poor are accused because they are the people who have resisted and ignored gossip. A witchcraft accusation is an escalation of gossip, a further effort to control the stubborn deviant.

Gossip and Scandal in Complex Societies

In urban complex societies, the effectiveness of gossip also depends on its consequences. Considerable research suggests that with increasing social complexity, informal social controls diminish in significance and are replaced by formal mechanisms of social control (e.g., Ayoub, 1965; Black, 1976; Nader and Todd, 1978). Yet, even within cities, the impact of gossip varies greatly according to the social structure of the community within which it occurs and the extent to which it leads to a consensus and to individual and collective responses. Wherever close-knit social networks exist, gossip occurs, but its impact is highly variable.

A detailed case study of a single American urban neighborhood demonstrates the differing roles gossip plays under varying social conditions (Merry, 1979; 1981). Dover Square is a pseudonym for a small housing project with 1200 inhabitants in the heart of a major Eastern city. Constructed in 1964 as a part of an urban-renewal program, the project caters to moderate-income families, but one-fifth are poor families eligible for public housing who receive rent subsidies. When studied in 1975–1976, the project was half Chinese, mostly immigrants from villages in rural China, one-quarter black, one-tenth white ethnic—of Syrian-Lebanese, Irish, Italian, and Greek ancestry—and one-tenth Hispanic, recently arrived from Puerto Rico. Despite this diversity, the population has been quite stable, with a turnover of only 5% a year. Ethnic groups were originally scattered throughout the project, and no ethnic clusters have emerged over the 10 years. Most residents find that they share a porch, stairwell, or balcony with one or more families ethnically different from themselves.

The project contains at least three distinct patterns of social organization, and in each gossip plays a different role. The Chinese residents form a relatively close-knit and bounded social world, highly economically interdependent, fairly normatively homogeneous, and closely linked to the political and economic institutions of the adjacent Chinatown. Most adult Chinese speak little English and are restricted to Chinatown for jobs, social life, recreation, and social, legal, and medical services. Of the Chinese heads of house, 86% work in Chinese restaurants or Chinatown shops or agencies and are subject to the control of the wealthy Chinese merchants or businessmen, a few of whom live in the project. A waiter or cook who aspires to start his or her own restaurant turns to Chinatown for partners or credit. Cooks and waiters shift jobs every 2 or 3 years, relying on contacts in Chinatown for information on better jobs and working conditions and new opportunities. Weddings are major social events, mobilizing large networks of kinsmen and friends in support and culminating in an elegant banquet in a Chinatown restaurant for as many as 500 guests. Chinese residents often belong to family associations, which offer social events, social services, and occasionally credit, as well as to smaller groupings of covillagers from China or Chinese Christian churches. In some ways, this community resembles a village: The overlapping social and kin groups create interconnected social networks; residents are economically interdependent; and moving away from the community is virtually impossible until one learns to speak English (see also Doo, 1973; Nee and deBary, 1974).

Gossip within the Chinese community is pervasive, frequently judgmental, and widely feared. Some Dover Square residents complained about the "goldfish bowl" quality of Chinatown and appreciated the anonymity of their multiethnic project. Gossip concerns women who gamble too much and fail to take care of their families, men who have affairs and desert their wives, women who fail to repay gifts of tea cakes, and kinsmen who fail to provide assistance for weddings. It can lead to ostracism, as it did for a woman who lived with both her lover and her handicapped husband, and to nicknames, such as *Juksing* Betsy for a very Americanized woman. Reputations for moral virtue are a central consideration in marriage choices. I heard of no case, however, where a consensus emerged and led to collective action of the type discussed above against a member of the Chinese community.

A few Chinese residents ignored gossip, but only those linked to white society, for whom exit from the Chinese social world was relatively easy. One young man rarely returned home to his Chinese wife and children, choosing to live instead with his white mistresses. Several American-born Chinese young people dated and married whites, despite community gossip. The more Americanized Chinese have broader job skills than cooking or waiting tables in Chinese restaurants and stitching in garment factories and are able to leave the Chinatown social and economic system. They are less tied to its values and have social networks stretching outside the Chinese community.

When urban conditions foster close-knit social enclaves with extensive economic and social interdependence and barriers to mobility out-

side the community, gossip seems to lead to powerful social consequences, just as it does in small-scale societies. Rural African migrants to
South African cities who are uncertain how long they can remain in
town display a similar responsiveness to urban and rural gossip, for
they must retain their ability to reclaim a home and social position in the
countryside (Mayer, 1961). Stable, working-class British families with
close-knit social networks among their neighbors experience frequent
gossip and worry about it, whereas those who are more mobile and do
not befriend their neighbors are little concerned with gossip or conformity to community norms (Bott, 1971: 75–76, 87). A Hausa trading quar-
ter in Ibadan (Cohen, 1969), a working-class neighborhood in East London (Young and Wilmott, 1957), and an Italian neighborhood in Chicago
(Suttles, 1968) all represent situations where a homogeneous, stable,
and economically interdependent population experiences consequences
from gossip and responds to its pressures.

The black residents of Dover Square illustrate a second pattern of
urban social organization: the loosely connected social network with
diverse norms, limited economic interdependence, and relatively easy
movement outside the community. Most black residents know all the
other black families in the project by name and reputation but socialize
only with a smaller group of friends with similar values. One of these
groups consists of people with stable nuclear families and jobs and
frequent church activities. They condemn those who are unable to keep
a steady job and who commit crimes. A second group of families lives on
welfare or marginal, temporary jobs but strives to maintain a stable
family home and keep their children out of trouble. Many are single
heads of house. The third distinct group are young people who spend
much time lounging together in public areas of the project and share
interests in the "fast life," drugs, petty crime, and avoiding regular
work.

Friendships rarely crosscut these social groups, although ties of kinship and acquaintance often do, and information flows easily between
them. Black residents work in a variety of jobs scattered throughout the
downtown area and nearby black community. Although they sometimes hear about jobs through friends and neighbors, they do not regularly get jobs this way. Black residents rarely belong to the same voluntary associations, churches, settlement houses, or social groups as their
black neighbors. Most residents have social ties with kinsmen and
friends outside the neighborhood as well as within it.

In the black community, gossip is pervasive and information flows
smoothly to all but the most isolated families. "Minding your own business" is a cardinal virtue, but one frequently neglected. Residents com-

plain about their neighbors who "see but don't see"; who notice illicit love affairs but not burglars. Yet, within each group, blacks care largely about gossip among their fellows and are indifferent to gossip in other groups. Several young men who were acknowledged burglars continued to steal in the project despite gossip about them by the family- and church-oriented black families. One youth even removed the gate from the back fence of a neighbor and installed it on his own fence, insisting to the irate victim that he had simply found the gate, not stolen it. Despite widespread gossip within the other black social groups, he refused to return it.

Because of the diversity of moral codes, information passing between groups rarely leads to a consensus. A young man who persuaded several women to work for him as prostitutes, for example, was viewed as a brutal exploiter of young women by the steady workers and church-goers and as a man of flash and style by the youth group. One young man who burglarized apartments in the project for some time appeared to be an incorrigible troublemaker to some neighbors, an unfortunate coping with an alcoholic mother and indifferent father to others, and an urban guerrilla to others. Individuals are rarely concerned about the reputations they earn in groups whose values differ significantly from their own and in which they are not members. Those who regularly defy the norms of the larger society, such as the youth group, simply form their own subsociety crystallized around those norms of loyalty and friendship they value while rejecting others.

Gossip does provide essential information on personal identities, however. It indicates who is trustworthy and who is not, who is a drug addict, who is a gossip, whom one can let into one's house, and who will use the opportunity to "case" it for a burglary. I heard of a few cases in which a victim used gossip to trace the person who burglarized his house. The burglar boasted about his exploits, and the information drifted back to the victim. Further, gossip serves as a means of political competition and rivalry within smaller friendship groups. Disputes are commonly accompanied by malicious gossip as each side attempts to place its own behavior in the most flattering light and its rival in the least favorable position. It can undermine the credibility of leaders and those aspiring to power.

Yet even very damaging gossip that leads to the loss of political position and expulsion is not necessarily socially devastating. One young man, for example, was an influential leader in the youth group as long as he could buttress his leadership with substantial gifts of money, rides in his fancy car, and offers of jobs. As his economic fortunes declined, his ability to deliver these favors dropped, and he gradually drifted to the periphery of his group. I began to hear gossip about him from those who before had been staunch supporters, and I noticed that he was often alone in the project, no longer surrounded by the familiar circle of eager youthful faces. A minor incident then tripped off what was, in effect, a public repudiation. He slapped his former girlfriend, a popular project resident, then fled the project. Her family, friends, and other members of the youth group gathered to await his return with threats of violence and court action. At the same time, they gossiped about him: "He does it with little boys, right here in the playground." "He never went to college at all, as he claims, but dropped out of school in the eighth grade and attended one semester of special remedial college." "He says he is your friend but you tell him your private affairs and he tells everyone else."

The young man was able to escape from this social disaster, however. He immediately moved out of the project, not even returning to pick up his clothes and furniture from his apartment. But he moved in with a friend only two blocks away and soon formed a new group of friends in the next park, including some old friends. Although he did not return to Dover Square during the next 5 months while I was able to follow the situation, many of his friends from the project went to visit him in his new "hangout," and he began to recreate a group of followers. Moving away from the dispute caused some hardship, but far less than for members of small-scale, bounded societies, who cannot join a new social group at all or, if they do, must remain perpetual outsiders.

The black residents of Dover Square represent the kind of urban community in which the structural preconditions for gossip—connected social networks—are present, yet the conditions for rendering it powerful are absent. The costs of expulsion are relatively small, and economic and political interdependence is limited. Because of the heterogeneity of norms, gossip does not lead to a consensus within the whole community, but only within smaller clusters of friends and kinsmen. Many ethnographies of urban communities describe similar situations in which gossip is pervasive yet has lost much of its virulence and power. This seems a common pattern in urban societies, where social networks are extensive enough to allow the flow of communication but are not sufficiently dense and durable to exert economic, political, and social power over their members. In other studies of low-income black neighborhoods, gossip performs an important social mapping function but rarely leads to consensus or collective action (Hannerz, 1967; 1969; Rainwater, 1970). Several other ethnographies describe urban communities with fragmented economic systems, normative diversity, and unbounded local social systems in which gossip seems impotent outside local friendship clusters, workplaces, professional associations, or other bounded groups (Frankenberg, 1957; Dore, 1958: 373–384; Szwed, 1966; Peattie, 1968: 57–60; Epstein, 1969; Roberts, 1973; Jacobson, 1973; Felstiner, 1974).

A third pattern of social organization found in Dover Square is relationships between strangers: those across social boundaries. In Dover Square, such boundaries occur between ethnic groups. Gossip does not flow across these boundaries. Members of each ethnic group in the project know few if any members of other ethnic groups, even though they live next door and share the same streets and stores. Because little gossip crosses these social chasms, members of one group know little about the personal identities and reputations of members of the other ethnic groups. Chinese residents, for example, know very little about the identities of the few black and white youths living in the project who commit crimes, and rarely can identify faces or know names, addresses, and family histories. The black residents, in contrast, generally know the names, places of residence, and something about the family situations of these youths. Consequently, the blacks know which youths to watch out for and which they can trust, whereas the Chinese lack this protective information. The Chinese residents feel far more vulnerable to crime than do the blacks. Based on a questionnaire of 101 people (40 Chinese, 23 blacks, 18 whites, 13 Hispanics, and 7 others), fear seems to be closely correlated to knowing the identities of these youths, regardless of ethnic identity or frequency of victimization (Merry, 1981). Thus, the absence of gossip fosters a sense of danger and lack of control. Nor is gossip in one ethnic group a concern to members of other ethnic groups. When I informed some of the youths about the small amount of gossip that did take place about them among the more Americanized, English-speaking Chinese residents, they were either indifferent or pleased with their notoriety.

Gerald Suttles argues that information about personal histories and reputations is essential to establish trusting relationships in a world in which individuals come to believe that their neighbors are untrustworthy people (1968: 8, 26). In the multiethnic urban neighborhood he studied, communication between ethnic groups was fragmentary and sporadic. Individuals kept to their own social groups, to the safer social worlds of individuals about whom they had social dossiers and protective information provided through the extensive gossip occurring within each ethnic group. Within ethnic groups, morality was judged in terms of personal precedent, not absolute standards. Although this information spread widely within ethnic groups, it appeared not to cross ethnic lines. Ethnic outsiders, those who lacked a gossip dossier, seemed dangerous and unpredictable (1968: 79). It is relationships between individuals in different social worlds that have been characterized as the essence of urban anomie and disorder (Wirth, 1938).

Gossip, even by strangers, is a serious concern for urbanites, however, when information about their rule breaking percolates into formal agencies of social control and elicits the sanctions of the state. Dover Square youths involved in crime complained constantly about "nosy" people who gossiped and accused them of crimes. In fact, this gossip did have consequences for the youths. Many of the gossipers were adult black women with friends, relatives, or acquaintances on the police force. Although I did not ask the police directly, they seem to have used this information to identify "troublemakers," who were carefully watched for any illegal misstep. One "known criminal" was arrested for carrying a marijuana cigarette behind his ear, an act that probably would have been ignored if committed by others. One victim trying to identify a purse snatcher said the police showed her a few pictures of known troublemakers in the neighborhood and pressed her to identify one of them. A police officer told a community group he was very pleased when one of these "bad characters" was arrested in a squabble with his neighbor. He felt that this case, at least, would stand up in court.

Other studies of police similarly suggest the use of gossip as a guide to decide how to handle individuals in urban neighborhoods. Egon Bittner describes the vast and detailed personal knowledge acquired by police working in skid row areas that enables them to keep peace and decide when and how to enforce laws (1967). While making rounds of the neighborhood, the police continually engage in small talk with the neighborhood inhabitants about the background, business, and intentions of local individuals (1967: 707–709). Donald Black reports that most police do not know the citizens they handle, but when they do have past experience or access to deeper social knowledge about them, it influences the way they handle the dispute (1980).

The kind of personal history encoded in gossip enters into the administration of formal sanctions in other ways as well. Sentencing and case-disposition decisions, as Lynn Mather observes, are influenced by information the defense or prosecuting attorneys provide about the family responsibilities, job situation, and general moral character of the defendants (1979). Like gossip, a prior criminal record, commonly used in case-disposition decisions, preserves the history of an individual's rule breaking. Both are used to determine if one instance of rule breaking is an occasional and nonserious event or if it represents a long history and indicates that the person is a "bad character" requiring more serious punishment (see also Buckle and Buckle, 1977). In one urban community, a Drug Screening Board evaluates persons accused in drug-related cases in terms of community norms, personal knowledge of the screening panel, and personal histories to provide disposition recommendations to the court (Yngvesson, 1978: 139–148). In some criminal courts, judges rely on information transmitted informally by trusted police officers about the moral character and community reputation of defendants and victims.

Gossip can also lead to serious consequences for individuals enmeshed in complex bureaucratic systems such as welfare or public housing (Rainwater, 1970: 72, 113–114; Stack, 1974; Valentine, 1978). Welfare recipients fear that their neighbors will report small outside jobs or a man present in the home; public-housing tenants fear the spread of information about extra inhabitants, additional income, or infractions of other myriad rules (see Rainwater, 1970: 113) to the housing office. Whenever individuals become involved in formal systems whose rules they sometimes break, whether a workplace, a housing complex, or the Internal Revenue Service, they become vulnerable to gossip about this deviant behavior which spreads to the formal agency itself.[4]

Conclusions

This analysis of gossip and scandal suggests that formal and informal social control are not distinct and unrelated processes. They have significant continuities. Informal gossip may lead to formal collective implementation or feed into formal institutions of social control. For example, when gossip leads to a consensus in small-scale societies, leaders convert this into a formal sanction such as banishment or execution. In complex societies, informal talk acquires power through its impact on formal agencies.

Further, the role of gossip and scandal in social control does not differ sharply between small-scale and complex societies. Gossip and scandal flourish whenever there are close-knit social networks and normative homogeneity. In both urban and rural societies, it serves as a way of drawing a social map of reputations and as a means of political competition and conflict.

[4]The mass media seem to perform many of the functions provided by gossip in small-scale societies and urban villages. Lawrence Sherman finds that the scandals that lead to police department reforms are spread principally through the media (1978). The newspapers in particular inform the public about widespread, organizational corruption, often elevating to public awareness facts already known to many citizens privately (1978: 62–68). Like the witch doctor, the media thus transform private suspicions into a public consensus (see also Allport, 1947).

In both urban and rural societies, those with power and wealth, those who are marginal, and those with contacts outside the local social system are insulated from the consequences of gossip and relatively indifferent to its pressures.

From this comparative analysis of the role of gossip and scandal several specific hypotheses emerge that suggest general conditions under which they lead to effective social control.

1. *The impact of gossip and scandal is greater in more bounded social systems in which the costs of desertion or expulsion are higher and the availability of alternative social relationships less.*

2. *The impact of gossip and scandal is greater in social settings where the members of the local social system are more interdependent for economic aid, jobs, political protection, and social support.*

3. *The impact of gossip and scandal is greater when it has the potential of producing a community consensus that can be converted into a variety of collective actions such as public shaming, ridicule, expulsion, or death.*

4. *The impact of gossip and scandal is greater when normative consensus about the behavior in question is more extensive.*

Clearly, "idle talk" is hardly of idle significance in many social settings in both simple and complex societies.

ACKNOWLEDGMENTS

I appreciate the comments of Donald Black and Jane Collier on an earlier draft of this chapter.

References

Abel, Richard L.
    1979   "The rise of capitalism and the transformation of disputing: From confrontation over honor to competition for property." *UCLA Law Review* 27: 223–234.
Abrahams, Roger D.
    1970   "A performance-centered approach to gossip." *Man* 5: 290–301.
Allport, Gordon W., and Leo Postman
    1947   *The Psychology of Rumor.* New York: Henry Holt.
Ayoub, Victor F.
    1965   "Conflict resolution and social reorganization in a Lebanese village." *Human Organization* 24: 11–17.
Bailey, F. G. (editor)
    1971   *Gifts and Poisons: The Politics of Reputation.* Oxford: Blackwell; New York: Schocken.
Balikci, Asen
    1968   "Bad friends." *Human Organization* 27: 191–199.

Barth, Frederik
    1959   *Political Leadership among the Swat Pathans.* London: Athlone Press.
    ·1961   *Nomads of South Persia: The Basseri Tribe of the Khamseh Confederacy.* London: Oslo
           University Press.
Baxter, P. T. W.
    1972   "Absence makes the heart grow fonder: Some suggestions why witchcraft
           accusations are rare among East African pastoralists." Pages 163–191 in *The
           Allocation of Responsibility,* edited by Max Gluckman. Manchester: Manchester
           University Press.
Benedict, Ruth
    1934   *Patterns of Culture.* New York: Mentor.
Bittner, Egon
    1967   "The police on skid-row: A study of peace-keeping." *American Sociological Re-
           view* 32: 699–715.
Black, Donald
    1976   *The Behavior of Law.* New York: Academic Press.
    1980   *The Manners and Customs of the Police.* New York: Academic Press.
Bleek, Wolf
    1976   "Witchcraft, gossip, and death: A social drama." *Man* 11: 526–541.
Bott, Elizabeth
    1971   *Family and Social Network: Roles, Norms, and External Relationships in Ordinary
           Urban Families.* 2d edition. New York: Free Press (1st edition, 1957).
Briggs, Jean L.
    1970   *Never in Anger: Portrait of an Eskimo Family.* Cambridge, Mass.: Harvard Univer-
           sity Press.
Buckle, Suzann R. Thomas, and Leonard A. Buckle
    1977   *Bargaining for Justice: Case Disposition and Reform in the Criminal Courts.* New
           York: Praeger.
Campbell, J.
    1964   *Honour, Family, and Patronage.* Oxford: Clarendon Press.
Cohen, Abner
    1969   *Custom and Politics in Urban Africa.* Berkeley and Los Angeles: University of
           California Press.
Collier, George A., and Victoria R. Bricker
    1970   "Nicknames and social structure in Zinacantan." *American Anthropologist* 72:
           289–302.
Collier, Jane
    1973   *Law and Social Change in Zinacantan.* Stanford, Calif.: Stanford University Press.
Colson, Elizabeth
    1953   *The Makah Indians: A Study of an Indian Tribe in Modern American Society.* Man-
           chester: Manchester University Press.
    1974   *Tradition and Contract: The Problem of Order.* Chicago: Aldine Press.
Cox, Bruce A.
    1970   "What is Hopi gossip about? Information management and Hopi factions."
           Man 5: 88–98.
Currie, Elliott P.
    1968   "Crimes without criminals: Witchcraft and its control in Renaissance Europe."
           Law and Society Review 3: 7–32.
Denich, Bette S.
    1974   "Sex and power in the Balkans." Pages 243–263 in *Woman, Culture, and Society,*

edited by Michelle Zimbalist Rosalso and Louise Lamphere. Stanford, Calif.: Stanford University Press.

Doo, Leigh-Wai
    1973   "Dispute settlement in Chinese-American communities." *American Journal of Comparative Law* 21: 627–663.

Dore, R. P.
    1958   *City Life in Japan: A Study of a Tokyo Ward.* Berkeley, Calif.: University of California Press.

Epstein, A. L.
    1969   "Gossip, norms, and social network." Pages 117–128 in *Social Networks in Urban Situations,* edited by J. Oyde Mitchell. Manchester: Manchester University Press.

Evans-Pritchard, E. E.
    1937   *Witchcraft, Oracles, and Magic among the Azande.* Oxford: Clarendon Press.

Felstiner, William F.
    1974   "Influences of social organization on dispute processing." *Law and Society Review* 9: 63–94.

Frankenberg, Ronald
    1957   *Village on the Border: A Social Study of Religion, Politics, and Football in a North Wales Community.* London: Cohen and West.

Gluckman, Max
    1955   *Custom and Conflict in Africa.* Oxford: Blackwells.
    1963   "Gossip and scandal." *Current Anthropology* 4: 307–316.
    1968   "Psychological, sociological, and anthropological explanations of witchcraft and gossip: Clarification." *Man* 3: 20–34.

Gluckman, Max (editor)
    1972   *The Allocation of Responsibility.* Manchester: Manchester University Press.

Goffman, Erving
    1959   *The Presentation of Self in Everyday Life.* Garden City, N.Y.: Anchor Books.

Gulliver, P. H. (editor)
    1978   *Cross-Examinations: Essays in Memory of Max Gluckman.* Leiden: E. J. Brill.

Handelman, Don
    1973   "Gossip in encounters: The transmission of information in a bounded social setting." *Man* 8: 210–227.

Hannerz, Ulf
    1967   "Gossip, networks, and culture in a Black American ghetto." *Ethnos* 32: 35–60.
    1969   *Soulside: Inquiries into Ghetto Culture and Community.* New York: Columbia University Press.
    1980   *Exploring the City: Inquiries toward an Urban Anthropology.* New York: Columbia University Press.

Haviland, John Beard
    1977   *Gossip, Reputation, and Knowledge in Zinacantan.* Chicago: University of Chicago Press.

Heppenstall, M. A.
    1971   "Reputation, criticism, and information in an Austrian village." Pages 139–167 in *Gifts and Poison: The Politics of Reputation,* edited by F. G. Bailey. New York: Schocken.

Herskovitz, Melville S.
    1937   *Life in a Haitian Valley.* New York: Knopf.

Hoebel, E. Adamson
   1954   *The Law of Primitive Man: A Study in Comparative Legal Dynamics.* Cambridge, Mass.: Harvard University Press.
Hotchkiss, John C.
   1967   "Children and conduct in a Ladino community of Chiapas, Mexico." *American Anthropologist* 68: 711–718.
Huntingford, G. W. B.
   1953   *The Nandi of Kenya: Social Control in a Pastoral Society.* London: Routledge and Kegan Paul.
Jacobson, David
   1973   *Itinerant Townsmen: Friendship and Social Order in Urban Uganda.* Menlo Park, Calif.: Cummings Publishing.
Kluckhohn, Clyde
   1944   *Navaho Witchcraft.* Boston: Beacon Press, 1967.
Koster, Ditte
   1977   "Why is he here? White gossip." Pages 144–166 in *The White Arctic: Anthropological Essays on Tutelage and Ethnicity,* edited by Robert Paine. St. John's: Institute of Social and Economic Research, Memorial University of Newfoundland. Newfoundland Social and Economic Papers, No. 7.
Liebow, Elliot
   1967   *Tally's Corner.* Boston: Little, Brown.
Loudon, J. B.
   1961   "Kinship and crisis in South Wales." *British Journal of Sociology* 12: 333–350.
Macfarlane, Alan
   1970   *Witchcraft in Tudor and Stuart England: A Regional and Comparative Study.* London: Routledge and Kegan Paul.
Mair, Lucy
   1969   *Witchcraft.* New York: McGraw-Hill.
Malinowski, Bronislaw
   1926   *Crime and Custom in Savage Society.* Paterson, N.J.: Littlefield, Adams, 1972.
Marshall, Lorna
   1961   "Sharing, talking and giving: The relief of social tension among !Kung Bushmen." *Africa* 31: 231–249.
Marwick, Max (editor)
   1970   *Witchcraft and Sorcery: Selected Readings.* Harmondsworth: Penguin.
Mather, Lynn M.
   1979   *Plea Bargaining on Trial? The Process of Criminal-Case Case Disposition.* Lexington, Mass.: Lexington Books.
Mayer, Philip
   1961   *Tribesmen or Townsmen: Conservatism and the Process of Urbanization in a South African City.* Capetown: Oxford University Press.
Mernissi, Fatima
   1975   *Beyond the Veil: Male–Female Dynamics in a Modern Muslim Society.* Cambridge: Shenkman.
Merry, Sally Engle
   1979   "Going to court: Strategies of dispute management in an American urban neighborhood." *Law and Society Review* 13: 891–925.
   1980   "Racial integration in an urban neighborhood: The social organization of strangers." *Human Organization* 39: 59–69.

1981   *Urban Danger: Life in a Neighborhood of Strangers*. Philadelphia: Temple University Press.

Moore, Sally Falk
1972   "Legal liability and evolutionary interpretation: Some aspects of strict liability, self-help, and collective responsibility." Pages 51–109 in *The Allocation of Responsibility*, edited by Max Gluckman. Manchester: Manchester University Press.
1977   "Individual interests and organizational structures: Dispute settlements as events of articulation." Pages 159–189 in *Social Anthropology and Law*, edited by Ian Hamnett. London: Academic Press.

Nader, Laura, and Harry F. Todd, Jr. (editors)
1978   *The Disputing Process—Law in Ten Societies*. New York: Columbia University Press.

Nee, Victor, and Brett de Bary
1974   *Longtime Californ': A Documentary Study of an American Chinatown*. Boston: Houghton-Mifflin.

Paine, Robert
1967   "What is gossip about? An alternative hypothesis." *Man* 2: 278–285.
1968   "Gossip and transaction." *Man* 3: 305–308.
1970a   "Lappish decisions, partnerships, information management, and sanctions—a nomadic pastoral adaptation." *Ethnology* 9: 52–67.
1970b   "Informal communication and information management." *Canadian Review of Sociology and Anthropology* 7: 172–188.

Parnell, Philip
1978   "Village or state? Communication legal systems in a Mexican judicial district." Pages 315–351 in *The Disputing Process—Law in Ten Societies*, edited by Laura Nader and Harry F. Todd, Jr. New York: Columbia University Press.

Peattie, Lisa R.
1968   *The View from the Barrio*. Ann Arbor, Mich.: University of Michigan Press.

Peters, E. Lloyd
1972   "Aspects of the control of moral ambiguities: A comparative analysis of two culturally disparate modes of social control." Pages 109–163 in *The Allocation of Responsibility*, edited by Max Gluckman. Manchester: Manchester University Press.

Pitt-Rivers, Julian A.
1971   *The People of the Sierra*. 2d edition. Chicago: University of Chicago Press (1st edition, 1954).

Pospisil, Leopold
1964   "Law and societal structure among the Nunamiut Eskimo." Pages 395–433 in *Explorations in Cultural Anthropology: Essays in Honor of George Peter Murdock*, edited by Ward H. Goodenough. New York: McGraw-Hill.

Radcliffe-Brown, A. R.
1933   "Social sanctions." Pages 531–534 in *Encyclopedia of the Social Sciences*, vol. 13. New York: Macmillan.

Rainwater, Lee
1970   *Behind Ghetto Walls: Black Families in a Federal Slum*. Chicago: Aldine Press.

Roberts, Bryan
1973   *Organizing Strangers*. Austin: University of Texas Press.

Roberts, John M.
1964   "The self-management of cultures." Pages 433–454 in *Explorations of Cultural*

Anthropology: Essays in Honor of George Peter Murdock, edited by Ward H. Goodenough. New York: McGraw-Hill.

Ruffini, Julio L.
  1978 "Disputing over livestock in Sardinia." Pages 209–247 in *The Disputing Process—Law in Ten Societies,* edited by Laura Nader and Harry F. Todd, Jr. New York: Columbia University Press.

Sahlins, Marshall
  1963 "Poor man, rich man, big-man, chief: Political types in Melanesia and Polynesia." *Comparative Studies in Society and History* 5: 285–303.

Sansom, Basil
  1972 "When witches are not named." Pages 193–227 in *The Allocation of Responsibility,* edited by Max Gluckman. Manchester: Manchester University Press.

Schwartz, Richard D.
  1954 "Social factors in the development of legal control: A case study of two Israeli settlements." *Yale Law Journal* 63: 471–491.

Selby, Henry
  1974 *Zapotec Deviance: The Convergence of Folk and Modern Sociology.* Austin: University of Texas Press.

Sherman, Lawrence W.
  1978 *Scandal and Reform: Controlling Police Corruption.* Berkeley, Calif.: University of California Press.

Stack, Carol B.
  1974 *All Our Kin: Strategies for Survival in a Black Community.* New York: Harper & Row.

Starr, June
  1978 *Dispute and Settlement in Rural Turkey.* Leiden: E. J. Brill.

Suttles, Gerald
  1968 *The Social Order of the Slum.* Chicago: University of Chicago Press.

Szwed, John
  1966 "Gossip, drinking, and social control: Consensus and communicaton in a Newfoundland parish." *Ethnology* 5: 434–441.

Turner, Victor W.
  1957 *Schism and Continuity in an African Society.* Manchester: Manchester University Press.

Valentine, Bettylou
  1978 *Hustling and Other Hard Work: Life Styles in the Ghetto.* New York: Free Press.

Wilson, Peter J.
  1974 "Filcher of good names: An enquiry into anthropology and gossip." *Man* 9: 93–102.

Wirth, Louis
  1938 "Urbanism as a way of life." *American Journal of Sociology* 44: 1–24.

Wolf, Margery
  1972 *Women and the Family in Rural Taiwan.* Stanford, Calif.: Stanford University Press.

Yang, Martin C.
  1945 *A Chinese Village: Taitou, Shantung Province.* New York: Columbia University Press.

Yngvesson, Barbara
  1976 "Responses to grievance behavior: Extended cases in a fishing community." *American Ethnologist* 3: 353–374.

1978   "The reasonable man and the unreasonable gossip: On the flexibility of (legal)
        concepts and elasticity of (legal) time." Pages 133–154 in *Cross-Examinations:
        Essays in Memory of Max Gluckman*, edited by P. H. Gulliver. Leiden: E. J. Brill.
Young, Michael, and Peter Wilmott
    1957   *Family and Kinship in East London*. Harmondsworth: Penguin.

11

Social Control from Below[*]

M. P. BAUMGARTNER

Among the advantages enjoyed by people of high status in dealings with their subordinates is ready access to the means of social control. Law, for instance, in the form of police, judges, jailers, and executioners, often stands ready to service those of high status when they have grievances against people with less wealth, authority, or other attributes of social standing. Discipline through violence—by the elites themselves or by retainers on their behalf—tends to flourish under socially stratified conditions as a way of dealing with recalcitrant underlings. At the same time, an ability to dispense or withhold the means of subsistence and other desired resources provides numerous opportunities for superiors to sanction less privileged individuals without recourse to physical coercion. Elites are thus well equipped to defend their interests and to deal with misconduct by their inferiors.

The situation of subordinates is different, for the obvious and preferred ways of pursuing grievances are not so readily available to them, especially against antagonists of higher standing. The unresponsiveness of law in such cases is well known; in fact, upward complaints (those by lower-status against higher-status people) are sometimes simply not al-

*Support for this work was provided by the Program in Law and Social Science of the National Science Foundation.

TOWARD A GENERAL THEORY OF SOCIAL CONTROL
Volume 1: Fundamentals

lowed (see Black, 1976: 28). There have even been times and places in which efforts to invoke the law against superiors have themselves been illegal. A decree of Catherine II of Russia (issued in the late eighteenth century), for example, made it "a criminal act for serfs to present petitions against their masters," and "those who violated this law were to be beaten with the knout and sent to forced labor in Siberia [Blum, 1961: 440]." In Roman Britain, slaves who complained against their masters were sentenced to gladiatorial combat (Pike, 1873: 14). Subordinates are generally limited in their right to exercise violence against their superiors as well, so that, for instance, the routine forms of disciplinary punishment that are so frequent downwardly—spankings, slappings, whippings, canings, and so forth—are strikingly uncommon in an upward direction. Those of low status also have comparatively few means of nonviolent coercion at their disposal, as the greater wealth and security of higher-status people insulate them from many material deprivations that aggrieved inferiors might wish to inflict on them.

From the point of view of the higher strata, all of this inequality in the distribution of normative resources should have clear implications for the behavior of the disadvantaged. As a Puritan clergyman of the seventeenth century explained, all subordinates ought to fear those above them—the specific character of this fear being "diversifyed according to the Nature of the Relationship which they stand in." Servants, for example, are ordained to "trembling, to express the kind of Fear belonging to Men in this Order, implying a sense of their Subjection, and the Power their Masters have over them [quoted in Morgan, 1966: 113]." Restricted in their capacity to influence or censure their betters, those of lower rank should recognize their weakness and simply comply with whatever might be expected of them. Indeed, when relating to their superiors, they should suspend moral judgment entirely.

Actually, people of lower status do not always behave in this way. Although the means available to them are limited by circumstances, and although in fact they often suffer offenses in silence, subordinates also can and do redress wrongs against themselves, dramatize grievances, and even punish those of higher status. Where social inequality exists, as elsewhere, normative order is defined and maintained by an interactive process, and superiors are rarely completely free of moral pressure from below. In developing a general theory of social control, it is important to recognize this fact, and to explore the techniques through which upward complaining and sanctioning occur. For too long, people have tended to assume that resentful inaction is the only significant response to be found when a social inferior suffers an offense. Accordingly, the present essay seeks to draw attention to the phenomenon of upward social control and to begin to specify how people handicapped by low status still manage to pursue grievances against the more powerful.

The following pages provide an inventory of some of the most characteristic forms taken by social control against status superiors, as seen across a variety of socially stratified settings. Under consideration are the mechanisms by which dependent wives express grievances against their husbands, children their parents, slaves and servants their masters, prisoners their guards, employees their employers, and diverse others of low status against those above them. Thus, although the survey of upward social control contained here may not be definitive, it is intended to be broad in scope. In fact, there emerges a great deal of similarity in the ways in which subordinates of all kinds proceed against their superiors, and this is true of people separated from one another by wide reaches of time, distance, and culture.

At one time or another, seemingly every kind of social control has occurred in an upward direction. Nonetheless, there are several characteristic forms of social control that appear to account for most of the regulation of superiors by those below them. Some of these forms are not peculiar to situations in which the offenders are of higher status than the aggrieved, whereas others are rarely if ever seen except under conditions of this kind. As a whole, the principal modalities of upward control stand as a testimonial to the ingenuity of people whose normative resources are meager, but whose demand for justice does not permit them to acquiesce in their own victimization. These modalities include rebellion, covert retaliation, noncooperation, appeals for support, flight, and distress.

Rebellion

Of all the forms of social control from below, rebellion is undoubtedly the most visible, the most spectacular, and the most feared by those of higher status. This is true even though rebellion—defined here as open violence against social superiors—is among the least common of the tactics discussed in this essay. It is usually difficult to initiate a rebellion, and in general it is even more difficult to carry off any rebellious undertaking without severe repercussions for those who participate. When a rebellion does turn out well, however, its results are generally more favorable to people of lower status than are those possible through any other means.

Because rebellion is such a well-known variety of upward social control, it is perhaps unnecessary to treat it in detail here. A few observations may suffice. One is that rebellion, as defined earlier, can entail varying amounts of organization, time, and damage. At one extreme are isolated acts of violence or intimidation committed against individual superordinates by lone avengers. Although less dramatic, these are far more frequent than other kinds of rebellion and perhaps deserve a few illustrations from among the very many that might be mentioned. An example from ancient history is found in the story of a Roman slave whose case became a cause célèbre in his day. This man, apparently in retaliation for being refused permission to buy his freedom at a previously agreed price, set upon his master in a rage and killed him (Hopkins, 1978: 126). In a fourteenth-century English case described in official records, a young man beat his stepfather to death with a staff for attempting to interfere with his inheritance (Hanawalt, 1979: 163). And in an Irish case from the beginning of the present century, a younger brother murdered an older one who had assumed ownership of the family farm at their father's death and who persistently refused to turn over a proper share of the farm's profits (Arensberg and Kimball, 1968: 112–113). In many societies, the rebellious character of homicides such as these is formally recognized by the state, which singles them out for special severity. English law, for example, traditionally applied the label of "petty treason" to murders committed by servants against masters or by wives against husbands (see, e.g., Green, 1972: 693). Apart from homicide, small-scale rebellions may involve others forms of aggression such as assault, intimidation, or overt property destruction.

One step beyond isolated rebellions by individuals are those involving small groups of aggrieved subordinates. In traditional agrarian settings, for example, unpopular landlords or bailiffs may be waylaid and assaulted by several or more enraged peasants (for examples, see Rockwell, 1974: 450–452; Hanawalt, 1979: 179). Sometimes the peasants involved are members of a troop of bandits who, having withdrawn from the ordinary rounds of agricultural life, exercise occasional violence against the persons or property of high-status individuals seen as oppressors and exploiters (see Hobsbawm, 1969). In prisons, uprisings of inmates may break out in response to grievances; on ocean-going vessels, disgruntled seamen may mutiny; households of slaves may turn violently against their masters, and so may villages of conquered people.

As the number and organization of aggrieved parties increases, and also the number and organization of elites, rebellion grows ever grander in scale. Riots, for example, may involve hundreds or even thousands of persons exacting revenge for perceived injustices by entire subpopulations. In these cases, the normative logic is often that of collective liability, with all members of a particular category—whether a class, occupation, race, or whatever—held accountable for the conduct of some. Extensive rioting has been triggered by unpopular actions of the police and military, owners and managers of factories, and merchants, among others (for accounts of actual riots, see, e.g., Rudé, 1964a; Hayden, 1967; Linebaugh, 1975).

The largest rebellions, involving the most people engaged for the longest periods of time in the most concerted activities, are found in revolutions. Successful or not, these represent an extreme in upward social control. Revolutions invariably express discontent with ruling elites and involve an effort to bring to an end conditions perceived as unacceptable. Specific grievances that have played a part in revolutions include the repression of dissent, religious practices, or other expression; taxation regarded as excessive or unfair; exactions of labor or other services regarded as intolerably burdensome or unjust (including the drafting of men to fight unpopular wars); corruption, or enrichment of elites at the expense of the public; and the inadequate or inequitable supply of land, food, and other essentials, due to what is seen as the greed or incompetence of elites. (It should be obvious that the mere existence of grievances such as these is by no means sufficient to ensure that a revolution will occur. Indeed, it seems that no form of deviant behavior, by anyone, ever leads automatically to a given mode of social control. In the case of revolution, there exists an extensive body of theory that seeks to specify the further conditions necessary for this phenomenon.) The degree of punishment inflicted on elite groups during revolutionary upheavals varies, but is generally considerable. Privileged people may suffer the confiscation of their property, expulsion from their homelands, internment, and violence against their persons, including assault, rape, torture, and execution. Applied widely, as they often are, these actions may approach a systematic effort to eradicate entire segments of a population.

Immense though the amount of upward social control imposed during rebellions may be, it is important to recognize that the effects of upward violence often extend far beyond the events themselves. Each rebellion establishes the possibility of others and tends to foster a dread of like treatment among all who are socially similar to those directly attacked. The fear thus aroused may be considered a sanction in itself. The worry of free citizens in classical Sparta that their serfs (or "helots") would rebel is still well known in history, for example (see, e.g., Michell, 1964: 33; Oliva, 1971: 47–48). The same applies to American slaveowners before the Civil War: "In answer to the question 'Are the masters afraid of insurrection?' [a slave] says, 'They live in constant fear upon this subject. The least unusual noise at night alarms them greatly. They cry out 'What is that?' 'Are the boys all in?' [quoted in Bauer and Bauer, 1942: 388]." For this reason, one scholar has characterized the slave-owning societies of the Caribbean and southern United States as "fear-ridden slavocracies [Davidson, 1966: 252]." It is also well known that the French Revolution of the eighteenth century aroused great anxiety among the aristocrats of European nations (see Rudé, 1964b: chap. 10).

In addition to the psychological burden imposed on elites, there are material costs associated with the fear of rebellion as well. Thus, many superordinates take preventive measures against rebellion, often at great trouble, inconvenience, and expense. They may hire bodyguards or watchmen, for example, sometimes even assembling private armies or police forces. They may install elaborate security systems to uncover or to hinder attacks and may invest heavily in weapons. For instance, in the modern world, there is a growing demand among wealthy industrialists, politicians, and others for armored automobiles and bulletproof clothing (see, e.g., Odening, 1981). The cost of such security measures and devices may be understood as a kind of exaction by lower-status people against their superiors.

In fear of violent social control from below, members of elite groups may also adjust their conduct. A rebellion in one setting may prompt the privileged in other places to increase surveillance and repression of their subordinates, but it may also lead them to make concessions. Much reform has been initiated or accelerated in the aftermath of outbreaks of violence. This has been true in the industrial workplace and the military, in prisons, cities, and entire nations. Changes may even follow rebellions that were not, from the viewpoint of their participants, successful. In light of this, acts of rebellion may be understood as ventures on behalf of an unknown number of subordinate persons beyond those directly involved, though they may rarely be intended as such. That this is so speaks to the community of interest—conscious or not—existing among people of low status in similar situations.

Covert Retaliation

One way to avoid the problems found in confronting a powerful antagonist is to proceed in secret. When an offender remains completely unaware that revenge has been taken or restitution exacted, or when he or she is at least uncertain about the circumstances surrounding an act of this kind (including who has committed it), countermeasures are impossible. Such a strategy may seem to perform rather poorly the educative function of social control, whereby moral boundaries are drawn and maintained for a population of potential transgressors (see Durkheim, 1893: book 1, chap. 2; Erikson, 1966: 8–19), but it does spare complainants many difficulties and allows them to impose a result that might otherwise be unattainable.

Covert retaliation is sometimes strictly punitive, whereas in other cases it may be calculated to secure compensation for the victim. In practice, it includes a wide range of actions that vary considerably in severity. Toward the mild extreme, for example, are pranks and related acts of mischief that can serve to harass, inconvenience, or annoy. Nicely illustrative of such behavior is a case from seventeenth-century Massachusetts, in which a servant, Mehitable Brabrook, "took revenge for a scolding, as she later confessed to a fellow servant, by putting a 'great toad' into a kettle of milk [Morgan, 1966: 124]." What she did has much in common with a practice proverbially attributed to disgruntled waiters and waitresses in more modern times—that of spitting in the food of offensive diners. Many other pranks and practical jokes, such as those committed by students against their teachers (see, e.g., Marsh, Rosser, and Harré, 1978) or young people against adult neighbors (see, e.g., Rees, 1961: 82–84), may be understood in this light.

A common and somewhat more serious variety of covert retaliation occurs when subordinates appropriate their superiors' property. This may have the character of compensation for injuries suffered, strictly calculated by the aggrieved, or it may be an act of sheer vengeance. Examples of the practice are numerous. In ancient Rome, for instance, people complained that their slaves were "light-fingered"; modern historians understand such theft as a form of resistance (see, e.g., Hopkins, 1978: 121). Peasants in late medieval England occasionally took their superiors' property to settle scores with them as well; in a specific case from the thirteenth century, four men burglarized an abbot's barn in an apparent effort to secure from their miserly victim the amount of bread that they and others felt he owed them for work done on his behalf (Hanawalt, 1979: 179). "Filching" from their masters' larders and barns seems to have been a common activity of Russian house serfs (Blum, 1961: 458), and, in traditional Danish peasant villages, "swindling" is said to have been the most frequent form of opposition against landlords (Rockwell, 1974: 452). Similarly, among colonists in New England,

> A master who wished to save . . . his goods from theft had to make some effort to win the good will of his servants, for he frequently had to leave them alone in the house, and unless they loved and respected him, no amount of care would secure

the cupboard or the cellar against them. The court records show that many thefts were committed by servants [Morgan, 1966: 124].

Covert retaliation through theft is a mode of upward social control found in more modern societies as well. High rates of theft from the workplaces of Nazi-occupied Poland seem, for instance, to have been related to a desire for retaliation: "People with ethical doubts could consider that all the means of production had, after all, been stolen from them by the Germans, so that they were simply 'expropriating the expropriators' [Gross, 1979: 114]." Likewise, much embezzlement by business employees in contemporary America appears to have its origin in grievances against employers. One man in prison for this offense told an investigator that he began taking money after being required to pay $1200 of his own in order to make up a shortage for which he was not responsible: "The manager was very nasty about it and said that I had to 'pay or else.' I thought it was a pretty rough deal. I'd been with the company ten years and everything. So I thought, 'If he's going to toss one at me I'll toss one at him.' So I did [quoted in Cressey, 1953: 65]." Another convicted embezzler explained to the same investigator how much he had disliked the head of his company and how he had stolen from him out of "rebelliousness." "If someone treats you wrongly," he said, "you can take it just so long and then you will start doing something to get even in one way or another [quoted in Cressey, 1953: 58]."

Beyond pranks and theft, property destruction committed covertly—often under ambiguous circumstances suggesting the possibility of an accident—also provides opportunities by which revenge may be exacted upwardly. The "carelessness" of slaves, for example, appears to be a plague to masters wherever the institution of slavery exists. Illustrations can be found in the history of the American South, where one slave-owner observed that "it always seems on the plantations as if they [the slaves] took pains to break all the tools and spoil all the cattle that they possibly can, even when they know they'll be directly punished for it [quoted in Bauer and Bauer, 1942: 393]." Special tools—such as the relatively indestructible but heavy and inefficient "nigger hoe"—were introduced onto the plantations because ordinary equipment was destroyed at such a rapid rate (Bauer and Bauer, 1942: 402). A southern physician, Dr. Cartwright, even proposed the existence of a mental disease distinctive to black people, *Dysaethesia Aethiopica,* to explain the extremely high incidence of property destruction by slaves. Among the symptoms of this affliction were the tendencies of its victims to "break, waste, and destroy everything they handle—abuse horses and cattle—tear, burn, or rend their own clothing," and to "cut up corn, cotton, and tobacco, when hoeing it, as if for pure mischief [quoted in Bauer and Bauer, 1942: 394]."

As the magnitude of property destruction increases, so does the amount of social control it represents. On the slave plantations of Madagascar and the East Coast of Africa during the eighteenth and nineteenth centuries, escaped slaves might surreptitiously enter the grounds and kill other slaves as a means of inflicting heavy losses on the masters (F. Cooper, 1977: 205). Another severe punishment inflicted through covert retaliation is arson. Indeed, even the mere threat of such action can be an effective sanction against the more powerful. Thus, in Hanoverian England, anonymous letters threatening burnings (and sometimes violence) to come were one means by which the grievances of the poor were given expression. They were received throughout this period by members of the rural gentry, the clergy, legal officials, industrial employers, and other superiors who had given offense (Thompson, 1975). The following rather poetic letter was directed to a merchant named Spragging:

> Spraging, remember thou art but Dust,
> And to thy Neighbour very unjust:
> Thou neither sticks at great nor Small,
> Till Vengeance once does on thee fall.
> I think how soon thou wilt be undone;
> In Flames of Fire thy Rafts shall burn
> [quoted in Thompson, 1975: 264].

Another was sent by "a good jurni-man shoemaker" to his master:

> You damd Insignificant Proud Impearias Rascal your are detested by every one that Works for you. . . . But I hope Soone to put an end to your pride by Eluminateing the Neighbourhood you live in . . . and if possible would Shove your damd Litle Self in to the midst of the Flames [quoted in Thompson, 1975: 274].

Many of these letters demanded money for the sender if the punishment were to be averted (to the authorities, this was the crime of "extortion").

Apart from threats, arson itself has been used to punish social superiors in many settings. Masters in colonial New England, slaveowners in the antebellum American South and on the clove plantations of the East Coast of Africa, as well as high-status Hanoverian Englishmen came to fear its commission (see, respectively, Morgan, 1966: 124; Bauer and Bauer, 1942: 403–404; F. Cooper, 1977: 200; Thompson, 1975). In Sicily to the present day, "every summer several thousand hectares [of reforested land] burn, sometimes ignited by displaced shepherds whose loss of grazing land to reforestation was never compensated to their satisfaction [Schneider and Schneider, 1976: 131]." And in contemporary New Jersey as well, in the Pine Barrens, where fire is a special ecological problem, residents occasionally set blazes for revenge. In fact, the chief fire warden of this area explained to an outsider that a fear of arson is one reason why illegal whiskey distillers, or "moonshiners," are not harassed by the government:

> We leave them [the moonshiners] alone. They leave us alone. Look at it this way: If we go in there and report them and they get arrested, they might spend six months in jail; then when they come out—if they wanted to get even—they could burn down half of New Jersey [quoted in McPhee, 1968: 87; see also 115].

A final example of covert retaliation, one generally intended by the aggrieved to inflict considerable harm on the offender, is seen in the practice of magical revenge. In many societies, people of low status have private recourse to supernatural techniques designed to cause physical harm, loss of property, or other misfortune to befall an offending superior. In ancient Rome, for example, magic "was particularly widespread among powerless and socially inferior groups, as a way of expressing resentment against a superior who they felt had wronged them"; it often took the form of curse tablets placed on tombs to ensure that an offender would die (Wiedemann, 1981: 189). Similarly, in at least one traditional Indian community, lower-caste people aggrieved by the conduct of their landlords might throw sand over their heads before a temple and pray to a goddess for vengeance on their behalf (Gough, 1960: 50).

In general, then, some form of covert retaliation—more or less severe depending on circumstances—seems to be an attractive sanction for underlings to use against deviant superiors. There are also other weapons in the arsenal of aggrieved subordinates. One, noncooperation, is the subject of the following section.

Noncooperation

Whereas covert retaliation involves an active and aggressive response to the conduct of a social superior, noncooperation simply entails a failure to do something ordinarily expected from a subordinate. In this sense, it is passive. It follows a logic of deprivation rather than infliction, though precisely what the offender is deprived of depends on the nature of exactions in any given stratified relationship.

One of the most frequent demands people make on their underlings is for labor, and so, understandably, one of the most frequent means by which upward grievances are expressed is withholding labor on a superior's behalf. Slaves, servants, employees, dependent wives, and other subordinates are all known to respond in this fashion when disgruntled. At its most dramatic and well known, this response may involve highly organized strikes or work slowdowns, actions that have been prominent in the workplaces of industrialized societies. In less developed form, this sort of behavior has played a significant role in many other settings as well. A study of farmer–laborer conflict in early twentieth-century England, for example, has documented the use of such techniques in a more traditional rural context (Howkins, 1977). In one job action there, which can serve to illustrate many, a group of workers who felt underpaid requested an additional shilling beyond what they had been offered to pull up some plants. When the farm's owner hesitated to agree, one of the workers, as he later explained to an investigator, told his fellows, " 'We mustn't work too hard today, otherwise we shan't get the shilling.' So we [the workers] went; we done a fair thing like, but not so much, and [the owner] did give us this other shilling [quoted in Howkins, 1977: 224]."

Less dramatic but more frequent as a form of social control by subordinates of all kinds is the simple slighting of tasks on a day-by-day basis. It, too, is one means by which employees express grievances against employers or managers who displease them. In Nazi-occupied Poland, for example, absenteeism from their jobs and a slow pace of work were among the major ways in which people responded to the conditions prevailing under the Germans. "These activities did not seem wrong; one was simply compensating for the ridiculous wages and expropriations, and the underground itself called for a 'turtle' work pace [Gross, 1979: 114]." Similar tactics are sometimes used by modern American workers. In discussing life in an Italian-American neighborhood of Boston, for instance, one investigator noted the following:

> When [exploitation on the job] does occur, considerable satisfaction is derived from fighting back. One [of the residents], who had once worked as a sweeper in a company that cleaned office buildings, spent considerable time in "goofing off" and methodically violating the rules set by management, because the wages were low, and the union was in a strong position. He intimated that the pleasure of his revenge reimbursed him for the poor wages [Gans, 1962: 123–124].

Other kinds of subordinates also punish superiors by neglecting their work on a routine basis. This, for instance, seems to account for the consistency with which slaveowners in diverse settings come to view their slaves as "lazy." Romans thought this (Hopkins, 1978: 121), and so did southern Americans before the Civil War. In the latter case, ample evidence remains to indicate the extreme reluctance of many slaves to engage in labor on behalf of masters. One northerner watching slaves transporting building materials commented that "it seemed as if they were trying to see how long they could be in mounting the ladder without actually stopping [quoted in Bauer and Bauer, 1942: 392]." Sometimes slaves succeeded in getting masters to perform tasks themselves in order to avoid the delay and shoddy workmanship that would otherwise occur, and the entire situation prompted another observer to exclaim that "it must be irksome and trying to one's patience, to have to superintend [slave] labor [Bauer and Bauer, 1942: 394]." Similarly, slaves among the Lozi of Zambia "slacked and worked as badly as possible, while doing the minimum to avoid whipping and semi-strangulation [Clarence-Smith, 1979: 231]."

In Puritan New England, servants were known to sanction their masters in the same way:

> [One contemporary] described what must have been a common practice: "My Master rebuked me sharply saies the Servant, . . . but I think I fitted them, they would have their way and wil, and would have it done after their manner, And I did it with a witness, so il-favoredly, that I know it vexed al the veyns of their hearts, thats the way to weary them" [Morgan, 1966: 123].

And prisoners, too, where required to work, sometimes express their dissatisfactions by failing to provide their labor. In one modern American prison, for example:

> [The] threats in the background appear to be sufficient to convince most of the inmate population that an outright refusal to work is unwise, but at the same time they appear to be incapable of preventing more subtle forms of rebellion. Apathy, sabotage, and the show of effort rather than the substance—the traditional answers of the slave—rise in the prison to plague the custodian-manager [Sykes, 1958: 28].

Finally, although it is not as central to the marriage relationship as to the tie between employer and employee or master and slave, labor (including such tasks as housecleaning, cooking, sewing, and child care) typically is expected of wives who are economically dependent on their husbands. Accordingly, one way that wives can sanction their spouses is by neglecting such work. In China, for example, a wife may "fight back" and "refuse to cooperate with [her husband], neglecting his clothing and food [Hsu, 1971: 251]." Among the Zinacanteco Indians of Mexico, being "slow in catering to her husband's needs" is a widely recognized means by which a wife may express a grievance (Collier, 1973: 183); this has also been true for the Cheyenne of North America (see Llewellyn and Hoebel, 1941: 183–185). And among the Tallensi of Ghana, wives sometimes use the same tactic:

> If [a husband] annoys [his wife] she can make a point of being too busy to attend to
> some want of his or too tired to cook the evening meal. This, men say frankly, is one
> of the strongest arguments in favour of keeping on good terms with one's wife
> [Fortes, 1949: 105].

Thus, although "poor housekeeping" may at first appear to be a potential *cause* of marital tension, something about which husbands may take offense, on closer examination it often proves to be a *response* to tension, and a way by which a wife may punish her husband.

Insofar as superordinates demand more than labor, social inferiors may withhold cooperation of other kinds as well. Where material resources are demanded, for instance, they may obstruct or frustrate the collection process. This may be accomplished through small gestures of defiance, such as the following one noted among Danish peasants:

> [A] source of resentment was the tithe, taken sometimes by the manor and always
> by the priest. [One person records]: "So that the tithe-taker should have as much
> trouble as possible in counting, they didn't stack their corn in rows as they do now
> [that tithes are no longer taken], but here and there all over the field, so it was very
> hard" [Rockwell, 1974: 446–447].

The withholding of taxes should often be considered a more extreme form of the same tactic. It might be an act of protest against specific governmental policies, or a response to demands for payment that seem excessive or unfair. In Mughal India, for example, villagers commonly balked at paying taxes levied on them by their rulers. If bribes to the collectors or to the armies that accompanied them failed to secure relief, those who had carried on the negotiations "would retire behind the mud fortifications of their village, in the hope of exhausting the patience of the Mughal collector [Kumar, 1977: 275]."

Noncooperation may take still other forms too, depending on what elites want from those below. Seemingly unreasonable commands of all kinds may be met with a simple failure to obey (for one among numerous possible examples of this strategy, drawn from Cambodia, see Steinberg, 1957: 317). And in societies where pariah populations perform specialized functions that the more powerful population groups shun, higher-status offenders can be sanctioned by denying them access to the services in question. Thus, in a study of Jewish life in Iran, it was found that when Muslim debtors refuse to honor loans from moneylenders (who are always Jews), "nothing can be done to repay the money, but this debtor is blacklisted by the entire Jewish community [Loeb, 1977: 86–87]." In general, the more numerous the demands made on subordinates by their superiors, the greater are the opportunities for noncooperation. Depending on circumstances, aggrieved parties who exploit these opportunities can inflict substantial material hardship on superordinates, thwart their plans, or simply drive them to exasperation.

Appeals for Support

Another way that a subordinate may exercise social control against a superior is by attempting to mobilize relatively powerful third parties to take up his or her cause. This may involve appeals to public opinion at large, and thus to the body of an offender's associates, or to particular individuals whose position makes them especially formidable. Such efforts may be made in a variety of ways, but in all cases the basic strategy is to equalize the power disparity by securing the services of one or more advocates, allies, or avengers (see Black and Baumgartner, 1983). (It is worth remarking that when low-status persons seek the involvement of third parties, it is unlikely to be *neutral* settlement behavior—such as mediation, arbitration, or adjudication—that they want performed. Rather, it is *partisan* intervention they seek. Perhaps the tendency of settlement agents to find ultimately for the higher-status people before them—on this point, see, e.g., Black, 1976: 21–24—explains why lower-status people choose to bypass them.)

Efforts to enlist support that are directed to an offender's colleagues in general usually take the form of "shaming." When this is the case, aggrieved parties try to attract widespread attention in order to publicize their problems and to arouse sentiment against the offenders. In ancient Rome, for example, at least two techniques were used by lower-status people for these purposes. One, known as *flagitatio* or *occentatio*, involved open ridicule by the aggrieved and a group of friends. This "took the form of an organized shouting of words in the offender's presence, words which normally consisted of, or were connected with, the aggrieved party's demand against the wrongdoer [Kelly, 1966: 22]." "The standard requirements for this abusive chant were that it should mention a name, be loud, and have alternating parts [Lintott, 1968: 9]." Such an action was likely to be effective because, in Roman society, an individual's reputation "counted for a great deal," and it "suffered if one were thought to be committing an injustice [Kelly, 1966: 21]." A Roman of the time remarked that public shaming—"done loudly and with a sort of chant to be heard far off"—"brought disgrace because it was thought to have good reason [quoted in Lintott, 1968: 8]."

The other way in which an aggrieved Roman might shame a higher-status opponent was by resorting to a practice known as "squalor" or "mourning." The basic forms of this strategy were *"immittere/summittere capillos,* to let the hair grow or dishevel it, and to wear shabby or dirty clothes, *vestem sordidam habere* [Lintott, 1968: 16]." So altered in appearance, the aggrieved party might begin to follow the alleged wrongdoer through the streets. By this means a person could excite pity on his or her behalf and arouse indignation against the object of the display (Kelly, 1966: 49–50; Lintott, 1968: 16). Squalor was used not only by low-status individuals against those of higher status but also by citizens against government officials and by weaker political factions against stronger ones. Thus, in a specific instance, the son of an exiled man, "letting his hair grow long . . . and with a beard and humble clothing, went round the forum pleading with citizens, and falling at their knees he asked for his father's return [quoted in Lintott, 1968: 19]." He was supported in his effort by his family, the Metelli, and those blocking the recall "had to suffer the odium of a column of Metelli dogging [them] [Lintott, 1968: 19]." More generally, political actors on the losing side of controversies sometimes assumed a pose of squalor "to indicate their disapproval of certain events which endangered the public interest and to inspire popular hostility and resistance [Lintott, 1968: 19–20]."

In ancient Ireland, one way of shaming a higher-status adversary (including a person of chieftain rank) was the practice known as "fasting." It was employed when the offender refused to settle a dispute, whether privately or through arbitration. Its immediate object was to pressure the offender into at least posting a surety, or pledge, that he would appear before an arbitrator and abide by the judgment rendered:

> It was done in this way. The plaintiff, having served due notice, went to the house of the defendant, and sitting before the door, remained there without food. It may be inferred that the debtor generally yielded before the fast was ended, i.e. either paid the debt or gave a pledge that he would settle the case. . . . This fasting process was regarded with a sort of superstitious awe; and it was considered outrageously disgraceful for a defendant not to submit to it:—[The law code states] "He that does not give a pledge to fasting is an evader of all: he who disregards all things shall not be paid by God or man" [Joyce, 1903: 204–205].

(Centuries later, Irish Catholic prisoners held in Ulster jails for their anti-British and anti-Protestant activities occasionally resort to "hunger strikes" in an effort to secure concessions from their jailers.)

The embarrassing spectacle of a social inferior planted outside one's door or following one through the streets, proclaiming all the while that he or she has been grievously victimized, has been the fate of the powerful elsewhere as well. In India, the practice of "sitting dharna"—or "sitting at the door of an opponent with the resolve to die unless the alleged wrong is redressed [Bondurant, 1965: 118]"—seems to have been used upwardly in practice at least some of the time. During the Victorian era, an Englishman noted that:

> "Sitting dharna," placed under the ban of British law, chiefly survives in British India in an exaggerated air of suffering worn by the creditor who comes to ask a debtor of higher rank for payment, and who is told to wait. . . , But it is still common in the Native Indian States, and there it is preeminently an expedient resorted to by soldiers to obtain arrears of pay [Maine, 1875: 304–305].

In the twentieth century, elements of the practice of "sitting dharna" were incorporated by Mahatma Gandhi into his campaign of nonviolent resistance against British colonial rule in India (see Bondurant, 1965: especially chap. 4). More generally, throughout the world today, the strategy of shaming a higher-status adversary finds expression in picket lines and sit-ins organized by workers against management, by citizens against government, and—as during the American civil rights movement—by minority group members against the majority.

Appeals to public sentiment through shaming may sometimes be made on behalf of lower-status people by others. In this case, mobilizing assistance becomes a multistep process, with one group of supporters seeking to recruit yet more. A fairly institutionalized form of this practice existed in fifteenth-, sixteenth-, and seventeenth-century France, for example, where groups of young men organized into associations called *societés joyeuses* took it on themselves to provide entertainment for the public and also to champion low-status victims of various kinds. One of the offenses that aroused the ire of the *societés joyeuses* was wife beating, and one of their methods of revenge was to shame the offenders by mocking them in public spectacles "with vile tinklings and varied clamours [Welsford, 1935: 204–205]." The groups also engaged in political satire, voicing grievances against those in power (Welsford, 1935: 206–207). To this day, some entertainers continue the tradition of shaming high-status offenders through ridicule; in less theatrical ways, members of the news media can disgrace the powerful simply by publicizing their misdeeds widely.

Apart from shaming, which is directed to an offender's public indiscriminately, another strategy of appeal exploited by lower-status grievants is to seek the assistance of one or a few specific high-status third parties who might be willing to take action on their behalf. In many societies around the world, for example, dependent wives turn to their fathers and brothers for help during conflicts with their husbands. This has been reported among the Zinacanteco Indians of Mexico (Collier, 1973: chap. 9), the Jalé of New Guinea (Koch, 1974: 101), the Yanomamö of Venezuela (Chagnon, 1977: 83), and in numerous other groups as well. Similarly, tenants, serfs, clients, and others of comparable status may seek help from one of an offending overlord's equals or betters. In fourteenth-century England, for instance, members of the gentry could sometimes be prevailed on to help a fellow member's serfs. In a particular case,

> Lord Adam de la Ford was indicted for receiving and protecting Walter le Moch of Edyngton, a runaway serf of John le Waleys. Walter paid Sir Adam two marks for his aid. Apparently Lord Adam had done this before because the indictment goes on to say that he is a "common maintainor and protector" [Hanawalt, 1979: 51].

In traditional India, a "means of redress for an aggrieved lower caste person, if his dispute was with his own patron, was to seek the help of his patron's enemies within the dominant caste [Cohn, 1965: 92]." And yet another example can be found in Thailand, where clients used the same strategy against their superiors: "*Nai* [patrons] who used the power that was legally theirs to oppress their *phrai* [clients] in practice lost out as their *phrai* sought protection elsewhere, namely, from powerful nobles feared by their *nai* [Rabibhadana, 1975: 118]." Appeals may also be made to individuals whose influence derives from sources other than wealth or military power. Cambodian peasants, for example, traditionally invoked the aid of *bonzes*, or Buddhist monks, in dealing with their superiors (Steinberg, 1957: 317), and championing the powerless has sometimes been the function of clergy in other societies as well.

The reasons why powerful third parties are willing to help aggrieved subordinates are quite various. Humanitarian concerns seem to prompt action in some instances, whereas a fear that failure to do something about an especially vicious peer will cause widespread unrest among a subordinate population seems important in others. In some cases, when the offended subordinate offers money or labor in return for assistance, the motive may be financial gain. In institutionalized patronage relationships, such service may be one of the obligations that patrons owe their clients when they have conflicts with other high-status people. If a long-standing enmity exists between the offender and the supporter of the aggrieved, revenge may be the impetus. And sometimes the reason seems to be that the supporter has been skillfully manipulated by the aggrieved individual into hostility against the offender. This is suggested, for example, in the following passage from an edict of Louis XIV of France:

> It does appear that there are persons of ignoble birth . . . who have never borne arms, yet are insolent enough to call out [to a duel] gentlemen who refuse to give

them satisfaction, justly grounding their refusal on the inequality of the conditions; in consequence of which these persons excite and oppose to them other gentlemen of like degree, whence arise not infrequently murders [i.e., dueling fatalities], the more detestable since they originate from abject sources [quoted in Baldick, 1965: 61].

Despite the many reasons why socially elite individuals might agree to cooperate with lower-status complainants, however, there are numerous reasons why they may refuse to do so, including friendship with the offender, solidarity with a fellow elite, and lack of concern for the problems of the lowly. Hence, although an appeal for influential support may seem worthwhile to the aggrieved and may have a good chance of success, it by no means leads automatically to the desired result.

Flight

Yet another widespread strategy by which people may express grievances against their social superiors is flight. It is seen when subordinates with complaints against those above them simply try to escape from future dealings with the offending parties, so opting for a kind of avoidance. In some instances, they ultimately relent and resume interaction with the offenders; in others, they disappear and are never seen again.

Whenever circumstances allow it, running away is an especially common tactic of slaves. The earliest law codes from ancient Mesopotamia include provisions for dealing with fugitive slaves and those who assist them (Siegel, 1947; Steele, 1948). In ancient Rome, likewise, the practice of escape seems to have been of great concern to the slaveowning class. Archaeologists have unearthed iron slave collars intended to distinguish human property from freemen—in a society where slaves were not physically unlike other people—and to facilitate the return of runaways to their owners. One such collar was engraved, "I have escaped; arrest me; take me back to my master Zoninus and you will be rewarded with a gold piece [Hopkins, 1978: 121]." Accounts by Roman citizens suggest that the number of fugitives was nonetheless quite large (Hopkins, 1978: 121; see also Wiedemann, 1981: 190–194). Chinese slaves, too, are known to have "run away by stealth [Hsu, 1971: 257]"; among the Ashanti of Ghana, a slave who had been "cruelly treated by his master could await an opportunity to run away [Rattray, 1929: 41]"; and on the clove plantations of eighteenth- and nineteenth-century Madagascar and East Africa, many slaves took flight, usually in response to particular grievances (F. Cooper, 1977: 201–202).

Slaves in the antebellum American South sometimes escaped to Canada via the "Underground Railroad"—a network of sympathizers and safe houses—although they suffered the disability of a distinctive appearance, which made unobtrusive movement difficult. Others ran away temporarily to wilderness areas in the vicinity of their masters' homes—to "the swamp." One observer of the time noted that "the manager told me that the people often ran away after they have been whipped or something else had happened to make them angry. They hide in the swamp and come into the cabins at night to get food [quoted in Bauer and Bauer, 1942: 400]." Occasionally slaves stayed away for extended periods of time. If their owner had hired them out to work for someone else, and this person offended them, they might remain in the swamp until their period of service (generally a year) had expired, then return to their owners, who hired them out to a different person. In some cases, negotiations took place between the fugitive slaves and their owners, through the intermediation of enslaved acquaintances on neighboring plantations, before the runaways consented to return (Bauer and Bauer, 1942: 399–401).

Elsewhere in the New World, including the Caribbean and Central and South America, the proportions of slaves who ran away were, if anything, larger. Those who engaged in flight, or the practice of *marronage*, often established their own communities in remote areas beyond the reach of Europeans; some of these settlements exist to the present day (see generally Price, 1979b). Efforts by colonial authorities to eradicate the so-called maroon societies met with many difficulties. Aside from those groups that successfully thwarted efforts at recapture or that eluded detection altogether, "new maroon communities seemed to appear almost as quickly as the old ones were exterminated, and they remained the 'chronic plague,' 'the gangrene,' of many plantation societies right up to the final Emancipation [Price, 1979a: 4]."

Servants in colonial New England were also known to express grievances against their masters by means of flight: "Strictness might even lead them to run away at a crucial time, perhaps at harvest, and even though [their master] recovered them and had their term of service extended by the court, he would not be able to repair his immediate loss [Morgan, 1966: 125]." Similarly, peasants bound to lords and patrons—whether as clients, serfs, or tenants—have often used escape as a way of handling their grievances. For example, in Russia before the emancipation of the serfs,

> flight [was] the most common form of protest. Just between 1719 and 1727 the far from complete official sources showed around 200,000 fugitives. Not only individuals or families but entire villages took off.

> Nothing the government or the serfowners did seemed able to check the stream of runaways. Scores of decrees, and harsh punishments of captured fugitives and of those who sheltered them, had no effect. There were more laws about runaways and their recovery than any other subject—a fact that in itself bears witness to the proportions of peasant flight [Blum, 1961: 553].

In Sicily and southern Italy at the turn of the twentieth century, "the ultimate response of [peasants] to the repression of the Crispi era, and to the deteriorated conditions which it forced upon them, is well known. Between 1876 and 1925, over 1.5 million people left Sicily, principally for North America [Schneider and Schneider, 1976: 124–125]." And in traditional India, one "method of peaceful demonstration against oppression is voluntary emigration—*hijrat* or *deshatyaga* (giving up the country). Where the people of an area were grievously oppressed and had no other recourse, they would all move from the place [Bondurant, 1965: 119]." The British encountered this tactic in India during the period of their colonial rule. Thus, when they greatly increased the tax burden "on the cultivating classes of Indapur, [the latter] resisted . . . through migrating in large numbers to . . . neighboring districts [Kumar, 1977: 276]." An eyewitness recorded what happened, for example, in the village of Oolhi:

> This place I well recall a flourishing village seven years ago, it had a couple of shops, and was to all appearances populous. It is now mostly deserted. The shops are ruined, all the trees disappeared, walls down and the place in ruins; and of 4000 acres 2,475 are waste, revenue fallen from 1,066 [rupees] to 618 [rupees]. . . . The rest of the over-assessed and mis-classed villages have all partaken more or less similar ruin [quoted in Kumar, 1977: 276].

Examples of the use of flight by disgruntled peasants can be multiplied (see, e.g., Lambton, 1953: 262, on rural Iran; Rockwell, 1974: 448, on Denmark); the practice appears widespread.

Under the label of "desertion," flight is also a well-known method by which aggrieved soldiers resist their officers. During the American Revolution, for instance, large numbers on the British side—particularly the mercenary Hessians, many of whom had been sold into service by their German rulers—escaped to remote areas and settled there. In France around the turn of the nineteenth century, military desertion reached monumental proportions as an expression of "increasing war weariness and of the alienation of important sections of the common people from a regime in which they no longer felt any stake and with whose declared aims they had become increasingly out of sympathy [Cobb, 1970: 93]." Entire companies of soldiers left their posts and simply walked home; reports from a variety of regions told of "every conscript from a given canton having returned home and living there unmolested [Cobb, 1970: 96]." Efforts by the government to put an end to desertion proved ineffective, leading a modern historian to remark that "there could have been no more eloquent referendum on the universal unpopularity of an oppressive regime [Cobb, 1970: 97]." Desertion also expressed the dissatisfaction of many Russian soldiers during the later years of the First World War; perhaps as many as 1.5 million men deserted, out of a total of 15 million who were mobilized (Thoden, 1971: 408, 427).

In the form of resignation, flight is a tactic often used in the political world as well. Lower-ranking and less powerful officials resort to it to protest policies or other actions by superiors that they find objectionable (see Hirschman, 1970). In the economic world, resignation is a common recourse of aggrieved employees. "Quitting" is very often a protest against the conditions of employment, and, in the aggregate, jobs that offer the lowest wages, poorest amenities, and least advancement experience the highest rates of turnover (see generally Peskin, 1973). (Note that employee turnover costs American businesses billions of dollars annually; see Peskin, 1973: chap. 5). Also in economic life, customer desertion, seen when buyers take their business elsewhere in protest over poor quality, high prices, or whatever, is a common means by which the ordinary citizens of industrialized nations sanction powerful corporations (see Hirschman, 1970).

Finally, it might be noted that flight is sometimes employed by dependent wives and children against their husbands and parents. Among the Samburu of Kenya, for example, flight is so commonly used by disgruntled wives that "it is almost a daily occurrence that some Samburu, seeing the wife of a fellow clansman some distance from her home, assumes she is running away from her husband and escorts her back [Spencer, 1965: 33; see also 46–50]." Other examples of running away by wives can be seen among the Jalé of New Guinea (Koch, 1974: 101–108), the Busoga of Uganda (Fallers, 1969: 106–107), the Tallensi of Ghana (Fortes, 1949: 85–87), the villagers of Lebanon (Rothenberger, 1978: 170), the Muslims of the Sudan (Fluehr-Lobban, 1977: 135), the Zinacanteco Indians of Mexico (Collier, 1973: 183), and many other groups. Even when the women involved do not go far, and when they ultimately can be persuaded to return, the inconvenience of their flight can be considerable to their husbands. From the male point of view, it is all the worse if the woman represents a financial investment that cannot be recovered unless she comes back. Among the Ashanti of Ghana, for instance, where wives were sometimes pawned to their husbands as sureties for loans given to the women's families, a pawned wife might run away if she were mistreated, resulting in the cancellation of the debt until she was recovered—a loss of both wife and money for the offending husband (Rattray, 1929: 50–51).

Because flight is such a common method of social control by those of lower status against their superiors, many of the latter take precautions against it. Extreme measures of this kind can be seen among slave-owners, prison officials, and government agents responsible for preventing the flow of people across a nation's borders. For example, huge sums of money may be expended to hire guards and to construct physical restraints. The cost and trouble entailed, regardless of results, must be considered impositions inflicted on the powerful by those who might choose to flee. The same applies to the heavy psychological burdens of vigilance.

Distress

One of the most distinctive ways in which people may pressure those above them is by engaging in conduct expressive of their own inability to function. In particular, they may display personality aberrations likely to elicit therapy, or they may inflict injury on themselves. Although superficially such tactics may not appear to be potent aggressive weapons, in fact they can effectively present a grievance against a superior. The value of distress derives partly from its incorporation of features characteristic of other means of upward social control—including covert retaliation, noncooperation, shaming, and flight—so that it might almost be considered a hybrid. Overall, however, it is quite different from these other forms.

Perhaps the most unusual thing about distress is that even while it is a dramatic and potentially effective upward weapon, it is also often a veiled one. To a greater or lesser degree in its various forms, it tends to sublimate conflict even while participating in it. Thus, it is frequently the case that all of the actors involved agree in placing the causes of distressed conduct beyond simple human control. For the weaker party, this definition of the situation means a release from responsibility—and accountability—for his or her actions. Much scholarly debate has centered around the questions of whether distressed persons actually choose to exhibit the behavior that they do, and if so, how freely and in what way. The uncertainty surrounding these issues sets distress apart from the other forms of upward social control discussed in this essay. For present purposes, however, the exact nature of the motivation lying behind such conduct is not made problematic. All that is claimed is that the various kinds of distress are responses to conflict, exploited by weaker parties against stronger ones, and capable of inflicting hardship on those who have given offense. Consider, first, the use of personality aberrations.

PERSONALITY ABERRATIONS

Elements of covert retaliation, noncooperation, and shaming appear whenever an aggrieved party exhibits behavioral symptoms likely to elicit therapy—such as hyperactivity, prolonged weeping, listlessness, or the persistent violation of situational proprieties (see Goffman, 1969)—during the course of conflict with a social superior. The therapy in question may be magical, designed to exorcise or placate supernatural spirits, or psychiatric, designed to cure mental illness. In each case, the display of symptoms indicative of a need for healing can be a powerful tool. The disturbed individual may be deemed unable to handle the tasks ordinarily expected of him or her, for example, so that others must assume the burden. At the same time, associates of the victim (among whom the person who has given offense is generally to be found) may fall under community pressure to take every step necessary to restore the afflicted to normality, and various concessions and accommodations are likely to be involved as part of this helping process. Should therapeutic sessions become necessary, a heavy expenditure of material resources may well be demanded from those most responsible for the patient, for healing everywhere tends to be expensive. In practice, this imposition is also apt to fall (at least partly) on the offender.

Across history and cultures, spirit possession seems to be more widely recognized than mental illness. Symptoms of supernatural problems frequently occur in the context of domestic conflict, where they may be useful to wives who are unhappy with their husbands. Among the Malagasy speakers of Mayotte, for example, wives who become possessed are often able—ostensibly through the spirits who invade them—to extract promises from men not to engage in such offensive behavior as sexual relations with other women. This is true even though, at least among men, second marriages are otherwise considered perfectly appropriate. It is believed that if a husband should break a promise to a spirit, or neglect to supply it with occasional luxuries, it will take revenge—perhaps by making his wife ill, or perhaps by retaliating against the husband directly, causing sickness or impotence. Thus, on Mayotte, spirits are granted a sort of leverage over men that women lack, and, when they become possessed, wives gain access to a source of power and control denied them under ordinary circumstances (see Lambek, 1980).

Similar patterns are seen in spirit possession in other societies. Plateau Tonga women in Zambia, for example, are subject to the possession of spirits who demand expensive gifts and curing ceremonies as the price for allowing their victims to resume normal lives. It falls to the husband and other relatives of the possessed woman to pay for these things, which might include soap, perfume, and other Western goods highly prized by Tonga women. Moreover, one of the most common circumstances under which possession arises is after a prolonged period of disputing between husband and wife (Colson, 1969). Somali women of the Horn of Africa are frequently afflicted with possession as well, and the *djinns* that invade them also require expensive curing rituals before they will allow the women involved to return to normality. If a Somali husband makes plans to marry a second woman, he may find his first wife stricken by possession, and by the time he has paid for her cure, the money he needs for his second marriage is likely to be gone. Not surprisingly, therefore, Somali men are often reluctant to accept a diagnosis of spirit possession and may believe that their wives' symptoms are intended to take advantage of them. Even so, they are under considerable pressure not to jeopardize the women's well-being by neglecting to appease the *djinns*. An anthropologist who studied the Somali has concluded that spirit possession there and elsewhere serves as a significant means of social control for afflicted women, largely because they find many alternative sanctions "blocked or culturally inappropriate" (Lewis, 1969: 189–190; see also Lewis, 1971: chap. 3).

Although spirit possession as a technique of upward social control seems especially likely to be used by wives against husbands, it is found in other contexts as well. Thus, one scholar has observed that it occurs widely among low-status men in a variety of societies, where it acts "like an X-ray to throw into relief areas of subordination in a social system [Lewis, 1971: 107]." Male slaves, clients, strangers, and ethnically marginal individuals may all have recourse to spirit possession, "regularly [doing so] in situations of stress and conflict with their superiors, and, in the attention and respect which they temporarily attract, [influencing] their masters. Thus adversity is turned to advantage, and spirit possession of this type can be seen to represent an oblique strategy of attack [Lewis, 1971: 117]." Spirit possession also occurs in the work settings of some modernizing societies. In Malaysia, for instance, women who work in the factories of multinational corporations are especially prone to attack by evil spirits while they are on the job, and when this happens management is forced to close the factory temporarily and to hire a ritual expert to perform an exorcism. As part of the purification process, an animal may be sacrificed and the cooked meat distributed to the workers, who in any case enjoy a brief holiday. A Malaysian psychiatrist who has consulted on many industrial spirit-possession cases terms the "hysteria" of the afflicted workers "an expression of hostility without physical violence [Newman, 1980: 1]":

> At a shoe factory in Malacca that [experienced outbreaks of spirit possession] 40 times, two down-to-earth researchers found that mass hysteria may also have something to do with industrial peace. Pay was $1.90 a day. The place was mismanaged. It had no medical benefits, no grievance procedures and, of course, no unions—but it did have a spy system, and the women complained of an atmosphere of intimidation. Outbreaks of hysteria followed rumors of layoffs, including one rumor that men would replace the women to put a lid on hysteria. . . .
>
> The academics, who don't want to be named because Malaysia's government dislikes labor organizers, came to the conclusion that mass hysteria is a form of "covert industrial conflict" [Newman, 1980: 1, 27].

Like spirit possession, mental illness can often be interpreted as an instance of upward social control. In industrialized society, neuroses and psychoses mostly replace attacks by malevolent spirits in the repertoire of tactics available to those of low status. Thus, one psychiatrist has described mental illness as a means of communication used by weaker against stronger persons in situations where blunt confrontation would be unproductive for the aggrieved parties and has remarked:

> In the modern world many people prefer to believe in various kinds of mental illnesses, such as hysteria, hypochondriasis, and schizophrenia—rather than admit that those so diagnosed resemble plaintiffs in court more than they do patients in clinics, and are engaged in making various communications of an unpleasant sort, as might be expected of plaintiffs [Szasz, 1974: 119].

In common with people who receive therapy for spirit possession in tribal settings, a disproportionate number of those who turn to psychiatrists and psychologists are women (see, e.g., Szasz, 1961; Chesler, 1971; Gove and Tudor, 1973). Such people have often experienced extensive tension in their interpersonal relations. In one American suburb, for instance, wives sometimes develop psychiatric symptoms and turn to psychotherapy during the course of conflict with their husbands. Grievances expressed in this way include perceived indifference or neglect by the men in question, their overly frequent absences, and their unfair demands for housework or other services (Baumgartner, forthcoming). In the same community, children also pursue grievances against their parents through mental illness (Baumgartner, forthcoming). A psychiatrist who has analyzed many cases of schizophrenia suggests that elsewhere, too, sons and daughters employ psychiatric symptoms as a means of responding to fathers and mothers who have offended them (see Laing and Esterson, 1964; Laing, 1969).

Like spirit possession, mental illness may also be used upwardly between unrelated persons. This is seen, for instance, in the prison, where a variety of aberrant behaviors known as "prison psychoses" frequently arise. Symptoms include paranoia, delusions, sudden rages, and persistent querulousness (Noyes and Kolb, 1958: 555–556). At least one form of mental illness, the "Ganser syndrome," is held to be distinctive to certain prisoners. In this case, a person awaiting trial begins to exhibit signs of mental irresponsibility, answering simple questions vaguely or absurdly (a phenomenon known as paralogia or *"Vorbeiriden"*) and performing simple tasks incorrectly, such as by attempting to write with the blunt end of a pencil. The Ganser syndrome is classified as a kind of dissociative reaction (see Noyes and Kolb, 1958: 503–504, 555–556). In general, prisoners are often able to secure improvements in their treatment when they develop psychoses, and it has been remarked how frequently they recover altogether on transfer from a prison environment to the presumably more congenial conditions of a hospital (see Noyes and Kolb, 1958: 556).

SELF-INJURY

One of the most dramatic forms of upward social control, and also perhaps the one with least appeal to people in more fortunate circumstances, is the deliberate infliction of injury by aggrieved parties on themselves. Although the techniques of suicide and self-mutilation might at first appear to be irrational, compounding rather than redressing offenses, in fact they are powerful weapons that the weak can turn against the strong. They have the special value of being available even when more ordinary means of upward sanctioning are restricted or entirely absent. Like the display of personality aberrations discussed earlier (with which it has a great deal in common and partly overlaps), self-injury derives much of its effectiveness from its capacity to combine features of more common tactics such as covert retaliation, noncooperation, shaming, and flight.

Suicide, for example, imposes the costs of flight but typically adds other burdens as well, notably a measure of disgrace for those believed to have driven the victim to such desperation. One anthropologist has suggested the label of "Samsonic suicide," or suicide of revenge, for self-inflicted deaths that have as their primary motive the desire to create difficulties for someone else (Jeffreys, 1952). In practice, Samsonic suicides are often directed upwardly—as, indeed, in the unusual case of

Samson himself, an Israelite judge who destroyed a building in which he was standing so that the leaders of the Philistine army, which had conquered his people, might be crushed to death along with him. Thus, for instance, dependent women and children may commit suicide as a way of taking revenge against husbands, fathers, or other figures of authority. In China, the suicide of aggrieved wives has been one traditional response to extreme conditions (Hsu, 1971: 251), and women in India also sometimes use it against their husbands and in-laws (see Ullrich, 1977: 101). In New Guinea, women may resort to suicide as a way of shaming adversaries and of placing them in the unenviable position of being held accountable for the death. Among the Kaliai of New Britain, for example, those deemed responsible for driving a woman to suicide—"killing her with talk"—are required to compensate the victim's family with blood money or face violent retaliation (Counts, 1980). An anthropologist who studied the Kaliai describes suicide by women there and elsewhere as an "indirect use of power" that "may neutralize more obvious displays of force and may . . . be ultimately more effective and enduring [Counts, 1980: 335]." On the Polynesian island of Tikopia, many suicides are committed by young people as retaliation for reprimands or beatings by their parents (Firth, 1961: 128–129).

Suicide is also used by slaves and serfs against their masters. In these cases, it may be understood as property destruction as well. In the American South before the Civil War, slaveowners

> had much trouble with slaves fresh from Africa, the new slaves committing suicide in great numbers. . . . A planter writing on the handling of slaves mentions the difficulty of adjusting the Africans to slavery: "It too often happens that poor masters, who have no other slaves or are too greedy, require hard labor of these fresh negroes, exhaust them quickly, lose them by sickness and more often by grief. Often they hasten their own death; some wound themselves, others stifle themselves by drawing in the tongue so as to close the breathing passage, others take poison" [Bauer and Bauer, 1942: 414–415].

In Russia before the emancipation of the serfs, "some peasants found the only way of escape from the intolerable conditions of their lives was through suicide. These were officially reported as 'sudden deaths.' After the emancipation a notable decline was reported in the suicide rate [Blum, 1961: 560]." Suicide has also been used as a tactic in the political arena—for example, in Vietnam during the war years of the 1960s by Buddhist monks and nuns, who occasionally resorted to self-burning as a way of dramatizing their dissatisfaction with American policy in their country (see, e.g., FitzGerald, 1972: 386). In addition to cases of successful suicide in these and other contexts, there are also many suicide attempts that fail—often by design—but that nonetheless effectively express grievances against the more powerful. (One particularly intriguing attempt has been reported from Tikopia, where a man tried to hang himself in an effort to take action against the neglectful or indifferent gods who had failed to cure his seriously ill son; Firth, 1961: 138. Perhaps this represents the extreme in upward social control.)

Self-mutilation, a lesser kind of self-destruction, is a related form of social control. Like suicide, it seems often an effort to accuse and shame offenders before a larger public. In some cases, it may be interpreted as a variety of noncooperation (insofar as it renders its perpetrators unfit to meet ordinary demands). It may also be a way to force superiors to expend time, effort, and resources in supplying medical (and perhaps psychotherapeutic) aid to the injured, and it may allow aggrieved parties to shock and disgust those with whom they are unhappy. Known and practiced among slaves (Bauer and Bauer, 1942: 414) and among those resisting induction into the military (Cobb, 1970: 96), self-mutilation appears to reach its highest levels of development in prisons and to become more extreme as inmate grievances are greater. To students of incarceration, it is a well-known phenomenon.

In the United States, for example:

> For many years preceding 1948, the extremely poor conditions under which Texas [prison] inmates lived and worked proved to be time and again more than ample reason for the most violent and savage attacks upon self. As protests against the excessive brutality, hands and feet were chopped off by desperate men. And, from sources now thoroughly concealed by the passing of time, inmates learned that slashing the Achilles' tendon with always available razor blades, or any other sharp instruments at hand, was an effective means of winning sympathy and support for their immediate protest, which at various times was directed against barbaric working conditions, putrid and tainted food, filthy and malodorous living conditions, etc. [Beto and Claghorn, 1968: 25].

In the prisons of contemporary Peru, self-mutilation is used primarily as "a device to escape or stop some form of corporal ill-treatment," at which it is quite effective (H. Cooper, 1971: 182–183). Peruvian prisoners also injure themselves as a way of "drawing attention" to other serious grievances (H. Cooper, 1971: 184).

Self-mutilation appears to be an especially prominent tactic of inmates in the prisons of the Soviet Union. There, swallowing foreign objects is a favored means of inflicting injury upon the self (Yaroshevsky, 1975: 443). A Soviet ex-prisoner has described some of this conduct:

> I have seen convicts swallow huge numbers of nails and quantities of barbed wire; I have seen them swallow mercury thermometers, pewter tureens (after first break-

ing them up into "edible" portions), chess pieces, dominoes, needles, ground glass, spoons, knives, and many other objects [Kuznetsov, 1975: 169].

A former Soviet prison physician has explained the circumstances under which such actions, as well as other kinds of self-injury, have occurred:

> [People] committed the mutilations as a result of the insufferable condition of their lives and the impossibility of obtaining their legitimate rights. For example, the administrator of the camp might arbitrarily not have permitted visits with parents or wives who could have travelled thousands of miles in vain, or he might have chosen to restrict mail or to subject the prisoners to physically abusive treatment [Yaroshevsky, 1975: 444].

The same writer has characterized self-injury in prisons as a way "to express grievances, with the realistic hope of obtaining some alteration in . . . circumstances," as "a protest against oppression," and as a way for prisoners "to remove themselves from the omnipotent control of their jailers, while simultaneously reproaching them morally [Yaroshevsky, 1975: 444, 445]."

Of all the forms of social control from below, none seems to speak more eloquently than self-injury of the extremes to which people are willing to go in the pursuit of justice. That suicides and self-mutilations occur as often as they do suggests the existence of an urge for fairness—or at least an urge for revenge—in human populations that may occasionally take precedence over the so-called urge for self-preservation.

General Observations

Although each of the forms of upward social control discussed in this essay has certain characteristics peculiar to itself, it is nonetheless possible to observe several patterns that apply in general to all. These are evident in the substantive nature of the social control imposed, in the procedures employed, and in the responses elicited. This section considers these commonalities in turn, then concludes by raising some remaining questions about social control from below.

SUBSTANCE

One of the most striking features of upward social control is how often and how much it imposes hardship on the people who exercise it as well as on those against whom it is directed. Although even social control occurring downwardly or between equals may require investments of time, trouble, or money, the costs associated with upward sanctioning are generally of a far greater magnitude. Indeed, the ways in which people of lower status pursue grievances against the more powerful might appear unpleasant and unappealing to any observer not personally confronted with a victimization by someone of higher social standing. Suicide and self-mutilation are especially extreme examples, but considerable sacrifices are also associated with such other tactics as flight from one's home, job, or nation; assorted varieties of shaming, including sitting for days outside someone's dwelling, perhaps without food, or following someone through the streets in rags; and participation in strikes and slowdowns, especially when these require a reduction in income or standard of living for an extended period. Thus, just as suicide may be called a Samsonic act when it occurs upwardly, entailing as it does a total sacrifice of the self in the interests of revenge, upward social control in general is notably Pyrrhic, for although it does not usually involve the complete destruction of the aggrieved party and although it frequently achieves a victory of sorts, it exacts a heavy price from those who employ it.

Another substantive feature of upward social control is its normative style. Recently, it has been proposed that across all settings, four major styles of social control may be identified: the penal, the compensatory, the therapeutic, and the conciliatory. Of these, the first two are accusatory, involving contestants who seek to further their own claims and to vanquish or coerce their opponents, whereas the last two are remedial, involving "methods of social repair and maintenance" that seek "what is necessary to ameliorate a bad situation" and to restore normality or tranquility (Black, 1976: 4–6). It has been generalized that social control in a downward direction—by a superior against an inferior—tends to be accusatory, and specifically penal, with its aim being to punish someone defined as an offender (see Black, Chapter 1 of this volume, p. 10). In light of the present materials, it may now be observed that the same is strikingly true of upward social control.

Thus, within the limitations imposed by restricted opportunities, people of lower status often seek retribution for the wrongs they experience. Extremes of the penal style are commonly found during rebellions such as riots and revolutions: for instance, executions, torture, beatings, burnings, and wholesale property destruction. A similar penal logic underlies most covert retaliation, whether it takes the form of an annoying prank or an act of arson. Penal behavior is also generally involved in cases of noncooperation, where offenders are deprived of services or resources because of their conduct. Finally, efforts to enlist support of third parties may also be designed to bring about the punishment of superordinates, and the infliction of costs appears to be an integral component of strategies of personal distress such as spirit possession and mental breakdowns.

When it is not penal, social control from below tends to involve accusatory and adversarial tactics designed to obtain compensation or at least an end to an unpopular course of action by a superior. Thus, as discussed earlier, covert retaliation may be tailored to secure a "settlement" to which the aggrieved individual feels entitled. In addition, compensation is often what a lower-status person hopes to achieve by mobilizing the support of a third party. When the aim is neither to inflict a punishment nor to collect restitution, but is simply to compel an offender to desist from offending, the style of social control is neither purely penal nor purely compensatory; it is nonetheless quite coercive. Such a goal may characterize acts of social control between people of any status; upwardly, it occurs in many cases in which noncooperation, appeals to third parties, flight, and emotional distress are used against superiors.

Noticeably absent from the list of techniques employed in an upward direction are those representative of the conciliatory and therapeutic styles of social control. The aggrieved parties in these cases appear unlikely to participate in hearings of their problems before mediators, for example, or in negotiation sessions. They are similarly underrepresented among those who impute to their opponents an abnormality requiring treatment and who seek to make that treatment available. These patterns do not necessarily express a distaste for conciliation or therapy on the part of lower-status people; rather, it is more likely that they reflect the difficulties inferiors have in securing the cooperation of their adversaries. Because both conciliatory and therapeutic social control depend more heavily than the other styles on the willingness of offenders to play a role in resolving a conflict at issue, they are more likely to flourish where the antagonists are equal in social status, or, in the case of therapy, possibly where the offender is of lower rank than the complainant (see generally Black, 1976: 29–30; Witty, 1980: 20, 23; Horwitz, 1982: 63–70; Merry, 1982; Felstiner, Chapter 9 of this volume, pp. 264–265).

Despite the predominance of coercive and adversarial elements in upward social control, the use of law—one of the most typically adversarial of all actions—is comparatively rare in cases of this kind. A relative absence of upward law has often been observed (see Black, 1976: 21–29), and it is now a widely recognized fact about legal life and the social order. When they exert social control, people at the bottom turn to tactics that may have much in common with law stylistically but that differ substantially in procedure. In the following section, some of the most striking procedural aspects of social control from below are discussed.

PROCEDURES

Closely related to variation in the content and substance of social control, though distinguishable from it, is variation in the procedures through which social control is applied. That is, apart from such issues as which standards wrongdoers are believed to violate, exactly how deviants are defined, and what sorts of sanctions are levied, there are also issues pertaining to the timing, sequencing, setting, and organization of the steps through which social control unfolds. It is possible to distinguish at least three general types of procedure, or modes of execution, that are widespread in normative life. These might be termed the *negotiatory,* the *legalistic,* and the *authoritarian.* It will be argued here that upward social control is mostly authoritarian in this sense.

The negotiatory mode is commonly found where the parties in conflict are socially equal and comparatively intimate. It is characterized by a dialogue between the parties—directly or through intermediaries—in which the problem in question is addressed on a shared basis (for an overview of this process, see Gulliver, 1979). Supervision of the affair lies ultimately with the antagonists themselves. Hence, negotiatory social control is a decentralized procedure and is associated with considerable variation across cases. Because nothing is a problem unless someone takes offense, for example, and because, on the other hand, anything can become a problem if it bothers someone else, there is little uniformity in standards where the negotiatory mode predominates. Accordingly, offenders may not know in advance how their conduct will be regarded. After a problem has arisen, many other features of the negotiatory process—the time, place, and structure of meetings about the contested issues, the number of third parties present, the scope of information deemed relevant, and so forth—are also variable. Finally, an outcome is achieved through the negotiatory procedure whenever the principals agree to a settlement. The exact terms can differ widely even in the face of similar offenses, depending on the ability and determination of the parties involved.

The second mode of procedure, the legalistic, has achieved its purest expression in the social control exercised by governments—hence its name. (Governments differ among themselves, however, in the extent to which their normative practices are legalistic in the present sense.) In this mode, the emphasis is on formality, regularity, and uniformity (see

Weber, 1925; Fuller, 1964; Selznick, 1969: 12; Unger, 1976: 53–54). Conflict is handled according to fixed protocols that are largely beyond the caprices and influence of either party. There is, for example, a concern to notify potential offenders in advance of what they cannot do without jeopardy; accordingly, a common practice is to promulgate statutes and codes in which prohibitions are made explicit. Once someone believes that a transgression has occurred, he or she can obtain satisfaction through a series of steps established in advance. These steps are more or less the same in all cases of a similar sort. Hearings about the issues may be limited to a particular setting, for instance, their organization and composition may be constrained within a narrow range, and the evidence they are allowed to consider may be narrow in scope. Offenders are generally given an opportunity to state their position, for conceptions such as "rules of procedure," "burdens of proof," "rights," "protections," and "due process" arise within the legalistic mode. It is also in this procedural context that "fairness"—like treatment for like offenders—is most emphasized as a goal; one consequence is that the range of variation across case outcomes is less than it is in other procedural modes. Where legalistic procedures dominate, often there are provisions for appeal by losing parties, providing a final check on disparities.

In the third mode of procedure—the authoritarian—the reaction of the aggrieved party is not limited by the search for a settlement agreeable to the offender (as in the negotiatory mode) or by standardized and publicized formulas established in advance (as in the legalistic mode). Rather, it is imposed. The injured party, possibly along with supporters, decides unilaterally what redress of the grievance is appropriate and when and how it will be achieved. The primary restrictions are those of feasibility, grounded in available resources and opportunities, and, to some extent, those established by broad cultural conceptions of what is permissible. Where the authoritarian mode prevails, then, which people are processed for what conduct depends heavily on the inclinations of those who are offended, even as these vary with the same person or group over time. Forewarning to potential deviants is correspondingly limited, and, in addition, the circumstances and outcomes of sanctioning tend to be highly variable and unpredictable. The responses may come at any time; they may occur in secret, in private, or in public; they may be mild or severe, customary or unprecedented.

Downward social control—by a person of higher status against one of lower status—is very often authoritarian in procedure. To a remarkably similar (or even greater) degree, so is upward social control. In fact, all of the strategies of upward sanctioning discussed in this essay tend to be authoritarian in practice. Generally the response is dictated by the aggrieved parties, without regard to the wishes of the offenders or to standards of procedural fairness. It is only the offended who decide what misconduct will be subject to social control, when this will happen, and how. Frequently, indeed, the redress of a grievance is planned and executed surreptitiously.

That the procedures found in upward social control—and also the normative styles represented—should be so similar to those of downward social control might at first seem anomalous. Superiors and inferiors are distinguished from one another by vastly different amounts of resources, influence, and strength and, from one perspective, may properly be considered opposites. Even so, the two are at the same time complementary parts of a single configuration—social hierarchy. In this light, the convergence in their conduct can more easily be explained. As one student of human behavior has observed:

> Since oppressed and oppressor form a functional pair, their respective orientations to human relationships tend to be similar. . . . Hence, each slave is a potential master, and each master a potential slave. It is extremely important to keep this in mind and to avoid the misleading contrast between the psychology of the oppressed and that of the oppressor. Instead, the similar orientation of each should be contrasted with the orientation of the person who wants to be neither slave nor master—but only his fellowman's equal [Szasz, 1974: 171–172].

It has been recognized, for example, that successful rebellions tend to establish new oppressive orders, similar in form to the ones they overthrow. Those previously on the bottom recreate the world to which they are accustomed but now place themselves in a more favorable position at the top. They treat their enemies and former superiors in the manner in which they themselves had always been treated (Freire, 1970: 29–31). Overall, then, there is considerable isomorphism between upward and downward social control—so much, in fact, that there appears to be a greater affinity between the two than between either of these and the forms of social control found among equals, which are far more likely to be conciliatory or therapeutic in style and negotiatory in procedure.

RESPONSES FROM ABOVE

In the sequence of events comprising a human conflict, an action that one party views as justifiable social control may be perceived as itself an offense by the side against which it is directed. It may then be met with a counteraction that, in turn, increases the moral outrage of the first party all the more. This chain of responses finally ends when a settlement is reached or imposed, or when one or both sides give up the struggle. The amount of time this process involves and the extent of hostilities it engenders vary considerably across instances.

Upward social control seems especially likely to generate indignation in its recipients. As people of higher status ordinarily have abundant means of social control at their disposal, subordinates who attempt to sanction those above them incur a substantial risk of retaliation in most cases. What is more, because the viewpoint of social elites is so likely to be adopted by others, it often happens that those who express grievances upwardly are seen as wrongdoers by observers not directly involved in the conflict. Even professional students of law and conflict management commonly view social control from below as so much deviant behavior (but see Black, Chapter 1, Volume 2 of this work; Yngvesson, Chapter 9 of the same volume).

This is particularly clear where law is concerned. A great deal of what is regarded as crime is, from the criminal's perspective, an expression of a grievance:

> Far from being an intentional violation of a prohibition, much crime is moralistic and involves the pursuit of justice. It is a mode of conflict management, possibly a form of punishment, even capital punishment. Viewed in relation to law, it is self-help. To the degree that it defines or responds to the conduct of someone else—the victim—as deviant, crime is social control [Black, Chapter 1, Volume 2 of this work].

And nowhere can this be seen more clearly than in the case of upward social control. Much of what people of lower status do to sanction offending superiors has been labeled and processed as crime in practically every legal system. Indeed, although they are not all defined as illegal in every jurisdiction, the forms of upward social control discussed in this essay have been so commonly prohibited that they constitute a virtual litany of crimes. Nearly every form of rebellion, for instance, has been subject to legal repression. Covert retaliations are often treated as serious offenses such as theft, embezzlement, and arson. Acts of noncooperation—including strikes, work slowdowns, and refusals to pay taxes—have been widely banned and punished. Appeals for support have often been described in the language of law as harassment, slander, seditious libel, or incitements to riot and disorder. Flight—by slaves from masters, children from parents, prisoners from guards, or other social inferiors from those above them—is generally illegal. Even suicide and self-mutilation have been regarded as crimes in numerous societies, and symptoms of personal distress have resulted in prosecution for witchcraft (in many cases a capital crime) and commitment to mental hospitals.

What is true of law also applies to many other kinds of social control administered by or for elites. School principals and related authorities, for example, often punish pupils for conduct designed to sanction their teachers. Similarly, much behavior countered by employers with reprimands, demotions, and dismissals arises to express grievances on the part of the workers. Military discipline treats as insubordination or other deviance many of the acts by which enlisted men seek to exercise social control against their commanding officers, and prison discipline does the same for the techniques by which inmates show disapproval of their guards. In families, too, heads of households often punish children or dependent spouses for having the audacity to attempt to sanction them. Overall, then, many varieties of social control from below are defined and processed by those above as misconduct, such as stealing, cheating, rowdiness, carelessness, sloppiness, laziness, nastiness, cheekiness, disobedience, insubordination, incorrigibility, evasion of responsibility, troublemaking, lying, abandonment, desertion, absence without leave, malingering, and so on. This treatment is analogous to what occurs when law is used to handle upward social control as crime or other illegality, for in all these instances people who express grievances against social superiors become the targets of retaliation. And because those with social status tend to be given the benefit of the doubt in matters of all kinds, those branded wrongdoers by their teachers, employers, officers, guards, and fathers are likely to find themselves viewed as such by others. The tendency for definitions from above to prevail has influenced—the aggrieved might say it has distorted—the perception of upward social control across societies and history, and in modern times it has conditioned how sociologists, anthropologists, and criminologists have understood conflict in hierarchical relationships. Even if the sanctioning of their superiors results in a moral stigma and punishment for those who engage in it, however, many people of lower status continue to seek justice in their own way.

This essay has explored how people of lower status express grievances against those of higher social standing. The following techniques of upward social control have been discussed: rebellion, covert retaliation, noncooperation, appeals for support, flight, and distress. Several observations have been made about the phenomenon of social control from below:

1. *It tends to be adversarial, and particularly penal, in style.*
2. *It tends to be authoritarian in procedure.*
3. *It tends to be defined and processed as itself an offense by the superiors*

against whom it is directed, and often by a larger public that accepts their version of events.

Because the first two of these patterns seem also to be true of downward social control, it appears that upward social control and downward social control are significantly isomorphic. The third pattern, dealing with responses to social control from below, has implications for the study of stratified conflict by social scientists, who often have a tendency to adopt the language and perspective of elites.

Lastly, it should be recognized that there are many remaining questions about social control from below. For example, little is known about how often people of lower status refrain altogether from expressing grievances against offending superiors. And when they do exercise social control, little is known about how to predict exactly which techniques they will use. Also unclear are the comparative frequencies of the six tactics discussed in this essay, whether there are any other major forms of upward social control, and what explains the occurrence of relatively uncommon responses (such as law) at all. Matters such as these await further investigation. At present, it is possible only to draw the broadest contours of social control from below and to hope for more research on this long-overlooked phenomenon.

ACKNOWLEDGMENTS

For helpful comments on an earlier draft of this chapter, I thank Donald Black, Mark Cooney, and Calvin K. Morrill.

References

Arensberg, Conrad M., and Solon T. Kimball
    1968   *Family and Community in Ireland.* 2d edition. Cambridge, Mass.: Harvard University Press (1st edition, 1940).
Baldick, Robert
    1965   *The Duel: A History of Duelling.* London: Chapman and Hall.
Bauer, Raymond A., and Alice H. Bauer
    1942   "Day to day resistance to slavery." *Journal of Negro History* 27: 388–419.
Baumgartner, M. P.
    forth-   *The Moral Order of a Suburb.* New York: Academic Press.
    coming
Beto, Dan Richard, and James L. Claghorn
    1968   "Factors associated with self-mutilation within the Texas department of corrections." *American Journal of Correction* 3: 25–27.
Black, Donald
    1976   *The Behavior of Law.* New York: Academic Press.

Black, Donald, and M. P. Baumgartner
    1983   "Toward a theory of the third party." Pages 84–114 in *Empirical Theories about Courts*, edited by Keith O. Boyum and Lynn Mather. New York: Longman Press.
Blum, Jerome
    1961   *Lord and Peasant in Russia: From the Ninth to the Nineteenth Century.* Princeton, N.J.: Princeton University Press.
Bondurant, Joan V.
    1965   *Conquest of Violence: The Gandhian Philosophy of Conflict.* Revised edition. Berkeley, Calif.: University of California Press (1st edition, 1958).
Chagnon, Napolean A.
    1977   *Yanomamö: The Fierce People.* 2d edition. New York: Holt, Rinehart and Winston (1st edition, 1968).
Chesler, Phyllis
    1971   "Women as psychiatric and psychotherapeutic patients." *Journal of Marriage and the Family* 33: 746–759.
Clarence-Smith, W. G.
    1979   "Slaves, commoners and landlords in Bulozi, c. 1875 to 1906." *Journal of African History* 20: 219–234.
Cobb, R. C.
    1970   *The Police and the People: French Popular Protest, 1789–1820.* London: Oxford University Press.
Cohn, Bernard S.
    1965   "Anthropological notes on disputes and law in India." Pages 82–122 in *The Ethnography of Law*, edited by Laura Nader. Supplement to *American Anthropologist* 67 (December).
Collier, Jane Fishburne
    1973   *Law and Social Change in Zinacantan.* Stanford, Calif.: Stanford University Press.
Colson, Elizabeth
    1969   "Spirit possession among the Tonga of Zambia." Pages 69–103 in *Spirit Mediumship and Society in Africa*, edited by John Beattie and John Middleton. New York: Africana Publishing Corporation.
Cooper, Frederick
    1977   *Plantation Slavery on the East Coast of Africa.* New Haven, Conn.: Yale University Press.
Cooper, H. H. A.
    1971   "Self-mutilation by Peruvian prisoners." *International Journal of Offender Therapy* 15: 180–188.
Counts, Dorothy Ayers
    1980   "Fighting back is not the way: Suicide and the women of Kaliai." *American Ethnologist* 7: 332–351.
Cressey, Donald R.
    1953   *Other People's Money: A Study in the Social Psychology of Embezzlement.* Glencoe, Ill.: Free Press.
Davidson, David M.
    1966   "Negro slave control and resistance in colonial Mexico, 1579–1650." *Hispanic American Historical Review* 46: 235–253.
Durkheim, Emile
    1893   *The Division of Labor in Society.* New York: Free Press, 1964.
Erikson, Kai T.
    1966   *Wayward Puritans: A Study in the Sociology of Deviance.* New York: Wiley.

Fallers, Lloyd A.
   1969   *Law without Precedent: Legal Ideas in Action in the Courts of Colonial Busoga.* Chicago: University of Chicago Press.
Firth, Raymond
   1961   "Suicide and risk taking." Pages 116–140 in *Tikopia Ritual and Belief.* Boston: Beacon Press, 1967.
FitzGerald, Frances
   1972   *Fire in the Lake: The Vietnamese and the Americans in Vietnam.* New York: Vintage Books, 1973.
Fluehr-Lobban, Carolyn
   1977   "Agitation for change in the Sudan." Pages 127–143 in *Sexual Stratification: A Cross-Cultural View,* edited by Alice Schlegel. New York: Columbia University Press.
Fortes, Meyer
   1949   *The Web of Kinship among the Tallensi: The Second Part of an Analysis of the Social Structure of a Trans-Volta Tribe.* London: Oxford University Press.
Freire, Paulo
   1970   *Pedagogy of the Oppressed.* New York: Herder and Herder.
Fuller, Lon L.
   1964   *The Morality of Law.* New Haven, Conn.: Yale University Press.
Gans, Herbert J.
   1962   *The Urban Villagers: Group and Class in the Life of Italian-Americans.* New York: Free Press of Glencoe.
Goffman, Erving
   1969   "The insanity of place." Pages 335–390 in *Relations in Public: Microstudies of the Public Order.* New York: Basic Books, 1971.
Gough, E. Kathleen
   1960   "Caste in a Tanjore village." Pages 11–60 in *Aspects of Caste in South India, Ceylon, and North-West Pakistan,* edited by E. R. Leach. Cambridge: Cambridge University Press.
Gove, Walter R., and Jeannette F. Tudor
   1973   "Adult sex roles and mental illness." *American Journal of Sociology* 78: 812–835.
Green, Thomas A.
   1972   "Societal concepts of criminal liability for homicide in medieval England." *Speculum* 47: 669–694.
Gross, Jan Tomasz
   1979   *Polish Society under German Occupation: The Generalgouvernement, 1939–1944.* Princeton, N.J.: Princeton University Press.
Gulliver, P. H.
   1979   *Disputes and Negotiations: A Cross-Cultural Perspective.* New York: Academic Press.
Hanawalt, Barbara A.
   1979   *Crime and Conflict in English Communities, 1300–1348.* Cambridge, Mass.: Harvard University Press.
Hayden, Tom
   1967   *Rebellion in Newark: Official Violence and Ghetto Response.* New York: Random House.
Hirschman, Albert O.
   1970   *Exit, Voice, and Loyalty: Responses to Decline in Firms, Organizations, and States.* Cambridge, Mass.: Harvard University Press.

Hobsbawm, Eric
   1969   *Bandits.* New York: Dell.
Hopkins, Keith
   1978   *Conquerors and Slaves. Sociological Studies in Roman History,* vol. 1. Cambridge:
          Cambridge University Press.
Horwitz, Allan
   1982   *The Social Control of Mental Illness.* New York: Academic Press.
Howkins, Alun
   1977   "Structural conflict and the farmworker: Norfolk, 1900–1920." *Journal of Peasant
          Studies* 4: 217–229.
Hsu, Francis L. K.
   1971   *Under the Ancestors' Shadow: Kinship, Personality, and Social Mobility in China.*
          Stanford, Calif.: Stanford University Press.
Jeffreys, M. D. W.
   1952   "Samsonic suicide or suicide of revenge among Africans." *African Studies* 11:
          118–122.
Joyce, P. W.
   1903   *A Social History of Ancient Ireland,* vol. 1. London: Longmans, Green.
Kelly, J. M.
   1966   *Roman Litigation.* Oxford: Clarendon Press.
Koch, Klaus-Friedrich
   1974   *War and Peace in Jalémó: The Management of Conflict in Highland New Guinea.*
          Cambridge, Mass.: Harvard University Press.
Kumar, Ravinder
   1977   "The transformation of rural protest in India." Pages 268–281 in *Dissent, Pro-
          test, and Reform in Indian Civilization,* edited by S. C. Malik. Simla: Indian In-
          stitute of Advanced Study.
Kuznetsov, Edward
   1975   *Prison Diaries.* London: Vallentine, Mitchell.
Laing, R. D.
   1969   *The Politics of the Family and Other Essays.* New York: Pantheon Books.
Laing, R. D., and A. Esterson
   1964   *Sanity, Madness and the Family: Families of Schizophrenics.* Baltimore: Penguin
          Books, 1970.
Lambek, Michael
   1980   "Spirits and spouses: Possession as a system of communication among the
          Malagasy speakers of Mayotte." *American Ethnologist* 7: 318–331.
Lambton, Ann K. S.
   1953   *Landlord and Tenant in Persia: A Study of Land Tenure and Land Revenue Administra-
          tion.* London: Oxford University Press.
Lewis, I. M.
   1969   "Spirit possession in northern Somaliland." Pages 188–219 in *Spirit Mediumship
          and Society in Africa,* edited by John Beattie and John Middleton. New York:
          Africana Publishing Corporation.
   1971   *Ecstatic Religion: An Anthropological Study of Spirit Possession and Shamanism.* Bal-
          timore: Penguin Books.
Linebaugh, Peter
   1975   "The Tyburn riot against the surgeons." Pages 65–117 in *Albion's Fatal Tree:
          Crime and Society in Eighteenth-Century England,* by Douglas Hay, Peter Line-
          baugh, John G. Rule, E. P. Thompson, and Cal Winslow. New York: Pantheon
          Books.

Lintott, A. W.
1968 *Violence in Republican Rome.* Oxford: Clarendon Press.
Llewellyn, K. N., and E. Adamson Hoebel
1941 *The Cheyenne Way: Conflict and Case Law in Primitive Jurisprudence.* Norman, Okla.: University of Oklahoma Press.
Loeb, Lawrence D.
1977 *Outcaste: Jewish Life in Southern Iran.* New York: Gordon and Breach.
McPhee, John
1968 *The Pine Barrens.* New York: Farrar, Straus & Giroux.
Maine, Sir Henry Sumner
1875 *Lectures on the Early History of Institutions.* London: John Murray.
Marsh, Peter, Elisabeth Rosser, and Rom Harré
1978 *The Rules of Disorder.* London: Routledge and Kegan Paul.
Merry, Sally Engle
1982 "The social organization of mediation in non-industrial societies: Implications for informal community justice in America." Pages 17–45 in *The Politics of Informal Justice,* vol. 2, edited by Richard I. Abel. New York: Academic Press.
Michell, H.
1964 *Sparta: τὸ κρυπτὸν τῆς πολιτείας τῶν Λακεδαιμονίων.* Cambridge: Cambridge University Press.
Morgan, Edmund S.
1966 *The Puritan Family: Religion and Domestic Relations in Seventeenth-Century New England.* Revised edition. New York: Harper & Row (1st edition, 1944).
Newman, Barry
1980 "Malaysian malady: When the spirit hits, a scapegoat suffers." *Wall Street Journal* (March 7): 1, 27.
Noyes, Arthur P., and Lawrence C. Kolb
1958 *Modern Clinical Psychiatry.* 5th edition. Philadelphia: W. B. Saunders (1st edition, by Arthur P. Noyes, 1934).
Odening, Gerald
1981 "Arms and the man." *Forbes* (July 6): 135–136.
Oliva, Pavel
1971 *Sparta and Her Social Problems.* Prague: Czechoslovak Academy of Sciences.
Peskin, Dean B.
1973 *The Doomsday Job: The Behavioral Anatomy of Turnover.* New York: AMACOM.
Pike, Luke Owen
1873 *A History of Crime in England: Illustrating the Changes of the Laws in the Progress of Civilization,* vol. 1: *From the Roman Invasion to the Accession of Henry VII.* London: Smith, Elder.
Price, Richard
1979a "Introduction: Maroons and their communities." Pages 1–30 in *Maroon Societies: Rebel Slave Communities in the Americas,* edited by Richard Price. 2d edition. Baltimore: Johns Hopkins University Press (1st edition, 1973).
Price, Richard (editor)
1979b *Maroon Societies: Rebel Slave Communities in the Americas.* 2d edition. Baltimore: Johns Hopkins University Press (1st edition, 1973).
Rabibhadana, Akin
1975 "Clientship and class structure in the early Bangkok period." Pages 93–123 in *Change and Persistence in Thai Society: Essays in Honor of Lauriston Sharp,* edited by G. William Skinner and A. Thomas Kirsch. Ithaca, N.Y.: Cornell University Press.

Rattray, Captain R. S.
  1929   *Ashanti Law and Constitution.* Oxford: Clarendon Press.
Rees, Alwyn D.
  1961   *Life in a Welsh Countryside.* Cardiff: University of Wales Press.
Rockwell, Joan
  1974   "The Danish peasant village." *Journal of Peasant Studies* 1: 409–461.
Rothenberger, John E.
  1978   "The social dynamics of dispute settlement in a Sunni Muslim village in
         Lebanon." Pages 152–180 in *The Disputing Process—Law in Ten Societies,* edited
         by Laura Nader and Harry F. Todd, Jr. New York: Columbia University Press.
Rudé, George
  1964a *The Crowd in History: A Study of Popular Disturbances in France and England,
         1730–1848.* New York: Wiley.
  1964b *Revolutionary Europe, 1783–1815.* New York: Meridian Books.
Schneider, Jane, and Peter Schneider
  1976   *Culture and Political Economy in Western Sicily.* New York: Academic Press.
Selznick, Philip (with the assistance of Philippe Nonet and Howard M. Vollmer)
  1969   *Law, Society, and Industrial Justice.* New York: Russell Sage Foundation.
Siegel, Bernard J.
  1947   "Slavery during the third dynasty of Ur." *Memoirs of the American Anthropologi-
         cal Association* 49: 1–54.
Spencer, Paul
  1965   *The Samburu: A Study of Gerontocracy in a Nomadic Tribe.* Berkeley, Calif.: Univer-
         sity of California Press.
Steele, Francis R.
  1948   "If a slave girl fled . . . : Being an account of how the law code of Lipit-Ishtar, a
         Sumerian king who ruled 19 centuries before Christ, was found to antedate the
         code of the great Hammurabi." *Scientific American* 178: 44–47.
Steinberg, David J.
  1957   *Cambodia: Its People, Its Society, Its Culture.* New Haven, Conn.: HRAF Press.
Sykes, Gresham M.
  1958   *The Society of Captives: A Study of a Maximum Security Prison.* Princeton, N.J.:
         Princeton University Press.
Szasz, Thomas S.
  1974   *The Myth of Mental Illness: Foundations of a Theory of Personal Conduct.* 2d edition.
         New York: Perennial Library (1st edition, 1961).
Thoden, Edward C.
  1971   *Russia since 1801: The Making of a New Society.* New York: Wiley.
Thompson, E. P.
  1975   "The crime of anonymity." Pages 255–344 in *Albion's Fatal Tree: Crime and
         Society in Eighteenth-Century England,* by Douglas Hay, Peter Linebaugh, John
         G. Rule, E. P. Thompson, and Cal Winslow. New York: Pantheon Books.
Ullrich, Helen E.
  1977   "Caste differences between Brahmin and non-Brahmin women in a south Indi-
         an village." Pages 94–108 in *Sexual Stratification: A Cross-Cultural View,* edited
         by Alice Schlegel. New York: Columbia University Press.
Unger, Roberto Mangabeira
  1976   *Law in Modern Society: Toward a Criticism of Social Theory.* New York: Free Press.
Weber, Max
  1925   *Max Weber on Law in Economy and Society,* edited by Max Rheinstein. 2d edition.
         Cambridge, Mass.: Harvard University Press, 1966 (1st edition, 1922).

Welsford, Enid
  1935   *The Fool: His Social and Literary History.* London: Faber and Faber.
Wiedemann, Thomas
  1981   *Greek and Roman Slavery.* Baltimore: Johns Hopkins University Press.
Witty, Cathie J.
  1980   *Mediation and Society: Conflict Management in Lebanon.* New York: Academic Press.
Yaroshevsky, Felix
  1975   "Self-mutilation in Soviet prisons." *Canadian Psychiatric Association Journal* 20: 443–446.

Author Index

Numbers in italics indicate the pages on which the complete references are listed.

Subject Index

А